NEW FORMATIONS

EDITOR
Jeremy Gilbert

REVIEWS EDITOR
Peter Buse

EDITORIAL BOARD
Shahidha Bari
David Bennett
Timothy Bewes
Peter Buse
David Glover
Ben Highmore
Cora Kaplan
Nicky Marsh
Mandy Merck
Scott McCracken
Brett St Louis
Jenny Bourne Taylor
Nicholas Thoburn

PRODUCTION CO-ORDINATION AND ADVERTISEMENTS:
For enquiries/bookings contact Lynda Dyson, Lawrence & Wishart.

SUBSCRIPTIONS:
UK: Institutions £350.00, Individuals £40.
Single copies: £15.99 plus £3 post and packing.
Back issues: £15.99 plus £3 post and packing for individuals; £80 plus £3 post and packing for institutions.
Payments can be made by credit/debit card (no American Express).

CONTRIBUTIONS AND CORRESPONDENCE:
Send to: Jeremy Gilbert: j.gilbert@uel.ac.uk

BOOKS FOR REVIEW:
Send to: Peter Buse, Reviews Editor, *New Formations*, School of Performance and Screen Studies, Kingston University, Penrhyn Road, Kingston-Upon-Thames, KT1 2EE, P.Buse@Kingston.ac.uk

New Formations publishes themed issues, themed sections and discrete articles. Contributors are encouraged to contact the editors to discuss their ideas and to look at the contributor information at http://www.newformations.co.uk/journals/newformations/contributors.html before submitting. Experts in the relevant field will referee all proposals anonymously.

The collection as a whole © Lawrence & Wishart 2017
Individual articles © the individual authors 2017

No article may be reproduced or transmitted in any form or by any means, electronic or mechanical, including photocopying, recording, or any information storage and retrieval system, without the permission in writing of the publisher, editor or author.

ISSN   0 950 237 8
ISBN   9781 9120649
Printed by Halstan Printing Group in the UK.

New Formations is published three times a year by
Lawrence & Wishart, Unit 1, Heath Park Industrial Estate, Freshwater Road, London RM8 1RX
Website: www.lwbooks.co.uk/new-formations

Orders and Subscription payments to: subs@lwbooks.co.uk

New Formations is indexed in British Humanities Index, Questia, ProQuest CSA, EBSCOhost, Literature Online database (ProQuest CSA), eLibrary database (ProQuest CSA), MLA bibliography, InfoTrac (Thomson Gale), First Search (OCLC)

ADVISORY BOARD

David Alderson
Ien Ang
Claudia Aradau
Angelika Bammer
Michèle Barrett
Clive Barnett
Andrew Barry
Vikki Bell
Tony Bennett
Jody Berland
Lauren Berlant
Homi Bhabha
Clare Birchall
Anita Biressi
Lisa Blackman
Lucy Bland
Rachel Bowlby
Rosie Braidotti
Joe Brooker
Ian Buchanan
Caroline Burdett
Victor Burgin
Eleanor Byrne
Lesley Caldwell
Kirsten Campbell
Hazel Carby
Ben Carrington
Erica Carter
Iain Chambers
Laura Chrisman
Phil Cohen
Claire Colebrook
Diana Coole
Joan Copjec
Nick Couldry
Tim Cresswell
David Cunningham
Lidia Curti
Tony Davies
Kay Dickinson
James Donald
Stephanie Donald
Alexander Dunst
Alan Finlayson
John Fletcher
Simon Frith
Andrew Gamble
Keya Ganguly
Natalia Gerodetti
Andrew Gibson
Andrew Goffey
Peter Hallward
Carrie Hamilton
Dick Hebdige
David Hesmondhalgh
Barnor Hesse
Andrew Hurley
Jayne Ifekwunigwe
Leila Kamali
Sarah Kember
Tim Lawrence
Vicky Lebeau
Jo Littler
Judy Lochhead
Roger Luckhurst
Graeme Macdonald
Suhail Malik
John Marks
David Marriott
Martin McQuillan
Angela McRobbie
Peter Middleton
Drew Milne
Joe Moran
Simon Morgan Wortham
Jo Morra
Frank Mort
Stephen Morton
Mariam Motamedi-Fraser
Mica Nava
Keith Negus
William Outhwaite
Benita Parry
Alasdair Pettinger
Sylvie Prasad
Nick Prior
Gillian Rose
Renata Salecl
Jani Scanduri
Lynne Segal
Stephen Shapiro
Debra Shaw
Lorenzo Simpson
Sujala Singh
Josie Slater
Marquard Smith
Judith Squires
Barbara Marie Stafford
Gillian Swanson
Tiziana Terranova
Andrew Thacker
Fran Tonkiss
David Toop
Alberto Toscano
Neil Turnbull
Nira Yuval-Davis
Valerie Walkerdine
Cary Wolfe

Contents
Number 89/90

Death and the Contemporary

5	*Georgina Colby*	Introduction: Death and the Contemporary
12	*Warren Montag*	The Prisoners of Starvation, or *Necessitas dat legem*
30	*Elizabeth Rottenberg*	Deconstructing Death: Derrida and the Scene of Execution
48	*Jonathan Platt*	Zoya Kosmodemianskaya between Sacrifice and Extermination
71	*Timothy Secret*	The Face of the Good Death: Euthanasia and Levinas
85	*François Debrix*	Horror beyond Death: Geopolitics and the Pulverisation of the Human
101	*Roger Luckhurst*	Why Do the Dead Keep Coming Back?
116	*Andrea Brady*	Drone Poetics
137	*Lisa Downing*	Dying for Sex: Cultural and Forensic Narratives of Autoerotic Death
153	*Jennifer Cooke*	The Violations of Empathy
170	*Georgina Colby*	Imaginary Intimacies: Death and New Temporalities in the Work of Denise Riley and Nicholas Royle
192	*Peter Boxall*	Blind Seeing: Deathwriting from Dickinson to the contemporary
212	*Robert Hampson*	Sites of Death in Some Recent British Fiction

Reviews

230	*Janet Wolff*	Car Thoughts
234	*Ben Highmore*	Capacious Aesthetics
243	*Ruth Preser*	Un-learning to See Palestine
247	*Karin Lesnik-Oberstein*	ARTs and the Unconscious
252	*Sheena Culley*	A Place for Practice
256	*Kevin M. Potter*	Expansion/Expulsion
260	*Julia Vassilieva*	Boris Groys: The Intruder
268	*Conor Heaney*	Inventing New Lines
272	*Dougal McNeill*	Psychoanalytic Stimulus Packages
276	*S. Trimble*	Trust Sylvia Wynter

new formations

is freely available online to all subscribers

Benefits include:

- ♦ Document to document linking using live references, for fast, reliable access to wider, related literature.
- ♦ Journal content that is fully searchable, across full text, abstracts, titles, TOCs and figures.
- ♦ Live links to and from major Abstract and Indexing resources to aid research.
- ♦ The ability to conduct full-text searching across multiple journals, giving you a wider view of the research that counts.
- ♦ Powerful TOC alerting services that keep you up to date with the latest research.

Set up access now at:
www.ingentaselect.com/register.htm

and follow the online instructions*

Subscription Enquiries:
help@ingenta.com

*Access is provided by Ingenta Select, an Ingenta website

Introduction: Death and the Contemporary

Georgina Colby

This double issue of *New Formations* addresses death in contemporary culture from a number of interdisciplinary and international perspectives. Since Michel Foucault aligned the 'power of sovereignty' with the disqualification of death in his 1975 essay 'Society Must be Defended', death has been at the forefront of biopolitical and geopolitical debates.[1] Through a contemporary lens Achille Mbembe, writing in 2003, stated that the expression of sovereignty ultimately resides 'in the capacity to dictate who may live and who may die'.[2] Yet Mbembe's necropolitics also questions the sufficiency of biopolitics to account for the question of death and sovereignty in the twenty-first century. This themed issue extends Mbembe's challenge by taking up the complex, often contentious subject of death in present-day culture as it is thought, and as it operates, within and beyond biopolitics. In bringing together articles from scholars across the fields of politics, law, philosophy, and literature, the issue interrogates the conceptual status of death in biopolitical discourse by considering emerging post-biopolitical and post-human contexts.

Foucault understood the status of death in 1975 as 'something to be hidden away' (*Society*, p68). With twenty-first century global conditions, death as a subject has become more visible, imbricated with, and paramount to ideas of the postcolonial, necroeconomics, the necropolitical, and ethical and legal debates surrounding the right-to-die. At the same time, new technologies of warfare in the 'War on Terror' have meant that death has acquired new forms, through modes of violence that often annihilate the body. Such forms of death challenge traditional ritualisations of death and render death increasingly invisible. The issue intervenes at the intersection of biopolitical and post-biopolitical fields of knowledge, entering current debates on critical social and political issues such as euthanasia, the death penalty, and contemporary geopolitics. A number of the essays collected in the volume examine new forms of geopolitical violence, reveal unacknowledged states of exception, and engage with liminal states of death created by medical advances. These articles are brought into a transdisciplinary dialogue with studies that explore the way in which contemporary visual art and literature offer new ways of representing death and emerging bio-medical phenomena. The issue places bioethical questions in relation to critical cultural developments and socio-historical events: the Syrian Civil War; the deaths of detainees in Guantánamo Bay; the shooting of Trayvon Martin and the #BlackLivesMatter campaign; Hurricane Katrina; the use of drones in contemporary warfare; and the Anthropocene. The essays in the collection also situate contemporary issues surrounding death within the context of the history of the twentieth-century: the European colonies and post-colonies; the Holocaust; the Soviet forced-

1. Michel Foucault, 'Society Must Be Defended', *Biopolitics: A Reader*, (eds.) Timothy Campbell and Adam Sitze, Durham and London, Duke University Press 2013, pp61-81; 67. (Hereafter *Society*).

2. Achille Mbembe, 'Necropolitics', (trans) Libby Meintjes, *Biopolitics: A Reader*, pp161-192; 161.

labour camps, and the executions carried out by Nazi forces in Stalinist Russia. In doing so, the scholarship of this issue offers theoretical means to navigate contemporary conceptions of death at the juncture of biopolitical and post-biopolitical discourses.

The starting point of the issue is Warren Montag's discussion of necessity and the law. The essay explores the maxim derived from Roman theorising about law: *Necessitas non habet legem*, or 'necessity has no law', in relation to the problem of the necropolitical order. Montag compares two books: Franz Fanon's *Les Damnés de la terre* (1961) (*The Wretched of the Earth*), and Gilles Couvreur's little known text *Les Pauvres ont-ils des droits? Recherches sur le vol en cas d'extrême nécessité depuis la Concordia de Gratien (1140) jusqu'à Guillaume d'Auxerre (1231)* [*Do the poor have rights? An inquiry into theft in the case of extreme necessity from Gratian's Concordia (1140) to William of Auxerre* (1231)]. The contemporary world, in which whole countries are left to starvation and 'zones of exception' proliferate, spaces abandoned to violence and destitution in the name of the necessity of killing and letting die, is addressed through the prism of Roman law. Montag offers an account of Couvreur's text, which retrieves the historical moment in which the jurists of medieval Christian Europe, the Decretists and Decretalists, agreed that the laws of property cannot be invoked to deny food to the starving who will not wait to be fed but will take what is necessary to their survival. Such a state of exception that prioritised the right of the destitute to existence over the rights of ownership suspended the law, and linked sovereignty with necessity. This maxim Montag brings to bear on contemporary issues, exposing the power of Couvreur's text in the contemporary moment.

Elizabeth Rottenberg's essay moves the enquiry into sovereignty to present-day America and the debates surrounding the death penalty. Rottenberg frames the scene of execution in Jacques Derrida's *Death Penalty Seminar* (1999) and Foucault's analysis of capital punishment in *Discipline and Punish* (1975), with 'the American scene' of execution in Norman Mailer's *The Executioner's Song* (1979), a true-life story of the events surrounding the execution of Gary Gilmore by the State of Utah in 1977. Alluding to Mailer's remarks regarding the need for the scene of execution to be made visible, Rottenberg interrogates the virtual or phantasmatic scene of execution in Derrida's *Death Penalty Seminar* and the 'coming-to-visibility' of sovereignty itself. Her article reveals two economies of visibility: one inherent to a society of the spectacle, the other emerging in the recent cultural shift to a society of surveillance. The death penalty, which for Derrida, Rottenberg points out, is the epitome of sovereign power, will survive its abolition because of the persistence of the phantasm that sustains it.

Another very different scene of execution: that of the Soviet guerrilla fighter Zoya Kosmodemianskaya, is the subject of Jonathan Platt's essay. Platt examines the photograph of Zoya Kosmodemianskaya taken by Sergei Strunnikov, which first appeared on the page three of *Pravda* on 27

January, 1942, after her execution by German Nazi forces on November 29, 1941. Platt considers two possible attitudes to Kosmodemianskaya's death and the contexts that support them. On the one hand the image is read as emblematic of maiden sacrifice; on the other it has been regarded as a picture of revolutionary militancy. Platt's reading of the image gives breadth to the ambivalence of Kosmodemianskaya. Apprehending her as the last Soviet militant, the paper challenges the typical interpretation of the photograph that reinforces the gender stereotypes that are usually escalated during wartime. Taking up the idea of chronotopic hybridity in Stalinist culture, the essay argues for a reconsideration of Kosmodemianskaya as more than an emblem of Stalinist ideology. The article explores this position from a psychoanalytic perspective, arguing that the mutilated Stalinist hero can be understood as a non-phallic subject in the Lacanian sense. Platt illustrates his argument through analyses of four different moments in the memorialisation of Kosmodemianskaya, demonstrating that the ambivalence of Zoya Kosmodemianskaya remains open.

Timothy Secret's essay offers a philosophical approach to the ethical issues surrounding assisted dying. Drawing on recent legislation and the shifting position of the British Medical Association in relation to assisted dying, the essay explores the contemporary debates within the fields of philosophy and medical ethics. Assessing the extent of engagement with the subject of euthanasia in these fields, Secret exposes the lack of discourse on assisted dying in contrast to the abundance of scholarship on issues such as abortion or intersexuality. As a means to address this gap, Secret takes up the work of Emmanuel Levinas to explore whether there is an approach to ethics in Levinas's work that might circumvent established ways of framing the questions surrounding euthanasia's ethical status and legislation. Engaging with Torben Wolf's work on suffering, the essay explores the role philosophy might play in mediating between public and specialised debate. Secret's essay on what a Levinasian ethics might illuminate in terms of the debates surrounding euthanasia offers a model of such enquiry.

François Debrix extends biopolitical and necropolitical discourses by shifting the focus on individual bodies in contemporary instances of geopolitical violence and destruction to what he terms 'the pulverisation of the human'. Borrowing Adriana Cavarero's language, Debrix opens out the term as a radical violence, the objective of which is the destruction of the uniqueness of the body. Two forms of contemporary geopolitical annihilation are the focus of Debrix's study: suicide bombings and drone attacks. Through these modes of violence, Debrix explores Cavarero's idea of 'horrorism' and the effect of horror on human lives and bodies in the twenty-first century.

Roger Luckhurst's article outlines the return of the physical dead body and the materiality of the corpse across a range of aesthetic practices, particularly contemporary photography: the work of Sally Mann, Annie Leibovitz, Luc Delahaye, Gilles Peress and other war reportage. Luckhurst explores the contexts for this return: the transformation of mourning practices since the 1960s; the challenge to what Anthony Giddens calls the 'sequestration' of extreme experience and the rise in fascination with ruined bodies in contemporary trauma theory; the medical redefinition of death and the emergence of a series of liminal states between life and death created by medical advances - from 'beating heart cadavers' and the debates in medical ethics around sustaining life 'after' death; the crisis of the 'real' induced by digital photography and the rise of the wounded body as a new marker of 'authenticity'. Death's insistent return in the photograph, the essay argues, needs to be grasped in formal, historical, social and medical frameworks that mutually reinforce each other. That which has been called the New Death by recent critical-medical theorists, Luckhurst contends, is necessarily an interdisciplinary object of concern.

In a time of 'everywhere war', Andrea Brady's essay sets out to assess the effects that drones may have on the committed lyric. The essay focuses on contemporary poetry since 2010, revealing six ways in which drones are revolutionising perspective and relation. Brady suggests ways in which these changes in perspective and relation might be applied to the theorisation of contemporary poetry. Situating the investigation within the context of twenty-first century American foreign policy in the Obama and Trump administrations, the essay traces the radicalisation of viewing, seeing and being seen that emerges in drone aesthetics back through the effects of aerial technology on the visual arts that began with modernism. This genealogy is extended in the essay from a contemporary perspective to encapsulate the textual engagements with the ideologies that accompany drone warfare. Brady offers a critique of Catherine Taylor's 'Inanimate Subjects' (2013), and brings this analysis into comparative dialogue with a close reading of Solmaz Sharif's poem 'Look' (2016). The final part of the argument outlines a 'drone poetics' that takes up the perceptual, legal, and phenomenological specificities of drones, and brings these aspects of drones to bear on a reconceptualisation of lyric form. Examining the implementation of structures of splitting and compartmentalising, the essay illuminates the artificial intimacy of drone warfare, and brings this into relation with the lyric's illusion of collapsing spatial and temporal distances. The perspective of drones is reflected, Brady argues, in the contemporary lyric that offers a way of magnifying selected objects from 'the safe container of a radical aesthetic'. The essay, through such an analysis, examines drone aesthetic in relation to the role of the lyric poet in contemporary culture.

Lisa Downing considers a very different form of death. Her essay examines the practice of erotic asphyxiation and representations of erotic fatalities, taken from a range of discursive fields including forensic pathology, the psy sciences, media coverage of celebrity deaths, and humorous internet e-cards. In particular, the essay closely reads the way in which erotic asphyxiation is problematically depicted in Tim Winton's novel, *Breath* (2008). The essay argues that contemporary discourses and representations of erotic asphyxiation and autoerotic death offer an explication of the establishment and inscriptions of cultural norms and sexuality. Downing moves the focus of the debate onto those who pronounce on normal and abnormal sexual practices, ascribing to the Foucauldian logic that the classification of sex is coterminous with the exercise of power. Through a number of case studies, the essay explores the way in which media, fiction, the internet, and popular culture, alongside the more recognised authority discourses of sexual science and medico-legal institutions, contribute to and reinforce the creation of sexual norms and the imposition of limitations in terms of acceptable and unacceptable degrees of the risk of bodily harm, in line with normative socio-cultural agendas. Calling into question dominant assumptions prevalent in contemporary society, Downing traces practices of erotic asphyxiation back to the Mayan period. Addressing the cultural anxieties surrounding erotic asphyxiation, the essay discloses two distinct conceptions of masculinity: either failed or weak masculinity, or excessive risk taking hyper-masculinity. Downing reveals that the concept of pathological erotic asphyxiation is even more pronounced when the practitioner is a woman. The cultural association between erotic asphyxiation, effeminacy and shame, transpires to be a contemporary phenomenon.

In her essay 'The Violations of Empathy', Jennifer Cooke addresses the limitations of empathy. She argues that empathy is not always benign and can involve violation, despite the extensive amount of scholarship extolling the ways in which empathy is improved by literature. Rob Halpern's *Common Place* (2015) is the first example, a poem about the death of a Guantánamo detainee, which is read in close relation to Vernon Lee's work on empathy. The essay argues that Halpern's work matches empathy in Lee's work, and embodies a refusal of empathy in its common sense. Both of these facts, the essay argues, lead to a violation of the dead Islamic man. The second example the essay draws on is Andrea Brady's 'Song for Florida 2' (2014), a poem that addresses the killing of Trayvon Martin. Cooke's reading of Brady's poem probes how empathy can obscure what is at stake in injustice by replacing or supplanting the one empathised with. The ending of Brady's poem attempts and fails to imagine the death of Brady's son. It fails, Cooke contends, because such a form of empathy would obscure the racial and economic injustice that means Brady's white son is safe in a racist world.

Georgina Colby also draws on a form of empathy in her essay on new temporalities in the work of Denise Riley and Nicholas Royle. In her essay *Time Lived, Without Its Flow* (2012), and her collection of poetry *Say Something Back* (2016) Riley inscribes her experience of the death of her son, and the attending experience of being flung into a new temporality, that which Riley terms a-temporality. Royle's work *Quilt* (2010) is centred on the death of the narrator's father. In both works there is a collapsing of the narrative voice and the deceased. Through experimental writing practices, both Riley and Royle depict new temporalities related to death that occur outside of linear time yet are experienced by the living person who has lost a loved one. For both Riley and Royle these temporalities run counter to death as it is experienced in contemporary culture: what Riley calls the 'sweetened overlay' of sentiment, and the experience of contemporary funeral practices. In each of the writers' works, such new temporalities are imbricated with geological time or 'deep time'. The essay contextualises these new non-linear models of time via the attempts in the field of phenomenology to theorise the relations between temporality and finitude. Colby brings the experimental works into dialogue with Stephen J Gould's work on deep time, *Time's Arrow, Time's Cycle: Myth and Metaphor* (1987) to navigate the ways in which such an imbrication of the time of death / the time of mourning with geological time might illuminate the relationship between temporality and death in the early twenty-first century.

In his essay 'Blind Seeing: Deathwriting from Dickinson to the Contemporary', Peter Boxall provides a new account of the trajectory of 'blind seeing' that can be traced through the poetic tradition. Through an examination of Blanchot and Kafka's deathwriting, the essay considers Blanchot's idea that a generative principle accompanies the experience of death. Extending this analysis, the essay traces a thread from the work of Emily Dickinson to the contemporary. In this literary 'tradition' (a term renegotiated by this article) Boxall discerns both a form of negation in the approach to realised death, but also, importantly, a means of producing a new possibility, that which Dickinson understands as another way to see. This idea of deathwriting is brought into dialogue with what it means to be contemporary. Drawing on Heidegger's idea of the world picture and Agamben's idea of the contemporary, which demands us to see what is excluded from the visible and representation, Boxall theorises 'blind seeing' in contemporary fiction. Deathwriting summons us to rethink the literary tradition through the countersight inherent to seeing and therefore challenges the normalising cultural forms to which we have become accustomed.

Sites of death in recent British fiction are the focus of Robert Hampson's essay. Situating his analysis within the context of Michel Foucault's *The Birth of the Clinic* (1963), Hampson argues that death in contemporary culture is ubiquitous but in mediated forms. In the staging of the body in recent popular culture death has become characterised by the performance of the medical gaze, which separates the body from identity. Graham Swift's *Last Orders* (1996) yields a number of examples of the way in which contemporary fiction consistently returns to 'non-places' of death: the hospital, the funeral parlour and the crematorium. Hampson argues that these spaces of death in the novel are discontinuous with the life of the deceased. J G Ballard's *Crash* (1973) provides a further example of 'non-sites' in the form of motorway slip-roads, airport access roads, police pounds and reservoirs. From the technologised death of the car crash the essay moves to a consideration of Tom McCarthy's contemporary novel *Remainder* (2007) and technologised sites of death. Hampson offers an account of psychogeographical sites of death in the work of Iain Sinclair and Allen Fisher. Concluding with an analysis of spaces of autopsy and forensics in popular television, Hampson reveals the proliferation of technologised sites of death in contemporary popular culture.

In bringing these essays together, this issue of *New Formations* opens up the debates surrounding death in contemporary culture and positions death as an interdisciplinary subject of enquiry.

GUEST EDITOR

Georgina Colby is Lecturer in Contemporary Literature at the University of Westminster. She is author of *Kathy Acker: Writing the Impossible* (Edinburgh University Press, 2016), and *Bret Easton Ellis: Underwriting the Contemporary* (Palgrave Macmillan, 2011). She has published widely on contemporary literature, in particular experimental writing, in journals such as *Textual Practice*, *Comparative Critical Studies*, *Contemporary Literature*, and *Women: A Cultural Review*. From 2012 to 2013 she was co-organiser, with the artist Anthony Luvera, of the Arts Council funded project 'Death and the Contemporary'. She is currently working on a collection of essays, *Reading Experimental Writing*.

The Prisoners of Starvation, or *Necessitas Dat Legem*

Warren Montag

Abstract In 1961, the same year that Fanon's *Wretched of the Earth* appeared, Gilles Couvreur, a Jesuit, published *Les Pauvres ont-ils des droits* [Do the poor have rights?]. Couvreur's work offered a carefully researched examination of the debates within canon law particularly in the twelfth and thirteenth centuries concerning the right of those who are starving to steal food. At the heart of these debates is the question of whether the appropriation of food that is the property of another, under circumstances of extreme need, constitutes theft (albeit a theft whose criminality is immediately nullified by the law itself) or whether in such circumstances the legal status of property itself is suspended, in which case the taking of food can no longer be understood as theft. Finally, I examine the legal maxims "need has no law" and "necessity [or need] makes law," often cited in the period under consideration, to show how the concept of property was subordinated to the imperative of life in a way that appears unthinkable today.

Keywords food, hunger, property, exception, necessity, theft

> Debout les damnés de la terre
> Debout les forçats de la faim
> *L'internationale*

In France in 1961 two books appeared within a few months of each other. They were undoubtedly conditioned by the same events and, more importantly, offered powerful critiques of the established order that converged in certain important respects. The critiques, however, were composed in registers so fundamentally different that their political and theoretical commonalities have remained until now almost completely illegible, or would have remained illegible had anyone ever thought to compare them. From the moment of their publication, the struggles in France and elsewhere, whose intensity only increased in the years that followed, propelled them along radically divergent trajectories: one book became an international success, read and reread, commented upon and contested, translated into more than a dozen languages; the other has remained confined to a tiny scholarly world whose interests to all appearances have little relevance to the conflicts and tragedies of the last century. It lies buried in an obscurity from which, even now, it cannot easily be extracted.

The first, Frantz Fanon's *Les Damnés de la terre* (*The Wretched of the Earth*) published by the newly established Éditions Maspero, a publisher firmly rooted in the currents of resistance to the Algerian War (and in anti-colonialist and anti-racist movements internationally), spoke directly to and of the present.[1] It was as if Fanon, following Sartre's injunction in 'What is Literature', sacrificed the abstraction expected of a work whose importance will be felt beyond its time, to the urgency of the conjuncture whose genocidal violence had simply moved from Europe back to the colonies where it had begun.[2] Sartre was right in his controversial preface, to see Fanon's last work as a discourse about the European that is not addressed to him and which interpellates him as an eavesdropper who will try in vain to comprehend what he has overheard.[3] Fanon's work is not a discourse on the right to rebel and thus on the conditions under which rebellion can be considered just or unjust. Rather, it is an attempt to articulate the philosophy immanent in the forms of struggle through which anti-imperialist movements sought to free themselves from the deadly grip of Western civilisation. What Fanon attempts to capture is the meaning of that moment when obedience to the law, specifically the regime of rights, requires individuals to expose themselves to death at the hands of those endowed with and able to enjoy the right to govern or the exclusive right of ownership. What is at stake in *Les Damnés de la terre* is not human dignity, nor even the recognition (Hegel's *Anerkennung*) that is central to *Peau noire, masques blancs*. Instead, Fanon's last work arrives at the disturbing conclusion that the central problem of politics from the perspective of the colonised is nothing more or less than their continued existence in the face of what Achille Mbembe has called the 'necropolitical order'.[4] This is the world, only too familiar to us today, in which entire populations are abandoned to starvation, and in which survival itself becomes a de facto violation of the law that demands that property rights (including the ownership of food and water supplies) and national sovereignty (the right to exclude those who do not possess citizenship rights) be respected at any cost, including that of the lives of those made destitute by war or climatic events. And nowhere was the imperative to protect property exercised with more violent abandon than in the European colonies and post-colonies.

The second book, published that same year by the small Catholic press, Editions SOS, was an only slightly embellished version of the author's doctoral thesis, and bore the intimidating title *Les Pauvres ont-ils des droits? Recherches sur le vol en cas d'extrême nécessité depuis la Concordia de Gratien (1140) jusqu'à Guillaume d'Auxerre (1231)* [*Do the poor have rights? An inquiry into theft in the case of extreme necessity from Gratian's Concordia (1140) to William of Auxerre (1231)*]. Its author, a Catholic priest and member of the Jesuit order, Gilles Couvreur, would later join the ranks of *les prêtres ouvriers* or worker priests who followed the proletariat into the factories, not so much to preach the 'Good News' or imitate the poverty of those who worked for little more than bare subsistence, as to share their hardship by becoming one of them. The author

1. Frantz Fanon, *Les Damnés de la terre*, Paris, Maspéro 1961.

2. Jean-Paul Sartre, *What is Literature?*, (trans) Bernard Frechtman, New York, Philosophical Library 1950.

3. Jean-Paul Sartre, 'Préface,' Fanon, *Les Damnés de la terre*, Paris, Maspéro 1961, pp17-36.

4. Achille Mbembe, 'Necropolitics,' *Public Culture*, Volume 15, Number 1, Winter 2003, pp 11-40.

of *Les pauvres* was soon to toil alongside Muslim immigrants and accompany them to the *bidonvilles* or shanty-towns that surrounded French cities. He would observe, and choose to share, their hunger. He would also observe what he could not share: the daily violence and racist hatred directed against them, which on 17 October, 1961 took the spectacular form of a massacre of hundreds of Algerian demonstrators in the heart of Paris.[5] Rather than directly denounce the horrors and injustices of a dying colonialism both in France and in its colonies and former colonies, Couvreur sought to inscribe in the institutional memory of the Church (and thereby of Europe itself) a moment, all but forgotten, that is only from the most superficial view unrelated to the wretchedness of Fanon's 'wretched of the earth'. It is the moment at which the great jurists of medieval Christian Europe, the Canonists, Decretists and Decretalists, who had both recovered Roman jurisprudence and sought to assemble the rulings of earlier Christian authorities into a coherent and consistent body of law, came to agree that the destitute in a condition of dire need could legitimately take what was necessary to their existence, even if it was the property of another.[6] It is to this consensus (arrived at from very different starting points and justified in different ways) that his title refers.

Couvreur thus chose to articulate in the guise of learned commentary on a medieval controversy concerning the right of the destitute to go on living, the principle, often passionately asserted, what the poor, not simply the allegorical figures who populated the parables of the gospels, but the increasing numbers of the landless and homeless, the starved and the half-starved, through the magnitude of their suffering and their resistance, succeeded in imposing as a moral and quasi-legal right: the priority of their right to existence over the rights of ownership. From this controversy, eight centuries before the appearance of *Les Pauvres ont-ils des droits?* there emerged a critique of a notion whose pertinence to our own time cannot be doubted: a conceptualisation of economic order and the form of property it requires. Above all, there developed a will to interrogate and examine in minute detail the emerging concepts of the *dominus* or proprietor who is exempted from any legal responsibility to those who cannot pay for the necessities of life, and a legal or quasi-legal definition of property right that immunises the owner against the claims of the poor, irrespective of the magnitude of their need or his surplus. It is important to note that the terminology concerning property and ownership in the great debates of the latter half of the twelfth and the first half of the thirteenth centuries is almost exclusively drawn from Roman law: most commonly *dominium* and *dominus*, rarely *possessio*, with little or no mention of the complexities of feudal notions of property. The conceptual precociousness of these debates confers upon them an uncanny familiarity that allows them to speak to us directly.

In part, Couvreur's detour through a medieval debate on the right of the desperately poor to steal was a strategic choice imposed by his position in the church at a time, before the changes introduced by Vatican II, when

5. Jim House and Neil Macmaster, *Paris 1961: Algerians, State Terror and Memory*, Oxford, Oxford University Press 2006.

6. Gilles Couvreur, *Les Pauvres ont-ils des droits? Recherches sur le vol en cas d'extrême nécessité depuis la Concordia de Gratien (1140) jusqu'à Guillaume d'Auxerre (1231)*, Rome, Libreria Editrice dell'Università Gregoriana 1961. (Hereafter *Les Pauvres*).

fears of internal communist influence were at their height and the mass radicalisation that arose from the increasing opposition to the Algerian war pushed sectors of the church to the left.[7] But the controversy he examined was not a mere pretext: on the contrary, his detailed reconstruction of the theological and legal positions in the disjunctive synthesis they form makes visible the currents of thought that, if gradually and unevenly, had finally to be rendered invisible in order to allow the emergence, or rather the imposition, of the specific hierarchy of law, property and life that characterises modernity. Such a strategy, of course, involves the risk that it will be ignored by precisely the audience it hopes to move and thus without effect. But perhaps we underestimate both the work and the strategy immanent in it. In the face of the Algerian war, its unrelieved violence and carefully engineered starvation, Couvreur chose to intervene by fashioning the theological and political materials that he gathered together into an untimely work whose meaning could be disclosed only in a time other than its own, a time whose hour has perhaps only now arrived.

7. Etienne Fouilloux, 'Intellectuels Catholiques et guerre d'Algérie,' *La guerre d'Algérie et les intellectuels français*, Paris, Éditions complexes 1991.

But what allows us to link Fanon to Couvreur, given that the work of the former spoke to millions of rebels and revolutionaries round the world, while that of the latter seemed to have been written *sub specie eternitate*, and thus with a serene indifference to its historical moment, as if it were a pure exercise in scholarship that could be relevant only to historians of Canon law? Couvreur's decision to examine a particular controversy over a ninety-one year period (1140-1231), the dates of which were placed conspicuously, perhaps ostentatiously, on the book's cover, seemed almost to have been designed to deter readers, or at least lull them into disregarding the threat that the book poses to their - and our - political/conceptual order. Indeed, Couvreur's work is unsparing: it contains nothing that would help orient the reader in the face of the arguments and counter-arguments concerning the question of theft in cases of extreme necessity or need. More seriously, apart from a single and somewhat ambiguous paragraph at the beginning of the work, Couvreur makes no attempt to suggest the ways in which these debates might be relevant to the great struggles of 1961-1962 in France or, for that matter, what relation these debates from the twelfth and thirteenth centuries had to the histories that followed them, the histories of sovereignty, property right, criminality and criminal law. It is hardly surprising, then, that *Les Pauvres ont-ils des droits?* fell almost immediately into obscurity, cited less than twenty times in the twenty years that followed its publication. What common ground could there be between Fanon's denunciation of 'Western values' and Couvreur's cautious excavation and reconstruction of theological and legal artefacts from eight hundred years earlier?

There are a few signs to be found in Couvreur's text. But identifying and deciphering them is not easy, given that the passages that might be construed as referring to the present are characterised by a constitutive ambiguity that not only allows them to be read in opposing ways, but prevents them from being reduced to either (or any) of their possible meanings. We need read no further than the book's title to find an example: written in the present tense, the question, 'Do the poor have rights?,' as opposed to something like 'The rights of the poor' or even 'the question of the rights of the poor,' creates an equivocity, and more importantly a certain doubt, that cannot be entirely eliminated even by the historical specificity imposed by the subtitle *'Recherches sur le vol en cas d'extrême nécessité depuis la Concordia de Gratien (1140) jusqu'à Guillaume d'Auxerre (1231)'* (An inquiry into theft in the case of extreme necessity from Gratian's *Concordia* (1140) to William of Auxerre (1231). Further, the subtitle not only fails to address the question of rights in general or in some a priori sense, but addresses a particular right, the right to steal in cases of extreme necessity, that most European states ceased to regard as legitimate in the seventeenth or eighteenth century. It is at this point that the strategic function of the historical specificity of the subtitle begins to work. Couvreur incites us to ask if such a right might once have existed, and, if so, whether it was once defended with the same assurance with which it is today routinely dismissed as an absurdity, as if, elevated to the level of principle, such a right could only lead to the destruction of the rule of law and thus civilisation itself. Couvreur's reference in the subtitle to Gratian's *Concordia Discordantium Canonum* or *Decretum* (as it is commonly known in English), a compendium of canon law governed by the principles of coherence and consistency, undercuts the assumption that the right to steal is a contradiction in terms, a right to violate the principle of right and thus an assertion derived from faulty or even irrational premises. It is not simply his commitment to the church that leads Couvreur to turn away from millenarian sects or heretical movements, and instead to the need to demonstrate the recognition of such a right within canon law itself and to recover the diverse arguments and objections that led to the establishment of this right in a form so durable that it would take five centuries to abolish it or simply empty it of practical significance.

But to recover what amounts to the material form of the right to have rights, that is, life, requires a clear understanding of the degree to which the right of the destitute to steal what is necessary to their survival has been forgotten and perhaps rendered unthinkable.[8] When, just over ten years ago, Hurricane Katrina destroyed large parts of the city of New Orleans, it left conspicuously intact the generalised conviction that the destitute individual, without the means to purchase, or the opportunity to receive through donation, the food and water required for survival, who takes what is owned by another, no matter how urgent his need for nourishment or water may be, is guilty of theft. Further, the very natural disaster that produced or exacerbated the needs of the poor and led to a declaration of a state of emergency by the governor of Louisiana, not only did not mitigate the crime of theft of food and water (as dire need did both in scripture[9] and in canon law), but made theft under such conditions all the more heinous in the eyes of the public.

---

8. By 'the material form of the right to have rights,' I refer not to Hannah Arendt's famous formula but to what the socialist jurist Anton Menger called the 'Urrecht' to what is necessary to mere existence, without which all other rights, whether human or civil, are meaningless. Anton Menger, *The Right to the Whole Produce of Labour*, (trans) M.E. Tanner, London, Macmillan 1899, p29.

9. Proverbs 6:30-31: 'Do not despise a thief if he steals to satisfy his hunger'.

10. Rebecca Solnit, 'Looters and the Lessons of Katrina,' *LA Times*, 29 August 2010. It is worth noting, as I will discuss in greater detail later, that the theft of goods other than food, which could be sold to obtain food and other necessities, was widely accepted by the participants in the debates examined by Couvreur.

11. Todd Gray, *Looting in Wartime Britain*, London, Mint Press 2009.

12. Michele Estrin Gilman, 'The Poverty Defence', *University of Richmond Law Review*, Vol. 47 (2013), 495-548. As I was writing this essay, *la Suprema Corte di Cassazione*, Italy's highest court, set aside the conviction of a man earlier found guilty of the theft

The governor's declaration of a policy of 'shoot to kill' (applied to looters in a city without potable water), a policy implemented under the conditions of the state of emergency, was widely regarded as perfectly just.[10] While the use of extra-judicial force to stop looting during a state of emergency in which food cannot be legally acquired by those without it, enjoys the greatest support in the US, even nations such as Britain (in the Second World War) have imposed the penalty of death on looters, irrespective of what was looted or why, during states of emergency.[11] In fact, throughout the world, looters are shot and killed by agents of the state, usually, but not always, during states of emergency when legal restraints on the use of deadly force are suspended. In this sense we could say that the experience in New Orleans was not only not an anomaly, but the logical conclusion of centuries of opposition to the very notion that Couvreur has excavated, namely, that in cases of urgent need the destitute have a right to steal what is necessary to their survival, if, that is, the act can legitimately be considered theft at all. Today, at least in US courts, necessity or need, however, life-threatening, is not a legitimate defense in cases of theft, even if the arguments arrayed against it in the handful of cases in which the right to steal was invoked are strikingly vague and allusive, little more than invocations of 'law' or 'property' whose obviousness excludes any need for explanation.[12]

The repertoire from which the arguments against the necessity defence in cases of theft, larceny and forgery were drawn is itself organised around a contradiction. On the one hand, it is argued that in societies as advanced as ours, food, potable water and medicines are always available to those who need them, an argument that requires the systematic exclusion of the mass of evidence to the contrary, no matter how detailed or irrefutable. In fact, one of the first uses of the argument that no one need go hungry in an advanced society with its ample provisions for the poor is found in Matthew Hale's posthumously published *HISTORIA PLACITORUM CORONÆ*, written just prior to the food shortages of the 1690s and nearly sixty years before one of the largest famines in the history of the British isles (1740-41), as if the argument made its appearance as a kind of pre-emptive and a priori denial of the very possibility of acute food shortages.[13] On the other hand, confirming the underlying cynicism of this position, is its second line of defense: although there cannot be urgent, life-threatening need in a society such as ours, if (or when) urgent need does arise, the taking of necessities remains theft and thus a punishable crime. Who can say with any certainty that, even in the midst of a generalised crisis, a particular individual who has gone without, say, water for forty-eight hours and has no prospect of obtaining it by legal means, is really in physical danger? After all, individuals react differently to dehydration and cannot be considered reliable judges of the severity of their own condition. This is especially the case when such judgments are offered as a justification for the crimes of theft or looting. Individuals cannot be allowed to make judgments that justify a violation of the law as serious as theft and appealing

of four Euros worth of bread and cheese and sentenced to six months in jail, declaring that he had in fact committed no crime. The decision was immediately and widely reported not only in Italy but internationally. Commentators, above all in the English language media, regarded with some concern, what Italian legal scholar, Maurizio Bellacosa, called the 'novelty' of the decision. According to the court, the defendant's actions did not constitute a crime, because 'he took possession of that small amount of food in the face of the immediate and essential need for nourishment, acting therefore in a state of need [*in stato di necessità*]' (Gaia Pianigiani and Sewell Chan, *Can the Homeless and Hungry Steal Food? Maybe, an Italian Court Says*, New York Times, May 3, 2016. Referring to the same case, Massimo Gramellini wrote in his column in *La Stampa*, 5 May, 2016, that 'in America', the court's privileging of the right of survival over property right would seem like '*bestemmia*' (a word that could be translated as either 'blasphemy' or 'absurdity'), while in Italy it will conjure up fears of 'proletarian expropriation'.

13. Matthew Hale, HISTORIA PLACITORUM CORONÆ, London, E.and R. Nutt and R. Gosling 1736, p53.

to a general rule about human beings and their physiological requirements tells us nothing about a particular case.[14] It is important to note that the scepticism about individuals' assessments of the degree of danger they face in justifying or excusing acts of theft, does not carry over to the category of justifiable homicide. In the latter case, especially in a surprising number of states in the US today (which we might regard as the purest expression of this tendency) the faith in the ability of an individual to assess the degree of danger posed by other people approaches the threshold of a de facto, if not de jure, immunisation of the person who believes or says he believes that he is in mortal danger.

Couvreur, for his part, does not cite a single argument from modern law, French or otherwise, concerning the inadmissible right to steal in the case of extreme necessity.[15] In fact, there is no need to do so: he has organised his exposition with all the precision necessary to impress upon the reader what had to be forgotten for modern jurisprudence, at least insofar as it concerns the doctrine of a right to steal food and water in order to go on living, to impose the principle of the primacy of property over life, without acknowledging or perhaps knowing that it has done so. That the killing of looters is just and right appears obvious to all but a very few in the US today. To read Couvreur is to be given the knowledge necessary to question the obviousness of the obvious, the network of presuppositions that could have arisen only on the basis of the exclusion of the positions of all the parties involved in the medieval controversy. To gauge the difficulty his approach must confront, we might examine the note Couvreur appends to the first sentence of the book's first chapter, one of the very few acknowledgments of the work's contemporaneity:

> We know how many contemporary authors, struck by the heretofore unknown situations that have occasioned great conflicts, crises and upheavals, have insisted on the unprecedented and unique character of these concrete situations. Thus, some, struck by the exceptional character of revolutionary wars, are tempted to think that in a subversive war, it is not possible to urge fidelity to traditional moral norms (cf. Jean Perrin, *Rester des hommes en Algerie*, 1957) (*Les Pauvres*, p1).

At first glance this passage may very plausibly be read as a critique of Fanon (similar, in fact to that of Hannah Arendt), but such a reading may only be sustained by isolating it from what follows, that is, the entire web of textual readings and arguments of which the book itself is composed. His reference to 'situations of exception' in the sentence that precedes the note leaves little doubt that the reference here is to the conduct of the French in Algeria and the succession of states of exception (*l'état d'urgence* and *l'état de siège*) that set aside legal restraints on the violence determined to be necessary to the restoration of the rule of law. But more importantly, the note invokes 'traditional moral

14. George R. Wright, *Does the Law Morally Bind the Poor*, New York, New York University Press 1996.

15. On the case of France before the twentieth-century, see Joseph Fabisch, *Essai sur l'état de nécessité*, Lyon: Paul Legendre 1903; Virginie Berger, 'Le vol nécessaire au XIXème siècle. Entre réalité sociale et lacune juridique, une histoire en construction', *Revue d'histoire de l'enfance 'irrégulière'* [online],

norms,' without any explanation of what this phrase means: can what follows, that is, the book itself and its detailed excavation of the starving man's right to steal be understood as an attempt to recover a traditional moral norm? From Couvreur's perspective, the state of exception, decreed from above, appears as nothing more than the formal re-enactment of the forgetting of the right to subsistence. It removes any legal limit on the violence that may be applied to 'looters' without regard to the urgent need that drives them to risk their lives for a small quantity of food or water. It is thus clear that Couvreur is not appealing to a well-known set of Christian norms, even as a set of precedents from which a right to steal might somehow be derived. In fact, the problem of theft in the case of extreme necessity calls into question the very notion of an original moral foundation, recalling the terms of Althusser's critique, articulated less than five years after the publication of Couvreur's book, of the concept of origin: 'The function of the concept of origin, as in original sin, is to summarise in one word what has not to be thought in order to be able to think what one wants to think'. Is it really traditional morality, Christian or otherwise, that modern thought must not think in order to think what it wants to think? Couvreur suggests that, on the contrary, it is the inescapable absence of this morality, as if it had always already been revoked by the operation of necessity which deprives the words in which the law exists, the very words of the commandments, of an original and final meaning.

Accordingly, it is useless to search for the origins of the right of the starving person to steal in antiquity or early Christianity:

> Nothing permits us to assert that the medieval authors found the doctrine of the innocence of the thief impelled by hunger already constituted in the heritage of their predecessors (*Les Pauvres*, p5).

On the contrary, a review of the *Penitentials*, an extensive historical record of sins and the acts of penance prescribed to the sinner, reveals that while the church recognised in practice a distinction between the mere theft of food and the theft of food by reason of necessity, requiring for the former penance that was longer in duration and greater in intensity than for the latter, nowhere is it recorded that the condition of starvation renders the thief who steals food innocent of any crime. But neither did it occur to any of those whose judgments were recorded to impose or advocate the imposition of the penalty of death by the secular authorities, as was typically prescribed by common law for theft of anything worth more than a very small amount of money in Medieval Europe (*Les Pauvres*, pp 46-49). There were, of course, scattered assertions of 'the innocence of the thief impelled by hunger,' but the major rupture which marked a reversal of values only occurred in the twelfth century. The sudden theoretical problematisation of property and property rights, the existence of which was once understood as the necessary consequence of the introduction of sin into the world, combined with a transformation of the notion of poverty itself, were not solely derived from scripture or the reappropriation of the church fathers. It was rather the reverse that was true: the doctrine emerged at a time of famine, disease and revolt that not even the safety-valve of the Crusades could diminish and which sent jurists in search of the means to immunise the destitute from the accusation of theft. Couvreur notes that England experienced twelve serious famines during the thirteenth century, the most severe of which, in 1235, killed 80,000 people (p14). At the same time, the struggle of the lords to extract higher rents and longer service led to landlessness, poverty and vagabondage. It was the spirit of anger and desperation that led a section of the clergy to seize words and phrases and, tearing them out of their original scriptural or legal contexts, to inscribe new meanings on them.

There is perhaps no more important example of this than a group of Roman aphorisms, which initially described inevitable states of fact over which law had no power, but which reappeared in the Gratian's *Decretum* (1140) as legal principals or norms: *Necessitas non habet legem, sed ipsa sibi facit legem* (Because necessity has no law, it can itself make law), *Quod non est licitum lege, necessitas facit licitum*, (Necessity renders lawful that which was unlawful) and *Necessitas excusat* (Necessity excuses).[16] As Couvreur notes, these statements re-emerged in the debates over the question of whether it was permissible to celebrate the Mass in an unconsecrated place if necessity made it impossible to do otherwise, 'but Canonists soon used it as a general principle (*règle*) of law in the case of theft as in other domains' (*Les Pauvres*, p.67).[17] While Gratian did not directly suggest the application of the notion of necessity to theft in cases of starvation, he nevertheless opened the way to such an application by the inclusion of a statement he mistakenly attributes to Saint Ambrose (340-397): 'Feed anyone who is dying of hunger. For if you are able to feed him and do not do so, you have murdered him' (*Pasce fame morientem. Quisquis enim pascendo hominem seruare poteris, si non paveris, occidisti*).

In this way, Gratian, whose aim was to reconcile the apparently discordant judgments that together made up canon law, in fact established a divergence in the approach to the phenomenon, increasingly common in his time (the twelfth century), of those faced with starvation. On the one side, it is to those who are not starving, particularly the rich, with their large surpluses, that both agency and responsibility for the lives of the destitute are imputed by the law. This was for a time the dominant view, undoubtedly because, at least in part, it left the legitimacy of property, irrespective of the severity of the subsistence crisis, intact. But it placed the poor in the position of waiting for the bounty of the rich, their only satisfaction knowing that in the case of their death, the rich man who could have helped but did not, might be charged with murder or, more realistically, left to the judgement of God. On the other side, as hunger, homelessness and the diseases that followed became more common, there emerged a questioning of property itself, the conditions of and limits on the ownership of the necessities of life, above all, food, as well

16. See also Seneca the elder, *Controversiae IV*, 'Necessity is the law of the moment. Is anything illegal which is done on the law's behalf?' (*necessitas est lex temporis. Quicquam non fit legitime pro legibus?*) and Pollibius Syrus (85-53 BCE), Sententiae, 'Necessity makes law but acknowledges none' (*Necessitas dat legem, non ipsa accipit*). See also Joseph Fabrisch, *Essai sur l'état de necessité*, Paris: Paul Legendre, 1903 and Philippe-Jean HESSE, UN DROIT FONDAMENTAL VIEUX DE 3 000 ANS: L'ETAT DE NECESSITE, *Droits fondamentaux*, no. 2, janvier - décembre 2002.

17. Giorgio Agamben, *The State of Exception*, (trans) Kevin Attell, Chicago, University of Chicago Press 2005. (Hereafter *Exception*).

as the rights of those who are starving if the failure of the rich to do their duty has placed them in immediate danger. If, under these circumstances, they take surplus food that belongs to another, does the act constitute theft? Can those who are in danger of dying take what is necessary to their survival from those who are, and will not be, even as a consequence of the removal of their property, in any such danger, be condemned (by canon law to do penance or by common law to suffer the amputation of an appendage or the loss of life)?

HUNGER AND PROPERTY: TWO TENDENCIES

At this point, it is clear that words themselves, under the pressure of economic and political forces, become a terrain of struggle between antithetical meanings. Necessity, property and even law become contested territory in the struggle between rich and poor. The antagonistic positions are not always clearly demarcated, nor are their effects necessarily different or opposed. We can, however, provisionally identify two tendencies, both of which develop unevenly, converging at times only to diverge again, driven by internal conflict that was itself a continuation of the struggle outside, the war that was waged merely to go on living.

The first tendency is marked by the effects of the difficulty (which clearly increases with time) of simultaneously defending a constellation of concepts at the centre of which is property, and the lives of the poor whose survival in times of 'extreme necessity' is incompatible with the right of the proprietor to dispose of his surplus as he sees fit. Under such conditions, the very meaning of property (other than property in land which tended to be regulated by a complex combination of feudal and pre-feudal laws and customs), not only as a legal concept, but in its logical and perhaps metaphysical senses began to fracture under the weight of crises and resistance, if not revolt. Could the fruits of the earth given by God to all mankind be legitimately withheld from the destitute by their owner on the grounds of his ownership alone? Did the proprietor have the right as owner to sell his wheat at the highest price he could find or withhold it from the market altogether until the price rose to the level he regarded as its maximum, even if a significant part of the population could not pay that price? Was the proprietor immunised, that is, released from the responsibility of the *munus*, the shared sacrifice that made community (*communitas*) possible? The initial impulse of theologians and legal scholars was to save the institution of *dominium* from the owners themselves who were increasingly abandoning their duty to the poor. The founding theological reference here was Augustine: not only to his defence of private property as a bulwark against the covetousness and greed that entered the world with the first sin, but his very explicit declaration that the surplus of the rich cannot be justly taken from them against their will, even with the aim of distributing this surplus to the poor.[18] The idea of violating

18. Augustine, *Contra Mendaciam*, I.7.18

the prohibition against theft that is both a direct commandment by God and a universal principle of human law, to alleviate corporeal suffering appeared untenable. The solution lay in finding the means to place a part or, under certain circumstances, all of the rich man's surplus at the disposal of the poor without challenging his *dominium* over it.

Such a solution would require great ingenuity even from those skilled in casuistry. The first line of attack concerned the duty of the rich. The failure of the rich to take immediate measures to prevent their fellows from dying of starvation could no longer be regarded simply as a misfortune of the latter. Gratian had rescued from oblivion and thus made available the passage attributed to St. Ambrose cited above: 'Feed anyone who is dying of hunger. For if you are able to feed him and do not do so, you have murdered him'. While the poor man who steals what is necessary to his continued existence, or risks his own life to obtain food for a sick parent or child who is in danger of perishing without it, is guilty of theft and liable to punishment, the rich man who withholds food from an individual who later dies of starvation is to be held responsible for the death he could have prevented and therefore guilty of the far worse crime of murder. Couvreur notes how perplexing Gratian's rehabilitation of this doctrine proved to be for the Canonists: was the application of the category of murder to the rich man's indifference to the poor to be taken literally? But the assault, directed less against the legal definition of property than on the conduct of the proprietor, had just begun. Has not the rich man, by withholding from the destitute individual the food without which he and perhaps his dependents cannot survive, placed before the poor the choice of stealing or dying? And if so, unless we believe like Cicero that an honourable man would prefer death to the dishonour of committing a theft,[19] we must conclude that he who is able to feed the starving man by virtue of the surplus he possesses but fails to do so is at the very least complicit in the theft, if not its primary cause, in that his actions have helped create the state of need. Had he done his duty to the poor as he has been commanded to do by God, there would have been no reason for theft.

But the partisans of this perspective did not simply concentrate their efforts on the duties of the rich; they also sought ways to indemnify the poor or at least grant them dispensation after the fact for acts necessary to their survival but contrary to the law. Even if the participation of the rich man by virtue of his abandonment of those in dire need in the crime itself could not exactly exculpate those who committed theft, the ingenuity with which certain scholars were able not only within the law, but using its own terms, to protect those who stole to save their own lives or the lives of those they were duty bound to defend is striking. Couvreur notes that variants of a single hypothetical case were debated in London, Paris and Rome at the end of the twelfth century: cannot a man in all justice steal food to feed his starving father, to whom he owes filial piety, and who will die without it (*Les Pauvres*, p9-11)? Some scholars responded with the familiar argument that it is not

19. Cicero, De Inventione, I. 11, chapter 58.

permitted to commit sin in order to obtain a good and that it is repugnant to the respect owed to one's father to give him what has been stolen from another.[20] An obscure figure, Maître Martin, a lecturer in Paris about whom little is known, left a written record of his determined rejection of this view in the form of two arguments. First, because the man who steals to feed his starving father is not guilty of possessing or profiting from the stolen goods, he cannot be guilty of theft, on the condition that he later makes restitution (an allusion to Proverbs 6:30-31). Second, as long as the 'thief' made a thorough attempt to obtain the owner's permission to take the food his father needs, but was unable to find him or his heirs, taking the food under conditions of extreme necessity cannot be considered theft.

20. Pierre de Poitiers, *Sententiae* 2.16.

These arguments may appear surprising to many present-day readers, but they were thoroughly grounded in Roman law (see the Digest of Justinian, lxvii, 2-*de Furtis*) and its far more restrictive understanding of theft (*furto*) in assessing cases in which individuals take something over which another individual has *dominium*. Martin's argument in fact served to inspire one of the most passionate advocates for the poor at the end of the twelfth century, Huguccio of Pisa (d. 1210), to take the argument one step further. What if the starving pauper succeeds in finding the owner of the food he (or his ailing father) requires to go on living, but the owner explicitly refuses to grant him permission to take what is necessary for his survival? The proprietor of the food might at this point be condemned for his failure to do his duty to his fellows; he might even be judged guilty of murder if anyone were to perish as a result of his refusal. But what of the pauper? How can he justly take the food refused to him by its rightful owner, above all, if he can be sure that the owner will be duly punished by the proper authorities for his crime: is the pauper now condemned to acquiesce in his and his father's death whether he does so, following the advice of Cicero, out of honour, or because he cannot bring himself to violate God's own commandments and commit what remains an illicit act?

Huguccio's solution to this problem is quite extraordinary and merits some discussion:

> When someone acts out of necessity, he does not commit theft, in that he supposes, or ought to suppose, that the owner has given his permission' (*Si quis per necessitatem nec comittit furtum, quia aut credit, aut debet credere dominium esse permissurum*).[21]

21. Huguccio, *Summa Decretum*, Couvreur, 84-85.

Huguccio thus preserves the law but only by turning it against itself, carrying out what is in fact a revocation of the proprietor's dominium over the things he owns by crediting him with, or imputing to him, a will the existence of which the *dominus* himself does not recognise, to fulfil his duty to the poor. In this way, the starving man by taking food from the owner who perversely refuses to give it to him voluntarily, saves the owner from both the sin and the crime he would have been guilty of committing had the theft not occurred. This is obviously directly opposed to the sense of imputation developed by Kant six hundred years later, namely the attribution of responsibility to an individual who must be treated as, or rather as if, he were the *causa libera* or free cause of his actions in that he can be regarded as the sole author of the act for which he may then be held accountable. Huguccio offers instead the possibility that the pauper by imputing to the proprietor the will and intention to give him what the proprietor, according to the *munus* required of him, owes the pauper, and further by demonstrating the owner's just intention by taking the food he has requested, interpellates him as a just individual who has done his duty (by means of his agent, the pauper, whose actions must be credited to the account of the owner). In this way, both the pauper and the proprietor are saved by the former's taking what is necessary to his subsistence, the one from starvation and the other from criminality and sin.

Thus, we see in this tendency an attempt to preserve property right even in the state of need (*necessitas*), if only in a formal sense, as if its purpose were, by emphasising (and multiplying) the obligations of the proprietor to the starving, obligations that were legally enforceable, to defend the notion of property. The owner who refused to fulfil these obligations not only exposed himself to a legal complaint by the poor, but would be supplanted by the persona the law demanded him to be, he who consented to grant the poor access to his surplus in times of crisis.

Was the second, opposing, tendency then a rejection of law altogether, an approach according to which the solution to the unequal and, in a crisis, fatal distribution of food was the state of exception in which law as such is suspended (but only for the duration of the emergency) and the poor will take what they need from a supply that in the space of the exception belongs to no one? And we must be clear that 'belonging to no one' does not have the same significance as 'belonging to everyone,' if 'belonging' is understood as something more merely having something in one's possession without any privileged or exclusive/exclusionary relation to it. Such a solution, far from giving rise to a Hobbesian state of nature, that is, a condition of disorder and the war of every man against every other man, in this historical period rendered the poor, insofar as they took what was necessary to their survival, an instrument of divine providence and the means by which the order or equilibrium disturbed by war, famine or drought would be restored.

The second tendency may be differentiated from the first, above all, by the shift from the obligation of proprietors to the right of the destitute. In part there is an increasing distrust of the rights granted to the owners of the stock of food, given their inability or unwillingness to distribute their surpluses even in the case of famine. But from this fact, which occasioned outrage among the canonists, came the realisation that laying obligations upon the rich (with or without earthly penalties) in no way guaranteed that they would in fact open their granaries to save the poor from death by starvation. In essence, a position that relied on preaching to or, as time went on, threatening them with eternal damnation or acts of penance, simply abandoned the hungry to the vagaries of the proprietor's conscience. The only effective way to distribute the necessities required to allow the poor to survive in a condition of dire need was 'to authorise the destitute themselves to take what was necessary to save their lives' (*Les Pauvres*, p110). Even here, though, the legality of property was not necessarily called into question: Huguccio advanced an argument similar in form to the case of the starving man unable to find the proprietor of a supply of food. In this case, a pauper may not be able to find a magistrate to issue a legal order, a *condictio ex lege*, that is, a manner of enforcing an obligation in the case that there is no prescribed penalty for a failure to fulfil it (p118). The necessity of taking the food that belonged to another was compared to self-defence and just war, cases in which one is permitted to engage in what would otherwise be an illegal action when there exists an immediate threat to one's life. Thus, by the end of the thirteenth century, there had emerged a general sense that in cases of dire need it was both legal and just for the destitute to take another's property without permission. It was inevitable that property right itself would be called into question.

It was precisely in this conjuncture, around the beginning of the thirteenth century, that the pronouncements of Basil the Great (330-379), who himself lived through a time of famine and drought in the Eastern empire, took on a renewed significance. The sermons that had earlier appeared as exhortations to the rich to use their wealth to relieve the sufferings of the poor, began to seem as if Basil had in fact proposed a radical reconceptualisation of property, especially as it was understood in Roman law. Indeed, few of his commentaries so directly and dramatically spoke to these concerns as the following:

> Now, someone who takes a man who is clothed and renders him naked would be termed a robber; but when someone fails to clothe the naked, while he is able to do this, is such a man deserving of any other appellation? The bread which you hold back belongs to the hungry; the coat, which you guard in your locked storage-chests, belongs to the naked; the footwear mouldering in your closet belongs to those without shoes. The silver that you keep hidden in a safe place belongs to the one in need. Thus, however many are those whom you could have provided for, so many are those whom you wrong.[22]

22. Basil, 'In Divites'.

What is striking in this well-known passage is not simply the obligation laid upon those who are able to help the poor, nor even the criminalisation of the failure to carry it out, as if the rich by withholding their surplus have hidden what no longer rightfully belongs to them. More important is the fact that Basil does not declare a nullification of property necessitated by a state of need, but rather reconceptualises property per se, especially property in those consumable goods, above all, food, that are necessary for survival, in order to destabilise the categories based on Roman law. To understand exactly how Basil does this, it is necessary to examine the text of his sermon, whose specific characteristics cannot easily be rendered in English. The line 'the bread which you hold back belongs to the hungry' exhibits a construction that will be repeated three more times in the sentence, in relation to a coat, shoes and silver. First, we should note that the terms Basil uses to designate the form or mode by which the rich man (to whom Basil has addressed his sermon) owns or simply 'has' food or a coat, only secondarily denote possession. In the case of bread, the verb in the original Greek (Τοῦ πεινῶντός ἐστιν ὁ ἄρτος, ὃν σὺ κατέχεις) is κατέχω, which suggests, apart from possessing or having, the act of withholding, holding on to, keeping (as opposed to giving something away) and even concealing what one is keeping. The semantic range of the term used in the Latin translation of Basil's works, *detineo* (the line is '*Esurientes est panis, quem tu detines*'), is similar to that of the Greek, in that it suggests that the object in question is held back and kept out of sight. Basil's language intimates that what is commonly understood as property, at least the property of the rich, consists of things necessary to, but illegitimately withheld and hidden from, the poor. In the case of the bread withheld by the rich, what renders the withholding of it unjust is the fact that, as the English translation puts it, the bread 'belongs' to the hungry person, which suggests that Basil regards that person as the true owner of the rich man's bread. In fact, 'belongs' is an interpolation: the line, in Greek or Latin, literally reads 'The bread that you withhold is that of the hungry person'. There is no word for owning, for property or even for possession at all in the passage cited above, except for the highly ambiguous κατέχεις in the Greek version and *detines* in the Latin.

In fact, food poses particular challenges to ideas of property. Unlike land, a dwelling, tools or even animals, food cannot be the object of a *jus utendi*, *usus et fructus*, the right to use and enjoy something owned by another but without destroying its substance. Moreover, these categories leave the position of proprietor or *dominus* intact even if, as maintained by the Franciscan order a century later, God was declared to be the absolute *dominus* and the world and everything in it his dominion. The destitute individual's food is his by virtue of *jus abutendi*, the right to 'abuse' (*abutor*, meaning to use up or consume and thus to destroy the substance of the thing). Indeed, without this right the mere possession of food would do nothing to aid in his survival. For Basil, it is rather the wealthy *dominus* who merely possesses the food without being able to use or consume it, as if he were temporarily holding another's property which must be restored to its rightful owner on demand.

But is this not another way of preserving the regime of property right by returning the goods in question to their true and legitimate owner to use and abuse as he sees fit, in which case, the poor stand to benefit from this regime? The answer lies in the nature of the origin and foundation of *jus abutendi* that Basil, and with him Gratian, denies the rich man and bestows upon the pauper. What gives the latter the right to take and consume the food which the rich man must yield to him is precisely the fact that it is an object of need for him, an object without which he cannot go on living, while for the rich man it is surplus. The effect here is to detach property in the fullest sense (*dominium* understood as *jus abutendi*) from the person and attach it instead to the condition of need or the relation of surplus to need. If the starving person is no longer starving, he ceases to have any claim to the surplus food another possesses, just as the existence of starving people deprives the possessors of any right over their surpluses and compels them to hand them over to those in need on demand. We are very close indeed to the notion of 'to each according to his need'. This also explains why Basil makes no mention of the right of the destitute to steal to survive. Such a right would be superfluous: the poor can no more be accused of theft in the act of taking what is necessary to their continued existence from the rich man's surplus, than someone retrieving lost property from the person who found it and is holding it for him. Once again, the implicit threat is quite palpable: if the rich man withholds from the poor what is theirs, he has stolen from them, in which case he can expect that they will come and take from him what is rightfully theirs by virtue of their urgent need.

Such might appear to be nothing more than an anachronistic projection of Marx onto one of the church fathers as read by Gratian and the Decretists of the twelfth century. But Couvreur, perhaps anticipating such a reaction, cites a 'violent' condemnation by the Archdeacon of Bath, Peter of Blois (1135-1203) of both the laws regarding theft by reason of severe poverty and the penalties typically imposed for such a crime. The particular case that outraged him was that of a pauper who, barely clothed and acutely malnourished himself, could not bear to see his wife and children dying before his eyes during a famine, and resolved to steal something of value that could be sold to obtain money for food. The pauper was caught during the commission of the crime and sentenced to death (the customary punishment for theft of an object of more than a minimal value). Peter demanded to know how is it that the theft of food (or the theft of an object whose sale would allow the thief to buy food) by a starving person could be called 'theft?' Is it not rather the wealthy who, by withholding their surplus from those who will perish from hunger without it, are guilty of a crime, namely the crime of murder? Further, can it be a crime for a person to steal food for a third party, whether one's family or a stranger, who is in danger of death by starvation? Is it a crime to steal an object in order to sell it if the proceeds are used to purchase food (or shelter or clothing)?

To understand the theologico-political positions inscribed in these statements, we might return to the maxim rescued from oblivion by Gratian: Because necessity has no law, it can itself make law (*Necessitas non habet legem, sed ipsa sibi facit legem*). The maxim takes the form of a paradox: Necessity *makes* (*facit*) but does not *have* (*habet*) law. Does it then 'have' the law that it makes? And if so, are we then to assume that having a law and being governed by it are the same thing? The precise wording of the maxim seems to suggest that necessity does not have, or perhaps more accurately have as its property, the law that it itself produces. In some sense, to designate law as something necessity does not possess, while declaring that necessity makes law and does so necessarily, is to draw a line of demarcation within the concept of law (*lex*). On the one side, law is defined as an edict or decree that establishes what should be, but in fact may not be; as such it is external to the existing state of affairs, as the norm is separate from fact. This is the law necessity does not have. On the other side, however, is not lawlessness but the law that necessity makes, a law that cannot be situated outside of what necessarily exists to establish rules that may be disobeyed. It is possible, then, to see in the maxim (or in the effects that it produces) the notion that if necessity *has* no law, it is because necessity *is itself that law*, as if necessity and law are one and the same thing. From this perspective, to make law is simultaneously to overcome its merely potential existence as a norm and bring about its realisation in fact. It is not enough to decree that the surplus supply of food held by the rich man is legally the property of the poor; the poor driven by vital need must be authorised to take it. This is the law that necessity makes, the law immanent in life itself, especially when it resists death that can exist only in an actualised form.

According to Giorgio Agamben, both Gratian and Aquinas regarded necessity as the means 'to justify single, specific case of transgression by means of an exception' (*Exception*). But such a reading sees in the maxim *Necessitas non habet legem*, a declaration of the necessary lawlessness of necessity: where necessity is, law cannot be, insofar as necessity for as long as it is present, suspends or negates what he calls the legal order. Moreover, the legal order is opposed to a natural order which, for Hobbes and later Schmitt, is in fact the absence of order, just as the life at stake in these disputations is from Agamben's perspective merely *la nuda vita*, the life, stripped of what is properly human, that we have in common with beasts. But nowhere in these debates do we find the notion of a setting aside of the system of law in order so that the violence necessary to the restoration of order will permit this system to operate once again. On the contrary, Aquinas, argues that to take another's property (literally 'thing' or 'things') in a condition of urgent need is not a sin. This is not because the law has been or indeed could be suspended, in which case no transgression could occur, but on the contrary because necessity makes the things that were otherwise 'another's' common (*propter necessitatem sibi factam commune*).[23] The fact that 'the division and appropriation of things... are based on human law', cannot be allowed to hinder an individual from taking what is necessary for life. Thus, for Aquinas, there is no lawless condition; such a condition would only allow the wealthy to continue to withhold their surplus from the poor. Instead, necessity operates within law to make it diverge from itself in the form of a counter-law, which here Aquinas calls natural law. But can we understand the relation between human law and natural law as a form of transcendence, as if natural law exists prior to and outside of human law, the set of norms against which human law may be judged? *Necessitas* neither nullifies 'law' as if law were, as Hobbes said, mere words, nor does it bring about a reversion to a more primary law, the real or more real law behind civil law. We should

23. Thomas Aquinas, Summa Theologica, II. II. 66, 7.

acknowledge the literal meaning of Aquinas's words, which echo the epigram: necessity makes law in the same movement by which it makes itself. The origin of law in this sense lies not in the groundlessness of sovereign decision, but in what necessity 'makes' or creates (the verb is '*facere*') from the materials salvaged from the wreckage of the existing law, shattered by the very operation of necessity itself. The outside of every law is another law, even if that other law, usually posited as discovered rather than made, as original and thus as the basis, even if superseded, of the present legal order, is invented after the fact and retroactively constituted as original. To answer Couvreur's question, the poor have rights only if the power to exercise these rights exists necessarily: there is no right without the power to realise its promise.

How are we to understand the meaning of Couvreur's book, not simply as a scholarly treatise on a now forgotten right, and perhaps on the idea of right itself, but as an intervention in the conjuncture in which he wrote? Perhaps it was his way of participating in that struggle so marked by Fanon, his 'prisoners of starvation' composed in counterpoint to *The Wretched of the Earth*. But unlike Fanon who often wrote without materials at hand as he moved from place to place and whose books were weapons designed to explode on contact, Couvreur slowly and patiently chose every scrap and fragment he could salvage from the ruins of that long-forgotten debate to fashion the theologico-political equivalent of a roadside bomb, an improvised explosive device. Disguised as a bundle of dust-covered papers on which are written lines of incomprehensible words, and placed carefully on the side of the road, it has remained to this day unexploded. Past it walk once again the millions who seek to go on living but whose mere existence is an affront to those who are convinced that their surplus is rightfully theirs to withhold from the destitute. The road these millions follow winds through the same deserts, over the same mountains, down to the same sea, across which awaits the same hatred and the same misery. What will detonate this book and release its power? We cannot know what or who will set it off or, once detonated, what armour it will pierce, what walls it will penetrate, what windows it will shatter. Unless, that is, the bomb that Couvreur constructed with such precision has already exploded, its fragments hurtling toward the fences that stand between life and death.

Warren Montag is the Brown Family Professor of Literature at Occidental College in Los Angeles. His last book is *The Other Adam Smith* (Stanford University Press, 2014). Other publications include *Althusser and his Contemporaries* (Duke UP, 2013); *Bodies, Masses, Power: Spinoza and His Contemporaries* (Duke University Press, 2013); *Louis Althusser* (Palgrave Macmillan, 2003) and *The Unthinkable Swift: The Spontaneous Philosophy of a Church of England Man* (Verso, 1998). Montag is also the editor of *Décalages*, a journal on Althusser and his circle, and the translator of Etienne Balibar's *Identity and Difference: John Locke and the Invention of Consciousness* (Verso, 2013).

Deconstructing Death: Derrida and the Scene of Execution*

Elizabeth Rottenberg

Abstract This paper focuses on the *scene* of execution, on the essentially theatrical and spectacular nature of the death penalty. It argues that this scene involves not a literal seeing but a virtual or phantasmatic seeing, i.e. a specific kind of visibility that has important consequences for thinking the death penalty (and its future). It highlights two moments of Derrida's reading of the death penalty in *The Death Penalty I* and *II*: the first is Derrida's insistence on the *virtualization* of the spectacle; the second is Derrida's appeal, in the penultimate session of *The Death Penalty I*, to the explicitly *phantasmatic* dimension of the death penalty. As the paper tries to show, there is no escaping the *scene* of execution because there is no escaping the *dream* of execution; one does not simply put an end to a phantasmatic truth. But if this 'ready-made phantasy' is the case, if there is something invincible about the dream of execution, then what would it mean, this paper asks, to think *beyond* the death penalty?

Keywords theatre, spectacle, visibility, virtualisation, primal phantasm

I would like to begin with a rather spectacular vision of the death penalty, one that brings together, with great irony, the death penalty, the possibility but also the impossibility of its abolition, and the 'American spirit'. Here is that vision:

> I would like to see a law passed which would abolish capital punishment, except for those states which insisted on keeping it. Such states would then be allowed to kill criminals provided that the killing is not impersonal but personal and a public spectacle: to wit that the executioner be more or less the same size and weight as the criminal (the law could here specify the limits) and that they fight to death using no weapons, or weapons not capable of killing at a distance. Thus, knives or broken bottles would be acceptable. Guns would not.
>
> The benefit of this law is that it might return us to moral responsibility. The killer would carry the other man's death in his psyche. The audience, in turn, would experience a sense of tragedy, since the executioners, highly trained for this, would almost always win. In the flabby American spirit there is a buried sadist who finds the bullfight contemptible - what

he really desires are gladiators. Since nothing is worse for a country than repressed sadism, this method of execution would offer ventilation for the more cancerous emotions of the American public.[1]

The author of this fight-club-phantasy - this unadulterated American-Gladiators-meets-Thunderdome scenario - is Norman Mailer. The same Norman Mailer who would, some twenty years later, go on to write the Pulitzer Prize-winning 'true life story' *The Executioner's Song* (1979), which depicts in 1109 pages the events surrounding the execution of Gary Gilmore by the state of Utah in 1977 (Gary Gilmore was the first person executed in the United States after the re-instatement of the death penalty in 1976). 'The Executioner's Song' is, of course, also the title of a 1982 NBC film starring Tommy Lee Jones and Rosanna Arquette.[2]

But before the book, and before the movie, Mailer wrote a short article, titled 'A Program for the Nation', from which I have just quoted an excerpt. This article was written in response to a survey from *Esquire* magazine in 1959,[3] in which 150 famous people were queried about the 1960 U.S. Presidential election: 'What, to your mind, should be the most important issues in the election' (*Presidential Papers*, p10)?

Now if I turn to Mailer's program for the nation here, it is not only because he addresses capital punishment as an important, presidential issue. It is also because he insists on the *scene* of execution in America. There is a scene, says Mailer, that is not being seen: a hidden and invisible and perhaps even disavowed scene. This scene, says Mailer, must be made visible; it must be *literally* seen (this is his irony). America must see what it refuses to see: the *scene* of execution. What Mailer goes on to describe, however, is a rather un-American scene: no lethal injection here (or to put it less anachronistically: no hanging, no electric chair, no gas chamber here). Instead Mailer stages his American scene of execution as an epic historical drama, as an archaic and sadistic scene.

Indeed, what Mailer's phantasy makes visible is not only a Roman scene. It is also a second (or even third) scene, which is really a kind of *primal* scene: 'In the flabby American spirit there is a buried sadist who finds the bullfight contemptible - what he really desires are gladiators'. In the deep, dark, fleshy recesses of the American soul lies a desire that is older, younger, more primitive, more archaic than a desire for (European) bullfights. It's a desire for cutting weapons and a desire for human, rather than animal, sacrifice. Thus, Mailer's insistence on the *scene* of capital punishment leads him, as it were, behind the scene(s), to the scene's latent structure: 'Since nothing is worse for a country than repressed sadism, this method of execution would offer ventilation for the more cancerous emotions of the American public'.

The scene, then, in Mailer's vision of it, would be something that exceeds its particular (empirical, social, political, historical) context. Or to put it more provocatively: there is no such thing as an *American* scene of execution (which

---

1. Norman Mailer, *The Presidential Papers*, New York, Bantam 1964, p11. (Hereafter *Presidential Papers*).

2. 'The Executioner's Song' had also been used as a title in two earlier works by Mailer: first as the title of a poem in *Cannibals and Christians* (1966) and then as a chapter heading in his documentary novel *The Fight* (1975).

3. In the end, Mailer's article was published not in *Esquire* but in *Dissent* magazine, in the winter of 1960. See Appendix B (*Presidential Papers*, p305).

does not mean that people are not executed in the United States). What it does mean, however, is that there remains something excessive, something fundamentally out of joint, temporally and spatially dislocated, about what is called the 'American' scene.

It should come as no surprise, therefore, if I move to another scene, another theatre, this time the Amphi*theatre* at the École des Hautes Études where, every Wednesday from 5:00 to 7:00 p.m., from December 1999 to March 2000 and then again from December 2000 to March 2001, Jacques Derrida delivered The Death Penalty Seminar. One might say that, like Mailer, Derrida calls our attention to the *scene* of execution - to the essentially theatrical and spectacular nature of the death penalty. Unlike Mailer, however, the scene in question involves not a literal seeing but a virtual or phantasmatic seeing, i.e. a specific kind of visibility that has important consequences for thinking the death penalty (and its future). In what follows, I will highlight two moments of this other visibility: the first is Derrida's insistence on the *virtualisation* of the spectacle; the second is Derrida's appeal, in the penultimate session of *The Death Penalty I*, to the explicitly *phantasmatic* dimension of the death penalty. As we will see when we get to the phantasm, there is no escaping the *scene* of execution because there is no escaping the *dream* of execution; one does not simply put an end to a 'phantasmatic truth'.[4] But if this 'ready-made phantasy' is the case,[5] if there is something invincible about the dream of execution, then what would it mean to think *beyond* the death penalty?

SCENE 1: THE STRATEGY

For Derrida, the idea of spectacle is analytically contained or included in the idea of legal execution. Here is what he says in the opening pages of *The Death Penalty I*:

> By definition, in essence, by vocation, there will never have been any invisibility for a legal putting to death ... there has never been, on principle, a secret or invisible execution for this verdict. The spectacle and the spectator are required. The state, the *polis*, the whole of politics, the co-citizenry - itself or mediated through representation - must attend and attest, it must testify publicly that death was dealt or inflicted, it must *see die* the condemned one (*Death Penalty I*, p2).

There can be no invisibility for a legal putting to death. Capital punishment - *by definition, in essence, in principle* - requires a public: 'the death penalty must be accessible to the public in its procedures of judgment, verdict, and execution ... Where this is not the case ... it is not certain that we can, in all rigor, speak of the "death penalty"'.[6] Nothing is more 'publicly theatrical or theatrically public' (*Death Penalty II*, p60) than a punishment that is administered by the state. Nothing is less private than the criminal

4. Jacques Derrida, *The Death Penalty, Volume I*, (trans) Peggy Kamuf, Chicago, University of Chicago Press 2013, p258. Jacques Derrida's The Death Penalty Seminar is being prepared for publication in French and English as follows: Jacques Derrida, *La peine de mort*, 2 vols, Paris, Galilée 2012-2015 and *The Death Penalty*, 2 vols translated by Peggy Kamuf (vol. 1) and Elizabeth Rottenberg (vol. 2), Chicago, University of Chicago Press 2013-17. Only the first volume of the seminar has appeared in English so far; the second volume is forthcoming in 2017. To oversee the English-language edition of *The Seminars of Jacques Derrida*, the Derrida Seminars Translation Project (DSTP) was formed in 2006. The six members of the DSTP - Geoffrey Bennington, Pascale-Anne Brault, Peggy Kamuf, Michael Naas, Elizabeth Rottenberg, David Wills - will be responsible for translating the first eight volumes of The Seminars of Jacques Derrida (of which The Death Penalty Seminar will be volumes 3 and 4). Hereafter, All references to *The Death Penalty, Volume I* will be given parenthetically las *Death Penalty I*, followed by a page number; all references to *The Death Penalty, Volume II* will be given parenthetically as *Death Penalty II*.

law in the name of which a person is condemned to death. 'The state', says Derrida, 'must *see die* the condemned one'. This *seeing-die* is, for Derrida, a *must-see*: it is essential to capital punishment. But let there be no literal or literalising misunderstanding here. When Derrida says 'the state, the *polis*, the whole of politics, the co-citizenry - *itself or mediated through representation*' it is clear that to be public does not mean, as it did for Mailer (or as it will for Foucault), that the public must *literally* see the execution or that the death penalty must be visible to everyone. Nor does it mean that it is *literally* possible to see die, i.e. to locate or pinpoint the 'objectifiable instant that separates the living from the dying' (*Death Penalty I*, p238). Rather, as we will see, a certain virtuality is already inscribed in the very act of witnessing an execution.

But the quotation continues. After pointing to the spectacular dimension of legal execution, Derrida shifts his attention to its *specular* dimension. In short, staging becomes *self*-staging:

> It is at that moment, in the instant at which the people having become the state or the nation-state *sees die* the condemned one that it best sees itself. It best sees itself, that is, it acknowledges and becomes aware of its absolute sovereignty and that it *sees itself* in the sense in French where 'il se voit' can mean 'it lets itself be seen' or 'it gives itself to be seen'. Never ... is the sovereignty of the state more *visible* in the gathering that founds it than when it makes itself into the *seer* and the *voyeur* of ... an *execution*. For this act of witnessing - the state as witness of the execution and witness of itself, of its own sovereignty, of its own almightiness - this act of witnessing must be visual: an eye witness. It thus never happens without a stage (*Death Penalty I*, p2-3).

In the scene of execution, sovereignty makes a spectacle of itself; it makes an absolute spectacle of itself. For it is 'at that moment, in that instant' in which the state sees die the condemned one, and perhaps not without jubilation, that it 'acknowledges and becomes aware of its absolute sovereignty'. In this sense, in the sense that the scene of execution is the site of the coming-to-visibility of sovereignty to itself, the scene of execution might also be called the *mirror-stage* of sovereignty. In a way too, and though I hate to say it, I do not think it can be avoided here, in this context of optics and self-reflection, the spectacle of capital punishment becomes a kind of *super-selfie*: it's the sovereign selfie.

But it is also through this sovereign selfie that the light of a more archaic or foundational scene begins to come into focus. Indeed, Derrida not only points to the coming-to-visibility of sovereignty (to itself) but also to the coming-to-visibility of sovereignty 'in the gathering that founds it': 'never', says Derrida, 'is the sovereignty of the state more *visible* in the gathering that founds it [*en son rassemblement fondateur*] than when it makes itself into the *seer*

All translations of *Death Penalty II* are my own. For more information on the translation of these seminars, see http://derridaseminars.org/index.html. Jacques Derrida.

5. Sigmund Freud, *The Interpretation of Dreams* in *The Standard Edition of the Complete Psychological Works of Sigmund Freud*, (trans) James Strachey in collaboration with Anna Freud, assisted by Alix Strachey and Alan Tyson, 24 vols, London, The Hogarth Press 1953-1974, 5, p495. Hereafter all references to Freud's works will be as *Standard Edition* followed by volume and page number.

6. Jacques Derrida, *For What Tomorrow: A Dialogue*, (trans) Jeff Fort, Stanford, Stanford University Press 2004, p145. (Hereafter *For What Tomorrow*).

and the *voyeur* ... of an *execution*' (*Death Penalty I*, p3). Never is sovereignty more visible in the gathering/assembling that is its dawn and first light, than in the state's act of witnessing an execution. To be most visible in its foundational gathering: what does this mean? What would it mean to see a *primal* gathering? Does one *see* a primal scene?

But let me return to the very beginning of *The Death Penalty I*:

> It is dawn, then. Early light, earliest light. Before the end, before even beginning, before the three blows are struck, the actors and the places are ready, they are waiting for us in order to begin (*Death Penalty I*, p3).

Why begin in this way? Why set the scene in such a 'deliberately pathos-laden fashion' (*Death Penalty I*, p2)? Derrida has in mind, of course, to 'analyse the "scene", the history of its visibility and of its "public" character generally' (*Death Penalty I*, xv). But if he marks the stage in this way, if he 'play[s] without playing at the theatre ... as theatrically but also as nontheatrically as possible' (*Death Penalty I*, p3), it is also because he desires to change the scene. It is because he wants to *bring down the curtain* on the death penalty: 'It is obvious that in my argumentation and in the pathos you will hear, my discourse is going to be abolitionist' (*Death Penalty I*, p5n7). That is, it's a strategy. It's a strategy for thinking a dramatic turn of events - a *coup de théâtre*. In fact, and despite his early programmatic statement to the contrary ('deconstruction ... is not the psychoanalysis of philosophy'),[7] Derrida's strategy here resembles nothing so much as that of an analyst who, in bringing the theatre of a patient's phantasies to the fore in an analytic setting, gives place to the non-theatrical at the heart of the theatrical, the place from which these phantasies can be analysed and thus potentially transformed.

Just like the analyst who plays without playing at the theatre, as theatrically but also as nontheatrically as possible, Derrida is laying the groundwork for thinking the possibility of change. But just as there can be no transference interpretation without transference, so too there can be no *coup de théâtre* without the theatre. In other words, we must begin, as Derrida does in The Death Penalty Seminar, by making the scene of execution as visible and as manifest as possible.

SCENE 2: THE VIRTUALISATION OF VISIBILITY

But we have already seen it - and right from the start. By insisting at every turn on visibility, Derrida disputes Michel Foucault's claims regarding the progressive disappearance of the spectacular visibility of torture and execution in *Discipline and Punish*.[8] Foucault's thesis, you will recall, is that at the end of the eighteenth and the beginning of the nineteenth century, 'punishment had gradually ceased to be a spectacle'.[9] 'Punishment-as-spectacle' (*Discipline and Punish*, p9) had disappeared and with it the theatre of public execution.

7. Jacques Derrida, *Writing and Difference*, (trans) Alan Bass, Chicago, The University of Chicago Press 1978, p196.

8. Although a student had presented on the chapter 'Right of Death and Power over Life' from Foucault's *History of Sexuality: Volume I, An Introduction* (see Editorial Note, *Death Penalty I*, xvi), and Derrida makes a passing reference to 'bio-power' in *The Death Penalty II* (see *Death Penalty II*, p42), *Discipline and Punish* is the only book by Foucault that is mentioned by name in Derrida's seminar.

9. Michel Foucault, *Discipline and Punish: The Birth of the Prison*, (trans) Alan Sheridan, New York, Random House 1977, p9. (Hereafter *Discipline and Punish*).

Hence, *Discipline and Punish* marks a division, a rupture, a passage from one *episteme* to another. Let me quote Foucault here:

> At the beginning of the nineteenth century ... the great spectacle of physical punishment gets erased; the tortured body was avoided; the theatrical representation of pain was excluded from punishment. The age of sobriety in punishment had begun (*Discipline and Punish*, p14, modified).

We move, in other words, from 'one art of punishing' to another (*Discipline and Punish*, p257) - from a society of spectacle and public execution to a society of surveillance where punishment 'tend[s] to become the most hidden part of the penal process' (*Discipline and Punish*, p9).

Now it is precisely this shift in the administration of penalties, a shift from the spectacular to the hidden, from the visible to the invisible that Derrida calls into question.[10] In fact, and it is somewhat compulsive, whenever Derrida mentions the name 'Foucault' in his writing on the death penalty, he does so in order to highlight another logic, another modality of visibility, one that extends the field of the visible beyond 'the "how", the "where", and especially the "when"' of the pre-modern 'spectacle' (*Death Penalty I*, p219).

This other logic, which is that of the 'virtual', follows closely upon any mention of 'Foucault'. I will give two examples of this. The first is from *The Death Penalty I*, and it is the only explicit reference to Foucault in the whole first year of the seminar:

> Foucault's book [*Discipline and Punish*] is not a book on the death penalty, but it is a book that deals among other things with the historical transformation of the spectacle, with the organized visibility of punishment, with what I will call, even though this is not Foucault's expression, the *seeing-punish* [voir-punir], a *seeing-punish* essential to punishment, to the right to punish as right to see-punish(ed), or even as duty-to-see-punish(ed) [*devoir de voir-punir*], one of Foucault's historical theses being that at the beginning of the nineteenth century, what 'gets erased' is, I quote, 'the great spectacle of physical punishment; the tortured body is avoided; the staging of suffering is excluded from the punishment. The age of punitive sobriety begins' ... I am not so sure of this, but perhaps there is here a technical, tele-technical, or even televisual complication of seeing, or even a virtualization of visual perception (*Death Penalty I*, p43).

The second is from Derrida's interview with Elisabeth Roudinesco (where he is speaking of The Death Penalty Seminar):

> Contrary to what Foucault says, I don't believe there is a shift from the visible to the invisible in the administration of penalties beginning in the eighteenth century. While I recognize the relative legitimacy of this

10. It is interesting to note that the work of the GIP (*Groupe d'information sur les prisons*) to which Foucault alludes in *Discipline and Punish* (see *Discipline and Punish*, p30-31) had, as its working principle, to expose the material conditions of prison life to the public, i.e. 'to make the invisible visible', as my colleague Kevin Thompson has put it. Though this work of revealing the deplorable conditions of detention (overcrowding, poor sanitation, lack of medical care, lack of privacy, etc.) certainly did make 'visible' what was 'hidden' and 'invisible' to the public, the notions of visibility/publicity to which the GIP appealed were, importantly, literal: the public must (be made to) see with its own eyes the material conditions of the prisons. Indeed, this literality was its force. But it is precisely this literal notion of visibility that Derrida challenges here.

analysis, according to certain limited criteria, I would be tempted to say that in the evolution of punishments, we shift not from the visible to the invisible but rather from one visibility to another, more virtual, one. In [my] seminar on capital punishment, I am trying to demonstrate that the same process is oriented toward another modality, another distribution of the visible (and therefore of the invisible) that can even, on the contrary, extend the virtual field of the spectacular and the theatrical, with decisive consequences (*For What Tomorrow*, p12).

By becoming virtual, the spectacle will have continued: 'today we can no longer speak of ... the death penalty without film and television; we have proof of this every day and it is an essential change in the given state of affairs' (*Death Penalty I*, p247). Film and television but also the media and the Internet will have transformed and extended the field of the visible. Never, says Derrida, 'have things been as "visible" in the worldwide space as they are today; this is itself an essential element of the problem - and of the struggle. Spectral logic invades everything' (*For What Tomorrow*, p159, modified). Spectral logic, here the logic of the 'virtual', makes it such that the scene of punishment and execution is never simply visible (or invisible) in Foucault's sense, but always marked by the trace of another visibility, of a non-present visibility (that is, the trace of something that is not visible determines our experience of the visible, so there is no pure visibility; visibility is always marked by the trace of another visibility). Thus, although it is true, *in a certain sense*, that punishment and execution have become less and less visible, less and less theatrical, more and more hidden and invisible, it is also true that we have more and more visibility through technical, tele-technical, and televisual means.

What this means, however, is that there is something *visibly unmasterable*, abyssal, and unattributable about the scene of punishment and execution. Such that Foucault's own masterful attempt to locate power in the organised visibility/invisibility of punishment finds itself unmastered by this logic. Now before I jump to the phantasmatic scene of execution in *The Death Penalty I*, I would like to turn briefly to a strange moment in *Discipline and Punish* where Foucault describes the 'real subjugation' that results from a 'fictitious relation' (*Discipline and Punish*, p202). In this passage, which is remarkable in many ways, one might say that Foucault sees without seeing, and knows without being able to take into account what Derrida has been saying all along, namely that 'capital punishment remains fundamentally ... a spectacle' (*Discipline and Punish*, p15) - and just to make my point in advance, I will note that this last quotation comes not from The Death Penalty Seminar but from *Discipline and Punish*. What Foucault describes in this passage is a fictional, a phantasmatic or virtual scene, an internalised spectacle in which the prisoner in the Panopticon sees himself being seen. Although Foucault sees only a 'calculated, organized, technically thought out' subjection in this scene of self-surveillance, I will suggest instead that it presents us with a scene from which we can begin to think an excess of play in the panoptic machine (*Discipline and Punish*, p26).

In the chapter that immediately precedes 'Panopticism' in the 'Discipline' section of *Discipline and Punish*, Foucault points to the importance of the examination in the rise of disciplinary power. The examination, says Foucault, 'combines the techniques of an observing hierarchy and those of a normalizing judgment' (*Discipline and Punish*, p184). Foucault devotes several pages to the examination in both its medical and educational applications before advancing a statement, which seems to follow directly and rather unproblematically from the central thesis of *Discipline and Punish*: '*The examination transformed the economy of visibility into the exercise of power*' (*Discipline and Punish*, p187). Such a sentence beautifully summarises the movement away from visibility that I have pointed to in Derrida's critique of Foucault. And yet, this is not what Foucault says, at least not in French. The French line reads: '*L'examen intervertit l'économie de la visibilité dans l'exercise du pouvoir*',[11] that is to say, *the examination reverses* (intervertit) *the economy of visibility in the exercise of power*. It is not, in other words, that we move from an economy of visibility, on the one hand, to an exercise of power, on the other, which is how the translator understands it (here, by being too Foucauldian, he forgets to read Foucault). Rather we move from one economy of visibility to another economy of visibility when we move from a society of spectacle to one of surveillance. The examination reverses or inverts that which is visible; it changes who or what is seen. Thus, the very process of despectacularisation is not only a move from visibility to invisibility; it is also, at the same time, a re-positioning or re-positing of visibility. What Foucault goes on to say makes this perfectly clear:

11. Michel Foucault, *Surveiller et punir: Naissance de la prison*, Paris, Gallimard 1975, p189.

> Traditionally, power was what was seen, what was shown and what was manifested ... Those on whom it was exercized could remain in the shadows; they received light only from that portion of power that was conceded to them, or from the reflection of it that for a moment they carried. Disciplinary power, on the other hand, is exercized through its invisibility; at the same time it imposes on those whom it subjects a principle of compulsory visibility. In discipline, it is the subjects who have to be seen. Their visibility assures the hold of the power that is exercised over them. It is the fact of being constantly seen, of being able always to be seen, that maintains the disciplined individual in his subjection (*Discipline and Punish*, p187).

Thus, Foucault describes the passage from relations of sovereignty to relations of discipline as a chiasmic reversal. The power that was visible ('Traditionally, power was what was seen') becomes invisible ('Disciplinary power, on the other hand, is exercised through its invisibility'), while the reverse is true for those who are on the receiving end of punishment. Traditionally, those on whom power is exercised remain invisible, 'in the shadows', whereas now they are driven into the limelight ('Disciplinary power ... imposes on those whom it subjects a principle of compulsory visibility'). But what remains constant and completely unchanged in this reversal is the principle of visibility/invisibility as a principle of power or mastery. Power (whether sovereign or disciplinary) is the power to make visible and/or invisible.

And nowhere is this power more explicit or more literal than in the 'political anatomy' of 'Panopticism' (*Discipline and Punish*, p208). 'The Panopticon', says Foucault, 'is a machine for dissociating the see/being seen dyad: in the peripheric ring, one is totally seen, without ever seeing; in the central tower, one sees everything without ever being seen' (p201-202). The Panopticon makes completely visible those in the peripheric ring while making completely invisible those in the central tower. The reason for this distribution of visibility/invisibility is that when it comes to the power of disciplinary power, less is more: the less visible, the less external, the less physical a mechanism, the more effective, the more efficient, and the more insidious its power. But nothing quite compares to the marvel that is the Panopticon - 'The Panopticon', says Foucault, 'is a marvellous machine [*une machine merveilleuse*]' (p202):

> [With the Panopticon] it is not necessary to use force to constrain the convict to good behavior, the madman to calm, the worker to work, the schoolboy to application, the patient to the observation of regulations ... He who is subjected to a field of visibility, and who knows it, assumes responsibility for the constraints of power; he plays them out spontaneously on himself; he inscribes in himself the power relation in which he simultaneously plays both roles; he becomes the principle of his own subjection. By this very fact, the external power may throw off its physical weight; it tends to the non-corporal; and, the more it approaches this limit, the more constant, profound and permanent are its effects: it is a perpetual victory that avoids any physical confrontation and which is always played out in advance (p202-203, modified).

12. Michel Foucault, *The History of Sexuality: Volume 1, An Introduction*, (trans) Robert Hurley, New York, Random House 1978, p140. (Hereafter *History of Sexuality*).

13. In this context, one might read Foucault's turn away from death and the death penalty in

What Foucault is describing here - and what he calls 'panopticism' - is the process whereby intersubjective relations are transformed into intrasubjective ones ('he inscribes in himself the power relation'). The power relation is transposed in phantasy from the 'outside' to the inside'; it is taken within the psyche such that the relation of subjection is lived out on the intrapsychic level. Freud called this process 'internalisation' and he too found it 'very remarkable' (*Standard Edition* 21: 123). Whether or not Foucault intends to limit this internalisation process to societies of surveillance (which would mean, I suppose, no superego before the eighteenth century), one thing is clear: there is a fictional and even theatrical dimension to this process. To be seen is at the same time - 'spontaneously', 'simultaneously' says Foucault

- to see oneself being seen. Thus, the disciplined individual (the convict, the madman, the worker, the schoolboy, the patient) sets up an agency within himself to watch over him, 'like a garrison in a conquered city' (*Standard Edition* 21: 123); he plays and replays for himself a scene of surveillance. In this scene, he *plays both roles*; he *plays them out* on himself: he occupies both roles, as one might in a dream - he is inmate *and* guard, schoolboy *and* examiner, patient *and* doctor, victim *and* executioner. Indeed, the echo is not only Freudian; it is also Baudelairian: 'Je suis la plaie et le couteau! ... Et la victime et le bourreau! [I am the wound and the dagger!... Victim and Executioner!]'. In becoming the 'principle of his own subjection', the convict, the madman, the schoolboy, the patient is also the *principal* actor or star *player* in a *scene* of subjection. Or to put it another way: in this phantasmatic scene of (self-)surveillance, the disciplined individual becomes the *master of ceremonies*.

To play both roles, to become the master of one's own subjection, where does this lead us? For Foucault it leads only to 'a real subjection' (*Discipline and Punish*, p202). By taking the Panopticon into himself and establishing his own private Panopticon, the prisoner *plays* into the hands of the other, of the external power, precisely because this external power is now inside him ('non-corporal' and invisible). In other words, Foucault sees the *play* between inside/outside, auto-surveillance/hetero-surveillance, auto-punishment/hetero-punishment as merely the effect of a disciplinary machination. Thus, although Foucault may rage against the machine and its 'calculated management of life',[12] the victory of external power is 'always played out in advance' (p203, modified). It is always played out in advance because we are part of its mechanism (*rouage*).

But what if we saw the 'fictitious relation', i.e. the phantasmatic scene of surveillance in a more Freuderridean vein? What if we saw the scene as precisely exceeding, or better yet e-luding (and the French here would be *déjouer*), the grip of our common sense (or conscious) belief in the oppositional distinction between inside/outside, internal/external, auto- and hetero? What if, in other words, we read the scene of self-surveillance not only as a scene of 'real subjection' but also, as I have suggested with and against Foucault, as a scene of *virtual mastery*? Indeed, what if what this scene of virtual mastery *made visible* was something essential to punishment?

Perhaps, then, we might read Foucault's disavowal of the theatrical nature of modern punishment - the fact that he sees without seeing that punishment remains fundamentally a spectacle - as a different sort of recognition.[13] One that would lead us to ask a different sort of question: What if there were something about the scene of virtual mastery that made it not only unthinkable for a thinker wedded to the modern detheatricalisation of punishment but also intolerable? Might there not be something intolerable about a virtual collusion (and to collude is to play with, *colludere*) with 'real subjection'?

History of Sexuality, published just one year after *Discipline and Punish*, as another example of such 'recognition'. It is as if Foucault had pinpointed the very condition of impossibility of his theory and had then simply excluded it. Thus, Foucault will argue that the procedures of power must turn away from death in order to focus on the management of life:

'How could power exercise its highest prerogatives by putting people to death, when its main role was to ensure, sustain, and multiply life, to put this life in order? For such a power, execution was at the same time a limit, a scandal, and a contradiction ... Now it is over life ... that power establishes its dominion; death is power's limit, the moment that escapes it; death becomes the most secret aspect of existence, the most "privat"'. (*History of Sexuality*, p138).

In a sense, then, by drawing attention to the death penalty in The Death Penalty Seminar Derrida begins with Foucault's disavowal, that is, he begins with the limit-case that Foucault has excluded from consideration and asks if the death penalty is not precisely the quasi-transcendental condition of sovereignty: included as excluded.

SCENE 3: THE DREAM OF DECONSTRUCTION

But here I would like to recall a difference, namely that, unlike Foucault for whom the death penalty becomes but another example of power-knowledge in a specific regime of punishment, Derrida considers the death penalty to be the example *par excellence* of sovereign power. Along with war, the death penalty remains the 'best emblem of the sovereign power of the state over the life and death of the citizen'.[14] This is why the deconstruction of the death penalty is not simply 'one necessity among others, a particular point of application' (*For What Tomorrow*, p148). Rather 'deconstruction is perhaps always, ultimately ... the deconstruction of the death penalty, of the logocentric, logonomocentric scaffolding in which the death penalty is inscribed or prescribed' (*Death Penalty I*, p23).

As a result, the theatre of the death penalty is not simply one theatre of punishment among others. Indeed, if Derrida returns again and again to the scene of execution, it is because, as we have seen, it is the primal or foundational scene of sovereignty; it is the moment in which sovereignty becomes most visible 'in the gathering that founds it' (*Death Penalty I*, p3). But if he insists on the logic of virtualisation - against Foucault's logic of 'devisibilisation' (p205) - it is because this primal scene of sovereignty is bound up with future scenes of punishment, that is, with the very question and possibility of abolition. To disavow the spectacle - to see without seeing the virtualisation of visibility, as Foucault does - is thus also to disavow the way in which the scene of the foundational gathering of sovereignty is *projected* into the future. It is to miss not only the foundational element of the spectacle but also its temporalisation: the relation between primal and future scenes of punishment. In the end, I hope to show how the linking of these questions (the question of what comes before with the question of what comes after) throws new light on the 'actual' theatre of the death penalty and on its future projections.

Derrida begins Session 9 of *The Death Penalty I* with a question: 'When to die finally?' (*Death Penalty I*, p218). When to die, in the end, since we are all fated or 'condemned to die'? 'What is the right age to die, if there is one?' (*Death Penalty II*, p5). These questions lead him to imagine a thought experiment: 'If ... I was given the choice between being condemned to death at age seventy-five (guillotined) or being condemned to die at age seventy-four (in my bed)' (*Death Penalty I*, p218), what would I choose? The point of course is not to choose but to show that what is at issue in this 'choice', and thus what is at issue when it is a question of the death penalty, is a 'certain modality, a certain qualification of living and dying ... a theatre, a scene of life-giving and of giving-death' (*Death Penalty II*, p6). So the choice is not between life and death; the choice is between two modes of an 'unavoidable and always imminent death' (*Death Penalty II*, p6), between two theatres of death, or - and Derrida will use the word 'intolerable' here to characterise

14. Jacques Derrida, *Without Alibi*, (ed. and trans) Peggy Kamuf, Stanford, Stanford University Press 2002, p245. (Hereafter *Without Alibi*).

both sides of the alternative - two relations to calculation, mastery, decidability, and the question of 'when':

> The alternative is terrible and infinite: I may deem it intolerable, and this is the case of the death penalty, to know that the hour of my death is fixed, by others, by a third party, at a certain day, a certain hour, a certain second, whereas if I am not condemned to death but only to die, this calculable knowledge is impossible. But conversely, I may deem it intolerable not to know the date, the place, and the hour of my death and thus I may dream of appropriating this knowledge, of having this knowledge at my disposal, at least phantasmatically, by getting myself condemned to death and thus by arriving in this fashion at some calculable certitude, some quasi-suicidal mastery of my death ... By knowing at what hour, on what day I will die, I can tell myself the story of how death will not take me by surprise and will thus remain at my disposal, like a quasi-suicidal auto-affection. (*Death Penalty I*, p218)

To know, or not to know 'when' - that is the question that divides, 'as with a knife blade, two deaths or two condemnations, the condemnation to die and the condemnation to death' (*Death Penalty I*, p219). Whether it is more intolerable to know the moment, the date, the precise hour of one's death (cf. the '"given moment" or the "designated place" of the given moment of "my death"' [*Death Penalty II*, p4]) or not to know at which instant death will come, and by opposing this non-knowledge with the calculable certainty of the death penalty, arrive at some quasi-suicidal mastery of my death.

However paradoxical it may seem, both positions are not only possible but also inseparable. For both are predicated on a relation to a force that comes 'into' me from a beyond that is greater than I am. Indeed, the point is that, *in both cases*, my time-of-life-and-death - the (im)possibility of my future - is determined by what comes to me from the outside, from the other. On the side of the death penalty, it is too obvious, but it is an 'obscure obviousness that one must begin by recalling' (*Death Penalty I*, p250). Let me quote, therefore, three short passages in order to recall this obvious fact - the fact that the death penalty is first and foremost *la mort venue de l'autre*, 'death that comes from the other':

> The death penalty, as the sovereign decision of a power, reminds us perhaps, before anything else, that a sovereign decision is always the other's. Come from the other (*Death Penalty I*, p1).

> Even in cases ... where the death sentence might be obscurely, compulsively, irresistibly sought, desired - as desire itself - by the condemned one ... the death penalty is always, by definition, death that comes from the other, given or decided by the other, be it the other within oneself. The possibility

> of the death penalty ... begins where I am delivered into the power of the other, be it the power of the other in me (*Death Penalty I*, p250-51).

> The death penalty ... [is] a death that comes from the other, decided and calculated by the other, in the hands of the other (*Death Penalty I*, p251).

The death penalty is death that comes from the other; it is death that is given, decided, calculated by the power of the other (be it the power of the other in me, the power of the outside inside me). It implies, in principle, 'that the other knows and sometimes that I know, to the second, to the minute, in a way that is therefore calculable, the moment of "my death"' (*Death Penalty II*, p4). To be condemned to death, in other words (and here we must distinguish the condemnation to death from the condemnation to die), implies the power of the other as the one who decides, sovereignly: 'you will die and you will die in such a way and you will die on this day, at this hour' (*Death Penalty II*, p137). And what is decided by the power of the other, what is 'delivered up to the calculating decision of the other', is my time of life and death: 'the time given or the time taken, time that becomes the calculation of the other' (*Death Penalty I*, p220). In the case of the death penalty, what comes to me from the other is, one might say, my death date, the given moment of my death.

But this death that comes to me from the other is also, says Derrida, the only example of a death whose instant is calculable by a machine or by machines - 'not by someone, finally, as in a murder, but by all sorts of machines: the law, the penal code, the anonymous third party, the calendar, the clock, the guillotine or another apparatus' (*Death Penalty I*, p257). This is why one must also speak, as Derrida does, of the 'machine of the death penalty' (p257) or, as Harry Blackmun did, of the 'machinery of death'.[15] But the worst, that is to say, the most intolerable, but also, as we will see, the most fascinating and the most seductive of these machines, is the clock. Indeed, one cannot think the torture and cruelty of the calculating decision without thinking its relation to clockwork: 'you will die ... in that calculable place, and from blows delivered by several machines, the worst of which is perhaps neither the guillotine nor the syringe, but *the clock and the anonymity of clockwork*' (*Death Penalty I*, p256, my emphasis).

In the end, what is intolerable (in the first sense) and what we oppose when we oppose the death penalty is not death, 'or even the fact of killing, of taking a life' (p256). What we oppose when we oppose the death penalty is the calculating decision, the calculation imposed on what is - and should remain - an incalculable future. And this is where the foundational element that distinguishes Derrida's thinking of the death penalty from Foucault's is also strangely - how shall I put it? - 'heartening', for what comes to us originally from the other is both death- *and* life-giving. For there is no way for me to speak of 'my life', that is, of my relation to an 'incalculable and

15. See Harry Blackmun's dissent from the U.S. Supreme Court's decision denying review in a Texas death penalty case (Callins v. Collins) on 22 Februar, 1994, at https://en.wikipedia.org/wiki/Harry_Blackmun.

undecidable future', without first naming what 'comes from the other', or from what Derrida lyrically calls the 'heart of the other' (p256):[16]

> The insult, the injury, the fundamental injustice done to the life in me, to the principle of the life in me, is not death ... it is rather the interruption of the principle of indetermination, the ending imposed on the opening of the incalculable chance whereby a living being has a relation to what comes ... It is because my life is finite, 'ended' in a certain sense that I keep this relation to incalculability and undecidability as to the instant of my death. It is because my life is finite, 'finished' in a certain sense that I do not know, and that I neither can nor want to know when I am going to die. Only a living being as finite being can have a future, can be exposed to a future, to an incalculable and undecidable future that s/he does not have at his/her disposal like a master and that comes to him or to her from [the] other, from the heart of the other. So much so that when I say 'my life' ... I have already named the other in me ... the other who ... lets me be me, the other whose heart is more interior to my heart than my heart itself. (p256-57, modified)

In other words, what comes to me from the other is not only death, calculation and decision, the calculable decidability of the instant of my death, but also life, the relation to incalculability and undecidability, the relation to the 'coming of the to-come [*venue de l'à-venir*]' (p256). What comes to me from the other, *from the heart of the other*, is thus a certain *undecidability* as to the instant of my death. And here we would have to think the heart *with* the machine, for a heart is also a machine: it's a time machine, a ticker. We would have to think the 'heart' as an excess in relation to the machine itself: at once a machine and something that eludes (*déjoue*) machinelike calculation. We might have to think the heart as something like the 'ghost in the machine'.

The 'I' is thus 'invested' by the other ('invested as one is by a force greater than oneself' [p257]). What comes to me from the other, from the heart of the other, is the *force* that affirms life in me (the force that 'lets me be me') rather than the *power* or the decision to give me death. 'Only thanks to the other', says Derrida, 'by the grace of the other heart that affirms life in me' (p257), can the finite being that I am have a future, be exposed to a future, to an incalculable and undecidable future that I do not have at my disposal like a master.

One might put this another way - and here we return to the other possible position, that of the second 'intolerable'. What is intolerable, and that of which I am relieved by the calculating decision, is precisely my exposure to an unmasterable future. By eliminating the principle of indetermination, by determining the instant of my death, by providing protection against what comes from the outside, the calculating machine has a strangely reassuring and pleasurable effect.[17] Whence its seductive power: we are 'fascinated by the

16. For a wonderful discussion of literature and the 'heart of the other', see Peggy Kamuf, 'At the Heart of the Death Penalty', *The Oxford Literary Review*, 35.2 (2013): pp241-251.

17. And how not to think of Freud here and his description of the death drive in *Civilization and Its Discontents*: 'Even where it emerges without any sexual purpose, in the blindest fury of destructiveness, we cannot fail to recognize that the satisfaction of the drive is accompanied by an extraordinarily high degree of narcissistic enjoyment, owing to its presenting the ego with a fulfilment of the latter's old wish for omnipotence' (*Standard Edition* 21, p121, modified).

power and by the calculation ... fascinated by the end of this anxiety before the future that the calculating machine procures' (*Death Penalty I*, p258). I may thus dream of appropriating or securing the power-knowledge of the calculating machine by getting myself condemned to death. For it is precisely in putting an end to *life* that the calculating machine gives the impression of putting an end to *finitude*: 'it *affirms* its power over time; it *masters* the future; it *protects* against the irruption of the other' (p258, my emphasis). But of course it only *seems* to do this; it only seems to do this because 'this calculation, this mastery, this decidability, remain *phantasms*' (p258, my emphasis).

To put an end to finitude, to put an end to the principle of indetermination that comes to us from the other (from some other), this would be our ultimate but also our most fundamental desire: 'It would no doubt be possible to show', says Derrida, 'that this [this desire for calculation, mastery, decidability] is even the origin of phantasm in general' (p258).[18] *Never is the origin of phantasm more visible, one might say, never is its foundational gathering more manifest, than in the scene in which we give ourselves death* (that is, in a scene in which the end of finitude is *represented* as the end of life). Thus, what the phantasm of the end of finitude makes visible is a primal or final scene of self-protection: self-destruction as self-protection against what threatens to irrupt or break into us from the outside. Why be anxious if there is no future, that is, if the future can be mastered?

But 'an end will never put an end to finitude', says Derrida, 'for only a finite being can be condemned to death' (p258). An end will never put an end to finitude, one might say, because it is already too late. The fear of irruption is the fear of an irruption that has already taken place - in a time before the beginning of time. We are always too late when it comes to the other: 'So much so that when I say "my life", or even my "living present" ... I have already named the other in me' (p257). I am invested by the other, says Derrida, 'as one is by a force greater than oneself and that occupies you entirely by pre-occupying you'; the other is 'before me in me' (p257).[19] What comes before, from the heart of the other, is the incalculability of the instant of my death. And it is to this *primal* incalculability that the calculating decision tries to put an end - by making a scene, as it were. Indeed, we would have to say that the virtuality of *any scene* of execution (e.g. the fact that the visibility of the death penalty is never simply literal but also always virtual) is already a sign or symptom of this primal relation to incalculability.

And now for the scene you have all been waiting for ... a scene that is not only a primal scene but also a primal projector. It is a much more unsettling scene than the scene of self-surveillance in *Discipline and Punish*:

> Since this phantasm is at work in us all the time, even outside any real scene of verdict and death penalty ... we cannot keep ourselves from permanently playing out for ourselves the scene of the condemned one whom we potentially are ... the fascination exerted by the real phenomena

18. As both primal scene and phantasm, the scene in which I give myself death would be both a scene of origin and a scene of closure. In this, it would differ interestingly from Freud's three primal phantasms, all of which are scenes of origin: the 'primal scene', which is the scene of the origin of the subject; 'castration', which is the scene of the origin of the distinction between the sexes; and 'seduction', which is the scene of the origin of sexuality.

19. In other words, the phantasm of the end of finitude - and here, it seems to me, Derrida is adding a new chapter to Freud's *Beyond the Pleasure Principle* - is the trace of 'my life' attempting (but forever failing) to return to the moment before there was the other in me, that is to say, to the moment before life began.

of death penalty and execution, this fascination of which we could give so many examples, has to do with its effect of truth or of acting out: we then see it <as> actually staged; we project it as one projects a film or as one projects a project; we see in projection actually enacted what we are dreaming of all the time - what we are dreaming of, that is, what in a certain way we desire, namely, to give ourselves death and to infinitize ourselves by giving ourselves death in a calculable, calculated, decidable fashion; and when I say 'we', this means that in this dream we occupy, simultaneously or successively, all the positions, those of a judge, of judges, of the jury, of the executioner or the assistants, of the one condemned to death, of course, and the position of one's nearest and dearest, loved or hated, and that of the voyeuristic spectators who we are more than ever. And it is the force of this effect of phantasmatic truth that will probably remain forever invincible, thus guaranteeing forever, alas, a double survival, both the survival of the death penalty and the survival of the abolitionist protest. (*Death Penalty I*, p258)

What keeps the death penalty alive is a dream, a desire, a fabulous and virtual scene of mastery in which we occupy all the roles, all the positions, all at once or successively. But if the death penalty fascinates and seduces us, if it promises us the fulfilment of our oldest wish for omnipotence, it is also because it allows us to *externalise* what is otherwise always *internally* occurring: in the real phenomena of death penalty and execution, we see *actually* staged, *actually* enacted, *in* projection what we are dreaming of all the time. What we are dreaming of all the time: what can this mean except that *the death penalty is a dream come true*. But to express it in this way is also, I hope, to convey something of its obscenity, for what the death penalty tries to play out as 'actual' theatre is a kind of 'internal' primal relation to an 'outside' that can never simply be located - and mastered or eliminated - in this way.[20]

In conclusion, I would like to return briefly to the American scene and to a rather remarkable episode in *The Executioner's Song*. Although Mailer's description of the scene of execution certainly accentuates its theatrical elements - 'Gary's end of the room was lit … and the rest of the room was dark. He was up on a little platform. It was like a stage'.[21] I would like instead to bring up an earlier and eerier scene in which Gary is preparing for his execution. In this scene, which takes place the day before the execution, Gary is insisting that his uncle deliver a posthumous gift to his girlfriend:

> Gary said, 'Look, take this watch. I don't want anybody to have it but Nicole'. He had broken it and taped it with the hands set at 7:49. (*Executioner's Song*, p1014).

Gary's parting gift to his girlfriend is a watch. But not just any watch. It's a watch he has broken and taped so that its hands are forever set at the given

20. Indeed, I would argue that the profound racialisation of the death penalty in the United States is the most outrageous and visible expression of this literalising violence.

21. Norman Mailer, *The Executioner's Song*, New York, Grand Central Publishing 2012, p1011-12. (Hereafter *Executioner's Song*).

DECONSTRUCTING DEATH 45

time of his death: dawn, 17 January, 1977.[22] It is a little as if he were trying to stage, from beyond the grave, his mastery over the 'clock and the anonymity of clockwork'.

But I don't want to end on a morbid note. So instead I will describe a new product on the market called 'Tikker'. Fredrik Colting, its inventor, calls it 'The Happiness Watch' and claims it was designed to help people make the most of their lives. Here is how the watch is advertised online (at mytikker.com):

> Anger or forgiveness? Tic-toc. Wearing a frown or a smile? Tic-toc. Happy or upset? Tic-toc.
>
> *THAT'S WHY WE'VE CREATED* Tikker, the death watch that counts down your life, just so you can make every second count.
>
> Tikker is a wrist watch that counts down your life from years to seconds, and motivates you to make the right choices. Tikker will be there to remind you to make the most of your life, and most importantly, to be happy.[23]

Mr Colting, who came up with the idea for the 'death watch' following the death of his grandfather, explains it this way:

> For all of us, life comes with a best-before date … While death is non-negotiable, life isn't. All we have to do is learn how to cherish the time and the life that we have been given; seize the day and follow our hearts … From years to seconds [Tikker] presents time ever moving, never standing still, and our lives dwindling towards the final rest … I think that if we were more aware of our own expiration … we'd make better choices while we are alive.[24]

However perverse we may find the Tikker and its maker - to say nothing of the algorithm that calculates the wearer's 'death date' - there is clearly a market for such products. Records indicate that 2162 backers pledged $98,665 on Kickstarter to help bring Tikker to life. For there's something unique, even if uniquely intolerable, about an everyday accessory that brings together 'this strange coincidence, this bizarre synchrony' (*Death Penalty I*, p250) of subjective and objective time, ticker and Tikker, heart and clockwork, the condemnation to die and the condemnation to death, the virtual event (Kickstarter) and the calculating machine, happiness and death. Indeed, for all its perversity, the 'death watch' puts a certain death penalty back on stage as if to submit it to the 'hypothesis of a mutation' (*Without Alibi*, p256). It is a little as if the Tikker campaign were saying: 'if there will always be "some death penalty"' (*Death Penalty I*, p282), if, as Derrida says at the end of *The Death Penalty I*, the future of the death penalty lies in the figures that will

---

22. The official time of death turned out to be 8:07 a.m.

23. See http://mytikker.com.

24. See http://www.dailymail.co.uk/health/article-2776230/How-long-YOU-got-left-live-New-Death-Watch-claims-calculate-life-expectancy-based-lifestyle-counts-death.html.

be invented for it, why not invent a figure for the death penalty, a symbolic deathwatch, we can live with? Why not a virtual death penalty?

And yet even this figure of the death penalty may give us pause. For it repeats, albeit symbolically, the illusion that the future is a countdown and the heart merely a ticking machine.

Since this essay is already too long, let me simply end by quoting my good friend and colleague Michael Naas who, bless his heart, had only this to say when I told him about the Tikker watch: 'Let's just hope', he said, 'your Tikker gives out before your ticker does'. By which I took him to mean - but who can say for sure, we were talking on the phone - that there would always remain something undecidable about what comes to us from the other.

*A longer version of this text appeared in the *Oxford Literary Review* 38.2, 2016, pp118-220.

Elizabeth Rottenberg teaches philosophy at DePaul University and is an advanced candidate at the Chicago Institute for Psychoanalysis. She is one of the six founding members of the Derrida Seminars Translation Project and the translator most recently of Jacques Derrida's *The Death Penalty II*. She is the author of *Inheriting the Future: Legacies of Kant, Freud, and Flaubert* (Stanford, 2005) and the translator of many books by Blanchot, Derrida, Lyotard. She is the editor of *Negotiations: Interventions and Interviews* (1971-2001) by Jacques Derrida (Stanford, 2001) as well as the co-editor (with Peggy Kamuf) of the two-volume edition of Jacques Derrida's *Psyche: Inventions of the Other* (Stanford, 2007/2008). Her forthcoming book is entitled *For the Love of Psychoanalysis*.

Zoya Kosmodemianskaya between Sacrifice and Extermination

Jonathan Brooks Platt

Abstract The article considers the posthumous representation of an eighteen year-old Soviet partisan, captured and executed by German forces during the Battle of Moscow in 1941. As the first woman honoured with the Hero of the Soviet Union award during the war, Kosmodemianskaya's story and image were deployed across the country as mobilisational propaganda, and she subsequently became a central figure in the pantheon of Soviet heroes, enduring in public consciousness to this day. My analysis focuses on moments of ambivalence in textual and visual representations of Kosmodemianskaya, specifically regarding the dialectic of gender and attitudes to the exterminatory violence of the war. I draw on psychoanalytical and anthropological models in my readings.

Keywords Zoya Kosmodemianskaya, stalinism, world war two, gender, Lacan, revolution, militancy

It is a photograph that begins the work of mourning: Zoya Kosmodemianskaya, a young Soviet partisan who was captured, tortured, and executed by German forces during the offensive on Moscow in 1941 (fig.1). The picture, taken by Sergei Strunnikov, first appeared on page three of *Pravda* on 27 January 1942 and was subsequently reprinted numerous times. The striking beauty of the executed woman, along with the uncomfortable eroticism of the harrowing image, made it one of the most memorable of the war. How should one read it? The erotic content suggests itself immediately - especially considering Stalinist culture's notorious prudishness - but it appears in a decidedly ambivalent way. This beautiful young girl has been savagely laid waste; her body appears horribly exposed, both to bestial violence and to the cold out of doors. At the same time, the bared breasts and thrown-back head suggest another kind of exposure as well - to consuming passion. The ambivalent conflict of these two readings is eerily reflected in the terrible binary of Kosmodemianskaya's right breast - inviting to a desirous gaze - and the left one, which has been 'lost', leaving a much more corporeal bareness, blocking erotic fantasy. The right breast beckons but can never be touched, establishing Kosmodemianskaya as a lost erotic object; the left breast marks the obscene enjoyment of her Nazi captors (as confirmed in a later poster based on the photograph - fig.2). Statues of Kosmodemianskaya often restore the left breast and clothe the right one, as if 'borrowing' the breast of fantasy to screen the wound (fig.3). But, again, such interpretations are only half the story. The missing left breast might also mark the trace of Kosmodemianskaya's own suffering passion, a *jouissance* of pain beyond pleasure.

In this essay I will first consider each of these two possible attitudes to Kosmodemianskaya's death, exploring the contexts that support them. Next, I will examine the ambivalence that allowed both attitudes to circulate in her myth, at times combining in striking ways. Stalinist culture has traditionally been interpreted in terms of a decline in revolutionary militancy, and the 'retreat' to more normative gender attitudes is typically seen as a central part of this tendency. However, the story and representation of Kosmodemianskaya suggest a more complex attitude. Through a reading of the anthropological models behind these images (informed in part by Lacanian psychoanalysis and its feminist elaborations), I hope to show how militant fidelity persisted through the post-revolutionary transformations of the 1930s such that it could be summoned up again, with renewed intensity, for the fight with fascism. The war, and not Stalinist Thermidor, was the final nail in the coffin of October, and Kosmodemianskaya can in many ways be called the last Soviet militant.

SACRIFICED FEMININITY

The most natural reaction to the Kosmodemianskaya myth is to read it as a story of female victimisation designed to motivate male soldiers. Such a message is clearly intended by 'Tania', the article by Petr Lidov that originally accompanied Strunnikov's photograph. Lidov enumerates Kosmodemianskaya's torments at the hands of the Nazis at great length - beatings with a belt, lips burned with a kerosene lamp, a saw drawn across

Fig 1: *The corpse of Zoya Kosmodemianskaya* (S. Strunnikov)

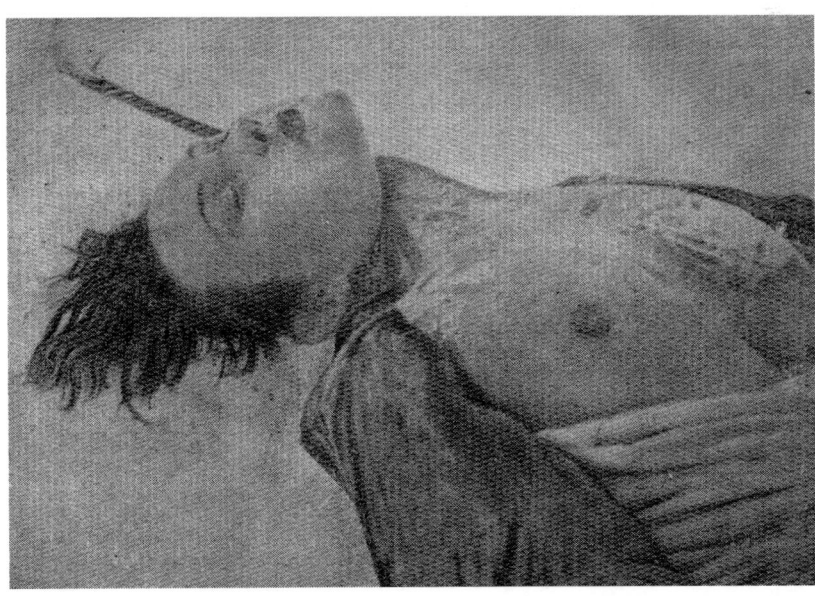

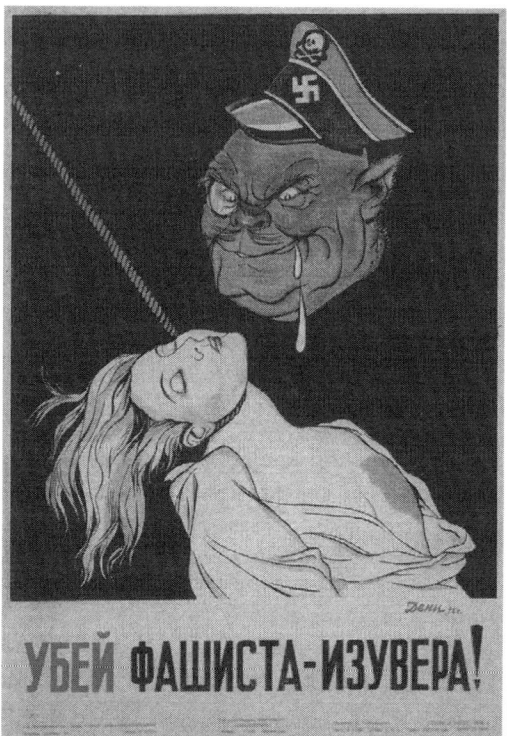

Fig 2: Kill the Fascist Monster! *(V. Deni, 1942)*

Fig 3: (O. Komov, 1986)

her back, forced marches through the snow undressed and barefoot, and finally hanging followed by the desecration of her corpse. Amid all this, Lidov devotes almost no attention to the partisan girl's activities as a combatant. When photographs of Kosmodemianskaya's execution were found among the effects of a killed German soldier, the filmmaker Aleksandr Dovzhenko wrote commentary for them, lingering on Kosmodemianskaya's suffering, feminine frailty (although she 'resembles' a male-gendered fighter):

> Zoya is cold. Her hands, swollen from the frost and the beatings, are clenched into fists like a fighter's [как у бойца]; her bare feet, only in stockings, have turned black from the frost during the terrible night. Her lips, bitten until bleeding, are swollen: two hundred blows from German belts tried to beat confessions out of these tender, girlish lips all night, but they did not succeed. She did not cry out, did not weep, did not groan. Mindless German violence, amorality, cruelty, and impotent hatred for the Russian people fell upon this girl with everything - but her young Russian soul withstood it all.[1]

1. Aleksandr Dovzhenko, 'Smotrite, Liudi!' *Pravda*, October 27, 1943, p3.

Soviet soldiers responded as hoped. They wrote letters to Kosmodemianskaya's mother promising to avenge her daughter's death. They inscribed the partisan girl's name on their tanks and planes, and they made a special point of hunting down the German regiment that had killed her. They carried photographs of the girl - even *that* photograph - in their breast pockets as they went into battle. It is also worth mentioning the particularly fierce libidinal economy of the Eastern front in general. Atrocity propaganda like the Kosmodemianskaya story no doubt played its role in the mass rape of women in East Prussia in the spring of 1945.

All of these facts impart a clearly gendered logic to the Kosmodemianskaya story. Its stark division between female sacrifice and male killing represents a classic example of how gender stereotypes are typically reinforced during wartime. Valorisation of military virtue may define codes of masculinity, but the actual experience of warfare tends to threaten male gender identities. This has doubtless always been the case, linked to men's assumption of domestic duties during wartime - preparing food, mending clothes, caring for the sick and wounded. However, in modern warfare -mass and mechanised - soldiers' heightened vulnerability is even less conducive to feelings of masculine power, and the Nazi-Soviet conflict was one of the most emasculating ever known. Gender thus becomes a central concern of wartime propaganda. The state promotes clearly defined roles for men and women, complementing images of masculine valour and aggression with, on the one hand, portraits of mothers dutifully sending their sons off to war, and, on the other hand, the horror (potential or actual) of women targeted by enemy violence.[2] Gendered images like these urge soldiers to defend not only their homes and families but the very social order that undergirds their power and authority as men.

Despite the changes of mechanisation, the continued manipulation of gender in modern war-making societies suggests the abiding influence of pre-modern cultural paradigms. Warfare arguably threatens men most by making them 'custodians of death' in a way that is typically reserved for women in peacetime. In a study of funerary practices in Madagascar, the anthropologist Maurice Bloch describes a gendered relation to death which he finds paralleled 'in all societies where authority is linked to an ideal, unchanging order'. In such societies, individual death is feminised:

> It is women who take on mourning for death. This they do [...] sitting on a pile of rubbish outside the home of the deceased, their hair undone, their clothes loose about them. It is they who receive the condolences of others and weep with the female visitors. It is women also who are associated with the pollution of death. It is they who must wash the corpse and then wash themselves and all the things in the house, and it is mainly they who ritually take on pollution by throwing themselves on the corpse. Individual burial is, therefore, a time of sadness, of pollution and of women.[3]

And yet, as the mourning process nears completion, it is men who make speeches and ask for blessings from the dead, placing the corpse into a familial tomb. The ultimate goal of such gendered practices is to overcome death's pollution, returning the spiritual substance of the dead to a patriarchal

2. Joshua S. Goldstein, *War and Gender: How Gender Shapes the War System and Vice Versa*. Cambridge, Cambridge University Press 2001.

3. Maurice Bloch, 'Death, Women and Power', in *Death and the Regeneration of Life*, ed., Maurice Bloch and Jonathan Parry, Cambridge, Cambridge University Press 1982, p223, 215.

realm of ancestral memory and controlled, collective fertility. Feminist critics like Elisabeth Bronfen have elaborated such anthropological observations, arguing that the formation and exchange of symbolic value itself demands the containment of death's indeterminate power through feminization. Bronfen further links the foundational suppression or sacrifice of the feminine other to such psychoanalytic concepts as Freud's death drive, the Lacanian Thing, and Kristeva's semiotic chora.[4]

If mourning rites domesticate death in peacetime, the unavoidable proximity of men to its polluting effects during war requires something more dramatic. Indeed, atrocity propaganda depicting violence against women suggests another mythic subtext. Anthropologist Walter Burkert - also cited by Bronfen - has described how the ancient ritual of maiden sacrifice has historically been used to launch military or hunting campaigns (most famously reflected in the myth of Iphigenia and the Trojan War). War requires a redirection of libidinal energies, deferring fantasies of sanctioned sexual union (love, marriage, children) to invest desire into the male collective's pursuit and slaughter of the enemy. Burkert explains why women are sacrificed to found this abstinent homosocial order:

> Man declines to love in order to kill: this is most graphically demonstrated in the ritual slaughter of the 'virgin'. [...] An irreparable act transforms an erotic game into fighting fury. Desperate 'searching' turns into 'hunting'. [...] In hunting myth, the sacrificed virgin becomes the bride of the quarry, [...] as a preliminary, maiden-sacrifice stands in contrast, and provides a balance, to the main sacrifice that supplies the food. It is a ritual of giving in order to get: in the main sacrifice fulfillment comes in the *sparagmos*, in cutting up and eating; during the preliminaries, however, there is an anticipatory self-denial which consequently requires other forms of destruction - submerging in water, hanging from trees.[5]

Burkert goes on to note that the great sacrifice of war or the hunt could also be 'motivated as a punitive expedition, as vengeance for the maiden's death' (*Homo Necans*, p65). Viewed through the interpretative lens of this tradition, the Kosmodemianskaya story seems all the more clearly designed to motivate male troops through a manipulation of the dialectic of gender. Indeed, Lidov's 'Tania' was only the most notable of a series of articles in *Pravda* about young female partisans captured and killed during the defence of Moscow. As the Soviet press struggled to make sense of the horrific onset of war, the death of 'maidens' occupied a central place in the public imagination.

Here it is important to recall that war and ritual sacrifice are closely connected as sanctioned violations of the taboo against bloodshed. The dialectic of gender in maiden sacrifice is interwoven with that of transgression. As Bataille reminds us, transgression 'suspends a taboo without suppressing it'.[6] The prohibition against murder marks the 'threshold beyond which murder is possible; and for

4. Elisabeth Bronfen, *Over her Dead Body: Death, Femininity and the Aesthetic*, Manchester, Manchester University Press 1992.

5. Walter Burkert, *Homo Necans: The Anthropology of Ancient Greek Sacrificial Ritual and Myth*, (trans) Peter Bing, Berkeley, University of California Press 1983, p64. (Hereafter *Homo Necans*).

6. Georges Bataille, *Erotism: Death and Sensuality*, (trans) Mary Dalwood, San Francisco, City Lights Books 1986, p36. (Hereafter *Erotism*).

the community war comes about when the threshold is crossed. If transgression [...] did not have this limited character it would be a return to violence, to animal violence. But nothing of the kind is so. Organised transgression together with the taboo make social life what it is' (*Erotism*, p64-65). René Girard similarly sees sacrificial violence as a ritual purification of blood, resisting explosions of violence that might threaten social distinctions with a free-for-all of contagious, reciprocal aggression. 'As long as purity and impurity remain distinct, even the worst pollution can be washed away; but once they are allowed to mingle, purification is no longer possible'.[7] Here Burkert's description of maiden sacrifice as a preliminary echo of the quarry's dismemberment acquires a precise chronotopic contour. The death of the maiden opens the extraordinary zone of ritual transgression in which war is waged. To return home and earn the right to a more ordinary, individual love, the members of the hunting party must complete the sacrifice and slay the beast.

From this perspective, whether Kosmodemianskaya is seen as the tragic victim of her Nazi captors or perhaps their polluted bride, the story of her death exposes Soviet soldiers to sacrificial guilt, binding them together with the spectacle of an irreparable act of violence. The feminine work of mourning is not sufficient to sublimate the maiden's loss into renewed fertility and the reaffirmation of social, symbolic codes. Instead, retribution is required - ultimately a vengeance against the self - traversing the extraordinary zone of transgression, suffering war's luxurious expenditure of life to re-establish the purity of social, territorial, and psychological distinctions through their ritual suspension.

7. René Girard, *Violence and the Sacred*, (trans) Patrick Gregory. Baltimore, Johns Hopkins University Press 1977, p38.

AN OTHER JOUISSANCE

However, there is also much about the Kosmodemianskaya story that suggests this gendered, sacrificial reading is not enough. First, it is important to note the peculiar militarisation of Soviet women - unique amongst the combatants in the Second World War. Anna Krylova has documented the emergence of an 'alternative - non-oppositional - gender system' in the 1930s, when military readiness was taught on an integrated basis in schools, in the Komsomol (Communist Youth League), and in paramilitary organisations like OSOAVIAKHIM (Society for the Assistance of Defence, Aviation, and Chemical Construction). Film characters like the machine-gunner Anka in *Chapaev* (1934) and the sword-swinging Vasilisa in *Alexander Nevsky* (1938) provided captivating images of women willing, able, and eager to kill. In a contradictory way quite characteristic of 1930s Soviet social policies, combat emerged as a shared gender space even as pro-natalist policies (like the 1936 law against abortion) encouraged women to define themselves as mothers first and foremost. When the war broke out, this contradiction was not resolved, and the state pursued a policy of 'discouragement without prohibition' with regard to female volunteers.[8] Many young Komsomol women (like

8. Anna Krylova, *Soviet Women in Combat: A History of Violence on the Eastern Front*, Cambridge, Cambridge University Press 2010, p70, 114.

Kosmodemianskaya) were thus able to make their way into combat, even though the mainstream press agitated for women to assume more traditional wartime roles on the home front or, at most, as medical orderlies. As the war progressed, however, more and more women were directly (if quietly) mobilised for combat, and many even assumed command roles.

Furthermore, while the *Pravda* articles on tortured partisans seem focused on narratives of female victimisation, the decision to make Kosmodemianskaya the first female Hero of the Soviet Union of the war suggests the recognition of gender-neutral forms of heroic self-sacrifice as well. Indeed, many treatments of the Kosmodemianskaya story also display non-oppositional gender dynamics, emphasising (even exaggerating) her military contributions rather than downplaying them in the manner of Lidov and Dovzhenko. For example, the earliest statues of the partisan, by sculptor Matvei Manizer, give her a steely, androgynous look and equip her with a rifle (fig.4). Lev Arnshtam's 1944 film *Zoya* contains several scenes of Kosmodemianskaya's life as a partisan, including one in which she shoots a German at point blank range to save a male comrade. In a subsequent montage sequence, the young woman is shown hurling grenades and firing an automatic rifle, superimposed over the flames of explosions she has caused.

It is this current of the Kosmodemianskaya myth that evokes associations with a different image of maiden sacrifice - Joan of Arc. Unlike the drowned or hanged virgins that initiate aggressive pursuit of the quarry, Joan of Arc represents an ecstatic, mystical defence against an invader. Moreover, while

Fig 4: (M. Manizer, 1942-47)

her power emerges from a feminine position, it ultimately transcends gender as the androgynous warrior unites a popular collective that is not specifically male. Unconditionally devoted to her king, enthralled by divine voices, the 'maid of Orleans' rallies the people behind her, leading them into war by example, rather than simply sending them off to avenge the death of an innocent. Her betrayal, capture, and execution do not mark the beginning of war, but the sublime limit of self-sacrifice that ensures victory if imitated by all who love France. Kosmodemianskaya is often called the Russian Joan of Arc, and she has always been surrounded with something of a mystical aura. Two central wartime depictions of her time in captivity - Arnshtam's film and Margarita Aliger's play, *A Fairy Tale about Truth* - show the partisan girl on the eve of execution visited by loved ones who bring her strength, culminating in a semi-divine visitation from Stalin:

> Who is that standing by the window? (*She looks tensely into the darkness.*) I cannot stand, Iosif Vissarionovich, my legs are burning, but I will listen to your order. Today, 5 December 1941, the divisions of the Red Army around Moscow have launched a general offensive. This means they will not take Moscow, they will never take Moscow! Thank you, Iosif Vissarionovich, for coming to tell me about this, now nothing can frighten me.[9]

9. Margarita Aliger, *Skazka o pravde*, Moscow, Iskusstvo 1947, p105.

As with Joan of Arc, the death of the maiden here marks the crucial turning of the tide from defence to attack, drawing on hidden resources of passion, enduring pain and even death to realise the will of the party.

The impulse to undermine rather than enforce gender oppositions has a rich pedigree in early Soviet culture. As several scholars have noted, this tendency typically manifests itself in the 1920s as a kind of revolutionary misogyny.[10] Polluted, feminised nature - the indeterminacy of death - must be rationalised and overcome to make way for the new culture of Soviet Man. For many Soviet subjects, this utopian rejection of femininity no doubt disguised the same denigration of women that traditionally undergirds the patriarchal order. For others, however, it reflected something different - a longing for a collective body free from fragmentation across the fissures of sexual difference. In the Stalinist period, even as more traditional feminine roles were being championed, this ideal of a genderless utopia remained actual in a number of ways, with integrated military readiness training as only one example. To be sure, as Krylova notes, female combatants did not abandon but often maintained feminine identities during the war (e.g. decorating their planes with flowers). Krylova thus interprets the policies she describes as 'regendering' rather than 'degendering'. In her view, the alternative system led not to gender's dissolution, but merely suspended the dialectic that defined masculine valour in opposition to feminine frailty. While this is certainly true, it is important to remember the overarching logic of Stalinism as a simultaneous struggle with left and right 'deviations' from the general line. It was just as important to avoid racing ahead too precipitously toward communism as it was to avoid stifling forward-looking impulses among the masses. In this way, the contradictory policies that allowed for the partial gender remapping Krylova has identified may suggest a similar attempt to steer between the Scylla of premature radicalism and the Charybdis of stifling conservatism. Non-oppositional gender may have only been a stage on the way to something more radical - the elimination of sexual difference - even if this utopian dream was still being actively resisted in the 1930s in many ways.

10. Eric Naiman, *Sex in Public: The Incarnation of Early Soviet Ideology*. Princeton: Princeton University Press 1997. Eliot Borenstein, *Men without Women: Masculinity and Revolution in Russian Fiction, 1917-1929*, Durham, Duke University Press 2000.

Perhaps the most significant manifestation of this degendering impulse in the 1930s is the emasculated hero of many socialist realist narratives - the mutilated proletarians and pilots Lilya Kaganovsky describes in *How the Soviet*

Man was Unmade. As Kaganovsky writes, quoting Kaja Silverman:

> More than a matter of displacement or return of the repressed, the blind, limping, paralysed, hysterical male body seems to be offered by Stalinist art as a new kind of masculinity, one that does not, at least on the surface, depend on 'collective make-believe in the commensurability of penis and phallus'- that is to say, of the male subject and power - but rather, one that stages the radical incommensurability of the two. [11]

Yet, while Kaganovsky sees the uncanny, zombie-like drive of Pavel Korchagin (from Nikolai Ostrovsky's *How the Steel Was Tempered*) as the relentless pursuit of his own castration - to discipline and interpellate himself into the symbolic order (surrendering *jouissance* to claim the phallic signifier, however unavailable it proves to be) - it is possible to read this drive and the wounds such heroes suffer as the mark of a different kind of passion. In his twentieth seminar, *Encore*, Lacan introduces the possibility of an 'other *jouissance*,' distinct from the two forms of phallic pleasure that typically define masculine and feminine desire. Lacan's well-known dictum that 'there is no such thing as a sexual relationship' describes the incommensurability of masculine fantasy, pursuing metonymic surrogates for *objet petit a*, and feminine interest in men who possess the symbolic phallus of social power. The other *jouissance*, by contrast, is available to feminine (but not necessarily female) subjects who reorient themselves away from the phallus, turning toward a different signifier - S(A̶), 'the signifier of lack in the Other'. Lacan associates this other *jouissance* with a mystic ecstasy (as in Bernini's famous statue of St. Teresa of Avila) 'beyond the phallus' and, by implication, beyond the pleasure principle, entering the domain of the death drive.[12] Instead of 'the idiotic enjoyment' of phallic pleasure, the other *jouissance* is localised much deeper in the body than anything produced by the cut of an erogenous zone. Ultimately, the subject encounters the *jouissance* of the Other itself, an unspeakable, unnamable, 'non-totalisable' truth (where 'God' is no longer the master signifier that founds the discursive order as a constitutive exception to the Law, but where, conversely, it marks the limit at which order and the Law collapse, and anything is possible). With this alternative in mind, I would argue that the hysterical masculinity Kaganovsky sees in Stalinist art in fact represents a subjectivity that emerges from the position Lacan describes as feminine, but which turns away from the phallus to encounter (witness, endure) the asexual *jouissance* of the Cause itself.

The fact that the mutilated Stalinist hero is a non-phallic subject, rather than a masculine one, is supported by the frequent association of Kosmodemianskaya with this figure. The partisan's various biographers make much of a diary entry in which she quotes Korchagin's famous words from *How the Steel was Tempered*: 'A man's most precious thing is life. It is given to him only once and he must live it so […] that in death he can say: I have devoted all my life and all my powers

11. Lilya Kaganovsky, *How the Soviet Man was Unmade: Cultural Fantasy and Male Subjectivity under Stalin*, Pittsburgh, University of Pittsburgh Press 2008, p22.

12. Jacques Lacan, *On Feminine Sexuality: The Limits of Love and Knowledge: Seminar XX (Encore)*, (trans) Bruce Fink. New York, Norton 1998, pp74-76.

13. L.T. Kosmodemianskaia, *Povest' o Zoe i Shure*, Leningrad, Lenizdat 1951, p182.

to the most wonderful thing in the world - the struggle for the liberation of mankind'.[13] These words were emblazoned on Kosmodemianskaya's tombstone when she was buried in Novodevichy Cemetery, and they also feature in Arnshtam's *Zoya*. In a related scene from the film, the young Zoya is deeply affected by the deaths of the crew of a stratospheric balloon. Asking her mother to explain the meaning of the word 'hero,' Kosmodemianskaya learns: 'A hero is someone who is always brave. Who is not afraid even to die in order to make others happy' (*Zoia* 1944).[14] Similar images of Kosmodemianskaya's captivation with heroic death can be found in the memoirs of her mother. In an article published in the spring of 1942, for example, Liubov Kosmodemianskaya recalled a funeral for martyred 'partisans' of the collectivisation campaign (i.e. activists killed by resisting peasants):

> They constructed the tomb in the centre of the village, near the local party headquarters. The coffins were placed in the crypt. They built a fence around the monument and set up benches, and children were the most common visitors to this tomb. [...] Sometimes Zoya would stand on a bench like it was a stage, and she would start declaiming in her childish way, remembering the speeches of the grownups. The kids fired pop-guns, pretending it was a salute. The marched off singing partisan songs.[15]

At the very least, such motifs confirm that Kosmodemianskaya's martyrdom was not only viewed as female victimisation. In my view, they also suggest that the partisan girl's death fit the gender-neutral paradigm of a Stalinist subject who invites (or even pursues) self-destruction in order to enter the 'life beyond life' of the Cause. Rather than Iphigenia, this position is more reminiscent of Sophocles' Antigone - a central example for Lacan, which Žižek has linked to Joan of Arc - who pursues her desire beyond the Law, beyond the limit of symbolic death, remaining ever faithful to an impossible calling.[16]

THE STALINIST IMPULSE TO CHRONOTOPIC HYBRIDITY: Φ/A AND S(A̶)/A

The duality of the Kosmodemianskaya myth - in which she is at once a female victim and a degendered (or at least alternatively gendered) hero - did not persist after the war. Images of the partisan become increasingly feminine in post-war years, following a general trend that demobilised women and suppressed the non-oppositional gender system of the 1930s.[17] This tendency continues in many representations of Kosmodemianskaya today, as can be seen in two monuments, erected in Kiev and Volgograd in the late 2000s, which focus on the partisan girl's forced march through the snow, depicting her barefoot and scantily clad. With the Soviet ban on erotic imagery long forgotten, these statues raise the partisan's skirt line significantly higher than a 1957 statue on the same theme (figs. 5 and 6).[18] It is also interesting that

14. In Lidov's account, Kosmodemianskaya cries from the scaffold: 'It is happiness to die for one's people'.

15. L. T. Kosmodem'ianskaia, 'Moia Zoia', *Komsomol'skaia pravda*, May 21, 1942, p3.

16. Slavoj Žižek, 'From Antigone to Joan of Arc', *Helios* 31 2004, 1-2, pp51-62. This figure also recalls Alain Badiou's description of the mystical 'fourth discourse', the discourse of 'unutterable utterances' which can 'only be experienced by the subject who has been visited by a miracle' in Alain Badiou, *Saint Paul: The Foundations of Universalism*, (trans) Ray Brassier, Stanford, Stanford University Press 2003, p51. In a more pragmatic vein, one may note that a principal goal of the Kosmodemianskaya story was to teach soldiers how to behave if they were taken captive - demonstrating total commitment to the cause through death. I am grateful to Aleksandr Semenov for this insight.

17. Adrienne Harris, *The Myth of the Woman Warrior and World War II in Soviet Culture*. PhD dissertation, University of Kansas, 2008.

18. For the Volgograd monument, see: http://nezabudem.net/obelisks/1788.

Figs 5 and 6: Monuments on the Minsk Highway (1957) and Kiev (2006)

the version of Arnshtam's *Zoya* shown after destalinisation in the ealry 1960s cuts both the reference to Ostrovsky's Korchagin and the line about a hero's willingness to die for the happiness of the collective.

What changed? How did the suppression of the non-phallic elements of Kosmodemianskaya's story affect the myth as a whole? Here it is useful to elaborate the Lacanian theory of sexuation in somewhat greater - and more speculative - detail. In *Encore*, Lacan offers the following diagram, relating the algebric symbols for the phallus, *objet a*, and the signifier of lack in the Other to the three orders of the Symbolic, the Imaginary, and the Real. In the centre of the diagram, *jouissance* bubbles forth from the vertex of the Real toward S(A̶):

Fig 7

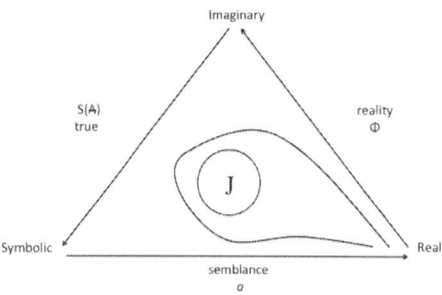

The structures represented by these three symbols share a fundamental similarity. Each in its own way describes an effect (or an opportunity) brought about by the gap in being suffered by speaking, desiring subjects - the gap between the subjective time-space of one's being - towards - death and the objective way in which one appears or is 'given' to another subject, as if already dead. It is the gap of incommensurability between these two positions that defines the Other as lacking, the subject as split, the *jouissance* of death as unknowable, and desire as insatiable. Indeed, all three symbols refer to the symbolic order's lack of that one signifier that would complete (and destroy) it - the subject herself, if she could choose her own name and bridge the gap that prohibits *jouissance*. *Objet a* represents the fantasy (or non-specular 'semblance') of a lost object left over from primordial separation (e.g., the maternal phallus). This object would complete the Other, but it can exist for the subject only as a hole in the Real that 'suffers from the signifier'.[19] The phallus, by contrast, is the signifier of this suffering - the *Non/Nom-du-Père* which founds the Law of castration, and which, if accepted, allows the subject to assume a place in the symbolic order and to desire (pursuing not the impossibility of *objet a*, but tracing a circuitous detour of fantasy around it). As mentioned above, the meagre (Lacan would say masturbatory) *jouissance* of normative, gendered sexuality depends on the interplay of these two figures. The masculine subject seeks metonymic shadows of the unnameable object in his partner, while the feminine subject urges hers to seize the phallus, the paternal name, as a metaphorical substitution for foreclosed *jouissance*. In either case, *objet a* remains as an intractable disturbance, preventing the consummation of phallic desire.

What then is S(A̶), especially since Lacan also calls the phallus 'the signifier of the Other's desire' in his essay 'The Signification of the Phallus'?[20] Perhaps it is a different kind of signifier, one more reminiscent of the logic of sublimation and, in some ways, fetishism. In his description of Antigone's 'sublime splendor' in the seventh seminar, Lacan associates her position - when she is entombed for her crime, banished from the life of the Law, yet still biologically alive - with that of an object raised 'to the dignity of the Thing,' the latter term usually taken as a predecessor of *objet a* (*Seminar VII*, p112). Lacan further describes this sublime object as a signifier beyond the pleasure principle - i.e., not a mere link in the signifying chain, but a signifier created *ex nihilo*, fabricated around the Thing and thus capable of representing it. What then does it mean for a feminine subject to orient herself not on the master signifier of desire (the symbolic phallus) but to turn toward this different signifier - that of the Cause-Thing beyond the Law. I would argue that it represents a simple chronotopic inversion - seeking not to claim the phallic signifier but to become one that is 'martyred'. In other words, it is a militant, eschatological subject position - truly inhabiting the gap of impossible desire rather than veiling or domesticating it. This place of martyrdom is also 'unconsummated' - it still marks the place of *objet a*, but it reverses the trajectory of phallic subjectivity. Antigone's position 'between two deaths' (symbolic and biological) is remarkable not for the position itself - which can be traced in the same gendered burial rites discussed above, in which one first surrenders bodily life to nature (mourned by women) and then spiritual life to the collective (mourned by men). Rather, it is the fact that Antigone uncannily dies in the symbolic order *before* she gives up her biological life. As a result, her second death is beyond the phallus, beyond gender, and in a sense truly 'authorised' by herself alone.[21]

19. Jacques Lacan, *The Ethics of Psychoanalysis: Seminar VII*, (trans) Dennis Porter. New York, Norton 1992, pp118-121. (Hereafter *Seminar VII*).

20. Jacques Lacan, *Écrits*, (trans) Bruce Fink, New York, Norton 2006, p583. (Hereafter *Écrits*).

21. Here it is worth noting Judith Butler's reading of Antigone as the queer subject *par excellence*, born beyond the incest taboo and staking her claim to the rights or 'aberrant, unprecedented future' of such a position. Judith Butler, *Antigone's Claim: Kinship between Life and Death*, New York, Columbia University Press 2000, p82.

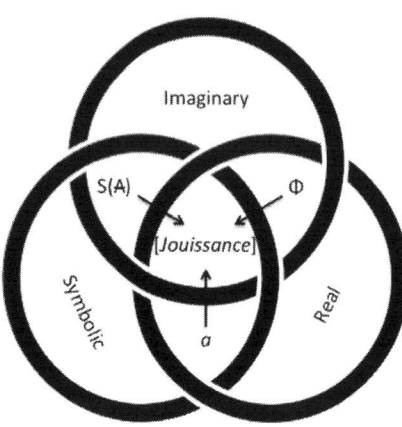

Fig 8.

22. Here the masculine position would be oriented on the suffering, feminised other, while the feminine position would be oriented on getting 'her man' to 'grow up' and claim the phallus. Such a categorisation only seems relevant to bourgeois modernity, however. By contrast, one might imagine a medieval gloss of the three pressure-points of *objet a*, the phallus, and S(A̶) as respectively referring to sin, tradition, and faith three different strategies for coping with the impossibility of absolute *jouissance*.

23. Claude Lefort, 'Outline of the Genesis of Ideology in Modern Societies', in *The Political Forms of Modern Society: Bureaucracy, Democracy, Totalitarianism*, (ed.) John B. Thompson, Cambridge, MIT Press 1986, pp205-14.

Although it requires taking some liberty with Lacan, it is useful here to superimpose the above diagram onto another one from later in the twentieth seminar - the Borromean knot, which also depicts the interrelation of the Symbolic, the Imaginary, and the Real (fig. 8). What this diagram represents, first of all, is the impossibility of absolute *jouissance*, the non-lacking Other or Thing. The central place where all three rings intersect is inaccessible, preserving the separation of the orders as well as their links. The places where two of the three rings overlap represent different 'pressure points' from which the subject may approach or organise herself around that impossibility. An orientation on the suffering of the Real under the Symbolic leads one to *objet a* - the lost object or semblance of being, present in the Imaginary only as the various 'part-objects' (like the breast). An orientation on normative 'maturation' from the Real to the Imaginary leads to the promise of the symbolic phallus - the master signifier of desire that does not complete the Other, but subdues its lack, or at least attempts to. The final pressure point would then be S(A̶) - the non-phallic signifier of lack in the Other, of the Other's own castration and desire, or of the fact that 'the Other does not exist'. The subject position corresponding to this point would be structured around the incommensurability of 'reality' (the Imaginary and the Symbolic orders taken together) and the Real, inhabiting the point of maximal tension between them, oriented on the Cause (of absolute *jouissance*) only as a truth-to-come, a truth defined by its untotalisable inactuality.

One could use the three subject positions in this account to produce a catalogue of gender, labelling them masculine, feminine, and 'other' respectively.[22] It is somewhat more interesting, however, to contemplate the difference between the phallic interplay of Φ and *a* and an inverted, 'non-phallic' interaction between S(A̶) and *a* (where an orientation on *objet a* would no longer represent a masculine position because of the lack of a feminine other). The importance of *objet a* as the common denominator of the phallic and non-phallic structures is to indicate the ambivalence and incommensurability they share. The bourgeois 'master' of modern life - the boss, family man, teacher, etc. - can never possess the phallus so completely that *objet a* ceases to haunt his subjectivity as the cause of desire.[23] Similarly, the militant subject of resistance can never fully become the signifier of the Other's lack. *Objet a* will always remain as the bodiless incarnation of the gap that makes subjectivity and desire possible, perhaps accounting for the signifier's unnamed status, as if anything could potentially fill its role. Again, the difference between the two structures is ultimately a simple inversion. The phallic structure of normative gender relations depends upon a foundational authority - the Law that condemns the subject to choose one of two genders and suffer the impossibility of their ever coming together to produce the

One. By contrast, the non-phallic structure, affording a mystical ecstasy beyond gender, looks ahead toward a signifier that cannot yet be uttered. The subject cleaves to the lacking Other but can never dissolve completely in an obliteration that would announce the realisation of the Cause. Elsewhere I have described these two structures - Φ/a and $S(\bcancel{A})/a$ - as the central chronotopes of modernity, referring to them respectively as ambivalent forms of monumentalism and eschatology.[24] As I see it, the guiding impulse of Stalinist culture (at least until the tide turned in the war in 1943) is to invoke both structures simultaneously, as if using the vacillation between them - and occasionally their hybridisation though chiastic superimposition - to create a makeshift, surrogate experience of absolute *jouissance* ('communism'), suppressing the disturbing effects of *objet a* without eliminating them (because without these effects the 'engine' of modern ambivalence would stall).

This, therefore, is the theoretical explanation for the vacillation between 'phallic' and 'non-phallic' representations of Zoya Kosmodemianskaya during the war - a vacillation that did not continue after Soviet militant subjectivity was exhausted by victory in 1945.

FOUR AMBIVALENT MOMENTS AND TWO AWKWARD MEMORIES

Beyond this overarching impulse to chronotopic hybridity in Stalinist culture, there was clearly something specific about the war years that promoted Kosmodemianskaya's ambivalent gendering. There is much to suggest the source was an equally ambivalent relationship to violence. Both sides of the Nazi-Soviet conflict believed they were involved in a 'war of extermination' (*Vernichtungskrieg, istrebitel'naia voina*), that is, in the words of a recent study, 'a war locked in a state of exception, in which each side fights (or insists it must fight) until one side is utterly and completely subjugated, incapable of renewing itself on its own devices. The victor survives as the 'last man standing'; the vanquished is not only dead, but also ravished'. The Eastern front's exterminatory character no doubt compromised its ability to serve as a purgative act of ritual transgression. Instead of reaffirming polluted boundaries through their temporary suspension, the conflict was more likely to foster a wholesale sense of chaos and indistinction. Even in strictly military terms, the Nazi-Soviet war was waged along a front that was more a zone of ambiguity than a clear division between combatants. This was 'a war that reached inside to remake the respective war-fighting society in a war of excisions much as it reached outside in order to subjugate and [...] exterminate the enemy'.[25] In other words, radical violence was practiced both internally and externally - a fact horrifically manifested in the Holocaust and perhaps best epitomised by the 'blocking units' used by both sides to deny doomed soldiers the possibility of retreat.

It seems possible, therefore, that sacrificed femininity did not exhaust the semantic potential of the Kosmodemianskaya story because it could not

24. Jonathan Brooks Platt, 2015. 'Snow White and the Enchanted Palace: A Reading of Lenin's Architectural Cult'. *Representations*, 2015, 129: 86-115. (Hereafter *Snow White*).

25. Mark Edele and Michael Geyer, 'States of Exception: The Nazi-Soviet War as a System of Violence, 1939-1945', in *Beyond Totalitarianism: Stalinism and Nazism Compared*, (eds.) Michael Geyer and Sheila Fitzpatrick, Cambridge, Cambridge University Press 2009, p350, 348.

overcome the exterminatory excess of the violence that had been visited upon her, a violence against bare, degendered life - as wordlessly spoken by the wounds on her exhumed body. Instead, Stalinist subjects drew on their own close acquaintance with exterminatory violence, having long expected to endure such pain as the cost of exposure to the *jouissance* of the Cause. After the war was won, Soviet society strove to forget this exterminatory excess (much like the Cause itself, one could argue).

These claims are highly speculative. However, I believe they justify further consideration of the ambivalence of Zoya Kosmodemianskaya as more than a sign of Stalinism's confused ideology. If we accept that during the war two distinct attitudes were available both to Strunnikov's photograph and to Kosmodemianskaya's story in general, the next logical step is to ask how these attitudes interacted with one another. In asking this question, I will now examine four different moments in which a certain unresolved conflict surfaces in the memorialisation of Kosmodemianskaya. I will first describe all four of the moments and then analyse them together.

1. *A large painting of Kosmodemianskaya's execution by the Kukryniksy collective.* The original painting, first exhibited in 1942, depicts the exact moment at which the box is kicked from under Kosmodemianskaya's feet (fig. 9). After the war, the artists revise the image to show the moment directly prior to this - presumably when Kosmodemianskaya is making her famous speech from the scaffold, urging the villagers to fight and promising Stalin will save them (fig. 10). The feeling of a captured moment in time is central to the painting, thematised by the German soldiers photographing the hanging. The position of Kosmodemianskaya in the 1942 version closely resembles Strunnikov's photograph.

Fig 9: Kukryniksy, Tania (1942)

Fig 10: Kukryniksy, Tania *(1947)*

2. *A strange impression created by the juxtaposition of Strunnikov's photograph and the last lines of Lidov's article.* The impression is strongest in one of the pocket-sized editions of materials about Kosmodemianskaya put out by *Pravda* and presumably distributed to soldiers at the front. Lidov ends his article with a description of the modest grave, under a weeping willow, in which the villagers laid the partisan girl's mutilated body. The final sentence of the article reads: 'And her unfading glory will spread across the entire Soviet land, and millions of people will think about that distant, snow-strewn grave with love, and Stalin will come to the grave of his loyal daughter in his thoughts'. In the pocket-sized edition, these lines appear directly opposite Strunnikov's photograph, revealing how the grave has been disturbed by exhumation and thus putting Stalin in a somewhat peculiar position (fig. 11). This moment is further complicated by the fact that, according to Lidov, Kosmodemianskaya's last words were 'Stalin will come!'

Fig 11: From Tania *(Pravda, 1942).*

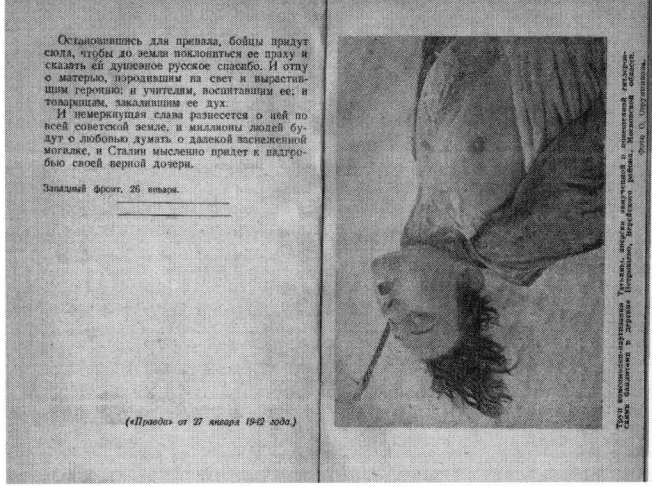

3. *A peculiar echo at the end of Margarita Aliger's narrative poem,* Zoya. Aliger ends the third and final chapter of her poem, written in 1942, with an ekphrastic description of Strunnikov's photo:

> Keep the photograph of Zoya forever.
> I don't think I will ever forget it.
> This girl's body,
> > neither dead
> > > nor alive.
> It is Zoya made of marble
> > lying quietly in the snow.
> There is a strange power in your thrown-back face [*в запрокинутом лике*].
> That's how one waits for a lover,
> > glowing with a secret beauty,
> from a mysterious feminine fire within.
> Only you didn't wait for him, snow bride.

Then, in the final lines of the poem's epilogue, Aliger imagines a sculptor chiseling the head of a statue after the war has ended:

> What does he want to say with his chisel?
> Why did he choose the most difficult stone?
> He abandoned his home, work, and peace,
> he fought alongside thousands of thousands,
> to return and carve the face of victory
> with the hand of one who has become a man.
> What distant horizons are you gazing at,
> still unknown,
> > already great.
> But we recognise Zoya's features
> In the thrown-back,
> > Marvelous,
> > > Eternal face [*в откинутом... лике*].[26]

4. *A new funerary monument erected for Kosmodemianskaya in 1986 by sculptor Oleg Komov (fig. 3)*. If one is not familiar with Strunnikov's photograph, the statue appears to depict the partisan girl falling in flight, 'like the cry of a bird, halted at its most sonorous note' as one journalist put it.[27] However, upon closer examination, it is clear that the statue is modeled directly on the photograph. Komov has simply raised the supine body into a vertical position and reversed its left-right orientation (fig.12).

What generalisations can be made about these four moments? In my view, each reveals the tension between the two available attitudes to Kosmodemianskaya outlined above. If we recall the model of double sacrifice in Burkert's description of ancient Greek hunting myth, the two sacrificial acts - the slaughter of the maiden and the dismemberment of the quarry - delineate a spatio-temporal zone of the extraordinary. This is the zone that must be traversed by the male collective if they are to return

---

26. Margarita Aliger, *Stikhi i poemy*. Moscow: GIKhL 1944, p170, 174. (Hereafter *Stikhi*).

27. I. Teplitskaia, 'Tvoi sled na zemle', *Kommunar* 1987, May, p1, 4.

28. Robert Hertz, 'A Contribution to the Study of the Collective Representation of Death', in *Death, Mourning, and Burial: A Cross-Cultural Reader*, ed. A.C.G.M. Robben, London, Blackwell 2004, p203.

29. For more on this structure, see Jacques Lacan, *The Ethics of Psychoanalysis: Seminar VII*, (trans) Dennis Porter, New York, Norton 1992, pp220-21, 247-49; Giorgio Agamben's

home, renewed and purified by the ritual. A similar structure can be seen in many burial rites. In the gendered practices Bloch describes, for example, the mourning process demarcates a specifically feminised period of pollution through which the deceased must pass before being reincorporated into the patriarchal order. The chronotopic aspects of this structure are even clearer in the related practice of double burial. Here the corpse undergoes decomposition in a temporary grave, after which the bare bones are exhumed and deposited in an ossuary. As Robert Hertz notes in his classic study of this practice, double burial treats the temporality of death as a zone of putrescence separating two bodies. In Hertz's words, the bifurcation of the funerary rite reflects a belief that 'death is not a mere destruction but a transition: as it progresses so does the rebirth; while the old body falls to ruins, a new body takes shape, with which the soul - provided the necessary rites have been performed - will enter another existence, often superior to the previous one'.[28] Thus, a first body, the body of death, departs from natural life, while a second body - sublime and deathless - achieves a new life beyond the natural cycles of transient being.

Fig 12: Komov's statue and Strunnikov's photograph.

Might we then think of the two attitudes to Kosmodemianskaya as distinct approaches to this zone of putrescence between the two bodies, or to the similar zone of transgressive pollution dividing Burkert's two sacrifices? One attitude - the 'phallic' one - distances itself from the extraordinary zone, domesticating it from outside through the work of mourning and memorialisation. The 'other,' non-phallic attitude, by contrast, identifies with the position inside the zone, where Kosmodemianskaya remains as long as the system has not completely 'digested' her bare life (*zoe*), returning her symbolic life (*bios*) to the collective.[29] From another perspective, one could say that the phallic attitude is interested only in what Kosmodemianskaya becomes after death - a sacrificial victim monumentalised in order to spur others on to avenge and redeem her loss, honoring her memory. By contrast, the non-phallic attitude focuses on Kosmodemianskaya's actual experience of exterminatory violence, going even so far as to contemplate (witness) the ecstasy of her suffering, as exposed in Strunnikov's photograph.

discussion of the Roman ritual of consecration in Giorgio Agamben, 1998. *Homo Sacer: Sovereign Power and Bare Life*, (trans) Daniel Heller-Roazen, Stanford: Stanford University Press 1998, pp91-103; and Bronfen's essay on the death of Mérimée's *Carmen* in Elisabeth Bronfen, *Over her Dead Body: Death, Femininity and the Aesthetic*, Manchester, Manchester University Press 1992.

Each of the four moments can be seen to vacillate between these two positions, either inside or outside the extraordinary zone. Such a shift is most evident in the two versions of the Kukryniksy painting. During the war, the painters identify with Kosmodemianskaya inside the zone and thus seek to capture the very threshold of her consummation and transcendence. By aligning this threshold with the moment of death, the extraordinary zone is marked as the span of time Kosmodemianskaya spends in captivity, and her torments can be mapped to the decomposition of the flesh. After the war, however, this position becomes too difficult to contemplate, and the painting must be revised. Now the image is itself a monumentalisation of the already 'digested' Kosmodemianskaya.

With the juxtaposition of Lidov's final paragraph and Strunnikov's photograph, vacillation occurs on a single page. Lidov clearly seeks a position outside the extraordinary zone - which is again the time of the partisan girl's torture and execution. However, the awkward contradiction with the photograph thrusts the reader back inside, revealing that Lidov's prediction of Stalin mentally visiting the grave of his devoted daughter has in fact already taken place. Stalin *did* come, just as Zoya promised. The ecstatic pose of her body is evidence of this fact.

Such awkwardness becomes somewhat more rigorous in Aliger's poem, which seems to strive for a full hybridisation of the two positions, doubling the sublime body that marks the end of the extraordinary zone. Linked by the motif of the thrown back head, the monument in Aliger's epilogue is shown to be a copy of Strunnikov's ecstatic corpse. Kosmodemianskaya thus simultaneously dons the peaceful body of monumental stillness and the convulsed body of suffering, non-phallic passion. Indeed, something similar can also be seen in the 1942 version of the Kukryniksy painting, in which Kosmodemianskaya again appears in a position that resembles her exhumed body. The Nazi photographers capture the partisan girl at the moment of death, and for them the picture will no doubt serve as a perverse memento of the atrocity. How is this memorialisation linked to the Soviet painting, which performs a similar, if nobler function? On the one hand, it suggests the artists' discomfort. Can they endure the guilt of having survived Kosmodemianskaya's sacrifice to transform her suffering body into a monumental image? Perhaps not, and thus they are drawn toward the ecstatic corpse, as if hoping to infuse their meager representation with its uncanny life. Like Aliger, the Kukryniksy move in both directions at once - inside and out - at least until after the war, when the monumentalist attitude becomes dominant.

Finally, Komov's sculpture is interesting because it seems to revive this impulse toward chronotopic hybridity some forty years after the end of the war. Again the ecstatic corpse serves as a model for the monumental image. The impression that Kosmodemianskaya is falling suggests identification with the moment of death even though the ostensible function of the sculpture is to provide an enduring 'afterlife' for the partisan girl, ensuring her memory is preserved. Yet here there is also a feeling that hybridity is somehow awkward and unintentional like the juxtaposition of Lidov's article and Strunnikov's photograph. Komov's plan seems murky - almost approaching a kind of *stiob* - rather than fraught with the conflicting desires that haunt Aliger's poem and the first Kukryniksy painting.[30]

The tendency to hybridise internalising and externalising attitudes to the zone of putrescence is in fact very characteristic of Stalinist culture in the 1930s. One need only think of the discourse and practices surrounding Lenin's embalmed body, for example (*Snow White*). With reference to my discussion of Lacan in the previous section, the external attitude depends on the phallic interplay of Φ and a, producing a monumental image of mastery over death. As the immortalised memory of a lost erotic object, Kosmodemianskaya comes to stand for the sacrifices required to uphold and exist within the symbolic order. By contrast, the internal attitude depends on the non-phallic interaction between $S(\cancel{A})$ and a. Now Kosmodemianskaya assumes the position of an eschatological subject, martyring herself not for the sake of the existing order but for a more sublime truth to come. Both attitudes are ambivalent. The monumental image requires the suppression of indeterminacy, domesticating the horrors of the partisan girl's torments, veiling the wound of her missing breast. Though hidden, this place of trauma remains a constituent part of the image, unsettling the work of mourning and demanding its repetition. The devotees of the Kosmodemianskaya cult must periodically return to the site of her sacrificial victimisation, recalling the obligation it entails. From the internal perspective, the partisan girl's martyrdom is also incomplete. Her body remains frozen in ecstasy, much as her corpse reportedly remained hanging for a month after her execution.[31] As long as the body of nature is suspended in this way, the full sublimity of truth must be deferred. Stalin may have come, making the partisan girl a witness to the Other's *jouissance*, but she is nonetheless still 'waiting for her beloved', as Aliger evocatively interprets Strunnikov's photograph in *Zoya*. Again, there is a suggestion of repetition here. One exterminated witness will not be enough to realise the Cause. All must imitate Kosmodemianskaya's descent into the extraordinary zone.

It is the shared ambivalence of the two attitudes - the common denominator of *objet a* - that enables their chiastic superimposition. First, the inversion can be examined in terms of violence. The external, monumentalist attitude finds its depiction of heroic sacrifice undermined by the trauma of exterminatory violence. Conversely, the internal, eschatological attitude must endure the fact that this violence did not run its full course. As long as Kosmodemianskaya's body lingers, her death has not yet truly been accomplished. Second, the relationship can be examined in terms of the extraordinary zone of putrescence. Here the monumentalist attitude treats the zone as if closed but is compelled to return again and again and reopen it. The eschatological attitude, by contrast, thrusts itself

30. *Stiob* refers to a common form of late socialist irony, typically deadpan. See Alexai Yurchak, *Everything was Forever, until it was no more: The Last Soviet Generation*, Princeton, Princeton University Press, 2006, pp249-54.

31. In the final scene of Aliger's play, *A Fairy-Tale about Truth*, the male lead promises to avenge Zoya's death while bizarrely standing next to the shadow cast by her hanged body.

into the zone as into an abyss, but finds it can never open it all the way. At most it can repeat the act of Kosmodemianskaya's martyrdom, enduring the interminable 'not yet' of the truth-to-come alongside her.[32] Thus the same wound haunts both attitudes in opposite ways. One mourns and veils it, while the other awaits its totalisation. As a result, the simultaneous embrace of both attitudes becomes imaginable, if paradoxical, enabling the pursuit of total mastery and martyrdom at once.

As noted above, the examples I have presented do not all suggest a willful impulse toward such hybridity. In the juxtaposition of Lidov's article and Strunnikov's photograph, the coalescence of the two attitudes seems almost accidental; it could even be read as a kind of revealing parapraxis. In Aliger's two endings, however, the doubling constitutes a genuine part of the poem's aesthetic fabric. When Kosmodemianskaya's monument and corpse are fused to produce a sublime body of undying ecstasy, the ambivalence that haunts both attitudes is subdued. It is as if the extraordinary zone were at once opened to engulf the entire symbolic order and closed completely, never to threaten the subject again. Somehow it is through the monumental image that the martyr achieves her dream of consummation and resurrection in the Cause. By the same token, the monument no longer hides the wound of castration but embraces it ecstatically as exposure to the power that founds the Law. Desire mingles with drive, and preservation of the lacking Other becomes identical to its totalisation and supersession.

At the same time, this paradoxical fusion of monumentalism and eschatology is not an actual accomplishment, but only a tragically optimistic image of total mastery and martyrdom. As suggested above, the true realisation of this paradox would mean both returning home from the great sacrifice of the war and enduring its exterminatory excess in full - as the total expurgation of collective guilt, ushering in the new age through self-immolation. Indeed, it is the manifest impossibility of this dual achievement that produces the impulse to chronotopic hybridity. Zoya's ecstatic monument is in the end only a makeshift surrogate for the sublime body that would simultaneously open and close the extraordinary zone in total consummation. Hybridisation arises as a strategy of subduing ambivalence without eliminating it, projecting an image of total victory while still waging the war.

With the Kukryniksy we see how Soviet culture tended to efface the traces of this tendency after the war was won. The 1942 painting suggests a hybridity similar to Aliger's, contaminating the moment of sacrificial victimisation with the ecstatic body of Strunnikov's photograph, suspended between life and death. After the war, however, ecstasy is dampened, and only the trauma of the partisan girl's suffering remains, veiled behind the enduring stillness of the lull before death. Nonetheless, in Komov's 1986 sculpture, some element of the old Stalinist logic still seems to be operative. It is hard to explain this resurgence, although one is tempted to associate it with the attempt to renew the Soviet experiment one last time before its final collapse with

32. In the section of *Zoya* preceding the description of Strunnikov's photograph, Aliger imagines such accompanying the partisan in this way: 'Burn me, suffering of the other, / become my own torture. / I would like to write about Zoya / in such a way that I might be strangled with her. / I would like to write about Zoya, / so that Zoya could begin to breathe, / so the famous Russian mother / would become stone and mean' (*Stikhi*, p168). The association in these lines of Zoya's position between life and death with the defeminisation of the mother is striking.

perestroika. Whatever the source, it is interesting that Kosmodemianskaya's image is still capable of producing uncanny effects today. On the anniversary of the October Revolution in 2011, the Zaporozhe regional committee of the Communist Party of Ukraine erected two statues to decorate their headquarters. The three-quarter figures stand in the windows on either side of the building's entrance - to the right is the generalissimo, Stalin, and to the left is Kosmodemianskaya, honored for her 'immortal, prophetic words: 'Stalin is with us! Stalin will come!' Unlike other post-Soviet monuments, the image of Kosmodemianskaya is martial and androgynous rather than feminine and frail. Whatever the intentions of the communists, it is fascinating how Kosmodemianskaya - standing in the traumatic position of the building's 'left breast' - is both immortalised by her sacrifice and yet still waiting for the ecstatic fulfilment of her prophecy. Stalin, meanwhile stands beside his loyal daughter, as if patiently waiting for the new life in which she will become his bride. But where does the door these sentries are guarding lead?[33]

Another recent appropriation of Kosmodemianskaya's image, also in Ukraine, appeared in an article written for the online news site, ridus.ru, about the artist-activist group, FEMEN. One of the photographs for the article, taken by Sergei Polezhaka, features three of the women standing in front of a recent statue to the Soviet partisan and mimicking her pose (fig.13). The point of identification for FEMEN is clearly Kosmodemianskaya's bound hands - symbolising the oppression of women.[34] Yet the peculiar resonance of their trademark topless attire at the various actions they stage and Kosmodemianskaya's own signature trauma is striking. While the women are clothed in the picture, one of them, Inna Shevchenko, wears a shirt with the image of Eugène Delacroix's famous painting of the bare-chested *Liberty Leading the People*. The connection to revolutionary violence is thus

33. The two statues were erected inside the building after a first version of the Stalin figure was blown up by members of the right-wing Svoboda party. In this context, Kosmodemianskaya's role is to guard her father-husband against fascists.

34. http://fototelegraf.ru/121405-pryamoj-razgovor-s-femen.html.

Fig 13.

directly implied. To lead the people to victory, the nurturing maternal breast must be transformed into its own kind of phallic weapon. Yet, what of Kosmodemianskaya's wound? What of her exposure to that other *jouissance*, the passion of Joan of Arc, ecstatically driven beyond the phallus? By inadvertently evoking the clash between these two feminine postures, the photograph seems to hint at the political awkwardness of the group's ideology - resisting male oppression without rejecting phallic norms of feminine beauty.[35]

35. In May 2010, FEMEN lovingly washed the Kiev statue of Kosmodemianskaya in preparation for Victory Day. The group described the gesture as commemorating all women who fought in the Second World War. See http://femen.livejournal.com/2010/05/07/.

Like Komov's statue, both of these recent Ukrainian flirtations with chronotopic hybridity do not seem fully thought out and tested in the manner of Aliger's poem or even the 1942 painting of Kosmodemianskaya's execution by the Kukryniksy. And yet, at the same time, they reveal the persistence of the impulse toward that hybridity in post-Soviet culture, despite the efforts to monumentalise the partisan girl as a feminine victim after the war. Does this mean that the Stalinist strategy of projecting a makeshift surrogate of communist victory upon the continuing struggle to achieve it still has its place in the post-Soviet imaginary? Perhaps - especially if one considers that the catastrophe of the war in the context of 1917. Stalinist culture in the 1930s waited with great eagerness for its total war of revolutionary consummation. Was the Nazi-Soviet conflict a missed opportunity to achieve this dream? Or did the dream in fact come to pass, halting the progress of bourgeois modernity and at last ending the 'heroic age' of revolutionary politics in industrial Europe? In either case, the meaning of this event remains unrecognised, and the extraordinary ambivalence of Zoya Kosmodemianskaya remains open.

Jonathan Brooks Platt is Assistant Professor of Slavic Languages and Literatures at the University of Pittsburgh. His articles have appeared in *Representations*, *Russian Review*, *Pushkin Review*, and *The New Literary Observer*, among others. His monograph *Greetings Pushkin: Stalinist Cultural Politics and the Russian Bard*, was published in 2016 by the University of Pittsburgh Press. His current research project focuses on Kosmodemianskaya and the memory of Soviet militancy in contemporary Russia.

THE FACE OF THE GOOD DEATH: EUTHANASIA AND LEVINAS

Timothy Secret

Abstract At various strata of the debate, the sense that arguments surrounding euthanasia are no longer making significant advances has provoked a variety of attempts to find alternative ethical approaches that might break with standard deadlocks. In this essay, we will trail one such move by giving a new account of what the ethical stance of Emmanuel Levinas might contribute towards the twin questions of the ethical justification and legalisation of euthanasia. Interpreting our fundamental relationship with the other in terms of the Biblical injunction 'Thou shalt not kill' and refusing to draw any distinction between murder and other forms of killing, Levinas is commonly taken to have offered an ethical stance that is strongly opposed to euthanasia. Without disagreeing with this interpretation, we will offer an account of a further twist on this perspective that renders euthanasia ambiguously the exemplary ethical failure and the supreme culmination of ethics, simultaneously separating this ethical question entirely from legality.

Keywords euthanasia, Levinas, death sacrifice, ethics

SOMETHING IS AMISS

The philosopher and medical ethicist Margaret P. Battin has published, adopting the term used in a well-known *New York Times Magazine* article about her life and work, 'wheelbarrows full' of book and articles championing the cause of euthanasia and physician-assisted suicide since entering the debate in the early 1980s.[1] It might be somewhat surprising, then, that she began her article on the topic for the 2003 *Oxford Handbook of Practical Ethics* with the statement: 'Something is amiss with the debate over euthanasia and physician-assisted suicide'.[2]

What makes this claim stand out is that those who support the legalisation of euthanasia, simply using this word from now on, tend to sound quite satisfied with a debate that they seem convinced they are winning or have effectively already won. Organisations in the UK such as the *Campaign for Dignity in Dying* champion statistics such as 82 per cent of the British population supporting a change in the law on assisted dying for terminally ill adults, rising to 86 per cent among the disabled and only falling to 79 per cent among those who identify as religious.[3] The former chairwoman of that of that group,

---

1. Robin Marantz Heing, 'A Life-or-Death Situation', *New York Times Magazine*, July 17 2013, available online at http://www.nytimes.com/2013/07/21/magazine/a-life-or-death-situation.html.

2. Margaret P. Battin, 'Euthanasia and Physician-Assisted Suicide', in (ed.) Hugh LaFollette, *Oxford Handbook of Practical Ethics*, Oxford, Oxford University Press 2003, p673. (Hereafter *Euthanasia*).

3. Campaign for Dignity in Dying, *Assisted Dying: Setting the Record Straight*, August 2015, available online at http://www.dignityindying.org.uk/wp-content/uploads/2015/08/DiD_MythBuster_Aug2015_A5_12pp_WEB.pdf.

Margaret Branthwaite, expressed a common sentiment among campaigners when she stated that 'it's only a matter of time before it's legalised'.[4] While rival organisations such as *Care Not Killing* marshal rather different statistics and the UK parliament recently rejected a proposed 'right to die' in England and Wales by a significant enough majority that the issue is unlikely to return for some time, the tone of campaigning in the legalisation movement remains that the march of history is on their side and inexorable. If it is only a matter of time, what, then, is amiss?

According to Battin, the primary problem with the ongoing debate relates to established patterns of discourse in which the issue is posed in for-and-against terms. While adversarial debate is vital for social and ethical issues that are 'just breaking open' - a situation where for-and-against analysis isolates, identifies, catalogues and critiques relevant elements - 'once a debate begins to mature, it becomes time to pursue attempts at resolution'.[5] Rather than an interminable back and forth over already well-churned ground that promises at best to unearth only an occasional new subtlety, the call for the debate to move from infancy to maturity is a push for not only theoretical but practical consensus. The obvious obstruction to such a development is that the euthanasia debate barely merits its definite article, being highly stratified between a public debate where the strong majority support change and specialised debates in legal, political and medical circles where such consensus is lacking. For example, while the British Medical Association shifted its position on assisted dying to neutrality in 2005, it returned to opposition in 2006 and since then the proposal for adopting a neutral stance has been put to the vote and rejected a further five times.

In such a situation, it is not uncommon to hear philosophers promoting their own block of the debate as the keystone around which harmony might be established. As Thomas Nagel wrote in his review of L.W. Sumner's *Assisted Death: A Study in Ethics and Law*, such a book:

> provides a superb example of the relevance of philosophy of public policy. The reason is that public policy governing treatment at the end of life is to a great extent shaped by philosophical confusions. It may not be too much to hope that a book such as this will help to rectify the situation.[6]

Indeed, such a hope does not seem entirely unrealistic when sources ranging from the public-facing website *NHS Choices* to *Medical Ethics Today: The BMA's Handbook of Ethics and Law* do indeed engage with the issues and a vocabulary that was developed in the adversarial debates of philosophers. However, without giving too much credence to traditional divisions between analytic and continental philosophy, it is notable that both public and specialised discussions engage with a relatively limited spectrum of thought in terms of its provenance, style and range of references. Although we encounter a certain Kant, we rarely encounter thinkers who might be referred to as post-

---

4. Margaret Branthwaite quoted in 'TTF director debates euthanasia in Ireland' Patients' Rights Council Update 036 Volume 20 Number 2 (2006) http://www.patientsrightscouncil.org/site/update036/

5. Margaret P. Battin, 'Euthanasia and Physician-Assisted Suicide', in Hugh LaFollette (ed), *Oxford Handbook of Practical Ethics*, Oxford, Oxford University Press 2003, p693.

6. Thomas Nagel, 'In Whose Interest?', *London Review of Books*, Vol 33, No. 19, 6 October 2011.

Hegelian or the currents of thought that take place more broadly within the critical humanities. Indeed, insofar as this lack of engagement is mutual, one might speculative that a wide spectrum of academics outside of the specialist confines of applied and medical ethics do not register the euthanasia debate as politically charged in the same manner as the debates surrounding such issues as abortion or intersexuality, in which we often find interventions form the critical humanities that disrupt established debates in medical ethics.

The underlying inspiration, or at least suspicion, that motivates this article is that insofar as the debate among philosophers has become reified, if not ossified, through standard distinctions, patterns of engagement and a canon of relevant articles and approaches - evidence of which can be readily found in any introductory applied ethics textbook or in the tens of thousands of essays produced annually by undergraduates on formulaic questions such as whether an act utilitarian ought to support active involuntary euthanasia for terminally ill patients or not - to that very extent philosophy loses its chance to play an active mediating role between public and specialised discourse and to prove itself truly relevant to public policy.

Some of the most promising moments in the euthanasia debate have been when a philosopher renews the debate through rejecting its accumulated concepts and concerns via adopting an alternative ethical approach in which they simply do not register. A strong example of this would be the distinctive account of virtue ethics offered in Liezl van Zyl's book from 2000 *Death and Compassion*, in which the dominant stream of discussion relating to the ethics of euthanasia is dismissed as rooted in 'monistic' or 'principalist' ethics.[7] Where van Zyl's work becomes even more interesting, however, is in her 2002 article 'Euthanasia, Virtue Ethics and the Law', in which she turns on the basis of her earlier work to the question of whether euthanasia should be legalised in a manner that simply bypasses the common issues that cause discussion to stagnate around apparently irresolvable aporias.[8] Without engaging further with the fascinating work of van Zyl, in this article I would like to test whether there is a way of pitching the distinctive approach to ethics offered by the philosopher Emmanuel Levinas that might also bypass traditional ways of setting up the distinct questions of euthanasia's ethical status and legalisation.

To briefly step ahead of ourselves, a common structure that we find in almost all strands of the euthanasia debate is that the question of whether euthanasia is ethically permissible is a simpler matter than the question of whether it should be legalised, simply because whether it should be legalised depends on (a) whether it is ethical and (b) some further concern. If euthanasia is ethically impermissible, then most would agree it should not be legalised. If euthanasia is ethically permissible, then there may still be good reasons for it remaining illegal. For example, that once legalised an inevitable 'slippery slope' would mean that people who do not want to die would be pressured into euthanasia. After addressing Levinas in the following two sections, we will see in the closing section how the position we develop on a Levinasian

7. Liezl van Zyl, *Death and Compassion*, Farnham, Ashgate 2000.

8. Liezl van Zyl, 'Euthanasia, Virtue Ethics and the Law', *New Zealand Bioethics Journal*, February 2002.

approach to euthanasia breaks with this structure of relating the two questions, possibly offering a route for engaging with the question of legalisation that does not depend on a simple, positive resolution for the question of ethical permissibility.

FACING THE DEBATE ANEW

The centennial celebration of the birth of Emmanuel Levinas in 2006 exhibited the continued relevance and influence of his work across the globe, with thirty-two conferences across thirteen countries. For better or worse, Levinas has commonly come to be seen through the lens of one dimension of his work. Stealing Hilary Putnam's appropriation via Isaiah Berlin of a fragment attributed to Archilochus, unlike those thinkers akin to foxes who knows many little things, Levinas is a hedgehog who knows one big thing: that 'one big thing' that his entire philosophy can be seen as unpacking is the claim that 'ethics is first philosophy'.[9]

The priority of *being first* can be taken quite literally here: when we engage in a genetic phenomenological analysis of experience, we discover at the root of the progressive constitution of our intelligible lived world the structure of an ethical relation to another human being rather than an ontological relation to Being. Our existence as isolated, independent self-sufficient egos is not false, but it is derivative. To capture this notion of the originary status of the ethical encounter in terms amenable to phenomenology, Levinas famously uses the terminology of the other's face. In our analysis that starts from the constituted world as an apparently consistent and meaningful totality, 'we can proceed from the experience of totality back to a situation where totality breaks up, a situation that conditions the totality itself. Such a situation is the gleam of exteriority or of transcendence in the face of the Other'.[10] Nevertheless, this imagery of encountering a face is analogical since the originary relation to the other is not actually given to the phenomenological gaze. The 'ultimate event of being' is 'essentially nocturnal' and cannot be brought to light and comprehended (*Totality*, p28). 'The Other is the principle of phenomena' without being given as a phenomena through 'disclosure' or even 'revelation' (p92).

Despite involving a rather elaborate account of the stages involved in the progressive synthesising and structuring of experience, a post-Kantian assumption that might be disputed by many forms of contemporary realism, I take it that what Levinas offers to ethical thought is a compelling account of motivation. If the world taken as meaningful totality *could* be constituted *without* having arisen from an originary ethical relationship - if the Other were not the principle of all phenomena - then an independent ego might legitimately ask questions such as 'Why does the other concern me? What is Hecuba to me? Am I my brother's keeper?'[11] In such a universe, Levinas claims that a concern for the other who remains outside-of-me would be

9. Hilary Putnam, 'Levinas and Judaism', in Simon Critchley and Robert Bernasconi (eds.), *The Cambridge Companion to Levinas*, Cambridge, Cambridge University Press 2004, p.58.

10. Emmanuel Levinas, *Totality and Infinity*, Pittsburgh, Duquesne University Press 1969, p24. (Hereafter *Totality*).

11. Emmanuel Levinas, *Otherwise than Being or Beyond Essence*, Pittsburgh, Duquesne University Press 2006, p117.

incomprehensible. Levinas thus offers an archaeology of a common ethical substructure, applicable as much to virtue ethics as to principalist normative approaches, in which we are at root individual animals driven to persevere in our being by what Spinoza would have called the *conatus essendi*, creatures who then find this disrupted by some further specifically human element - reason, virtue, divine revelation, etc. This further element can supposedly compel us, at times, to act against our own egoist self-preservation and self-interest. Although the surface narrative of *Totality and Infinity* appears to go along with this schema - the enjoyment and nourishment of a dwelling and loving egoist described in Section II having its mode of being radically subverted by the election via the face to a properly human mode of being that is dedicated to the Other in Section III - that apparent chronological narrative is properly an account of rediscovering the Other who is always-already acting as the nocturnal principle of the world as totality. Levinas is flatly sceptical about any other account of ethical motivation where that which demands ethics comes through a higher faculty to an original *conatus*. For example, he denies that something like the 'respect for formal universality', offered by Kant as the cause of our only following maxims that we would legislate for all others, could subdue our rapacious animal drives were it not for this original ethical relation.[12]

Whether one is convinced by Levinas's approach or not, as one of the major, distinctive thinkers of ethics in the twentieth-century one might expect there to already be plenty of scholarship on Levinas and euthanasia. This expectation would only be heightened when we consider Jacques Derrida's famous claim that 'all of Levinas's thought, from the beginning to the end, was a meditation on death'.[13] However, while Levinas gives us a great deal of material about the role of the ethical relationship in the constitution of experience, it is notoriously difficult to draw concrete ethical judgements from his work. As Dermot Moran forcefully put it at the beginning of the chapter on Levinas in his *Introduction to Phenomenology*:

> it must be made clear at the outset that Levinas has nothing to say about ethics as it is traditionally practiced in Western philosophy, since he thinks this tradition has either ignored ethics or made it secondary and provisional. Indeed, he explicitly repudiates the traditional understanding of ethics as a discipline within philosophy which examines different ways of motivating and justifying certain forms of behaviour. He deliberately avoids such topics as the nature of ethical justification, the various forms of ethical theory (e.g. utilitarianism, deontology), or the meta-ethical analysis of ethical discourse.[14]

If Moran is right, it would go without saying that Levinas's ethics also has 'nothing to say' about applied topics such as euthanasia. Simon Critchley offered a slightly less extreme account of how Levinas's work connects with

12. Emmanuel Levinas, *Entre Nous*, London, Continuum 2006, p135.

13. Jacques Derrida, *Adieu: To Emmanuel Levinas*, California, Stanford University Press 1999, p120.

14. Dermot Moran, *Introduction to Phenomenology*, London, Routledge 2000, p320.

practical ethics by saying that its relation:

> to conventional moral philosophy, or even applied ethics, will at best be oblique, and perhaps even critical. […] [F]or Levinas, the construction of a system, or procedure, for formulating and testing the moral acceptability of certain maxims or judgements […] is itself derived and distinct from a primordial ethical experience that Levinas's work seeks to describe.[15]

Levinas himself certainly seemed to reject the idea that his ethical work produced concrete ethical judgements, asking:

> Is my discourse deficient in concern with concrete reality? Does all this metaphysics of mine have the ability to solve actual ethical problems? I have no ambition to be a preacher […] it is not my purpose to moralise or to improve the conduct of our generation […] I have been speaking about that which stands behind practical morality.[16]

Furthermore, as he famously stated in a conversation later recounted by Derrida: 'You know, one often speaks of ethics to describe what I do, but what really interest me in the end is not ethics, not ethics alone, but the holy, the holiness of the holy'.[17] His status as a reluctant thinker of ethics can be further shown through the fact that his first tentative articulation of the originary role of ethics comes in the 1951 article 'Is Ontology Fundamental?' sixteen years after expressing the problem of being riveted to Being in 1935's *On Escape*. In the intervening years Levinas made attempts at breaking with the fundamental ontology endemic to philosophy that culminates in the climate of Heideggerian thought almost every approach *except* the ethical relation.

Against the statement above from Moran, the so-called 'Third Wave' of Levinas scholarship, which announced itself in Peter Atterton and Matthew Calarco's introduction to their 2010 edited volume *Radicalising Levinas*, demands tangible ethical results. Opposed to the supposed 'navel gazing' of previous Levinas scholarship, it is a movement concerned with 'the wider practical and applied dimensions of Levinas's work' and focuses primarily on 'exploring progressive socio-political issues' in the face of Levinas's characterisation of a 'world in pieces'.[18] Although the texts in *Radicalising Levinas* do not pose themselves directly in terms of applied ethics, the topics that emerge in this volume such as animal liberation and environmentalism overlap with the concerns of many applied ethicists. Nevertheless, the euthanasia debate does not figure.

A possible cause of the relative dearth of material on Levinas and euthanasia is that the most obvious reading of Levinas's ethical position would contribute an answer that is not the one people exploring so-called progressive socio-political issues are likely to welcome. Whatever the value of oppositions such as conservative and progressive when it comes to ethical rather than political issues, Levinas's actual statements on life and death, rooted as they are in the Hebrew scriptures, frequently lend themselves to defending quite traditional stances. When fellow phenomenologist of ethics Pope John Paul II evoked Levinas's work as 'a testimony for our age' in *Crossing the Threshold of Hope*, it was in the context of defending a pro-life stance on the issue of abortion.[19] It is perhaps unsurprising, then, that if Levinas's name is mentioned in the euthanasia debate at all, it is by those opposing the legalisation of euthanasia. Paul Schotsmans, for example, evokes Levinas in the context of defending a secularised version of the catholic stance on palliative care in which: 'ultimately there is nothing I can do against this inexorable enemy but answer "here I am" with freely-willed and sincerely concerned proximity, and hold her/his hand tightly, thus lightening her/his death and making it more bearable'.[20] In one of the only English-language Levinasian texts defending the partial legalisation of euthanasia, Torbens Wolfs notes his article's exceptional status: 'Some authors have explained their vision on euthanasia by reference to the philosophy of Emmanuel Levinas. It is striking that they either reject euthanasia categorically or approve of it only in so-called states of necessity. It seems that only opponents of euthanasia appeal to the philosophy of Levinas'.[21]

That Levinas is quite correctly - although we will enact a small twist on this point in the next section - understood as a thinker whose account of ethics, if it has anything to say about such issues, would be opposed to euthanasia, derives from the manner in which the commandment 'Thou shalt not kill' plays an elevated role in his philosophy. When Levinas comes to flesh out his notion of the face, he states directly that: 'The first word of the face is the "Thou shalt not Kill." It is an order'.[22] Indeed, the 'face is that possibility of murder, that powerlessness of being and that authority that commands me: "Thou shalt not kill."'[23] This is not simply a negative prohibition for Levinas since we kill far more often through inaction than action, meaning that 'Thou shalt not kill' is equivalent to 'Thou shalt cause thy neighbour to live' - not a prohibition to respect but an unending labour of care.[24]

The easiest way to avoid such a blanket rule against killing is to clarify that the biblical injunction against *ratsakh* is more accurately rendered 'Thou shalt not murder'. Thus, just as killing in war or when carrying out a legal sentence of execution is not *ratsakh* in the Hebrew scripture, if euthanasia is agreed to constitute something other than murder then the injunction encountered in the other's face would not forbid it. However, while this is an option for many divine command theorists who hold to the fundamental status of this commandment, it is not an option for Levinas. Although this precise formula arises in the context of killing someone by accident, Levinas is clear throughout his work that 'there would be only one race of murderers'.[25] The distinction between the race of murderers and the race of manslayers only occurs to us because: 'Our conscience is not yet wholly conscience. It is a twilight. The transition from the non-intentional to the intentional is noticeable. We are not awake enough'.[26]

I have long found this to be among the most striking phrases in the history of ethical thought. If there is only one race of murderers, then the distinctions that we have developed through engaging in back-and-forth debate - all of the sophisticated issues we tutor undergraduates in - would be the product of a half-sleep. Indeed, with each additional nuance, the twilight we produce around ethical debates becomes murkier. Perhaps this explains why Levinas had little interest in supporting his account of the primordial ethical experience with a particular account of ethical system building. When we wake up to the ethical demand, there will be no excuses or nuances of the kind ethical systems are built to recognise. To awaken is to see things in black and white rather than shades of grey. Yet, far from this awakening resolving into a strict distinction between saints and sinners, the consequence is the overwhelming guiltiness testified to in one of Levinas's most frequently quoted literary references, Zosima's claim from *The Brothers Karamazov* that: 'Each of us is guilty before everyone and for everything, and I more than all the others'.[27] In less hyperbolic terms, every person in the first world fails the commandment 'Thou shalt cause thy neighbour to live' daily by enjoying the rewards of the economy. We are all of the race of murderers in a world where: 'Every death is a murder, is premature, and there is responsibility of the survivor'.[28] Nevertheless, according to Levinas what one cannot do on the basis of this is reason like Macbeth that we are so steeped in blood, and furthermore so inevitably steeped in blood, that we may as well commit one more atrocity.

THE ULTIMATE SACRIFICE

The primordial ethical experience that Levinas describes as opening the world of phenomena does not simply play out in our world. Nobody directly feels infinite ethical election and nobody does everything they could to cause their neighbour to live. Nobody - to use another of Levinas's favourite references - gives the other the bread from out of their own mouth, or at least not all of it. Indeed, insofar as anyone truly and fully did give the other the bread from out of their own mouth, they would soon not be around to do so further. Yet this insatiable and excessive demand is used to explain moments ranging from the occasions a person actual does reject the *conatus* to die for another (Levinas frequently refers to the Franciscan friar Maximilian Maria Kolbe who volunteered to die in place of a stranger at Auschwitz) to the moment we take a second to hold a door open for a stranger. Above all, our underlying ethical election explains the very existence of a guilt that we become attached to, and it is in this context that we will address euthanasia below.

It has already been mentioned that Torben Wolfs offers one of the only attempts to defend the Levinasian legalisation of euthanasia in particular circumstances. According to Wolfs:

26. Emmanuel Levinas, 'Cities of Refuge', *Beyond the Verse: Talmudic Readings and Lectures*, Bloomington, Indiana University Press 1994, p43.

27. For example, Emmanuel Levinas, 'Interview with François Poirié', *Is it Righteous to Be?* California, Stanford University Press 2001, p56.

28. Emmanuel Levinas, *God, Death and Time*, California, Stanford University Press 2000, p72.

> Suffering [...] is inhuman, and this is to be understood literally: it depersonalises. The patient is no longer who he used to be. It is as if the patient himself does not live, but that 'something' has taken over, something anonymous: 'it lives'.[29]

Wolfs is not saying that *ratsakh* does not cover all acts of killing humans - as some divine command theorists claim killing in war is not *ratsakh* - rather he accepts that all killing of humans - including all letting die of humans - is murder. However, in extreme suffering Wolfs claims one can cease to be human. This approach can be found in traditional euthanasia debates, for example in the work of James Rachels for whom it is morally indifferent if a creature stops biologically *being alive*, what is ethically unaccepting is killing someone who *has a life*.[30] For Wolfs it is wrong to murder a human being, but it is not necessarily wrong to put an end to a depersonalised 'it lives'.

Although this argument makes sense in the context of a hospital ward, it strikes me as untenable for Levinas. Surely the most depersonalised, suffering figure we find in the work of post-holocaust writers such as Levinas is the *Muselmann* in a concentration camp? As described by Giorgio Agamben:

> Nothing 'natural' or 'common', however, is left in him; nothing animal or instinctual remains in his life. All his instincts are cancelled along with his reason. Antelme tells us that the camp inhabitant was no longer capable of distinguishing between pangs of cold and the ferocity of the SS.[31]

Although Levinas bases his phenomenological account of responsibility explicitly on the *responsiveness* of the other - the expressiveness of the face and the absolute loss that occurs when the face ceases to respond and becomes a death mask - he cannot allow that in extreme suffering death would already effectively have occurred during biological life without absolving those who put the body of the *Muselmann* out of its misery. Levinas will in fact go out of his way to insist on the possibility of shreds of light in even the most depersonalised spaces. For example, Levinas refers to the account of the gulags in Vasily Grossman's *Life and Fate* as offering 'a complete spectacle of desolation and dehumanisation. The book reflects absolute despair, and I see no horizon, no salvation for the human race', yet even here in 'the decay of human relations' he holds that 'goodness persists' albeit as a goodness that, in Ikonnikov's words, 'is beautiful and powerless, like the dew' (*Proximity*, pp106-109). This powerless beauty expressed even in a situation of absolute despair suggests Levinas is more likely to follow Schotsmans statement above about staying with the dying, holding their hand tightly in freely-willed and sincerely concerned proximity. So, is there an alternative way of accounting for euthanasia using Levinasian resources?

It is rarely sufficiently appreciated that Levinas's philosophy is not simply

29. Torben Wolfs, 'Levinas, Euthanasia and the Presence of Non-Sense' in Roger Burggraeve (ed) *The Awakening to the Other: A Provocative Dialogue with Emmanuel Levinas*, Leuven, Peeters 2008, p317.

30. James Rachels, *The End of Life: Euthanasia and Morality*, Oxford, Oxford University Press 1986, p5.

31. Giorgio Agamben, *Homo Sacer: Sovereign Power and Bare Life*, California, Stanford University Press 1998, p.104.

selfless. Although infinite ethical responsibility involves immense guilt as we recognise ourselves as murderers, we are nevertheless deeply attached to this growing guilt and the mode of being beyond *mere* being that we attain as creatures subject to such guilt - that is, as entities elected to properly human status. Election as 'total altruism' empties 'the I of its imperialism and egoism' in an engagement that is 'happy' - albeit with 'an austere and non-complacent happiness that lies in the nobility of an election that does not know its own happiness'.[32] Although we need bread and would enjoy it, this finite need and its satisfaction is as nothing compared to the desire that only grows in giving bread. In platitudinous terms, it is better to give than to receive. Put differently, although we might appear to be engaged in an act of giving when we serve the other, it is the other who gives us the greater gift. The other elevates us from the carefree life of an egoistic animal following the *conatus* and partaking in finite enjoyments to being an upright human who stands in relation to the infinity of the good beyond Being.

Although in the hyperbolic terms of Levinas's description of ethical election we are compelled by a pure desire to care *for the other*, the commitment to 'cause thy neighbour to live' is driven by terror at what would happen to us should we lose them. If the other ceases to be, we will lose ethical election and return to the carefree life of animal enjoyment that, although it might sound superficially attractive, can only be a horrifying prospect to a human who has nurtured their desire for the other:

> I did not know I was so rich, but I don't have the right to keep anything anymore. Is the Desire for Others appetite or generosity? The Desirable does not satisfy my Desire, it hollows me, nourishing me somehow with new hungers. Desire turns out to be bounty. […] As if the compassion […] were a hunger […] nourished beyond all saturation, by increasing that hunger, infinitely.[33]

It is beyond the scope of this article to give a full account of the relation between enjoyment, desire, responsiveness, responsibility and death at stake in Levinas's texts.[34] One simple way of characterising our relation to the other, at least before Levinas produces the concept of the trace, is that they are the only free element in our existence. Every other entity we encounter is, ultimately, simply a measurable portion of matter that obeys the deterministic laws of physics. It is only when I engage with the other in a face-to-face relationship through language that I encounter responsiveness rather than reaction. Although some scientific worldviews might deny the above claim, seeing humans as only very complicated machines, Levinas is likely to respond that insofar as we view another human in these terms we are not engaging with them in a face-to-face relationship. The death of the other can thus be seen as a transfer from a universe in which responsiveness between free beings exists to a cage of absolute causal determinism:

32. Emmanuel Levinas, 'Transcendence and Height', *Basic Philosophical Writings* Bloomington, Indiana University Press 1996, p18.

33. Emmanuel Levinas, *Humanism of the Other* Chicago, University of Illinois Press 2006, p30

34. For a significantly more detailed account of many of these issues in relation to the key yet slippery notion of the 'trace', see chapter 3 of my *The Politics and Pedagogy of Mourning*, London, Bloomsbury 2015.

Death is the disappearance in beings of those expressive movements that are always responses. Death will touch, above all, that autonomy or that expressiveness of movement that can go to the point of masking someone within his face. Death is the no-response. Those movements both hide and inform the vegetative movements.[35]

In another vocabulary, there is no significant sense of time in a universe of causal necessity - the future is simply the outcome of the present - it is only the other who brings the possibility of a future.

It is at this point, where keeping the other alive as a locus of responsiveness is as much a matter of protecting my own human existence from annihilation as that of the other, that euthanasia reveals itself to entail the most Levinasian of anti-Levinasian twists. Although it seemed that we would do anything for the other *except* the act of euthanasia, we might begin to worry that the reason we would not do this is because it would impoverish us rather than them. What if the fury to keep the other alive, even when the other states they do not wish to remain alive, stems from horror at the prospect of living-on without them? Do we not, then, in killing or in simply letting the singular other die, enact the ultimate personal sacrifice: willing returning to a mode of being that is properly unliveable for the sake of obeying the other's demand? Euthanasia would be the end of ethics - the end of the possibility of ethical living, of a life worthy of living - for the sake of one last service to the other. It seems then to be both the worst and best of acts - we cut ourselves off from the good beyond being, that relationship to infinity that constitutes the holy dimension of being human and that Levinas claimed to be his real interest rather than ethics, in favour of helping a concrete other. While Levinas will claim that we only relate to the divine Other through serving a human other in their simple mortal needs, here we choose the human other at the expense of the divine Other. While all other ethical acts implicitly serve our own interests, here we have an act that is utterly opposed to our own interests - to both our physical needs and our metaphysical desire. To help the other die can therefore be seen as the ultimate sacrifice both in terms of being the highest sacrifice and as last sacrifice. Although everything in Levinas's work suggests it would be the highest scandal, perhaps it is also the only death that is not scandalous.

The above is certainly not the only way to approach euthanasia on the basis of Levinas's work. Indeed, an alternative way of approaching the issue might seem to reject the above. If we consider the act of euthanasia from the perspective of the one who asks to die rather than the one asked to help, we encounter a quite different set of issues relating to Levinas's pre-ethical work on the impossibility of suicide. Indeed, this is the approach largely taken by A. T. Nuyen in 'Levinas and the Euthanasia Debate', who only considers euthanasia from the perspective of the one asked to assist in the act very briefly.[36] Although Levinas's aim in these texts was to reject the romanticised

35. Emmanuel Levinas, *God, Death and Time*, California, Stanford University Press 2000, p9.

36. A. T. Nuyen, 'Levinas and the Euthanasia Debate', *The Journal of Religious Ethics*, Vol. 28, No. 1 Spring 2000.

Heideggerian image of the existential hero who seizes death resolutely - a figure we are more likely to find choosing death rather than divulging the secrets of the Resistance in Sartre or Camus than begging for an end to their suffering in a hospital ward - the claim that suicide is 'a contradictory concept' frustrates any Levinasian attempt to approach or justify euthanasia from a first-person perspective. 'My mastery, my virility, my heroism as a subject can be neither virility nor heroism in relation to death' and in a world where the 'whole acuity of suffering lies in this impossibility of retreat' that limitation testifies against those discourses on euthanasia that pose the issue in terms of *autonomy*, *taking control* or *dying on one's own terms*.[37] The very intelligibility of euthanasia for Levinas would depend on death being conceived as release from Being, as a return to nothingness, yet against this Levinas suggests death to be a mystery on the basis of the Bergsonian argument that nothingness is a modification of being:

> *Hamlet* is precisely a lengthy testimony to this impossibility of assuming death. Nothingness is impossible. It is nothingness that would have left humankind the possibility of assuming death and snatching a supreme mastery from out of the servitude of existence. "To be or not to be" is a sudden awareness of this impossibility of annihilating oneself.[38]

Does the impossibility of annihilating oneself, with help or not, impose consequences on the one who is asked to help? It is unclear that it does. That the Other might be deceived in their belief that they can escape Being is no obvious reason for refusing to assist them, since my obligation is not limited to carrying out those acts I endorse as rational. Furthermore, to assume that the whole mechanism of desiring to escape Being and inevitably failing to do so would apply to the Other would be to assume that the Other is existentially the same as me, which Levinas strongly rejects: the Other is 'absolutely foreign to me - refractory to every typology, to every genus, to every characterology, to every classification' (*Totality*, p73).[39]

ETHICS AND LEGALITY

What then are the consequences of the line of thought expressed in the previous section for the euthanasia debate? What is most notable is that questions of ethics and legality are completely severed in Levinas's approach. That is to say, to address the legalisation of voluntary active euthanasia we will certainly not first ask 'Is voluntary active euthanasia ethical?' and then, if it passes this test, ask the further question of whether there are any additional factors that mean we ought to nevertheless maintain its illegality.

We can see why this cannot work in a Levinasian context by considering the broader category of murder, which we have argued euthanasia always remains for Levinas and that we have seen to be equally the demand that we cause the

---

37. Emmanuel Levinas, *Time and the Other* Pittsburgh, Duquesne University Press 1987, p43, 72, 69.

38. Emmanuel Levinas, *Time and the Other* Pittsburgh, Duquesne University Press 1987, p73.

39. This claim is discussed and apparently endorsed by Nuyen in 'Levinas and the Euthanasia Debate' p130, yet he then proceeds to apply claims that emerge from the experiential relation to suicide of the self (such as its concept being contradictory) to the suicide requested by the other.

other to live. One clearly cannot form a law in relation to such an account of murder, an account that states there is only one race of murderers and that this race encompasses everyone insofar as we participate in the unfairly distributed products of the global economy. Putting the entire population of a country in jail for murder as they have failed to cause the other in the Third World to live might have a beautiful poetic truth, yet it serves little practical purpose and might well be taken as a *reductio ad absurdum* of Levinas's position. That it is not such a *reductio* is because he never suggests a direct connection between these forms of responsibility. While Levinas declares that those who draw an ethical distinction between manslaughter and murder or between negligence of the starving other and their violent annihilation are not awake enough, this does not mean that such distinctions are irrelevant in a court of law. Levinas has no interest in forgiving and forgetting the deeds of concentration camp guards or stating equal legal culpability for the one in the gas chamber and the one who locked the door. This is just one aspect of the distinction between the incalculable ethical dimension of our primordial existence and calculable political reality. This lack of a direct relation is not, however, a claim that there is no relation. The ethical conditions legal responsibility and explains its possibility: the metaphysical guilt that accounts for the very fact that we are not living in a world without law or with only a Hobbesian law based on fear of violence.

Where ethical justification was a precondition for legal justification, here ethical accusation is a precondition for legal accusation. Nevertheless, freed of a direct correlation between what is ethical and what can be legal, the basis for legislation becomes entirely practical. Though ethics does not distinguish between murder and manslaughter, the law is right to do so and the legislation depends more on what works than what is right. Indeed, what is right is not merely unattainable but undesirable if imposed by law - as in the case of a country with its whole population imprisoned.

Although the above was our primary target, it is worth noting that a second consequence of the above way of viewing euthanasia is that, even if it was to become legalised or tolerated, in a Levinasian perspective it cannot ever become routine or professionalised. If someone carrying out euthanasia is not merely committing murder but being asked to abandon a distinctly human mode of being and cut themselves off from the good beyond Being, then this act is final and unique. If every death is experienced simply an absolute scandal but an apocalypse - the end of the world - then the repeated enactment of such a task can never become part of a job description. A third consequence would be that - unlike the Levinasian justification of euthanasia found in Wolfs - there seems to be little basis for such distinctions in the debate such as whether the other is terminally ill and in pain or neither of these things, or whether we are killing them or letting them die. Although these may be practical issues for legislators to consider in terms of what works, as they do with where to draw the boundaries between self-defence, manslaughter and murder, in ethics drawing such lines is simply evidence of remaining in a state of half-sleep.

In closing, let us clarify that it was never the aim of this essay to convert those engaging in the euthanasia debate to Levinasian ethics rather than some purportedly opposed ethical theory such as deontology or utilitarianism. The purpose of engaging in a study such as the above is to see that some of the deeper structures that ethical theories are formulaically plugged into - such as the assumption that whether euthanasia should be legalised is a matter of whether it is ethically permissible plus some further practical concerns - can be shaken by seeing that they are unintelligible in certain other ethical theories. In using an alternative approach to ethics to shake ourselves out of such common patterns of thought, we need not necessarily be committed to the truth of that theory or remain bond to it afterwards. The assumption that there is a set way of going about the interrogation of a dilemma in applied ethics, a method that we can run through with one ethical theory and then run through with another before tabulating the differing answers they give, produces a field of expertise rather than provoking philosophy. If philosophy is to play a role mediating between public and specialised debates, at the very least there is cause to hope that it will be through philosophers interrogating the deep strata of the debate rather than simply sketching and clarifying confused concepts on its surface.

Timothy Secret is Senior Lecturer in Philosophy and Religion at the University of Winchester. His first monograph was *The Politics and Pedagogy of Mourning: On Responsibility in Eulogy* (London: Bloomsbury, 2014). He is currently working on his second monograph, which focuses on questions of ethics, film and the gaze.

Horror beyond Death: Geopolitics and the Pulverisation of the Human

François Debrix

Abstract From territorial conquests or wars of attrition to the concentration camps or policies of control of displaced populations, the biopolitical capture of human life in configurations of geopolitical power has often involved the putting to death of populations. While, following Foucault's work, we can argue that late modern political power has been concerned with the management of people's lives or with the 'health' of a population, this capacity to 'make live and let die' (as Foucault put it) is never separate from a modality of force premised upon a right to put to death. Thus, the distinction between biopolitics and what has been called thanatopolitics or necropolitics can no longer be guaranteed. The goal of this essay is to push further the biopolitical/necropolitical argument by showing that, in key contemporary instances of geopolitical violence and destruction, the life and/or death of populations and individual bodies is not a primary concern. What is of concern, rather, is what I have called the pulverization of the human. I consider this targeting of the human, or of humanity itself, to be a matter of horror. Horror's aim, when it enters the domain of geopolitical destruction, appears to be to put bodies to death. But, more crucially, its aim is to render human bodies, beyond the fact of life and death, unrecognizable, unidentifiable, and sometimes undistinguishable from non-human matter. Horror does not care to recompose human life or humanity. This essay briefly details the argument about horror and horror's 'objectives' beyond death. It also takes issue with recent theories that have argued that traces of human life can be recovered from contemporary instances of geopolitical violence and destruction. Finally, this essay offers two contemporary illustrations of horror's targeting of the human by examining the role and place of horror in suicide bombings and in drone attacks.

Keywords biopolitics, necropolitics, horror, pulverisation of the human, suicide bombing, drone attacks

Biopolitics often enters the sphere of geopolitics in the form of a series of necropolitical or thanatopolitical interventions.[1] From territorial conquests or wars of attrition to the concentration camps or policies of control of displaced populations, the biopolitical capture of human life and bodies in configurations of (geo)political power has generally involved the putting

1. See, for example, Michael Dillon and Julian Reid, *The Liberal Way of War, Killing to Make Life Live*, London, Routledge 2009; François Debrix, *Tabloid Terror: War, Culture, and Geopolitics*, London, Routledge 2008; Derek Gregory 'The Biopolitics of Baghad: Counterinsurgency and the Counter-City', *Human Geography* 1 (1) (2008), pp6-27.

to death of large swaths of populations, whether they are directly targeted or they happen to be 'in the way'. Michel Foucault argued that biopolitics emerges when the power of the sovereign shifts from a 'right to take life' to a capacity to 'let live'.[2] Thus, political power, the power of the geopolitical sovereign (generally), becomes concerned with the management, control, and enhancement of people's lives, with the 'health' of a population/body politic, and with the efficient utilisation and incorporation of individual bodies into political preoccupations (including the concern with the survival of the state or sovereign). Yet, as Giorgio Agamben and Achille Mbembe, among others, have also argued, while Foucault's recognition that biopolitical power is primarily concerned with the maintenance of life is crucial, this capacity to 'make live and let die' is never completely separate from the old modality of sovereign power and geopolitical force that was/is premised upon a right to put to death. Thus, as Mbembe puts it, biopolitics is also about the 'subjugation of life to the power of death'.[3] Agamben adds that 'if there is a line in every modern state marking the point at which the decision on life becomes a decision on death, and biopolitics can turn into thanatopolitics, this line no longer appears today as a stable border dividing two clearly distinct zones'.[4] The distinction between biopolitics and thanatopolitics/necropolitics can no longer be guaranteed. When biopolitics - the concern with the enhancement of human life/living - is the main object of geopolitical operations, what Mbembe calls 'the creation of death worlds' often becomes modern and late-modern geopolitics' primary objective (*Necropolitics*, p40).

This essay, however, is not interested in reprising the many biopolitical arguments that have been advanced to demonstrate the close connections between biopolitics and necropolitics. It is clear and, in a way, it was so already for Foucault that, in order to maximise the life/living potentials of some populations and bodies, other populations or other bodies have to be sacrificed or must disappear (*Society*, pp254-258). Put differently, what brings geopolitics and biopolitics together is their devotion to making populations and bodies die (in other words, their attachment to necropolitics). This essay is also not concerned with the many necropolitical dimensions of late-modern geopolitics (whether we are looking at World War II and the camps, for example, or, more recently, at techniques of exclusion of bodies and disappearance of life in the long era of the global war on terror). Again, many studies have targeted this late modern condition of (geo)political life.[5] Instead, my goal in this essay is to push further the biopolitical/necropolitical argument by showing that, in key contemporary instances of geopolitical violence and destruction, the life and/or death of populations and individual bodies is not a primary concern. What is of concern, rather, in some contemporary geopolitical configurations is what I have called the pulverisation of the human,[6] or, to borrow Adriana Cavarero's language, a radical violence that, 'not content merely to kill because killing would be too little, aims to destroy the uniqueness of the body'.[7] What is at stake in some geopolitical scenarios

2. Michel Foucault, *'Society Must Be Defended': Lectures at the Collège de France, 1975-1976*, New York, Picador 2003, p241. (Hereafter *Society*).

3. Achille Mbembe 'Necropolitics', *Public Culture* 15 (1) (2003), p39. (Hereafter *Necropolitics*).

4. Giorgio Agamben, *Homo Sacer: Sovereign Power and Bare Life*, Stanford, Stanford University Press 1998, p122.

5. See, for example, Julian Reid, *The Biopolitics of the War on Terror*, Manchester, Manchester University Press 2013; Elizabeth Dauphinee and Cristina Masters (eds), *The Logics of Biopower and the War on Terror: Living, Dying, Surviving*, London, Palgrave 2007; Brad Evans, *Liberal Terror*, Cambridge, Polity 2013.

6. François Debrix, *Global Powers of Horror: Security, Politics, and The Body in Pieces*, London, Routledge 2017.

7. Adriana Cavarero, *Horrorism: Naming Contemporary Violence*, New York, Columbia University Press 2009, p8. (Hereafter *Horrorism*).

is 'not the end of human life, but the human condition itself' (*Horrorism*, p8). With Cavarero's help, I have called this targeting of the human condition, of the fact of the human, or of humanity itself a matter of horror.[8] Horror's aim, when it enters the domain of geopolitical violence and destruction, may appear to be to put bodies to death. But, more crucially, it is to render human bodies and lives, beyond the fact of life and death, unrecognisable, unidentifiable, and sometimes undistinguishable from non-human matter. Moreover, beyond the life and/or death of bodies and populations, horror does not care to recompose human life or humanity, unlike what some theorists have sought to argue lately.

8. See François Debrix and Alexander D. Barder, *Beyond Biopolitics: Theory, Violence, and Horror in World Politics*, London, Routledge 2012.

The first section of this essay briefly exposes the argument about horror, horror's objectives beyond death, and some of the opportunities that geopolitical creations of 'death worlds' give to horror. It also challenges perspectives offered by theorists like Didier Fassin (via Jacques Derrida) and Judith Butler who have argued that human traces and/or fragments of life and living can still be recovered from contemporary instances of geopolitical power, violence, and destruction. The next section offers two possible instantiations of horror's targeting of the human (beyond the life or death of human bodies) in the recent geopolitical context of the seemingly unending war on terror or crusade to fend off the evil of radical Islamism (which, often these days, becomes the new geopolitical mission and label for the West's and, perhaps, humanity's fight against terror and terrorism). One such instantiation of horror in the geopolitical sphere is suicide bombing. The other, coming from the alleged 'other' side of the terror divide, is drone attacks and what they are said to achieve. The last and concluding section offers a brief reflection on what it might mean to no longer have the human/humanity as a recognisable objective and, perhaps, to have no choice but to turn to horror itself to look for new forms or traces of life, even if it is about a life beyond the human/humanity.

HORROR BEYOND DEATH

In her well-known treatise on horror and what she calls 'horrorism,' Cavarero draws an important distinction between horror and terror. Whereas terror forces human bodies to run away in the face of violence and destruction, horror freezes or paralyses. To be terrorised is a visceral fear that pushes humans to turn their back to the terrifying sight or event and to rush away from it so that they can try to survive. The preservation of life - trying not to die - is key to terror. By contrast, for Cavarero, horror is beyond human survival (*Horrorism*, p9). The sight of horror brings with it a 'state of paralysis' for the human body and, in the process (not being able to move), horror dismantles human life. Yet, this dismantling of life is not done, Cavarero intimates, in the name of death. Horror does not merely replace biopower with necropower. Rather, horror directly attacks the human/human life, including its capacity to die. This does not mean that horror seeks to keep alive (although, in a perverse way, horror can keep 'alive,' as Agamben, for example, has argued about the horrors of the concentration camps[9]). Horror does not concern itself with the question of whether the human body is alive or dead. Again, beyond the fact of life or death, the horrifying event or sight leaves the human 'body undone,' a 'body undone' that further 'loses its individuality' (*Horrorism*, p9). The loss of the 'ontological dignity of the human figure' is what horror is after (p9). Or, as Cavarero adds, 'extreme violence, directed at nullifying human beings even more than at killing them, must rely on horror rather than terror' (p9).

One may be tempted to think of horror as an additional degree of violence, a supplementation of terror, or a modality of destruction and death-making that may be even more unbearable to witness or fathom than terror itself. Cavarero's own phrasing about 'extreme violence' may lead one to think so. But to place terror and horror in the same category of geopolitical 'death-making' or along a continuum of devastation is incorrect. It is incorrect because terror and horror have drastically different objectives. Whereas terror seeks to scare off or force away (often by killing, and killing gruesomely), horror does not care whether humans (alive or dead) are scared or not.[10] Put differently, for terror to fulfil its objectives, it is imperative that humans (at least, some of them) remain alive, that they and their bodies remain active or in motion (they can still run away), or that some of them continue to live in fear. As I have argued elsewhere, it is also imperative for security (terror's alleged counter-force) that terror be about putting certain bodies to death while preserving others. Security politics' own mobilisation of bodies and lives is premised upon terror's or terrorism's capacity to take lives away, to make death worlds.[11] By contrast, horror has the ontological unity or individuality of human life as its main target. Horror wishes to do away with human ontology altogether, perhaps with what some have called the 'metaphysics of substance'.[12] Thus, it attacks the human by seeking to 'undo its figural unity' (*Horrorism*, p9). Whereas the human is often defined or recognised through the image of the one or unique human body (in life as well as in death), horror's violence pulverises the human's 'figural unity'. It renders it indistinct from all sorts of matter and materials. It dismembers it or turns it into bits and pieces that may get mixed up with non-human things and objects. Put differently, horror targets unity, individuality, integrity, and identity.[13] Thus, the human body or human life, often a key figure of ontological unity and individuality, is what horror aims at, even if the human body has already been deprived of life (horror often employs means of annihilation that are well in excess of techniques that would simply guarantee that bodies have been killed). And, unlike terror, what horror often leaves behind is, to borrow philosopher Eugene Thacker's language, a 'world-without-us,' that is to say, a world without humans or, better yet, a world in which to be human no longer holds any privilege.[14]

---

9. Giorgio Agamben, *Remnants of Auschwitz: The Witness and the Archive*, New York, Zone Books 2002.

10. Thus, the concept of horror that I, via Cavarero, seek to mobilise cannot be confused with, for example, Elaine Scarry's notions of human torture and pain. For Scarry, what could be construed as the horror of human torture (and the pain to the human body torture inflicts) always makes sense in relation to the continued assumed presence of a 'person's body' (Scarry's phrasing). For Scarry, torture and pain remain within the realm of terror, per Cavarero's nomenclature, particularly to the extent that torture and pain still target responses at the level of the human body, or of humanity in general. At best, for Scarry, 'horror' (a term that, by the way, to my knowledge, Scarry does *not* use) is merely an 'amplification' of human/bodily terror. See Elaine Scarry, *The Body in Pain: The Making and Unmaking of the World*, Oxford, Oxford University Press 1985, pp27-28.

11. François Debrix 'Katechontic Sovereignty: Security Politics and the Overcoming of Time', *International Political Sociology* 9 (2) (2015), pp143-157.

12. Judith Butler, *Gender Trouble: Feminism and the Subversion of*

Some theorists have recognised the extremely destructive power or force of many contemporary geopolitical events. They have also admitted that, in contemporary geopolitics, precisely because geopolitics is always about both biopolitics *and* necropolitics, the integrity/individuality/unity of the human body is often targeted. Yet, in the face of what others (starting with Cavarero) would call horror, these theorists have also insisted that traces of the human/ humanity and, further, a new capacity for life/living can be rediscovered. Chief among these theorists are Didier Fassin and Judith Butler who, confronted with instances of extreme violence onto the human, seem to refuse to give in to necropolitics, but also wish to resist 'horroristic' perspectives. Fassin turns to Derrida to try to resist Agamben's notion of bare life (a life that can be killed without such a killing constituting a criminal offense or being construed as a sacrificial offer to a deity). Fassin insists that 'Derrida's conception of life as survival... may offer an alternative to conceptions of life' found in biopolitical and necropolitical perspectives.[15] In a conventional way (but one does not need to invoke Derrida to claim this), to survive is to fend off the power of death or, in a geopolitical context, the making of death-worlds. But there is more to Fassin's attempt at reclaiming Derrida's argument about survival. Indeed, Fassin adds that '[t]o survive is to be still fully alive *and to live beyond death*' (*Ethics*, p83). The second part of the statement, 'to live beyond death,' is also a wish to see survival function as a response to horror. To live beyond death is, just like horror, to place a target or objective (about humanity, about geopolitics) beyond the fact of life or death, beyond both biopolitics and necropolitics. But, unlike horror, to construe survival beyond death is to seek to maintain (human) life active, productive, and meaningful beyond actual instances of destruction and disappearance of human bodies. It is about insisting on the power of life/living in a manner that, in fact, transcends the physical human body and its possible undoing. Indeed, Fassin adds that this kind of survival is an 'unconditional affirmation' (Derrida's turn of phrase) in the face of a horrifying annihilation of the human body, and it is a 'hope' where there seems to remain no place for such hope. As Fassin declares: 'it is the hope of 'surviving' through the traces left for the living' (*Ethics*, p83).

When life and the body have been blown to pieces or, perhaps, left as traces, there is still a hope for survival for Fassin, and this is a hope for another or a more-to life. Even when confronted or mixed with what is not human, there is an insistence here (and a desperately hopeful one at that) on not giving up, and not so much on not giving up on life, but on *human* life. In fact, according to Fassin's reading of Derrida, life seems to continue to matter, even beyond death and destruction, because life is about humanity. Thus, bits and pieces of the human, recognisable or remembered as human or not, must be sufficient to maintain that there still is life, that there *must* be (human) life, or that humanity will live on. Whereas 'horroristic' perspectives 'erase much of the complexity and richness of life' (p93), traces and fragments, including written, pictorial, or variously representational signs, keep life

Identity, London, Routledge 1990, pp.20-21; Elizabeth Povinelli, *Economies of Abandonment: Social Belonging and Endurance in Late Liberalism*, Durham, Duke University Press 2011, pp106-107.

13. This understanding of horror and, in particular, horror's removal/targeting of humanity or of the ontological unity of the human are what some theorists of the so-called condition of 'evil', such as Maria Pia Lara, reject, primarily on moral grounds. For example, for Lara, the problem with the notion of horror is that it makes 'us' (humans) 'lose our capacity to pose questions about responsibility and accountability'. See Maria Pia Lara, *Narrating Evil: A Postmetaphysical Theory of Reflective Judgment*, New York, Columbia University Press 2007, p76.

14. Eugene Thacker, *In the Dust of This Planet: Horror of Philosophy, Vol. 1*. Winchester, UK, Zero Books 2011, p46. (Hereafter *Dust*).

15. Didier Fassin 'Ethics of Survival: A Democratic Approach to the Politics of Life', *Humanity* 1 (1) (2010); p82. (Hereafter *Ethics*). See also Jacques Derrida 'Living On', in Harold Bloom et al, *Deconstruction and Criticism*, New York, Continuum 1979, pp75-176.

and humanity 'alive' and vibrant, engaged and purposeful, and, perhaps, politically and ethically resistant too. For Fassin, reformulating survival this way, through traces, fragments, and signs of a (human) life that refuses to go away, is a recognition of the enduring presence of 'multiple forms of life'. But it is also, and probably more crucially, a guarantee about the changing but still powerful 'everyday expression of the human' (p94).

Judith Butler pursues this line of thinking about survival in the face of horror. Perhaps more so than Fassin, Butler finds in survival or over-living (*survivance* is the French term mobilised by Derrida) a way of resisting the powers of destruction, death, and perhaps horror of contemporary geopolitical forces. Similar to Fassin, for Butler, survival/over-living/*survivance* is about traces and fragments of human life. Those traces of life, beyond death but also beyond the horror of annihilation of bodies, are, as Bonnie Honig explains, 'a dividend - that surprise extra, the gift that exceeds rightful expectations, the surplus that exceeds causality'.[16] Survival or over-living as a recognition of the presence of human life traces, fragments, or surpluses is a felicitous outcome, something that should never have been available once death took place and, furthermore, once horror performed its deeds. Life and humanity remain or, rather, 'live on' as lucky surprises or unexpected gifts, beyond common sense and indeed beyond causation/causality, when and where one could not rightfully expect to see humanity. Hope for the human and human life is thus the product of chance, of an event nobody could have planned for (since horror dismantles any possibility for human plans, for human futurity). Yet, despite this unpredictable outcome - humanity lives on/survives in, through, and as traces, fragments, or signs of the living that horror both created and failed to fully erase - it takes a certain disposition to insist on seeing those traces, fragments, and surpluses as evidence of a human life that refuses to disappear.

Butler clearly possesses such a disposition. For Butler, after death, after destruction, after terror, and perhaps after the horrors inflicted upon human bodies, words often take on the vocation of survival/over-living/*survivance*. Words become the traces and fragments of life and humanity, the surplus gifts that guarantee that there is and perhaps must still be human life and humanity. In her reflections on the US war on terror's detention and torture camps (Guantanamo's Camp Delta, for example), Butler poignantly highlights the relevance of the 'Guantanamo poems,' short texts or aphorisms written by some of the prisoners (many of whom were beaten up and tortured, and others who would never be seen or heard of again).[17] She hails those poems/writings as 'words… carved in cups, written on paper, recorded onto a surface, in an effort to leave a mark, a trace, of a living being - a sign formed by a body, a sign that carries the life of the body' (*Frames of War*, p59). Words carry life with them, beyond death, beyond human disappearance, beyond the body's devastation, even if words have no way of knowing where life or humanity will be taken or end up. Butler adds that, 'even when what happens to a body

16. Bonnie Honig, *Emergency Politics: Paradox, Law, Democracy*, Princeton, Princeton University Press 2009, p10.

17. Judith Butler, *Frames of War: When Is Life Grievable?* London, Verso 2009. (Hereafter *Frames of War*).

is not survivable, the words survive to say as much' (p59). Not even horror, Butler seems to suggest, can undo the endurance and survivability of human life traces. For Butler, as traces or fragments, words cannot be stopped or erased. They are always in surplus. And, in a way, the life that those written traces/fragments have become cannot be stopped or erased either. This is what I take to be Butler's predisposition towards human life, towards seeing and wanting to believe that neither death nor horror can ever foreclose the promise, gift, or surprise that is life, a life that can still be found even through the presence of non-human things and inanimate matter (a cup, a sheet of paper, a brick wall, a piece of wood, etc.). Or, to put it differently, things like these can be seen as alive, as life itself, perhaps because at one point they were in contact with human bodies, because they performatively embody suffering and precarious lives, even if these lives have been brutally terminated. Here, words and objects may become alive or life because they can be construed as traces or fragments of a no longer visible (but still hoped for and willed to be alive) humanity. Indeed, as Butler affirms, in the poems and other markings, 'the body…is what lives on, breathes, tries to carve its breath into stone' (p61).

The desperate hopefulness that one finds in Fassin's and Butler's rediscoveries of human survival/over-living/*survivance* is an expectation that, even in horror, even when the body, life, and the human have been frozen and left in place to be dismantled and reduced to dust, something will live on. Yet, ultimately, this something that lives on can and perhaps must be seen as a someone, as a *human* body or life that has been transferred to or transmuted into things, objects, words, and all their traces. The will to human life and to humanity is, for Butler and Fassin, a force that needs to remain greater than horror, greater than the undoing of the human body and human unity. Still, inspiring and uplifting as Butler's and Fassin's perspectives may be, many instances of geopolitical destruction often leave us with nothing but traces, traces that are neither human nor non-human. As horroristic perspectives may suggest, it takes a certain will to believe to insist on seeing those traces of the human and the non-human alike as stubborn signs of human survival or as guarantees for a humanity-driven future. In the next section, I examine two unfortunately all too common modalities of contemporary geopolitical annihilation - suicide bombings and drone attacks - that confront us with horror and its effects on human lives and bodies. Horror, I suggest, may force us to suspend the belief in or hope for human survival through a supposed endurance of life traces.

MODALITIES OF GEOPOLITICAL HORROR

Suicide bombings

In his study of war violence and its effects on war itself as well as on human bodies (soldiers, to start with) beyond the actual death of these bodies, Steven Miller offers a supporting argument for the claim that the violence of geopolitics is not just about necropolitics. Geopolitical violence always seeks to reach beyond the death of bodies. It is, in Miller's language, 'nonlethal' or, better yet, 'extralethal'.[18] Miller claims that, often, in extreme circumstances of geopolitical violence, this 'extralethal dimension... becomes the object of political discourse' (*War after Death*, p3). Geopolitical violence (including war) becomes extralethal when it 'disregards the distinction between the living and the dead, persons and things, combatants and noncombatants' (p5). Miller concludes that 'the problem with war [and with other instances of destructive geopolitics, I would add]... is not killing as such' (p5).

Interestingly, it is when Miller introduces the phenomenon of suicide bombing that his study turns to the notion of horror. Miller relies on Jacqueline Rose's analysis of suicide bombing as a 'special horror' (p108). What seems especially horrifying for Rose and, by extension, for Miller about suicide bombing is 'the fact that the attacker also dies'.[19] Crucially, why the death of the attacker becomes a matter of horror for Rose is because the attacker and the victim are conjoined in death. They are inseparable in their concomitant death. Their bodies become intimate as they suddenly and violently are killed. They form what Rose terms a 'deadly embrace' whereby attacker and victim are now identifiable as one. Powerful yet troubling as Rose's insight may be, I believe that it does not quite manage to capture what is horrific about suicide bombing's alleged deadly embrace. Indeed, what horrifies about suicide bombing is precisely that it renders identification - of the one, victim or attacker, or of both, together, embraced - impossible. Rose and, to some extent, Miller still wish to find identification, identity, and identifiable bodies in the immediate aftermath of suicide bombing, even if it is an abhorrent form of identification and bodily unity. Yet, the outcome of suicide bombing and, indeed, its moment of horror are a direct offense to identity, an attack on bodies and lives as marks of human identification, recognition, and existence.

A witness account of a suicide bombing attack in Afghanistan in 2008 against a NATO military convoy details the following scene:

> That morning we set off from Jalalabad in a convoy of about eight vehicles, green Ford pickups and one small truck with fifty to sixty laborers. About forty minutes later we came to a small town, Khogyani... We stopped. The driver and the commanding officer got out, and everyone started jumping off the back of the flatbed, all the police meeting each other... Paul and I waited in the truck. We had the windows down and were smoking, talking, when I heard a huge bang. Then I saw black. I still don't know if it was smoke or if I actually blacked out... Crouched with me was an Afghan cameraman and some police officers. Then I looked toward the vehicles, twenty yards from where the bomb had gone off, and I saw six or seven bodies... All around people were shredded like minced meat, mangled bodies missing heads, legs and arms. I didn't see many

18. Steven Miller, *War after Death: On Violence and Its Limits*, New York, Fordham University Press 2014, p3. (Hereafter *War after Death*).

19. Jacqueline Rose 'Deadly Embrace', *London Review of Books* 26 (21) (2004), pp21-24.

wounded. I remember one guy alive sitting among all these bodies. I think it made an impression just because he was alive in this mess. I started taking pictures. I felt I was taking pictures of evidence… Eventually, the Americans… gave us a medevac flight to Bagram Air Base, outside Kabul. Paul is here, too. He's got five holes in the back of his head, two the size of golf balls. There's a bone fragment stuck inside one. They don't know if it's his or somebody else's.[20]

In this description of the immediate aftermath of a suicide bombing attack, Rose's 'deadly embrace' becomes a heap of 'mangled bodies missing heads, legs and arms' and 'shredded like minced meat'. Identification is impossible. Bodies are beyond recognition. Attacker and victim, other and self, and enemy and friendly bodies are categories that have become meaningless. While there may be some sort of intimacy, it is one that involves bits and pieces of bodies, body parts, and perhaps shreds of flesh or meat mangled and mingled with non-organic matter (for example, a skull has been cracked and a head has been penetrated by a bone fragment that may not even be human). The horrifying fusion and confusion of matter, human or non-human, takes over from any form of identification. Cavarero had already noted this powerfully destabilising effect of the horror of suicide bombing when she recounted the story of Rachel Levy, a sixteen year-old American Israeli, who perished in a suicide bombing attack in Jerusalem in 2002 (*Horrorism*, pp104-105). The suicide bomber was another sixteen year-old girl, Palestinian Ayat al-Akhras. Both girls had walked into a grocery store in Jerusalem at about the same time. Witnesses had thought that they were related since they looked alike. When Ayat detonated her explosive belt into the grocery store, many bodies were pulverised. Ayat's body and body parts were nowhere to be found. And neither were Rachel's who had been closest to Ayat when the bomb exploded. Then, a head was found. It was identified as Ayat's and shown on the news on TV later that day. Watching the news that same evening, Rachel's mother found out that her sixteen year-old daughter had been killed and destroyed in the attack on the grocery store as the head that was shown on TV was, in fact, Rachel's. As a result of suicide bombing, body parts, it seems, become interchangeable. Human bodies do not survive, nor do they stand the test of identification. The only traces and fragments that remain and, often, proliferate in suicide bombings are bits and pieces of formerly integral bodies and lives.

In his book *On Suicide Bombing*, Talal Asad explains why suicide bombing is about horror, beyond the death of the body, and even beyond any possible rediscovery of traces or fragments of human life. For Asad, horror 'has no object'.[21] Turning to an argument first developed by political theorist Stanley Cavell, Asad declares that horror has no object - at least, it has no object with regards to human bodies and lives - because, in horror, 'our origins as human beings…are unaccountable'.[22] This 'unaccountability' of the origins of things

20. Stephen Dupont 'Witness to a Suicide Bombing in Afghanistan', *The Lede: The New York Times News Blog*, May 9, 2008; accessed February 9, 2016. http://thelede.blogs.nytimes.com/2008/05/09/witness-to-a-suicide-bombing-in-afghanistan/?_r=1.

21. Talal Asad, *On Suicide Bombing*, New York, Columbia University Pres 2007, p68. (Hereafter *Suicide Bombing*).

22. Stanley Cavell, *The Claim of Reason*, Oxford, Oxford University Press 1999, pp418-419.

and matter that remain after the suicide bombing attack is in stark contrast to Rose's search for identity/identification. At best, after a suicide bombing, as a result of the horror of the 'sudden shattering and mingling of physical objects and human bodies' (*Suicide Bombing*, p69), one is left with what Asad calls a 'confounding of the body's shapes' (p70). Again, this 'confounding of the body's shapes' often does not enable a reconstitution of human bodies and identities. But, more crucially perhaps, it leaves one highly uncertain as to the possibility that one might claim that this confounding of shapes is still about traces or fragments of life, or about opportunities for survivability, as Fassin or Butler tried to argue. Indeed, the horror about this 'confounding of the body' in the instance of suicide bombing is twofold. First, as we saw above, bodily integrity and identity have been undone. Parts of human bodies and lives have been mangled and mixed up with all sorts of organic and non-organic materials that make human lives, even as traces, unaccountable. And second, in the act of mingling or confounding caused by the sheer force and proximity (and, indeed, intimacy) of the explosion, new entities, new shapes, and perhaps newly arranged or composed forms of life may have been formed that owe their existence to horror itself, to horror's extreme violence, to the catastrophe, but not to humanity or human life since human life is, at the most, a mere component of those newly formed shapes and thus no longer holds any ontological privilege. Beyond death and devastation, what horrifies about suicide bombing is both the de-composition of human bodies and lives *and* the re-composition of shapes, forms, and materials/matter - the recognition and re-making of a vibrant actancy perhaps, as Jane Bennett, via Bruno Latour, might put it - that do not have any recognisable or accountable human origins.[23] As we will see next, in the death-making and horror-spreading geopolitical context of the unending global war on terror, predator drone attacks are other illustrations of this offense on human life and death and on the *ontos* of the human.

23. Jane Bennett, *Vibrant Matter: A Political Ecology of Things*, Durham, NC, Duke University Press 2010. (Hereafter *Vibrant Matter*).

DRONE ATTACKS

Miller notes that, in contemporary instances of violent geopolitics, 'disfigurement… entails a violence whose extremity is measured by the fact that it goes further than killing' (*War after Death*, p112). This statement seems to be a fitting description of what attack drones, as weapons of war and horror, are about. One of the first well publicised stories about drone attacks by the US military in Afghanistan in the aftermath of 9/11 detailed the fate of three Afghan men (including one often referred to as a 'tall Afghan man'), who turned out to be villagers looking for scrap metal, and whose bodies had been pulverised over and over by a succession of predator drone attacks that came back to hit them well beyond their death (caused by the first strike) because they had been mistakenly thought to be Taliban sympathisers.[24] Although steered by human operators (US military 'drone pilots') thousands of miles

24. See, for example, John Sifton 'A Brief History of Drones', *The Nation*, February 7, 2012; accessed February 9, 2016. http://www.thenation.com/article/brief-history-drones/.

away on a US military base (often Creech Air Force Base in Nevada), predator drones used by the United States in its global war on terror in Afghanistan, Pakistan, Iraq, Yemen, or Syria (among other places) characteristically display this over-killing zeal. Either because of their fairly close proximity to the human target when they hit or because they circle back a few times and relaunch their 'hellfire' destruction, drones often leave nothing of the bodies and the lives they are directed to eliminate.

The following account of a drone hit is a case in point.[25] In North Waziristan in October 2012, Pakistani grandmother Mamana Bibi was working in the fields behind her village with several of her grandchildren when, out of nowhere, and only a few seconds after its typical hum was heard, a predator drone dropped from the sky, launched its missile, and blew Mamana Bibi's body to pieces. Right in front of her grandchildren, the sixty-eight year-old Pakistani grandmother totally vanished. Not only was she disfigured and dismantled, but nothing of her remained except for a few shreds of matter similar to what one might find after a suicide bombing attack. There may not have been enough traces or fragments of her body and life for recomposition or identification. And there was no time, in this case, for a recording (on paper, through the image) of what had happened either, even though several drones do possess the capacity to capture and record images (images that supposedly remain under the tight control of the US military and government). Some of the predator attack drones such as the one that destroyed Mamana Bibi have been aptly but chillingly named by the US military 'Gorgon Stare' drones since they can take a snapshot of the 'kill' as it hits its target, but also because to stare in the face of this drone (supposing there is any time to do so) implies immediate annihilation (similar to the mythological Gorgon's gaze). In a field in North Waziristan in October 2012, a Gorgonian gaze in the form of a drone 'kill' made it certain that no human image/trace would remain of the body of the mistakenly targeted Pakistani grandmother. Mamana Bibi, suddenly, faced the Gorgon and its horror. But so did her surviving grandchildren for whom horror in the faceless form of an attack drone entered their world and their life.[26]

Perversely, one of the main reasons the United States uses drones in its war on terror is 'to save lives'.[27] Both for US soldiers and local populations, drones are said to be humanitarian. They are not meant to be machines of death or, better yet, machines of horror. They supposedly seek to preserve human life by precisely targeting those other individuals and bodies (terrorists, potential suicide bombers, etc.) who seek to offend human dignity and are a threat to many human lives (in the West, in particular). In his critical theory of drones and drone technology, Grégoire Chamayou cites an expert in drone warfare who affirms that '[d]rones save lives, American and other' (*Theory of the Drone*, p136). Based on the claim that an attack drone is a weaponry of selective death-making, drones are seen by their proponents and users as biopolitical and necropolitical instruments. They kill some bodies and

25. See 'Amnesty International and Human Rights Watch Blast US Drone Strikes'. *Time Online*, October 22, 2013; accessed February 9, 2016. http://world.time.com/2013/10/22/amnesty-international-and-human-rights-watch-blast-u-s-drone-strikes/.

26. For more on this story, see François Debrix, *Global Powers of Horror: Security, Politics, and the Body in Pieces*, London, Routledge 2017.

27. Grégoire Chamayou, *A Theory of the Drone*. New York, The New Press 2015, p136. (Hereafter *Theory of the Drone*).

erase some lives cleanly in order to 'let life live' (to use Foucault's slogan, once again). As former US secretary of defense Robert Gates once argued, why put US fighter jet pilots' lives in danger when drones can do the job more cleanly and precisely? 'From now on,' Gates enthusiastically stated, 'the watchword is: drones, baby, drones!'[28] Yet, Chamayou asks, '[h]ow can one claim that war machines with no human being on board are a 'more humane' means of destroying life?' Better yet, '[h]ow can one describe as 'humanitarian' procedures designed to annihilate human life?' (*Theory of the Drone*, p135). For Chamayou, the tension between the alleged humanity of the drone and the goal of preservation or even enhancement of human life is untenable since not even drone technology (let alone the drone pilot) has the capacity to discriminate between a life that is worth living and one that must be sacrificed. As Chamayou puts it: 'A drone can distinguish shapes [including human shapes] more or less imprecisely' (p49).

28. Quoted in Andrew Cockburn, *The Rise of the High-Tech Assassins*, New York: Henry Holt 2015, p215.

Yet, is the drone's inability to distinguish shapes and forms (human or otherwise) with precision not the point? Is the point about drone attacks and their Gorgonian stares precisely that they are *not* meant to decide between good lives/bodies and evil ones, that they are *not* about separating biopolitics from necropolitics, and that indeed they *are* about horror? Put differently, the threshold of life and death is of no importance or consequence to the drone and its technology. Attack drones are about the devastation and obliteration of bodies and, in fact, beyond bodies, of shapes and forms. Attack drones, despite the humanitarian alibi, have no consideration for human life or human death. This is why drones pulverise from relatively close range and why they sometimes return several times to ensure that nothing remains. Likewise, for the drone pilot, while his/her life is allegedly spared (by being safely placed thousands of miles away), the body of the soldier/pilot disappears too as it is now replaced by a flying horror-inducing object with a camera on top. Thus, the argument made by some that the drone, like all technology perhaps, is about the augmentation of the human and human life by way of autonomous technologies and robotisation turns out to be false.[29] The attack drone is about the diminution of human life and bodies to the point of extinction since its objective is to make human targets indistinguishable from all the non-organic matter that may have been around them while they were still standing. In this manner, the objective of the drone attack (one of the West's or even humanity's weapons of choice in the war on terror and its long aftermath) is not fundamentally different from what suicide bombing seeks to achieve with regards to the human.

29. Adam Rothstein, *Drone*, New York, Bloomsbury 2015, p120.

In the geopolitics of horror, whether the explosive device or the tool of pulverisation is intimately attached to or even placed inside the body or whether it is a 'decorporealised destructive technology' (as with the drone), the outcome and objective are one and the same: human life and human death are to be rendered immaterial or, at least, inconsequential (*Horrorism*, p95). The human, including its traces and fragments, is what must be the object of an unending onslaught to the point that, if anything is ever to be re-composed out of the extremely violent and gruesome de-composition, it will come only out of the moment of horror itself. Some have been tempted to see this geopolitics of horror-making not as the making of new forms of (no longer just human) life but, rather, as the dawn of 'a world of unreason,' a world that, as Jenny Edkins puts it, 'begins to resemble the world that Foucault sees in Goya's paintings... where [a new kind of] madness... "eats away faces, corrodes features; there are no longer eyes or mouths, but glances shot from nowhere and staring at nothing... or screams from black holes"'.[30] It is somewhat unfortunate that Foucault never really found the time to theorise the making of this new world or this geopolitics of unreason, madness, and horror (other than in a few passages about Goya in *Madness and Civilisation*) and that, instead, he went on to bury this reflection on horror and its eradication of human features behind a growing concern with biopolitics. Yet, I also wonder if something about the powers of horror does not get lost if one only sees horror (and its extreme geopolitical violence) as a radical and utter negation of human ontology and not as something, some force, some humanly unbearable and perhaps unaccountable explosive and destructive event that nonetheless can produce new matter, new vibrancy, and perhaps new life too, even if this new life is no longer clearly identifiable as or traceable to a human creation. The concluding section of this essay touches upon this possibility or, perhaps even, this hope for some sort of life of matter with and after horror, and it also tries to differentiate it from the hopefulness for remaining traces or fragments of life (as survival) that we found above in Fassin's and Butler's writings.

30. Jenny Edkins, *Face Politics*, London, Routledge 2015, p6.

HOPING FOR SOME FORM OF LIFE AFTER HORROR?

Perhaps one of the most shocking remnants of the September 11, 2001 attacks on the World Trade Centre in Lower Manhattan are what have been called composites. Composites are objects/things/materials of various sizes that, from a distance, may appear to be rocks or boulders. They are made of several floors of one of the World Trade Centre towers 'that collapsed into a stack, like pancakes, and then fused together'.[31] As a result of the force of the initial explosions, the searing heat they caused, and the crushing pressure on all sort of organic and inorganic matter present in the buildings at the time of the collapse, composites have been formed as an amalgamation of unrecognisable stuff. The debate as to whether there may be human remains in these composites still has not been closed.[32] While many forensic experts and scientists affirm that traces of human matter are not present in the composites, they also admit that what would be left of the utter pulverisation of the human in those new forms or objects would likely be undetectable.

What sort of forms or objects are the 9/11 composites? What materiality do they contain? Do they exude any life and, if so, what kind of life? Are they just what horror has left behind, once again, as unidentifiable or unaccountable

31. Patricia Cohen, 'At Museum on 9/11, Talking through an Identity Crisis', *The New York Times*, June 2, 2012; accessed February 9, 2016. http://www.nytimes.com/2012/06/03/arts/design/sept-11-memorial-museums-fraught-task-to-tell-the-truth.html?_r=0.

32. See, for example, Chip Coldwell-Chanthaphonh, 'Forgetting the 9/11 Victims' *HuffPost Impact*, August 10, 2014; accessed February 9, 2016. http://www.huffingtonpost.com/american-anthropological-association/forgetting-the-911-memorial-victim_b_5447250.html.

residues perhaps? Interestingly, the recent controversy over the appropriate display of one of the composites at the 9/11 Memorial Museum at Ground Zero in Manhattan has had to do with the question of the exact nature of the composite as a new type of matter and, possibly, as a life form. Some 9/11 families whose loved ones perished on that day and whose remains have been to this day unidentified have insisted that, out of this horrifying thing/form that is the composite, a trace of life may still persist or perhaps be re-invented.[33] The undecidability about the composite, the inability to ascertain whether it contains human fragments (even if too minuscule to be accounted for) or not, becomes an opportunity to not so much claim that life can spring out of death or destruction, but rather that some way of living and hoping can emerge out of a new matter that results from the annihilation or is born out of horror. The hope for life/living, after horror, is a hope for a life/living that is beyond death but also, and crucially, beyond the human. There is nothing recognisable as human anymore, nothing that makes us understand that we are in the presence of humanity, when we are faced with the composite. Yet, the composite still has and is matter/materiality. It is vibrant, active, and, in a way, it has life. It has and is a life beyond human life and death, a life as a sediment of human life or, better yet, as 9/11 documentary photographer Francesc Torres puts it, 'the sediment of the sediment of [human] history'.[34]

In her essay on Antigone, Judith Butler questions what sort of person, what sort of humanity, and what sort of life is/was Antigone, a figure/body whose condemnation to death prior to having committed any crime becomes an opportunity to make claims about humanity and life more so than if she were free, alive, or not deprived of her humanity. Antigone, Butler claims, is 'the less than human [that] speaks as human'.[35] With Antigone, what it means to be human 'has entered into catachresis: we no longer know its proper usage' (*Antigone's Claim*, p82). Might some of the figures of geopolitical horror, such as those we have encountered above, not be only about the dismantling of the human/humanity, but also about some form of re-composition, a re-composition of and with the human and, yet, beyond the human too? Might something like the 9/11 composite or the horrific embrace of a suicide bombing attack's body parts not be akin to what Butler saw in Antigone: a catachresis of human life (and death), an impossibility to know the proper usage or even the utility of human life, but also an opportunity to rethink life beyond the so-called ontological fact of the human, beyond (human) identity/integrity/unity/primacy? Butler brings her own thought (and Antigone) to the edge of this human/life precipice. But, on the verge of taking the plunge into horror and horroristic thinking, Butler shies away from it, and she chooses to return to the life and death (biopolitics and necropolitics) debate. She tells us that, after all, this place beyond the human (and from which both the human and life can be re-composed) is always, for Antigone, a 'vacillating boundary' that is found

33. See 9/11 Museum, '2013 Museum Planning Conversation Series Report,' pp4-6; accessed February 9, 2016. https://www.911memorial.org/sites/all/files/2013ConversationSeries.pdf.

34. Quoted in Robin Cembalest, 'A Terrible Beauty?' *ArtNews*. August 15, 2011; accessed February 9, 2016. http://www.artnews.com/2011/08/15/a-terrible-beauty/.

35. Judith Butler, *Antigone's Claim: Kinship between Life and Death*, New York, Columbia University Press 2000, p82. (Hereafter *Antigone's Claim*).

to be 'between life and death' (*Antigone's Claim*, p78). Here again, as we saw above with her insistence on rediscovering traces of human life out of written fragments or objects, Butler refuses to give up on humanity, or at least on humanity as survival/over-living.

But no longer knowing the proper usage of human life is what horror does. It is also what the so-called distinction between life and death, biopolitics and necropolitics, can never achieve. When instances of geopolitical horror leave us with very little chance to survive - even as or through traces/fragments of humanity - any hope for some sort of life in and with horror may depend on our ability to accept that humanity/the human has been undone and that the life of matter has been remade. Being open to the fact that life still lives and matters even without us, without humanity being an essential part of it, that is to say, being open to what Thacker has called the 'world-without-us' (*Dust*, p5), may be the necessary condition for life in the aftermath of horror. In an attempt to rethink life away from humanity's imprint, critical anthropologist Eduardo Kohn has asked: 'Why ask anthropology to look beyond the human?'[36] One possible answer, Kohn ventures, is that a critical anthropology that is curious about what lies beyond humanity/human life can tell us that what is beyond the human 'also sustains us and makes us the beings we are and those we might become' (*How Forests Think*, p221). This answer, however, is still very much a matter of what Kohn refers to as 'salvage anthropology' (p227). Indeed, it is about deploying an anthropological gaze (albeit beyond human life and bodies) to try to rescue or re-assert humanity's role and presence. As we saw above, Butler and Fassin are often unable or unwilling to rid themselves of this salvage anthropological gaze or imagination. But another answer to the question about the purpose of 'looking beyond the human' is provided by Kohn too. One may want to look beyond the human and at what takes life beyond the human - including horror, I would add - because, as Kohn puts it, even if humanity is no longer in the frame or matters, 'it is not as if all life will end' (p227). Not even horror seeks to end all life and matter (in fact, as we saw, horror can re-create some sort of life/vibrancy too). Thus, being open to a gaze beyond the human - and beyond human life as well as human death - can also be a way of 'attending to the living logics that are already part of how forests [or, in addition to forests, things, matter, the world, and so on] think themselves through 'us'' (p227). This gaze beyond the human may well see an awful lot of human devastation, and often it will be tempted to call this devastation of the human and human life horrifying. Yet, this gaze enabled by horror, like the gaze about possibilities to rethink life enabled by the presence of composites, for example, may also help us to 'listen for the hopes that that kind of reality houses as well' (p227). Perhaps there is hope beyond death but also beyond the human after all.

François Debrix is Director of the Alliance for Social, Political, Ethical, and

36. Eduardo Kohn, *How Forests Think: Toward an Anthropology beyond the Human*, Berkeley, CA, University of California Press 2013, p221. (Hereafter *How Forests Think*).

Cultural Thought (ASPECT) and Professor of Political Science at Virginia Tech. He researches social and political theory, international relations theory, critical geopolitics, and media and visual studies and is the author, among other books, of *Tabloid Terror: War, Culture, and Geopolitics* (Routledge, 2008) and *Beyond Biopolitics: Theory, Violence, and Horror in World Politics* (Routledge, 2011). He is currently completing a manuscript on the politics and theory of horror and bodily dismemberment. He has also translated several of Jean Baudrillard's essays for the journal *C-Theory*.

Why have the dead come back? The instance of photography

Roger Luckhurst

Abstract This essay examines how the critical theory of photography has, at least since Barthes and Sontag, developed a default position that is routinely suspicious of the political and aesthetic value of images of the dead, even as the archive of images of the dead continues to accumulate and to shock. Photographic theory seems to share the post-war assumptions that death has been eclipsed by modernity, sequestered away and rendered taboo. The project here is to give a sense of the array of photographic practice that exists in stark opposition to these assumptions, and indeed in the contemporary moment seems actively to stage an argument with the thesis of the 'eclipse of death'. It considers work ranging from Sally Mann and Luc Delahaye to the recent projects of Edgar Martins.

Keywords Sontag, Barthes, critical theory, photography, death

THREE POST-MILLENNIAL SNAPSHOTS

Sally Mann's photographic series and book, *What Remains* (2003) is a sequence that begins with a dispassionate lens focusing on the body of her beloved greyhound Eva, exhumed after fourteen months in the ground. 'Was it ghoulish to want to know? Was it maudlin to want to keep her, at least some part of her? Was it disrespectful to watch her intimate decomposition?'[1] The sequence included an exploration of the woodland visible from her kitchen window where the police had chased, shot and killed a young man who had escaped arrest. Does a landscape hold the memory of violence or atrocity? It also included a section of Mann's experiments with early photographic collodion techniques from the 1860s to capture ravaged glimpses of the landscape of Antietam, site of the bloodiest battlefield of the American Civil War, brooding on the landscape's 'underpinnings of death'.[2] Wet collodion was used to coat glass negative plates from 1851, but had been first used as a treatment for war wounds: form graphically followed content.

Most memorably, *What Remains* centred on her record of the 'Body Farm' at the University of Tennessee in Knoxville where patterns of decay in human corpses in different environments are researched using bodies that have been volunteered to science. In her memoir *Hold Still*, Mann recalls:

> pausing by a body and waiting until the rustling of the leaves quieted,

1. Sally Mann, *What Remains*, New York Bulfinch Press 2003, p6.

2. Sally Mann, *Hold Still*, New York, Little Brown 2015, p414. (Hereafter *Hold Still*)

I could hear the maggots noisily eating, a sound sometimes like the crackling of Rice Krispies in milk and other times, like raw hamburger being formed by hand into patties. The bulging skin roiled with their movements beneath it (*Hold Still*, pp425-6).

Mann relishes the abject, the stench of bodies, the bloated flies, the skin cells sloughed off onto her clothes as she wrestles with the corpses:

I had slipped on chunks of fatty adiopocere and found hair stuck to the brake pedal of the Suburban as I drove home at night (p433).

Mann, already a controversial figure for capturing the life of her children too intimately for some critics ten years before in her *Immediate Family* project, when that work got caught up in paedophile panic and political posturing over public art funding, now courted controversy for her portrayals of death.

In 2005, Luc Delahaye was awarded the Deutsche Börse Photography prize for his 'History' series of monumental images, all vast eight by four metre prints. It included *Taliban*, an image of a dead soldier lying shoeless in a ditch, shot from a high angle above so that the body appears weirdly to be floating above the viewer, looking down, eyes glassily open. Delahaye was an embedded photojournalist during the Afghanistan war in 2002, providing images for *Newsweek*, but was also taking parallel images for a wholly different end. His photojournalism was on a standard 35mm camera, but *Taliban* was taken with a tripod-mounted, large format Linhof panoramic camera. Delahaye considers that slowness, precision and monumentality of this work attains an aesthetic detachment he suggests evokes a greater objective truth than the selected, captioned and often re-purposed newspaper image. He wanted to achieve a certain neutrality, 'measuring of the distance that separates me from what I see', he stated.[3] Delahaye's claim inevitably provoked controversy in a war where the circulation of images of dead bodies has remained a consistently politicised matter.[4]

In 2006, Annie Leibovitz displayed at the Brooklyn Museum her last photographs of her partner Susan Sontag in the later stages of dying of leukaemia, the series concluding with *Susan Sontag at the Time of her Death, December 28 2004*. She also included photographs of the body of her father in the show, another major affective attachment for Leibovitz and who had died six weeks after Sontag. These images were published as *A Photographer's Life 1990-2005*, a project dogged by questions of taste and transgression, since Leibovitz was in part turning the camera on the dead body of one the premier theorists of photography's melancholic function, but also one who repeatedly returned to the question of the capacity of the image to shock.[5] Sontag's son David Rieff condemned the photographs as 'carnival images of celebrity death', but did so in his agonised memoir *Swimming in a Sea of Death: A Son's Memoir*, in which he detailed his own horrified post-mortem investigation of

3. Mark Durden, 'Luc Delahaye: Global Documentary', in *Deutsche Börse Photography Prize 2005*, London, Photographers' Gallery 2005, p13.

4. See discussion in Erina Duganne, 'Photography after the Fact', *Beautiful Suffering: Photography and the Traffic in Pain*, (eds.) M. Reinhardt, H. Edwards and E. Duganne, Chicago, University of Chicago Press 2006, pp57-74. (Hereafter *Beautiful Suffering*).

5. Janny Scott, 'From Annie Leibovitz: Life, and Death, Examined', *New York Times*, 6 Oct 2006. For commentary, see also Caitlin McKinney, 'Leibovitz and Sontag: picturing an ethics of queer domesticity', *Shift* 3, 2010, pp1-25.

his mother's ravaged body.[6] In 2016, Katie Roiphe restaged all the details of Sontag's last months, her blind determination to defy death related to her earlier bouts with cancer, and her enduring theme in her writing of *la mort equivoque*, the fake death, the device of those presumed dead returning to life. Roiphe added her own riff to the seemingly interminable disputes over the afterlife of Susan Sontag's corpse and corpus.[7]

David Lillington notes in 'Death Ltd' that there was a resurgence in contemporary art focused on death and dying between Deborah Boardman's 'Mortal' exhibition in Chicago in 2001, the Wellcome Collection's 'Death: A Self-Portrait' (2011-12) - an exhibition of the art dealer Richard Harris's personal collection of death art - and Lillington's own 'Death and Dying' in Vienna (2014), an extensive survey of over forty artists.[8] The dead, like the zombie horde popular culture so insistently imagines, had very determinedly come back into the image culture. This essay explores why this might be so.

6. David Rieff, *Swimming in a Sea of Death*, London, Granta 2008,

7. Katie Roiphe, *The Violet Hour: Great Writers at the End*, New York, Dial 2016. Citation from Rieff, p47.

8. David Lillington, 'Death Ltd'. *Art Monthly*, November 2016, pp5-8.

THE ECLIPSE OF DEATH?

The question needs to be posed in this way because a generation ago it was widely argued that death, and the social practices attending it, had been definitively eclipsed. Geoffrey Gorer influentially argued in the 1950s that there had been a rapid collapse in the West of social rituals around death and mourning, and that there was now a 'fear of the expression of grief on the part of the English professional classes'. Within a generation, he proposed, 'social recognition of mourning has practically disappeared'.[9] Gorer, who remembered the rituals around the mass deaths of the Great War (and his own father's death on the *Lusitania* in 1915) suggested a kind of dialectic at work: the restrictive prudery in social mores on the subject of death at once silenced and yet actively fostered a compensatory 'pornography of death' in popular culture. In his influential article in *Encounter* in 1955 called 'The Pornography of Death', Gorer suggested with patrician disdain:

9. Geoffrey Gorer, *Death, Grief and Mourning in Contemporary Britain*, London, Cresset 1965, pp15 and 113.

> While natural death became more and more smothered in prudery, violent death has played an ever-growing part in the fantasies offered to mass audiences - detective stories, thrillers, Westerns, war stories, spy stories, science fiction, and eventually horror comics.[10]

The moral panic about the tasteless recurrence of the dead in American comics soon saw this gleeful outlet almost entirely suppressed by the end of 1955, the Comics Code stamping out any corrupting depictions of the dead, at least for a time.[11]

Gorer's line proved very influential on the last section of Philippe Ariès's important study, *The Hour of Our Death*, first published in France in 1977. After five hundred pages excavating the history and ritual of the 'good death', Ariès called his last section 'Invisible Death' in which he argued:

10. Geoffrey Gorer, 'The Pornography of Death', *Encounter*, 1955, pp49-52. (Reprinted as an appendix in *Death, Grief and Mourning*, p173).

11. See Jim Trombetta, ed., *The Horror! The Horror! Comic Books the Government Didn't Want you to Read!* New York, Abrams 2010.

> In the course of the twentieth century an absolutely new type of dying has made an appearance in some of the most industrialised, urbanised and technologically advanced areas of the Western world.[12]

Ariès amplified and systematised Gorer's thesis, suggesting a rapid set of transformations that had effectively banished death. Medicalisation replaced the priest with the doctor and the familial deathbed with the anonymous hospital ward and the 'cellular discipline' of atomised death-care pathways. In the clinical machine, the body is disarticulated into separate systems, each managed by specialists, dividing and subdividing the moment of death into a series of technical calibrations:

> Technology erodes the domain of death until one has the illusion that death has been abolished. The area of the invisible death is also the area of the greatest belief in the power of technology and its ability to transform man and nature (*The Hour of Our Death*, p595).

It is a position that still hovers behind Anthony Giddens' notion of the 'sequestration of experience' in *Modernity and Self-Identity* (1991), the 'protective cocoon' of a technologically advanced, reflexive modernity that supposedly smooths violent extremes away, handing them over to experts and institutions; death as risk management.[13] Surprisingly perhaps, Ariès also directly inflects Michel Foucault's formulation of 'biopolitics' in his Collège de France lectures. Biopolitics is 'a matter of taking control of life and the biological processes of man-as-species and of ensuring that they are not disciplined but regularised'. This results, Foucault says, unusually relying on received wisdom, in 'the famous gradual disqualification of death'.[14] Asserting the self-evidence of Ariès, Foucault explains: 'Power has no control over death, but it can control mortality'. This is why power does not recognise death, but brackets it and gets on with its *vital* politics. Post-Foucauldian biopolitical theory has thus concentrated on the politics of 'life itself', as Nikolas Rose calls it, or the ceaseless management and control of a regime of biopolitical production and reproduction, as described by Michael Hardt and Antonio Negri in *Empire*.[15]

It is the partiality of this position that has redoubled the sense that the dead have come rushing back *in spite of* our theorisations. After biopolitics, the next generation of critical theorists has had to add a 'thanatopolitics', to use Giorgio Agamben's coinage. In *Homo Sacer*, he observes that if 'one of the essential characteristics of modern biopolitics ... is its constant need to redefine the threshold in life that distinguishes and separates what is inside from outside', then this must lead to a necessary administration of the category of the socially and biologically dead. 'It is as if every valorisation and every "politicisation" of life ... necessarily implies a new decision concerning the threshold beyond which life ceases to be politically relevant', Agamben

12. Ariès, *The Hour of Our Death*, trans. H. Weaver, London, Allen Lane 1981, p560. (Hereafter *The Hour of Our Death*).

13. Anthony Giddens, *Modernity and Self-Identity: Self and Society in the Late Modern Age*, Cambridge, Polity 1991. (Hereafter *Modernity*).

14. Michel Foucault, *Society Must Be Defended: Lectures at Collège de France, 1975-6*, (trans) D. Macey, London, Penguin 2004, pp246-7.

15. Nikolas Rose, *The Politics of Life Itself: Biomedicine, Power, and Subjectivity in the Twenty-First Century*, Princeton, Princeton University Press 2007 and Michael Hardt and Antonio Negri, *Empire*, New Haven, Harvard University Press 2000.

concludes.[16] In the neo-colonial context of the murderous extraction of even bare life from labour, Achille Mbembe terms this 'necropolitics':

> the creation of *death-worlds*, new and unique forms of social existence in which vast populations are subjected to conditions of life conferring upon them the status of the *living dead*.[17]

New formations of global Empire are not just biopolitical; they have also set up circulations of hugely profitable body parts and corpses, broken down into commercialised elements where transferable tissues and organs can be worth tens of thousands of dollars.[18] Although the trace of the dead labour of these bodies is classically obscured by the magic of commodity fetishism, it does not simply vanish. Even Gorer acknowledged back in the 1950s that alongside an eclipse of the dead body representation spilt out in other ways. At least since the 1960s (since the mechanical repetitions of Andy Warhol's 'Death and Disaster' silkscreen sequences), there has been a steady growth of a 'pathological public sphere' that organises conceptions of community around the spectacular display of injured, ruined or dead bodies.[19]

In place of Ariès, the monumental tome on death of our time is Thomas Laqueur's *The Work of the Dead* (a strikingly thanatopolitical title), which argues that the cultural work of the dead does remain foundational to human community, and that this has long outlived the alleged 'disenchantments' or eclipses of the dead associated with modernity:

> The dead remain active agents in this history even if we are convinced they are nothing and nowhere.[20]

Judith Butler now places *grievability* at the core of human community.[21] The spectacle of death is not confined to a 'pornography' of excessive ruination, but has become culturally ubiquitous. Photographic theory has been late to this change.

DEAD THEORY

The photograph has become intrinsically linked with the deathly due to the influence of Roland Barthes' *Camera Lucida* (1980), a book indebted to André Bazin's 'The Ontology of the Photographic Image'.[22] Barthes insists on the signification of chemical photography as indexical, the record of the literal trace of light bouncing off the referent: 'This is its pathos, its melancholy'. Every photograph does not capture life, but instead builds a monument to an anticipated, future anterior death. Barthes stares in morbid certainty at the photo of his mother, a violent image, brute and undialectical, that 'fills the sight by force' and slashes at him with 'lacerating emphasis': her death will have already been encoded in the photograph.[23] A generation (and

16. Giorgio Agamben, *Homo Sacer: Sovereign Power and Bare Life*, (trans) D. Heller-Roazen, Standord, Stanford University Press 1998, p131 and p138.

17. Achille Mbembe, 'Necropolitics', *Public Culture* 15: 1 (2003), p40.

18. See Nancy Scheper-Hughes and Loic Wacquant (eds), *Commodifying Bodies*, London, Sage 2002.

19. Mark Seltzer, 'Wound Culture: Trauma in the Pathological Public Sphere', *October* 80 (1997), pp3-26.

20. Thomas W. Laqueur, *The Work of the Dead: A Cultural History of Mortal Remains*, Princeton, Princeton University Press 2015, p18.

21. Judith Butler, *Frames of War: When is Life Grievable?* London, Verso 2009.

22. André Bazin, 'The Ontology of the Photographic Image', (trans) H. Gray, *Film Quarterly* 13: 4 (1960).

23. Roland Barthes, *Camera Lucida*, (trans) R. Howard, London, Vintage 1993, pp90-91 and 93.

technological revolution) later, some critics still centre photography's intrinsic truth on Barthes's insistence on melancholia, traumatic absence and death.[24]

Susan Sontag equally spoke of the photograph's essential role as a *memento mori* in the same language of scarring, piercing or wounding in *On Photography* (a book completed when doctors had given her a death sentence for her first bout of cancer). Her foundational shock encounter with photography, to which nothing can subsequently compare, was seeing images from the Dachau concentration camp in 1945, images that 'cut me', left Sontag 'irrevocably wounded'.[25] Everything after this initiation, she (sometimes but often inconsistently) argues, is a kind of falling away, the shock effect rippling into passivity or, even worse, indifferent *ennui*. Both Barthes and Sontag invoke an originating traumatic realism to the power of photography, and this has been installed as the dominant paradigm ever since, even through and beyond the digital transformation of the ontological condition of the photographic image. As Laura Mulvey argued in *Death 24x A Second*, 'the digital still thinks with the idea of the index' - even or perhaps because of the ontological status shifting underneath the image.[26]

It is Sontag's modernist suspicion of the apparent transparency of the photograph, through its fatal *reality-effect*, that puts this paradigm in such continually tortured, self-cancelling positions. Trauma theory at once demands representation and insists on the erasures of that ghastly presumption. This tension has the highest stakes in discussions of Holocaust photography, and can be carefully formulated as a productive paradox, generative of ethical photographic theory and practice.[27] But the suspicion of photography's seductive ease can end up in extreme places, where any direct photographic representation is condemned as 'kitsch' or 'mute cliché' and only anti-representational abstraction or voids can properly convey the crisis in any possible 'explanatory referential frames and contexts for understanding'.[28] Ulrich Baer's demand of the (non-)image is that 'representations of trauma cannot constitute evidence', but that the approved image 'documents precisely the abolition of referential systems on which the notion of evidence depends' (p117). This peculiar iconoclasm willingly embraces its own anti-historicism to defend the rigour of its aesthetic demands.

These positions haunt the troubled contributions to the catalogue of the 2006 exhibition at the Williams College Museum of Art, *Beautiful Suffering: Photography and the Traffic in Pain*. This exhibition had a contemporary focus on photojournalism and art generated from the conflicts of the 1990s and beyond. This inevitably meant that it began to circle around the politics of images from the Iraq War. One of the curators and editors, Mark Reinhardt, offers a useful interrogation of the Sontagian line on numbing passivity, pointing out her symptomatically confusing shifts of position from book to book, and almost from paragraph to paragraph in the knotty inconclusiveness of her later work *Regarding the Pain of Others*.[29] To her position that photography can only aestheticise death so that it can only be met with

24. Jay Prosser, *Light in the Dark Room: Photography and Loss*, Minneapolis, University of Minnesota Press 2005.

25. Susan Sontag, *On Photography*, London, Penguin 1977, pp15, 20.

26. See Laura Mulvey, *Death 24x A Second: Stillness and the Moving Image*, London, Reaktion 2006, p21.

27. See, for example, Marianne Hirsch, 'Surviving Images: Holocaust Photographs and the Work of Postmemory', *Yale Journal of Criticism* 14: 1 (2001), pp5-37; Michael Rothberg, *Traumatic Realism: The Demands of Holocaust Representation*, Minneapolis, University of Minnesota Press 2000.

28. Ulrich Baer, *Spectral Evidence: The Photography of Trauma*, Cambridge, Mass, MIT Press 2002, pp69-70.

29. Susan Sontag, *Regarding the Pain of Others*, London, Penguin 2004.

'passivity or contentment,' Reinhardt contends that this is 'neither obviously true nor even obviously clear', and continues:

> I suspect few viewers really believe this, at least not consistently. And yet, when struggling to articulate what disturbs them about particular pictures or photographic tendencies, some critics (Sontag among them) are sometimes tempted by this position.[30]

Even so, it is significant that Reinhardt and one of the other curators, Erina Duganne, ultimately end up with a similar modernist model of work that at once opens and yet closes the question of the representation of death. The exemplary work for this exhibition is Alfredo Jaar's practice that emerged from his *Rwanda Project*, exploring the 1994 genocide in a series of installations in the following years. Jaar's lightboxes at once illuminate and deny representation. In his 'Real Images' installation, for instance, Jaar selected his most powerful one hundred images from his journey through Rwanda, but then buried them in black linen archival storage boxes with a description of the picture in words silk screened on the top of the box. 'The boxes were then arranged within the darkened space of the gallery so as to create a "cemetery of images."' In Jaar's installation, text trumps image, just as it always does in Sontag's writing on photography because she so insistently mistrusts the reality-effect. Duganne goes on to suggest, in very familiar language, that this tactic 'rendered explicit the sheer impossibility of representing this tragedy' *(Beautiful Suffering*, p69). We have been here before.

The dead have come back so insistently in contemporary photography, I propose, precisely to target this doctrine of difficulty or refusal, this demand that images of atrocity and its aftermath self-cancel themselves. As I've argued in *The Trauma Question*, it is problematic to fix a single ahistorical aesthetic from the Holocaust image, as Sontag does, when the contexts and situations of image production have undergone such profound transformation in the post-1945 era.[31] In the case of war, it has long been documented that the catastrophe of the Vietnam War, in particular, transformed the management and control of images in the Western media, with progressively tight restrictions by military and government authorities ever since.[32] In such a situation, further escalated in the Gulf Wars, the imperative of the violent image can be ethically charged in multiple, overdetermined ways. The necessity of the violent image can redouble the shock of *needing to see* in the most naïvely 'realist' representational terms what is otherwise suppressed or massaged by media management.

But this is not just an argument about framing or the imperative to burst a managed frame. As Walter Laqueur is careful to insist, death itself has a history rather than standing sentinel outside it, and death itself has been steadily redefined by the medical revolutions of our era. This, surely, has been one of the main factors behind renewed photographic investigations:

30. M.Reinhardt, 'Picturing Violence: Aesthetics and the Anxiety of Critique', *Beautiful Suffering: Photography and the Traffic in Pain*, (eds) M. Reinhardt, H. Edwards and E. Duganne, Chicago, University of Chicago Press 2006, p21.

31. See Roger Luckhurst, *The Trauma Question*, London, Routledge 2008.

32. See Caroline Brothers, *War and Photography: A Cultural History*, London, Routledge 1997.

death is not a static object, but a mobile, highly articulated process. Let's take these two contexts, war and medicine, in order.

THE WAR ON DEAD IMAGES

The ethical pressure on the aesthetics of photography is always time-and-context-specific, never more so than the changing conditions of the very possibility of making images in war. In 1972, John Berger dismissed 'photographs of agony' as having no effect on the course of the Vietnam War, possibly diverting activism into merely sympathetic passivity (a position that clearly influenced Sontag).[33] The military evidently did not agree, thinking perhaps of the damning power of Nick Ut's image of a napalmed girl or the impact of Ron Haeberle's unofficial record of the My Lai massacre that galvanised the anti-war movement. Caroline Brothers and others have carefully traced emergent strategies of containment in the taking and circulation of images in subsequent wars, the authorities continually narrowing the aperture, as in the Falklands War or the first Gulf War of 1991, where the press pack were held far back from the front line and fed nose-cone images of smart bombs in an attempt to virtualise or dematerialise the conflict.[34] This management was why Kenneth Jarecke's unofficial photograph of a charred, grimacing corpse caught in the fire-storm unleashed by U.S. forces on the Basra Road was such a shocking intervention. Initially rejected by American newspapers as too graphic, *Incinerated Iraqi* was reproduced around the world as a powerful counter to the tactic of derealisation of asymmetric remote warfare. The context of containment *amplified* the need for the image to transgress military control.

The second Iraq War used a different tactic. The U.S. military embedded the press with units on the ground, but with permission granted only through 'embed agreements' that put tight controls on the kinds of images taken and circulated. These agreements were significantly tightened as the American occupation turned into guerrilla and civil wars in 2005, and especially during the 'surge' in 2007, when American casualties were high. Particularly taboo were images of wounded or killed American soldiers. While conventions have emerged on how to represent images of dead Iraqis, there was an almost complete ban on the representation of the American war dead (and both have inevitably been criticised for their aestheticisation of violence).[35] Even the release of images of coffins was restricted. There was a long dispute over the publication of a photograph taken clandestinely by an employee of Maytag Aircraft, an image of coffins draped in flags being repatriated in a cargo hold from Iraq to America in 2004.

These restrictions meant that a succession of photographers and news units were put under pressure by the military command. Chris Hondros (a photojournalist who was later killed covering Libya in 2011) was attached to a night patrol that accidentally shot and killed the parents of six children, who

33. John Berger, 'Photographs of Agony', *About Looking*, New York, Vintage 1991, pp41-4.

34. See Caroline Brothers, *War and Photography: A Cultural History*, Routledge, London 1997 and also the contributions to the monumental *War/Photography: Images of Armed Conflict and its Aftermath*, (eds) Anne Wilkes Tucker and Will Michels, Houston, Museum of Fine Arts/Yale University Press 2012.

35. For critique of newspaper representations, see David Shields, *War is Beautiful: The New York Times Guide to the Glamour of Armed Conflict*, New York, powerHouse books 2015. See also Roger Luckhurst, 'Iraq War Body Counts: Reportage, Photography, and Fiction', *Modern Fiction Studies*, forthcoming 2017.

were in the back seat of the family car. His photograph of the five year-old Samar Hassan, covered in her parents' blood, with the boots and gun-barrel of an American soldier towering over her, was published in *Newsweek* and syndicated around the world. This was only after he had ensured that he had taken careful measures to send the images back to his agency in New York, since the military command feared 'that some kind of seminal, career-ending photo might have been taken, so they had wanted to delay our distributing the photos'.[36] In 2007, Zoriah Miller, after weeks of being denied permission to leave base, accompanied a security patrol that was caught by a suicide bomber. He took several images of the aftermath before being ushered away. There were immediate demands to delete his memory cards, and after he had posted a number of images on his website, in spite of their strict adherence to the code to ensure that the bodies could not be identified. Miller was threatened with permanent blacklisting from covering any type of military operation 'anywhere in the world' (p174). Although the military backed away from this decision, further close policing of his activities, allegedly for his own protection, made work very difficult. Other photographers reported continual harassment and threat, particularly when photographers got anywhere near wounded soldiers. By 2008, it was estimated that although there were 150 000 U. S. troops in Iraq and several factional armies at war, the danger, expense and military restrictions on photojournalists meant that there were only ten officially accredited photojournalists left in the theatre of war.[37] There was rarely any explicit censorship, but restrictions effectively curtailed reporting of the war.

It is this specific context that produced responses like Thomas Hirschhorn's 'The Incommensurable Banner' (2008), an installation that presented an overwhelming array of photographs of ruined and devastated bodies from the Iraq War across a continuous eighteen metre-long banner. The images had all been rejected as too graphic to appear in the media and Hirschhorn intended to confront the politics of that exclusion. Nina Berman's portraits of severely injured veterans back home were difficult to place in newspapers and magazines, since they confronted the viewer with irresolvable aftermaths. Instead, she began to present them in exhibition spaces (London's Trolley Gallery eventually published them as *Purple Hearts: Back from Iraq* in 2004). This difficult context re-situates Luc Delahaye's decision to work, even inside the theatre of war, with a large format camera to escape the conventions of the fugitive image caught by the heroic, fearless photojournalist on the Robert Capa model. The era of global consolidation of media outlets under ideologically invested ownership made the development of other routes for display in the gallery, in artists' book, or on the web an outflanking tactic. Michael Kamber's anthology of interviews and images, *Photojournalists on War: The Untold Stories from Iraq*, a book 'about combat, the toll of war, censorship' with 'the goal ... to publish photos that had not been seen in the United States' was the work of a fellow photojournalist, but published through a university

36. Michael Kamber, 'Chris Hondros', in *Photojournalists on War: The Untold Stories from Iraq*, Austin, University of Texas Press 2013, p119. Hereafter *Photojournalists on War*.

37. Michael Kamber and Tim Arango, '4000 Deaths and a Handful of Images', *New York Times*, 26 July 2008, http://www.nytimes.com/2008/07/26/world/middleeast/26censor.html?_r=0.

press (p267).

Not just why, but *where* the dead come back is vital to examine, since the violence of the image of war can often be taken as a meta-commentary on the violence needed to bring it through the enunciative proscriptions that control entry to the public sphere. The impulse is of course prompted by the evidentiary, documentary imperative. But the Sontagian moral angst about this stance of a revelation through shock derives from the understanding of the image as an indexical sign of the actual body, and there are indications that this melancholic paradigm is shifting.

In Kaja Silverman's history of photography, she proposes tracing out a trajectory based on analogy and relationality, not that the image stabs down, as it were, back into the body, but that its effects take place between the image and the viewer, which in turn 'helps us to see that each of us is a node in a vast constellation of analogies'.[38] That photography is *disclosive*, in excess of the indexical, allows it to re-constellate sympathies in and across time. It is not stuck in melancholic fixation, but oddly reanimates the dead, bringing them back into play. It is significant that Silverman ends her chapter 'A Kind of Republic' with a discussion of John Reekie's *A Burial Party on the Battle-Field of Cold Harbour* (1865), an image of African Americans collecting the skeletons and body parts of Union Army dead. The black figure who looks out in the foreground, rhyming the glaring white skull next to him, 'invites us to join the republic' with a gaze 'headed toward the present: toward the here and now in which a potentially infinite series of later looks will both meet it and greet it' (*Miracle of Analogy*, p113). In several deft strokes, Silverman provides resources for thinking about images of the dead that step outside Modernist narratives of shock, angst or the urge to de-face the face, to undo representation. There is the prospect for theorising the complex set of relays of sympathetic identification so often disallowed in thought on the photography of death.

38. Kaja Silverman, *The Miracle of Analogy, or The History of Photography, Part 1*, Stanford, Stanford University Press 2015, p11. (Herafter *Miracle of Analogy*).

MEDICINE AND THE REDEFINITION OF DEATH

There is another corpus of photographic work that intimately confronts the dead body in medical contexts, inside enframement by the clinical environment, whether in the ward or, post-mortem, in the morgue. The fine art of morgue photography is a whole subset of practice, which might be considered to run from Stan Brakhage's extraordinary record of the autopsy, *The Act of Seeing with One's Own Eyes* (1971), or Jeffrey Silverthorne's parallel *Morgue Work* (1972-74, and again in 1986 and 1990-1), a series that was initially driven by a political imperative to reveal the bodies of American soldiers from the Vietnam conflict. At the same time, the English translation of Foucault's *The Birth of the Clinic* in 1973 emphasised the centrality of the clinical gaze and the autopsy in particular in morcellating the body's pathologies, distributing them in a new economy of the visible and the invisible.[39] Silverthorne has spoken of this compulsion and its limits in a recent retrospective:

> I photograph to understand, then do it again, go back and again, but in the morgue finally giving up trying to understand. There is too much life here, an absolute overload, and now I feel that if I can understand, there is something wrong with me.[40]

Twenty years later, controversy was deliberately courted in Andres Serrano's *Morgue Series* (first shown in New York in 1993), where familiar arguments over the aestheticisation of death attended his large cibachrome colour images of details of bodies from a New York city morgue, all callously titled with an abrupt cause of death (*Death by Drowning, Knifed to Death, Rat Poison Suicide,* and so on). Like Mann, Serrano had been the target of right-wing politicians for the provocations of his work on blood and bodily fluids at the height of AIDS activism. His morgue work was designed to provoke controversy.[41] It is in the nature of transgression to need continual re-staging: Cathrine Ertmann's series, *About Dying* (2014) offers its more oblique images in a considerably cooler climate of contention, but using the same language of 'lifting the veil of secrecy' on a working morgue deemed outside normal social signification.[42]

AIDS activism also drove an insistence on confronting the medical realities of dying and dead bodies in the 1980s and 1990s, when conservative governments deliberately under-funded medical research and care of an illness identified solely with a gay community considered by definition dissident from heteronormativity. In 1990, Therese Frare won the World Press Photo Award for her image of David Kirby on his death-bed in his father's arms, seen by some as a provocative echo of Christian *pietà* iconography. When the image was colourised and recycled for a Benetton advert and displayed on billboards and in glossy fashion magazines, it made unlikely allies of the Terence Higgins Trust and the *Sunday Times* in calling for a ban.[43] Insistence on tracking the very act of dying was foregrounded by artists from Derek Jarman to Hervé Guibert. Guibert transgressively breached aesthetic decorum, crossing between fiction and confession, image and text in the years before his death in 1991, recording every detail of his medical complications and treatments. He committed suicide to cheat the inevitable progress of the virus, an event he effectively filmed (in its carefully staged rehearsal) in his documentary *Pudeur ou L'Impudeur*.

A related area is the resurgence of post-mortem photography as a form of memorial, particularly in the area of neo-natal deaths. This was considered a morbid and gruesome practice exemplifying the Victorian cult of the dead, in the post-1945 paradigm of death's eclipse. In 1990, however, the Burns Archive of medical history photography issued the first volume of *Sleeping Beauty*, images of the posed dead from their substantial archive (which has been followed by two further volumes), and curator Audrey Linkman has traced this long history, coincident with the arrival of photography itself in

39. Michel Foucault, *The Birth of the Clinic*, (trans) A. M. Sheridan Smith, London, Tavistock 1973. (Hereafter *BoC*).

40. Jeffrey Silverthorne, 'Morgue Work' statement, *Working 1968-2013*, Berlin, Kehrer 2014, p64.

41. For commentary, see Andres Serrano, *Works 1983-93*, Philadelphia, ICA 1994.

42. Hayley McMillan, 'This is What Death Really Looks Like', *Refinery 29*, Feb 2015,

43. See Ben Cosgrove, 'The Photo that Changed the Face of AIDS', *Time Magazine*, 25 November 2014, http://time.com/3503000/behind-the-picture-the-photo-that-changed-the-face-of-aids/.

the 1830s, into the present. Post-mortem photographic practice has been fully re-integrated into grieving practices now recommended by neo-natal units.[44]

These kinds of practices might well be inscribed within the conventionalised idea that the hospital is the privileged locus for the 'sequestration of experience'. In Giddens' theory, when our protective cocoon of technical expertise is pierced by extremity, by death, the trauma is intensified: 'The frontiers of sequestered experience are fault lines full of tensions and poorly mastered forces,' Giddens warns. 'Where individuals are brought face to face with existential demands ... they are likely to experience both shock and reality inversion' (*Modernity*, pp168-9). In this formulation, the photograph reveals the truth of death concealed by the technical medical ensemble. The photographer Andres Serrano talks about the space of the morgue in exactly this way, as a 'private domain', a 'secret temple where few people are allowed' - 'some people feel shocked and outraged that I've presented it so directly'.[45]

But this still figures Death as an obtrusion from an outside, an implacable other poorly bracketed off by modernity's institutions. It conceptualises death as the other to biopolitical management of life and the body. What if we brought back death itself into history, grasping that it has been in the process of medical redefinition, its thresholds reworked and limits extended, throughout the contemporary period?

This is what has been happening since 1968, the crucial year when the Ad Hoc Committee of the Harvard Medical School was assembled to address 'obsolete criteria for the definition of death' and produced a hugely influential new paradigm, which changed medical and legal discourse on death in America and around the world.[46] Up to 1968, the legal definition of death was still defined as the cessation of the heart-beat, a fixed and incontrovertible *moment* in the eyes of the law. This was newly problematic, because medical advances in artificial respirators and ensembles of machines newly called the 'intensive care unit' had greatly improved resuscitative measures through the artificial maintenance of respiration. This created a novel problem: the cardiopulmonary system could be sustained entirely separately from the complete absence of cortical activity: people who were definitely living and breathing, yet 'brain dead'. These new beings, products of the intensive care unit, were sometimes called 'beating heart cadavers' or 'neomorts'. They were potentially an important source for another medical frontier - transplant surgery - except that the earliest transplant doctors were at risk of being prosecuted for wrongful killing because organs were being taken from bodies with still beating hearts. As a solution to this difficult situation, the Ad Hoc Committee relocated death from the heart to the brain, establishing the criteria for determining 'irreversible coma'. This condition was determined as a complete absence of responsiveness to stimuli in both autonomic brain systems and the higher neocortex.[47]

This proved extremely influential, but problems of definition were only

44. See Audrey Linkman, *Photography and Death*, London, Reaktion 2011 and Stanley Burns, *Sleeping Beauty: Memorial Photography in America*, New York, Burns Archive 1990.

45. Anna Blume, 'Andres Serrano', *BOMB* 43 (Spring 1993), http://bombmagazine.org/article/1631/andres-serrano.

46. Report of the Ad Hoc Committee of the Harvard Medical School to Examine the Definition of Brain Death, 'A Definition of Irreversible Coma', *Journal of the American Medical Association*, 5 August 1968, p337.

47. This paragraph draws on Stuart Younger, 'The Definition of Death' in *Oxford Handbook of Bioethics*,(ed.) Bonnie Steinbock, Oxford, Oxford University Press 2007, pp285-303. . (Hereafter *Definition of Death*). Dick Teresi, *The Undead: How Medicine is Blurring the Line Between Life and Death*, New York, Pantheon 2012.

addressed over a decade later when 'whole brain death' criteria were agreed in the 1981 American medical commission report *Defining Death*. When the patient met the criteria, brain death could be declared, respirators turned off, and a window of time was then opened for the harvesting of organs. Foucault's observations about the autopsy can folded back into this living/dead body now disarticulated into separate systems: 'Death is therefore multiple, and dispersed in time: it is not that absolute, privileged point at which time stops and moves back; like disease itself, it has a teeming presence that analysis may divide into time and space; gradually, here and there' (*BoC*, p142).

In the interval opened up between brain death and biological death has become a fraught terrain full of anomalies, ethical crises, and a host of new liminal beings that hover between life and death. In 1972, the Persistent Vegetative State (PVS) was coined for states where there is a catastrophic collapse of brain function, yet some neocortical activity persists. This condition is meant to transition to PVS after twelve months of stasis, yet the boundary has proved difficult to secure and the wider culture has become obsessed with anomalies and extraordinary recoveries or reanimations of those in coma, however vanishingly rare these instances are. Most know about Locked-In Syndrome, another liminal state in which higher cortical activity is preserved amidst the complete collapse of the voluntary muscular and nervous system, through Jean-Dominique Bauby's memoir (and later film), *The Diving Bell and the Butterfly*.[48] It was the record of his life that he blinked out letter by letter from his hospital bed, his eyelid the only muscle he could move voluntarily.

Attempts to resolve the difficulties of medical definition of these states resulted, in 1997, with an entirely new category, the Minimally Conscious State, which encompassed not just coma-states, but also late-stage dementia. The population existing between two deaths has been therefore continually expanding since 1968. Susan Squier suggests that these liminal lives 'test the boundaries of our vital taxonomies' and become 'powerful and dangerous representatives of a transformation we are all undergoing as we become initiates in a new biomedical personhood mingling existence and non-existence, organic and inorganic matter, life and death'.[49] Margaret Lock polemically terms this a process of making up new nosological categories for the 'Good-as-Dead', and wonders if these aren't categories of social rather than biological death. 'In late modernity,' Lock contends, 'the numbers of people recognised as candidates for social death have increased exponentially'.[50]

I have argued elsewhere that this expansion offers contexts for modern 'body horror' fiction and film, a newly graphic focus on bodily disintegration. It is no coincidence that 1968, the year of shifting death from heart to head, was the year of George Romero's redefinition of the zombie in the foundational underground classic, *Night of the Living Dead*. Since Romero, the zombie has been dispatched not like the older vampire by a stake to the

48. Jean-Dominique Bauby, *The Diving Bell and the Butterfly: A Memoir of Life in Death*, London, Vintage 1998.

49. Susan Merrill Squier, *Liminal Lives: Imagining the Human at the Frontiers of Biomedicine*, Durham, Duke University Press 2004, pp4-5.

50. Margaret Lock, 'On Making up the Good-as-Dead', in *Remaking Life and Death: Toward an Anthropology of the Biosciences*, S. Franklin and M. Lock (eds), Sante Fe, School of American Research Press 2001, p189.

heart but by a bullet to the head.⁵¹ It is also, I think, the frame for why the dead come back in photography that addresses the intimate condition of the body in hospitals and morgues. 'The public hardly has a monolithic view about what it means to be dead,' Stuart Younger observes. (*Definition of death*, p294). Photography is part of this conversation.

A final illustration of how this terrain has been picked up in photography is the extraordinarily rich project of photographer Edgar Martins, who has spent several years investigating the archive of Portugal's National Institute of Legal Medicine and Forensic Sciences in Lisbon. The archive, well over 150 years old, holds physical evidence, medical documents and photographic records of violent crimes and death scenes. The files contain autopsy findings, logged and often preserved the implements used in suicides and murders (ropes, cords, knives, guns), and included meticulous photographs of the scene, as well as suicide notes. The archive, overlooked, crumbling away, is also an accidental history of photography itself. Early reports include sketches or drawings, then hand-drawn details on primitive photographs, then a mournful acceleration through types of celluloid films, boxes of negatives, polaroids, rolls of undeveloped film, and ending up with mobile phones and digital cameras bagged for evidence. Martins began presenting different arrays of this work in 2016 in various exhibitions, starting in the UK with 'Flat Death' at the Open Eye Gallery in Liverpool, and also in the book, *Siloquies and Soliloquies on Death, Life and Other Interludes*.

Martins' taxonomic impulse clearly shows that he works in the wake of the New Topographical School of objective documentation, the serial cataloguing of forms celebrated by Bernd and Hilda Becher in their practice and teaching. Previous projects by Martins have focused on the non-places of modernity - airport runways, beaches at night, large industrial plants, European Space Agency laboratories - with a detached, neutral, formal precision. At the same time, the very precision of these topographies tips the real into the surreal, rending his representations at once transparent and enigmatic.⁵²

In this much more fraught terrain, Martins has re-documented the documents of the National Institute of Legal Medical and Forensic Science in hundreds of photographs, in a way that raises questions about how to represent such a catalogue of private pain and death. He catches a strange 'archive fever' in trying to order such disorder, the re-shuffling of taxonomies in different displays foregrounding this unnerving curatorial compulsion. There are sequences of images of ropes or garrottes, against neutral backgrounds, precisely coiled by medical investigators as they work through these chaotic scenes of death. There are puzzling, bizarre objects that have lost their notes and thus any framing discourse: a top-hat with a bullet hole, somewhere else, a skull with a matching bullet hole - a marvellous death, the actual circumstances long lost in the bureaucracy.

It is the suicide notes that feel to be the core of the project. In some sequences, Martins photographs only the very edges of the sheets of paper,

51. See Roger Luckhurst, 'Biomedical Horror: The New Death and the New Undead' in *Technologies of the Gothic in Literature and Culture: Technogothics*. (ed.) J. Edwards, London, Routledge 2015, pp84-98.

52. See Edgar Martins, 'In Conversation with David Campany' in *Topologies*, aperture, London 2007, pp115-22.

end on to the camera, offering delicate slivers of withheld knowledge; in others, original photographs of notes are digitally manipulated to remove the writing, whilst keeping the creases or blood-stains; in others, finally, we are gifted with the message, however banal, petty, vengeful or lovingly regretful ('someone let the cat out'), texts freighted with the knowledge that death inheres in the written mark. In *The Postcard*, Derrida argued that every letter becomes a dead letter, gets stuck in the dead letter office, no return to sender, no addressee found, because of the inherent quality of writing to detach from its author, to circulate and continue to signify, but also to err, to veer off course, long before death let alone long after it. This is the logic of *destinerrance*, where destination, destiny, and the inherent errancy of the letter converge.[53]

Martins' digital manipulations are inevitably contentious interventions - the history I have traced when the dead come back into photography guarantees that. But the Martins project, more than any other explored here, seems to inhabit deliberately that zone between what Kaja Silverman calls the indexical and the disclosive where affective networks are less predictable, more mobile. It wants to challenge assumptions about the fixity of the always-already wounding index, instead thinking about another possible relation between photography and death. André Bazin thought that the ontology of the photograph inhered in the long practice at the foundation of art, 'the practice of embalming the dead' - 'a mummy complex'.[54] Perhaps it is more attuned to registering the present crisis in the image and the transformation of death itself, to think of the photograph as existing in that liminal space *between* life and death, a weird zone with now decidedly fuzzy edges that is packed with all kinds of new provisional beings and dynamic relations.

Roger Luckhurst is Professor of Modern and Contemporary Literature at Birkbeck College, University of London. He has published extensively in the field of contemporary literature and cultural studies. He is the author of *Zombies: A Cultural History* (Reaktion Press, 2015); *Alien* (Palgrave/BFI, 2014); *The Shining* (Palgrave, 2013), *The Mummy's Case: The True Story of a Dark Fantasy* (Oxford University Press, 2012), *The Trauma Question* (Routledge, 2008), *Science Fiction* (Polity Press, 2005), and *The Invention of Telepathy* (Oxford University Press, 2002).

---

53. Jacques Derrida, *The Postcard: From Socrates to Freud and Beyond*, (trans) A. Bass, Chicago, Chicago University Press 1987. See also Hillis J. Miller, 'Derrida's Destinerrance', *Modern Language Notes* 121: 4 (2006), pp893-910.

54. André Bazin, 'The Ontology of the Photographic Image', (trans) H. Gray, *Film Quarterly* 13: 4 (1960), p4.

DRONE POETICS

Andrea Brady

Abstract 'Drone Poetics' considers the challenge to the theory and practice of the lyric of the development of drone warfare. It argues that modernist writing has historically been influenced by aerial technology; drones also affect notions of perception, distance and intimacy, and the self-policing subject, with consequences for contemporary lyric. Indeed, drone artworks and poems proliferate; and while these take critical perspectives on drone operations, they have not reckoned with the phenomenological implications of execution from the air. I draw out six of these: the objectification of the target, the domination of visuality, psychic and operational splitting, the 'everywhere war', the intimacy of keyhole observations, and the mythic or psychoanalytic representation of desire and fear. These six tropes indicate the necessity for a radical revision of our thinking about the practice of writing committed poetry in the drone age.

Keywords drones, aesthetics, lyric, aerial technology, psychoanalysis, Medusa, intimacy

---

This essay is a provocation, which seeks to determine the potential for lyric in the drone age. Prison and flight have long been important tropes for establishing the polarities of aesthetic constraint and liberty, but they also influence writing in more practical ways, as sites of literary production and ways of seeing. The airplane was particularly important in altering spatial perspectives and had far-reaching consequences for the visual arts. Gertrude Stein suggested that cubist landscapes approximated the view from an airplane.[1] Paul Virilio has written provocatively about the intimacy between aerial bombing and cinematic technique.[2] Planes are also an important influence on literary perspective (*Time and Space*, pp242-7).[3] Filippo Marinetti describes how:

> as I looked at objects from a new point of view, no longer head on or from behind, but straight down, foreshortened, that is, I was able to break apart the old shackles of logic and the plumb lines of the ancient way of thinking.[4]

The airplane produces a new vantage which leads Marinetti to fantasise about bombing language, seeking to 'destroy syntax and scatter one's nouns at random'. Planes are mythologised by Proust and Kafka as a form of

---

1. Stephen Kern, *The Culture of Time and Space, 1880–1918*, Cambridge, Harvard UP, 2003, p245. (Hereafter *Time and Space*).

2. Paul Virilio, *War and Cinema, The Logistics of Perception*, (trans) Patrick Camiller, London and New York, Verso, 1989.

3. Laurence Goldstein, 'The Airplane and American Literature', in *The Airplane in American Culture*, Dominick Pisano (ed.), Ann Arbor, University of Michigan Press, 2003; Anne Collins Goodyear, 'The Effect of Flight on Art in the Twentieth Century', *Reconsidering a Century of Flight*, Roger D. Launius and Janet R. Daly (eds), Chapel Hill, University of North Carolina Press, 2003, pp223-41.

4. Filippo Marinetti, 'Technical Manifesto of Futurist Literature', *Documents of Twentieth- Century Art: Futurist Manifestos*, trans. Robert Brain, R.W. Flint, J.C. Higgitt, and Caroline Tisdall, New York, Viking Press, 1973, pp100-106.

the technological sublime,[5] or (in the famous skywriting scene in Woolf's *Mrs Dalloway*) regarded by Mr Bentley as 'a symbol... of man's soul; of his determination ... to get outside his body, beyond his house, by means of thought, Einstein, speculation, mathematics...'[6] George Oppen worked as a tool and die maker for Grumman aircraft - later the company merged to form Northrup Grumman, producers of the Global Hawk drone.[7]

Since approximately 2010, many poets have engaged with drones in their lyrics, making use of drone operators' chatter, personifying drones (or robotising humans), and offering critiques of the destruction and alienation that drones produce. I will discuss a few of these projects, but the intention of this essay is not to offer a synopsis of poems about drones. Rather, it is to test what effect drones might have on the practice of committed lyric in a time of 'everywhere' war. To do this, I will summarise six ways in which drones are revolutionising perspective and relation, and suggest how they might be applied to the theorisation of contemporary poetry. My aim is not to sublimate the actual experience of assassination into an aesthetic topos; rather, I want to consider the limits of committed lyric through a detailed, materialist examination of the forms of warfare in which it is grounded.

Drones are an epochal technology, the consequence and drivers of profound changes to politics, law and warfare. They alter the way we see and relate to others, the way we conceive space and time. While drones continue to be scotomised by the US public, around the world they are a powerful symbol of US aggression.[8] Drones are the most conspicuous mechanism of American necropolitics, which Achille Mbembe defines as the sovereign power to dictate who may live and who must die.[9] They are also specifically related to carcerality, which has been a crucial metaphor for and site of poetic production for centuries. Although US prison populations have become grotesquely swollen since the early 1980s, in respect of foreign counterinsurgency operations, the US has moved to replace incarceration with assassination. Many historians have argued that the huge expansion of drone strikes under the Obama administration can be attributed to Obama's campaign pledge to close Guantánamo Bay and other US 'black sites'. Though rendition, military commissions and indefinite detention were preserved, Obama and his counterterrorism chief John Brennan pursued a policy of 'kill rather than capture' for suspected militants because - it is alleged - they did not want conspicuously to add to the numbers in Guantánamo.[10] (At the time of writing, Trump has tweeted his enthusiasm for expanding those numbers; his express aim to 'bomb the hell out of Isis' and kill the families of suspected 'terrorists' also makes him unlikely to scale back Obama's drone operations).[11]

This is not to say that drone executions have displaced the prison as the primary instrument of American and British aggression. Rather, drones have made whole territories in Afghanistan, Yemen, Somalia, and Pakistan into open-air prisons. A Waziri man from Datta Khel says that many people there 'have lost their mental balance ... are just locked in a room. Just like you lock

5. Sara Danius, *The Senses of Modernism: Technology, Perception, and Aesthetics*, Ithaca, Cornell University Press, 2002, pp121-2.

6. Virginia Woolf, *Mrs Dalloway*, London, Granada, 1976 [1982], pp26-7.

7. George Oppen, *Selected Letters*, ed. Rachel Blau Du Plessis, Durham, NC and London, Duke UP, 1990, xiv, p202.

8. Peter L. Bergen and Daniel Rothenberg (eds), *Drone Wars: Transforming Conflict, Law, and Policy*, Cambridge, Cambridge University Press, 2015, p95.

9. Achille Mbembe, 'Necropolitics', trans. Libby Meintjes, *Public Culture*, 15.1, 2003, 11-40, p34.

10. The thesis that the CIA and the Pentagon engage in targeted killing because they have 'few options for detaining terror suspects, and little appetite for extensive ground operations' is explored in Mark Mazzetti, *The CIA, a Secret Army and a War at the Ends of the Earth*, New York and London, Penguin, 2013.

11. Tom F. A. Watts, 'If Donald Trump takes control of the US drone fleet, he's made plans to commit war crimes', *The Independent*, 21 September 2016.

people in prison, they are locked in a room'.[12] Drones are a technology of carceral surveillance and punishment, and like the prison they manufacture self-policing subjects. They also resemble prisons in other ways, including their production of constant, inescapable noise. George Jackson described the clamour of an American prison as psychological torture:

> It destroys the logical processes of the mind, a man's thoughts become completely disorganised. The noise, madness streaming from every throat, frustrated sounds from the bars, metallic sounds from the walls, the steel trays, the iron beds bolted to the wall, the hollow sounds from a cast-iron sink or toilet.[13]

Similarly, many informants describe the ceaseless buzzing of drones overhead as a direct cause of mental suffering. A worker in Pakistan told the *Atlantic*:

> I can't sleep at night because when the drones are there ... I hear them making that sound, that noise. The drones are all over my brain, I can't sleep. When I hear the drones making that drone sound, I just turn on the light and sit there looking at the light.[14]

Drones are an apparatus of visual surveillance whose threatening presence is conveyed sonically. Noting that drone videos on YouTube focus on the explosion (the money-shot), Nasser Hussain argues that 'the experience of drone strikes from the ground cannot be understood as a singular moment but as a structuring reality' of constant sound.[15] While the victim can only hear and not see the drone, for the drone operators the visual feed is silent. This 'lack of synchronic sound renders it a ghostly world in which the figures seem unalive, even before they are killed. The gaze hovers above in silence'. This silence, combined with the ubiquitous 'overhead shot' which prohibits an exchange of the gaze inhibits empathy and encourages the use of force.

Like prisons, drones also modify their inmates' behaviour. Parents keep their children home from school; people avoid praying together or shopping at markets; they stop going to funerals, having meals together, or offering hospitality. As 'signature strikes' often target people not because of their identity, but because they exhibit 'patterns of life' which are considered suspect (these include praying, or standing to urinate)[16] people have changed their habits of moving and socialising to avoid showing a lethal signature (*Kill Chain*, p225).[17] Drones thus devastate traditional cultures where political, religious and social life revolves around gathering, producing atomised units of besieged and paranoid individuals.[18]

DRONE AESTHETICS

Polls regularly affirm that the majority of Americans approve of drone

---

12. International Human Rights and Conflict Resolution Clinic (Stanford Law School) and Global Justice Clinic (NYU School of Law), *Living Under Drones: Death, Injury and Trauma to Civilians from US Drone Practices in Pakistan*, Sept. 2012, pp87-8, http://chrgj.org/wp-content/uploads/2012/10/Living-Under-Drones.pdf

13. George Jackson, *Soledad Brother, The Prison Letters of George Jackson*, Baltimore, MD and London, Penguin and Jonathan Cape, 1970, p45.

14. Conor Friedersdorf, '"Every Person Is Afraid of the Drones": The Strikes' Effect on Life in Pakistan', *The Atlantic* 25 Sept. 2012.

15. Nasser Hussain, 'The Sound of Terror, Phenomenology of a Drone Strike', *Boston Review*, 16 October 2013, https://bostonreview.net/world/hussain-drone-phenomenology.

16. Andrew Cockburn, *Kill Chain, Drones and the Rise of High-Tech Assassins*, London and New York, Verso, 2015, p224. (Hereafter *Kill Chain*).

17. At the peak of drone operations in Pakistan in 2009 and 2010, half of all kills were classified as signature strikes (John Kaag and Sarah Kreps, *Drone Warfare*, Cambridge,

use, and substantial outcries about their use are confined to invasions of privacy and threats to civilian airspace by hobby drones. Drones deliver pizzas, dry cleaning and engagement rings, and one day will drop Amazon purchases on your doorstep. Drones are ubiquitous in feature films,[19] documentaries (*Kill/Capture* [2011]; Tonje Schei's *Drone* [2014]; *Unmanned: America's Drone Wars* [2015]); and even an astonishing 'black comedy' called 'Bugsplat' which briefly aired on Channel 4 in 2015. Drone performance and visual art has also proliferated since 2010. Visual art projects include Axel Brechensbuaer's Peace Drone, designed to administer OxyContin in rural areas from a creepy, clown-faced drone which plays music, like an ice cream truck; Baden Pailthorpe's MQ-9 Reaper series animations; Adam Harvey's stealthware; James Bridle's 'Drone Shadows' and 'The Light of God' projects; Tomas van Houtryve's 'Blue Sky Days' project; ESSAM's NYPD Drone Campaign posters; Lisa Barnard's 'Whiplash Transition' films and photographs; video artist George Barber's 'The Freestone Drone'; Mona Kamal's 'Drones in Waziristan' rugs; Trevor Paglen's relational and performative photographic projects; Omer Fast's film *Five Thousand Feet Is Best*; and Jananne Al-Ani's video series 'Shadow Sites'.[20] ANOHNI's 2016 album *Hopelessness* included a track called 'Drone Bomb Me'; in the video, Naomi Campbell (dressed in a swimming costume and military gear) sits weeping on an execution chair.

Many of these projects are critical of the militarisation of perspective and the barbarity of targeted killing. Some also seek to intervene in drone operations themselves: for example, a collective of artist-activists printed vast images of victims of drone strikes and set them out in fields in the areas susceptible to drone surveillance (the project was called '#notabugsplat'). However, some movements such as the 'New Aesthetic' regard drones as a potentially radical technology which can inspire new artistic practices. A panel at South by Southwest in March 2012 introduced The New Aesthetic as part of a discussion of 'Seeing Like Digital Devices', which focussed on how digital vision, including drones, represent an irreversible and potentially positive aesthetic development. As Joanne McNeil puts it in her notes for her talk, 'Technology creates new ways of seeing - with every advance we move closer to understanding what the world is about. With progress come new points-of-view, new perspectives, new possibilities'.[21]

One artist who has engaged extensively with the filmic implications of drone technology, and its role in state surveillance, is Laura Poitras. Her 2016 'Astral Noise' show at the Whitney in New York included a work called 'Bed Down Location' (military jargon for the places where targets sleep).[22] It consists of a platform on which viewers lie back and look up at a ceiling-mounted screen where footage of skies above Yemen, Pakistan and Somalia is displayed. Reclining and looking at the heavens recalls the pastoralism of one of Poitras's collaborators, Trevor Paglen, who (in Julian Stallabrass's estimation):

Polity, 2014, p32). (Hereafter *Drone Warfare*).

18. *The Civilian Impact of Drones, Unexamined Costs, Unanswered Questions*, Columbia Law School Human Rights Clinic and the Center for Civilians in Conflict, 2012, http://web.law.columbia.edu/sites/default/files/microsites/human-rights-institute/files/The%20Civilian%20Impact%20of%20Drones.pdf.

19. Henry Barnes, 'Kill shots, why cinema has drone warfare in its sights', *The Guardian*, 14 April 2016.

20. Some of these projects are discussed in Susanna Davies-Crook, 'Art in the Drone Age', *Dazed*, June 2013, http://www.dazeddigital.com/artsandculture/article/16183/1/art-in-the-drone-age.

21. http://www.joannemcneil.com/new-aesthetic-at-sxsw/. On the way 'machinic vision' changes consciousness, see also John Johnston, 'Machinic Vision', *Critical Inquiry* 26.1, Autumn 1999, pp27-48, 45.

22. Shimrit Lee reviews this installation, 'Astro Noise, War on Terror as Virtual Reality', *Warscapes Weekly*, 18 February 2016, http://www.warscapes.com/reviews/astro-noise-war-terror-virtual-reality.

evoke[s] both the mathematical and the dynamic sublime in your satellite imagery, particularly in images of the night sky and of trails over pristine landscapes that evoke nineteenth-century landscape photographs of the American West.[23]

The sublimity of the pristine skyscapes is undermined however by the chatter of drone operators, quietly broadcast in the background of Poitras's installation. This noise, and a single overpass by a Predator drone in the video, warn the viewer of a baleful presence in the otherwise clear skies. The work temporarily positions the viewer on the side of those living under drones, rather than replicating the perspective of the operators which has been represented fulsomely on YouTube. It invites us to identify with the victims of drone warfare, allowing us to *see* with those who are normally seen, but at the same time aligning us with the operators we can *hear* (and whose voices are normally unheard). Poitras's exhibition concludes with a *coup de théâtre* called 'Last Seen', a screen just near the exit which visualises current viewers of 'Bed Down Location' using heat-sensing cameras, alongside a screen which uses Sniffer software to pick up and broadcast the location and type of visitors' mobile devices.

It is perhaps unsurprising that the majority of artworks which respond to drone technology are visual. These works examine drones' radicalisation of viewing, seeing and being seen, and continue to register the effects of aerial technology on visual arts which began with Modernism. But there are also many textual engagements with drones and their ideology. Several poets have written drone poems to commemorate Barack Obama's 2012 inauguration, including 'To the Drone Vaguely Realising Eastward' by Michael Robbins, and Paul Muldoon's 'For Barack Obama, His Second Inauguration'. Teju Cole's *Seven Short Stories about Drones* is a twitter sequence which détournes literary texts by inserting drones into their narratives (e.g. 'Someone must have slandered Josef K., for one morning, without having done anything truly wrong, he was killed by a Predator drone').[24] Harry Giles developed a collaborative performance poem with sound artist Neil Simpson called 'Drone', which tells 'the fragmented story of a military drone's lives and fears', personifying the aircraft 'as part weapons system, part office worker, part tense background hum'.[25] Maxine Chernoff's poem 'Drones', which imagines the drone operator's overhead perspective to argue instead that 'the land has no boundaries, countries no borders. Objects of interest move on a grid'.[26] Chernoff's poem annotates 'the ache of the past', a time when 'Fear was small and hovered on lips', whereas in the present age 'Surgeons of excision, men enact death's plans'. She suggests that the work of the poem is to remember and set limits to the perpetuity and pervasion of war, a 'small' gesture which can restore the bodies to the washed out grids across which 'objects' (men, women, animals) move as targets.

Catherine Taylor's prose-poem sequence 'Inanimate Subjects' depicts

23. Julian Stallabrass, 'Negative Dialectics in the Google Era', pp3–14.

24. http://thenewinquiry.com/blogs/dtake/seven-short-stories-about-drones/

25. https://harrygiles.org/portfolio/drone/.

26. Maxine Chernoff, 'Drones', *Here*, Denver, Counterpath Press, 2014, p35; https://www.arts.gov/writers-corner/bio/maxine-chernoff.

an anthropomorphised drone whose 'bulging head with its swivelling eye' may be looking at you, or you looking through it.[27] The latter perspective is provided by the speaker's brother, a drone pilot, whose disembodied experience of piloting the aircraft is held in tension with the embodiment of the drone, and the overhead perspective of the poet herself. Taylor uses the figure of the puppet to comment on the relation between the drone operator and 'his' aircraft, as well as the relation of citizens to their governments. She writes that the pleasure of puppets lies in the paradox that 'they seem to act on their own. Autonomous. Alive. Once we glimpse the master, the puppet becomes merely an object' (*Inanimate Subjects*, p45). She questions whether drone technology is itself an ethical problem, or merely a symptom of 'an autonomous state run amok' (p55). Sketching scenes of children watching puppet shows of varying malevolence, Taylor considers the emotional effects on viewers of these fictions of autonomy. Though much of the poem draws on substantial research into the legality and technology of automised warfare, the pleasures of watching require a more precise examination, as I will argue later in this essay.

Taylor's poem also reproduces some troubling, if familiar, justifications of drone war: war has always been unfair, and relied on technological advantages and camouflage; drones don't cause more 'collateral damage' than ordinary bombing. These culminate in the astonishing claim that:

> perhaps one of the most significant things about drones isn't how they hide, but how they reveal our distaste for killing, or at least the killing of innocents. In this way, we might see drones as an ironically effective tool for peace-making if they can disclose that what their opponents oppose is not drones per se but unjust war. (*Inanimate Subjects*, p50).

This position is the consequence of considering drones not as a technology which creates intrinsic ethical problems, but simply as an indifferent tool. Taylor's text hopes that although not everyone will care about 'collateral damage' inflicted abroad, Americans might be moved to a selfish recognition that drones could pose a domestic threat: 'everyone can share the fear that the kill chain will end with us' (p56). The poem does not in itself work to overcome this indifference to foreign death. Instead, it concludes with a fantasy of

> put[ting] away the plaything of this metaphor in favor of a more active one, something that reminds us of the ways in which we are not puppets and that drones are not our masters, but we theirs. Maybe I'll cut the strings and turn all these puppets into effigies. Effigies are puppets that burn. (p59)

But this revolutionary fantasy is based on an overestimation of the poem's own capacity for surrogacy or metaphoric substitution. In a poem, drones

27. Catherine Taylor, 'Inanimate Subjects', *Seneca Review*, 43.1, Fall 2013, pp44-59, 44. http://www.hws.edu/academics/senecareview/43_1/taylor.pdf. (Hereafter *Inanimate Subjects*).

can easily become puppets:

> You can substitute a text for puppet.
> You can substitute a bomb for a text.
> You can substitute a swarm for a self (p51).

But who is this 'you' who can make these substitutions? Anyone with an imagination? Or, the privileged producer or reader of committed Anglophone lyric poetry? It is hard to imagine how such capacities for poetic substitution might be meaningful to the people targeted by drones. Rather, the fantasy of unlimited autonomous creative power in the derided field of poetic operations is consistent with the ideology which underpins drones: the poet, safe from harm, can perform her prosthetic acts of viewing and intervention, contemplating their consequences and ethics in the abstract, far from any actual encounter with her objects. The substitution of 'a bomb for a text' is anyway quite a specialised act of displacement, a form of cunning which may be essential to turning puppets into revolutionary things that burn, but in which the poem itself does not instruct us.

Taylor's poem attempts to engage with the legal and ethical complexities of drone operations, but it is limited by its failure to acknowledge that its perspective replicates that of the object of its critique. Jena Osman's book *Public Figures* is more successful in challenging imperialist warfare, specifically by problematising surveillance in the drone age through an artistic intervention in an American city.[28] Osman's text integrates found text from drone operators' chatrooms with photographs taken by a camera rigged up to replicate the perspective of statues of war heroes around Philadelphia. The text works to resist the heroic gaze and our habituation as citizens to the ubiquity of armed icons. Recognising the near-impossibility for Anglo-American poets of representing the perspective of people targeted by drones, Osman instead reveals how Philadelphians are both symbolically and actually the objects of a historical, militarised gaze.

As Osman's poem shows, the committed poet must acknowledge her complicity in the exclusion of the people most directly affected by drone warfare from the 'distribution of the sensible', which Jacques Rancière calls 'this distribution and redistribution of places and identities, this apportioning and reapportioning of spaces and times, of the visible and the invisible, of noise and speech'. Rancière has repeatedly insisted that 'the whole question' of politics is 'to know who possesses speech and who merely possesses voice':

> Politics occurs when those who 'have no' time take the time necessary to front up as inhabitants of a common space and demonstrate that their mouths really do emit speech capable of making pronouncements on the common which cannot be reduced to voices signalling pain.[29]

28. Jena Osman, *Public Figures*, Wesleyan, 2012.

29. Jacques Rancière, *Aesthetics and Its Discontents*, trans. Steven Corcoran, London, Polity, 2009, pp24-5. (Hereafter *Aesthetics*).

Drone poetics extend beyond the products of individuals who can lay claim to the leisure required to produce aesthetic objects and imagine metaphoric substitutions, and a media context in which the voices of the victims are translated as untranslatable trauma. Drone poetics must take into account what Gil Hochberg calls 'hypervisibility'. Describing the subjection of Palestinians in the Occupied Territories to Israeli surveillance, and the visualisation of their suffering by the global news media as 'an instrument meant to facilitate the ethical responses of others,' Hochberg argues that the problem for committed artists is how to challenge

> the dominant modes of representations through which the very visibility of others' suffering remains nothing but a spectacle, providing at best a momentary source of ethical speculation and, at worst, a source of voyeuristic pleasure.[30]

30. Gil Z. Hochberg, *Visual Occupations, Violence and Visibility in a Conflict Zone*, Durham and London, Duke University Press, 2015, p120.

This challenge requires an examination of the specific nature of the voyeuristic pleasure which drones liberate. But it also requires a recognition that the privileged artist in many ways replicates the perspectives and prosthetic violence which characterise drone operations, and that this relation between the artist and her objects cannot be simply inverted or wished away through acts of imperialising empathy.

This recognition is at the heart of my final example of a drone text, a sequence of poems which draws on the *Dictionary of Military and Associated Terms* for its vocabulary, and on both surveillance and family photographs for its imagery: Solmaz Sharif's *Look*.[31] In that dictionary, a 'look' is not a form of the gaze which constitutes an ethics of engaging with the Other, but 'a period during which a mine circuit is receptive of an influence'. Sharif draws on her own Iranian heritage, and juxtaposes the destructive militarised gaze with less remote acts of looking: at family photographs of an uncle peeling apples in a military camp during the Iran-Iraq wars (*Look*, p79), at a video of her father (p39), at the demolished houses of the 'martyrs' (p63) and the scattered effects of the dead. These visualisations are however entirely permeated by the military language, signalled in the book as a literal capitalisation of what seem like ordinary words that have been transmuted into much more sinister meanings as military jargon. This device shows how militarisation permeates ordinary speech: as Sharif writes about the disappearance of 'drone' from a later version of the *Dictionary*, 'the military definition is no longer a *supplement* to the English language, but the English language itself' (p95). This penetration of reality by the diction of war is also the inverse of the erasure of terms of intimacy from censored letters to prisoners of war in 'Reaching Guantánamo' (pp 49-51).

31. Solmaz Sharif, *Look*, Minneapolis, Graywolf, 2016. (Hereafter *Look*).

The mutation of intimacy in the presence of the military gaze is one of the book's major themes. In the opening poem, 'Look', the tender conversations of lovers are interspersed with references to drone operations:

Whereas years after they LOOK down from their jets and declare my mother's Abadan block PROBABLY DESTROYED, we walked by the villas, the faces of buildings torn off into dioramas, and recorded it on a handheld camcorder;

Whereas it could take as long as 16 seconds between the trigger pulled in Las Vegas and the Hellfire missile landing in Mazar-e-Sharif, after which they will ask themselves *Did we hit a child? No. A Dog.* they will answer themselves; […]

Whereas the lover made my heat rise, rise so that if heat sensors were trained on me, they could read my THERMAL SHADOW through the roof and through the wardrobe; (*Look*, p3)

This reading of the body's erotic heat is not a poetic fiction, but (as I'll explain in a moment) an actual aspect of the perverse intimacy of drone operations. The poem concludes with the wish: 'Let it be the exquisite face for at least 16 seconds. / Let me LOOK at you. / Let me LOOK at you in a light that takes years to get here' (p5). The poem carves out the briefest of interludes for the exchange of gazes, a moment which is expanded both by being bathed in the slow time of starlight, and as the pause before impact.

Sharif's book does not only stage the exquisite intensities of victimhood; the speaker is elsewhere also a perpetrator ('You begin to appreciate / the heft of your boot soles, / […] how they can kick in / a face -', (p60), or capable of exchanging gazes with power:

peepholes without a lens

so when the GUARD comes to inspect me,
I inspect him.

Touch me, you said.

And through that opening

I did. (p29)

Here, the 'you' is both an intimate interlocutor - a lover or family member - and the guard; the 'opening' is both the portal in a cell door, a camera aperture, and an opening in the body. (Lisa Guenther has written about the cuffport as both a mouth and an anus, a site of interchange for prisoner whose full participation in intercorporeality has been blocked).[32] The poem neither wholly circumvents, nor wholly surrenders, this desire to be touched, physically or emotionally, to this mediating carceral structure of surveillance.

32. Lisa Guenther, *Solitary Confinement: Social Death and Its Afterlives*, Minneapolis, University of Minnesota Press, 2013, p187.

Look makes use of military diction in order to challenge the technologies of perception and tyranny which are epitomised by drones. It carves out spaces for poetic reflection and memory in both the position of the object and subject of the militarised gaze, making trauma visible without turning it into spectacle. The remainder of this essay outlines a drone poetics which engages with the perceptual, legal and phenomenological specificities of drones and brings them to bear on a reconceptualisation of lyric form and relation. This essay does not allege that the aporias of the committed lyric can be fixed by a more empathetic (but still ventriloquized) representation of the voices of the victims, or only written by those - like Sharif - whose personal or familial histories are marked by a direct engagement with military violence. Rather, it contends that drones are a historic development which demonstrate the limits of lyric as a technology for imagining and relating to those others whose suppression is part of the general economy in which poetry can be written.

OBJECT RELATIONS

The drone operator's target is called an Object, and given a code name, a carceral procedure which replaces the person's individuality with an institutional identity. Targeted killing is a kind of lethal retrospective interpellation: simply by virtue of being a military-age male, or having been killed, the object is convicted as a combatant. The targeting process also produces a legal innovation, in which war is regarded not as aggression against enemies as a corporate body but as individuals - putting 'warheads on foreheads'. Samuel Issacharoff and Richard Pildesi argue that this individuation of guilt makes targeted killing more like an extrajudicial execution or police action than an act of war. Whereas traditionally the enemy was defined:

> not because of any specific actions he himself engaged in, but because he was a member of an opposing army - we are instead now moving to a world which implicitly or explicitly requires *the individuation of personal responsibility* of specific 'enemy' persons before the use of military force is considered justified, at least as a moral and political matter.[33]

For this reason, the use of the AUMF (Authorisation for Use of Military Force) as a legal justification for continuing US drone attacks has been widely criticised.[34] Derek Gregory also notes the paradox that while the enemy is individuated, the targeters and drone operators retain the traditional corporate status (and anonymity) accorded by the nation-state which has declared war.[35] For victims of drone attacks, there is also no trace of accountability.[36] This lack of accountability is typical of the U.S'.s refusal to make reparations for war crimes or hold its service personnel accountable for their crimes or mistakes. It also means that victims and their families cannot prove their innocence, having been convicted retrospectively by the mere fact of being killed.

33. Samuel Issacharoff and Richard Pildesi, 'Drones and the Dilemma of Modern Warfare', in *Drones and the Promise of Law*, ed. Peter Bergen and Daniel Rothenberg, Cambridge, Cambridge University Press 2013, p388.

34. See for example: 'US, Reassess War Model Against Al Qaeda; Apply Human Rights Law to End "Perpetual War"', *Human Rights Watch* https://www.hrw.org/news/2013/07/31/us-reassess-war-model-against-al-qaeda

35. 'The Individuation of Warfare?', *Geographical Imaginations* blog, 26 August 2013 https://geographicalimaginations.com/2013/08/26/the-individuation-of-warfare

36. *The Civilian Impact of Drones, Unexamined Costs, Unanswered Questions*, Columbia Law School Human Rights Clinic and the Center for Civilians in Conflict, 2012, http://web.law.columbia.edu/sites/default/files/microsites/human-rights-institute/files/The%20Civilian%20Impact%20of%20Drones.pdf

The remoteness of areas where drones strike also inhibit reporting of their effects on people on the ground. The British Ministry of Defence argued that it could not estimate casualties 'because of the immense difficulty and risks that would be involved in collecting robust data' (*Drone Warfare*, p27).

No (news) organisation wants to spend money on tribal journalists, and these people are living in conflicted zones. There are meagre resources. These areas are informational black holes. This is *ilaqa ghair* [out-of-bounds territory].[37]

The informational black hole also recalls standard psychoanalytic theories of trauma. Drawing on Freud's account of war neurosis in *Beyond the Pleasure Principle*, Hochberg has argued that traumatic witnessing is felt as a gap or a hole in experience, in part because the traumatic event produces a momentary shutdown of the senses, especially the eyes.[38] She contends that trauma is innately scopic, but that 'the traumatised individual appears to be caught in a vicious cycle of repeated failed witnessing' and attempt to overcome the failure to see (*Trauma*, p142).

Alongside this traumatic gap in witnessing, the 'black hole' where victims' testimony (and viewers' empathy) should be mirrors an emptiness in the viewing subject (the drone operator). Practically, this viewer is invisible; but in Lacanian terms, he vanishes when he is looked back at by the objects of his own gaze. This viewing subject projects his disappearance onto the *ilaqa ghair*, decrees it a *terra nullius* inhabited only by criminals and their spectres. Describing the Afghan landscape from his 'God's-eye view' three hundred miles up, drone operator Lt. Col. Mark McCurley waxes poetic:

> Deep valleys cut through the region like unhealed wounds. Small settlements spotted the terraced slopes at odd intervals. Dirt roads snaked through and around the ruined landscape, providing the only means of contact with the villages.[39]

The valley is an untreated, unhealed body; the landscape becomes a Kleinian array of primitive experiences of death-dealing and libidinal desire. Its emptiness also conveys a perspective which cannot find value in pre-capitalist landscapes and their inhabitants. As Moqbel Abdullah Ali al-Jarraah, a villager from Silat al-Jarraah, where a January 23, 2013 U.S. airstrike hit a civilian house, observed: 'I believe that America is testing its lethal inventions in our poor villages, because [it] cannot afford to do so at any place where human life has value. Here, we are without value'.[40]

VISUALISING THE OTHER

At extreme distances, there is essentially
no such thing as depth of field. - Trevor Paglen

McCurley's description epitomises what Nicholas Mirzoeff has analysed as

---

37. Sarah Imtiaz, 'What Do Pakistanis Really Think About Drones?', *Drone Wars, Transforming Conflict, Law, and Policy*, Peter L. Bergen and Daniel Rothenberg (eds), Cambridge UP, 2015, 89-110, p102.

38. See also Ruth Leys, *Trauma: A Genealogy*, Chicago and London, University of Chicago Press, 2000. (Hereafter *Trauma*).

39. Lt. Col. T. Mark McCurley with Kevin Maurer, *Hunter Killer, Inside the World of Drone Warfare*, London, Allen & Unwin, 2016, p107. (Hereafter *Hunter Killer*).

40. *Death by Drone: Civilian Harm Caused by U. S. Targeted Killings in Yemen*, Open Society Justice Initiative, p7. https://www.opensocietyfoundations.org/sites/default/files/death-drones-report-eng-20150413.pdf. (Hereafter *Death by Drone*).

the regime of 'visuality', a term which relates to the heroic leader's capacity to 'visualise history to sustain autocratic authority'.[41] Visuality collapses the complexities of the battlefield into a single domain which can be mastered by the commander. This permits the operator to experience the work of surveillance as a form of divine detachment and omniscience. In actuality, drone visuality is undermined by limited bandwidth, interruptions and delays in satellite transmission, 'latency' (not Freudian *Nachträglichkeit* but the gap between real time and transmitted time), 'blinking' (when a drone needs to move and another one cannot replace it immediately), resource constraints, and the 'soda straw' effect (the drone camera's inability to visualise more than a small proportion of the total field).

Nasser Hussain, whose remarks on the silence of the drone's visual feed I cited earlier, describes the ethical consequences of drone visuality:

> The camera angle is always the same: the overhead shot. By definition, the overhead shot excludes the shot/reverse shot, the series of frontal angles and edits that make up face-to-face dialogue. With the overhead shot, there is no possibility of returning the gaze.[42]

Yet there is some evidence that the drone's panoptic visuality can be challenged. Tellingly, drone operators are trained to look for 'eyes' in the visual field, in order to find the places where improvised explosive devices have been buried:

> He saw an eye, a shape in the asphalt. "I knew the eye from the training," he says. To bury an improvised explosive device in the road, the enemy combatants place a tire on the road and burn it to soften the asphalt. Afterwards it looks like an eye from above.[43]

McCurley also writes about the uncanny realisation that 'the face of your enemy was staring back at you in high-definition' (*Hunter Killer*, p134). On one mission, 'The pixels on the screen sharpened and I could make out the folds in his clothes…. In the HUD, it seemed like he was looking right at us. His gaze was locked in the targeting pod for a brief moment before he ran' (pp130-1). He complains of the psychic costs of such moments of visual intimacy: 'our targeting pods not only showed us everything, but also lingered over the carnage, searing the images into our brains' (p134). However, he argues that drone operators 'didn't lack humanity' because they 'took those images home' (p135), transgressing the split between the theatre of operations and civilian life which is supposed to insulate them against anxiety.

SPLIT OPERATIONS AND CONTAINERISED PSYCHES

Drones enforce structures of splitting and compartmentalisation. On a

41. Nicholas Mirzoeff, *The Right to Look: A Counterhistory of Visuality*, Durham and London, Duke University Press, 2011, p3.

42. Nasser Hussain, 'The Sound of Terror, Phenomenology of a Drone Strike', *Boston Review*, 16 October 2013, https://bostonreview.net/world/hussain-drone-phenomenology.

43. Nicola Abé, 'Dreams in Infrared, The Woes of an American Drone Operator', *Der Spiegel* 14 Dec. 2012, http://www.spiegel.de/international/world/pain-continues-after-war-for-american-drone-pilot-a-872726-2.html.

practical level, flight control is managed through 'split operations', with local crews in places like Chabelley Air Field or Camp Lemonnier in Djibouti overseeing take-off and landing, before transferring flight control to remote bases, the most well-known of which is Creech Air Force base outside of Las Vegas, Nevada, where crews operate from small mobile units in modified shipping containers. There is also the splitting of the operator's presence which prosthetic violence entails. Gregoire Chamayou has explored the phenomenological implications of 'tele-presence', or working in two places at once:

> faced with mixed and overlapping experiences of presence that are both local and distant, their problem is to cope, in a coherent fashion, with the horizons of this experience of a mixed reality. They do not take one reality for the other but take the one together with and within the other. There is not so much confusion, but rather an embedding, a partial superimposition or a problematic interarticulation between the two. Their experience is not of being captured in a particular presence, but rather of having two presences, the one on top of the other.[44]

Chamayou suggests that this embedding is experienced by drone operators as a duplication of presence or self; but drone operators also repeatedly attest to the necessity of splitting as compensation for such doubling in their labour. Many pilots speak of the problem of rapidly crossing between their day-jobs at war and their home life.[45] One drone operator speaks of the 'strange sensation' of stepping out of the Ground Control Station and realising,

> 'Ok, I am not there'. I'll go meet my wife for lunch. I'll step out from doing a mission and go off to my child's soccer game. So, I am there and then I am not there and then I am there again, an adjustment which can take only ten minutes - 'it's really that fast'. 'How do you operate in two different worlds? You compartmentalise'. (*Drone Wars*, p117)

Splitting is thus not only an operational mechanism; it is also a psychic adaptation.

Without alleging any equality between these situations, I would note that compartmentalisation is also intrinsic to colonial occupation. Frantz Fanon describes the colonial world as a 'world divided into compartments', its zones for settler and native occupation strictly policed.[46] The difference is that soldiers can freely cross between military and civilian zones. At the same time, the very fact of drones overhead erases any distinction between military and civilian zones in whole areas such as the FATA between Afghanistan and Pakistan. The privilege of containing harm within a split-off part of the psyche, or splitting the geography of war and home, is not universal.

The military faces significant challenges in recruiting and retaining

44. Gregoire Chamayou, *Drone Theory*, London, Penguin, 2015, pp258-9, n. 23. (Hereafter *Drone Theory*).

45. Frantz Fanon, *The Wretched of the Earth*, trans. Constance Farrington, New York, Grove Press, 1963, pp38-9.

46. See for example Mary Manjikian, 'Becoming Unmanned: The Gendering of Lethal Autonomous Warfare Technology', *International Feminist Journal of Politics*, 16, 1, 2014, pp48-65.

drone operators, in part because remote operations are not considered as honourable as direct engagement in combat; drone pilots are even represented as 'castrated' fighter pilots.⁴⁶ The work's stresses include hours upon hours of unalleviated boredom, followed by momentary flashes of adrenaline.⁴⁷ They resemble what Sianne Ngai calls 'stuplimity': 'a state of emotional deficiency paradoxically invoked in tandem with the emotional excess of shock or intense astonishment', in which dysphoria mixes with dread or awe.⁴⁸ Increasingly, drone operators are said to be suffering from PTSD. Chamayou suggests that the risks of PTSD have been magnified in order to prove that this work is honourable because psychologically, if not physically, dangerous (*Drone Theory*, p107). It is on this basis that drone operators have lobbied for combat pay and bravery awards (*Kill Chain*, p7). Drone crews are also alleged to suffer from a controversial condition sometimes known as 'perpetrator's trauma', in which the person who commits a violent act suffers a 'moral injury' to their self-identity.⁴⁹

EVERYWHERE AND ALWAYS WARS

Drone operations also distort conventional notions of time and space. The AUMF offers no temporal or spatial limits on executive's ability to target suspected terrorists. Moreover, whereas criminal law adjudicates on past events, targeted killings are largely oriented toward the elimination of risk in the future. The White House has said that it will use lethal force 'only to prevent or stop attacks against U.S. persons' and 'only against a target that poses a continuing, imminent threat to U.S. persons'.⁵⁰ As John Brennan admitted, 'We are finding increasing recognition in the international community that a more flexible understanding of "imminence" may be appropriate when dealing with terrorist groups'.⁵³ This extension of imminence into perpetuity - the expansion of the now - is matched by a distention of the spatial boundaries which conventionally define the theatre of operations, into what Gregory calls an 'everywhere war'. Andrew Cockburn quotes General Joseph Votel, commander of JSOC, who admitted that 'Since we can no longer draw a box on a map and say that's where the problem is, we must be everywhere, in the sense that we must be able to find the threat anywhere on the planet' (*Kill Chain*, p247): necropolitics expanded to a zone unbounded in time or space.

Another spatial effect which has been developed by drone operations is the reconceptualisation of the traditional two-dimensional field of battle as a deterritorialised three-dimensional space of performance, a kill box, which corresponds to what Eyal Weitzman describes as the 'politics of verticality'.⁵¹ The kill box is a specific tactical concept. The military defines it as a 'joint terrain reference system that may be used as a tool to facilitate rapid attacks'.⁵² Its primary purpose 'is to allow lethal attack against surface targets without further coordination with the establishing commander and without terminal attack control' and to ensure 'maximum flexibility while preventing fratricide'.

47. Pratap Chatterjee, 'Our Drone War Burnout', *New York Times*, 14 July 2015: http://www.nytimes.com/2015/07/14/opinion/our-drone-war-burnout.html?ref=topics.

48. Sianne Ngai, *Ugly Feelings*, Cambridge and London, Harvard University Press, 2005, p268.

49. Jonathan Shay, 'Moral Injury', *Psychoanalytic Psychology*, 31.2, 2014, pp182-91.

50. 'Fact Sheet, U.S. Policy Standards and Procedures for the Use of Force in Counterterrorism Operations Outside the United States and Areas of Active Hostilities', Office of the Press Secretary, 23 May 2013. https://www.whitehouse.gov/the-press-office/2013/05/23/fact-sheet-us-policy-standards-and-procedures-use-force-counterterrorism.

51. Eyal Weitzman, 'The Politics of Verticality', *OpenDemocracy* https://www.opendemocracy.net/ecology-politicsverticality/article_801.jsp.

52. Maj. James W. MacGregor, *Bringing the Box into Doctrine: Joint Doctrine and the Kill Box*, School of Advanced Military Studies Monograph, 2004. http://www.dtic.mil/cgi-bin/GetTRDoc?AD=ADA429320 .

A kill box can be opened, activated, and closed without the restrictions of conventional warfare on engaging at 'fronts' or in legally delimited zones of conflict. Chamayou describes kill boxes as 'temporary lethal microcubes' which can be opened 'wherever an individual identified as a legitimate target has been located' (*Kill Chain*, p56). The body of the individual might itself become a kill box, he argues, a miniaturisation of the field of fire which is at the same time extended 'to take in whole world'.

INTIMATE OBJECTS

> mon désir est là sur quoi je tire
> (Apollinaire, 'Lueurs des Tirs', Calligrammes)

The perpetuity and expansion of the war on terror is admitted in the metaphor, used by many counterterrorism experts, which equates killing 'bad guys' to 'mowing the lawn'.[53] As a former CIA analyst told the *Washington Post*, 'The problem with the drone is it's like your lawn mower. You've got to mow the lawn all the time. The minute you stop mowing, the grass is going to grow back'.[54] This image of constant, instinctive killing helps to counteract the intense libidinal exchange between operators and the visualisation of their targets which seems to be a regular consequence of drone surveillance. Operators refer to 'Pred porn' or 'Pred crack', reflecting the addictive nature of viewing 'Kill TV', the large plasma screens on office walls where video footage of air strikes and raiding parties streams.[55] These screens are watched by many members of the command hierarchy; lowly operators can feel their performances being scrutinised by (and enjoyed) by the military's big Other.

Another consequence of the drone's distortion of spatiality is that, despite their enormous distances from their targets, many operators speak of the space between themselves and the object as miniscule - 18 inches, or the distance from face to screen. As Col. Pete Gersten told a reporter, 'You're 8000 miles away. What's the big deal? But it's not 8000 miles away. It's 18 inches away…'[56] This artificial intimacy produces a feeling of exciting risk, even though the operator is safely segregated from the scene of violence. McCurley describes watching the video feed and feeling 'like a voyeur peeking through the curtain into another pilot's cockpit' (*Hunter Killer*, p59). In his famous anecdote of the keyhole, Jean-Paul Sartre stresses how it is the moment of being discovered which produces the 'irruption of the self' in a consciousness which, in the act of pure looking, is both unconstrained and lost in the world.[57] The shame, judgement and threat represented by this look - the look that catches me in the act - produces myself as an object for others, and reveals the Other's freedom 'across the uneasy determination of the being which I am for him' (p262). The existential consequences of becoming the object of the Other's gaze may be addressed in the context of drone warfare through the diagnosis of PTSD, but as I'll argue presently, they also return in the

---

53. Mattathias Schwartz, 'Like a Mosquito', *LRB* 35.13, 4 July 2013, pp13-15, http://www.lrb.co.uk/v35/n13/mattathias-schwartz/like-a-mosquito.

54. Greg Miller, 'Plan for hunting terrorists signals U.S. intends to keep adding names to kill lists', *Washington Post*, 23 October 2012.

55. Richard Whittle, *Predator: The Secret Origins of the Drone Revolution*, New York, Henry Holt, 2014, p101.

56. Megan McCloskey, 'The War Room: Daily Transition between Battle, Home Takes a Toll on Drone Operators', *Stars and Stripes*, 27 Oct. 2009.

57. Jean Paul Sartre, *Being and Nothingness*, (trans) Hazel E. Barnes, London, Routledge, [1958] 1993, pp259-60.

mythological names given to operations.

While the money shots of target obliteration may be most exciting for viewers, for most of the time these screens reveal nothing more than the mundane details of distant existences. The long duration of these operations allows time for reflection and familiarity with the target to develop. For military commanders, intimacy with the target is not an ethical opportunity but an operational obstacle. As Col. Hernando Ortega, who conducted a study on drone pilot stress, told the *New York Times*, 'You might gain a level of familiarity [through constant watching] that makes it a little difficult to pull the trigger'.[58] One commander testified:

> Flying an RPA, you start to understand people in other countries based on their day-to-day patterns of life. A person wakes up, they do this, they greet their friends this way, etc. You become immersed in their life. You feel like you are a part of what they're doing every single day. So, even if you're not emotionally engaged with those individuals, you become a little bit attached. I have learned about Afghan culture this way (*Drone Wars* p116).

This pilot presumes that visuality conveys cultural understanding, and elides the top-down perspective of the drone camera with 'immersion' in local life. Operators also identify with their objects through the recognition of shared routines. They even witness the private sexual moments of their objects: one pilot described watching two heat signatures become one on his screen (*Dreams*).

The ambivalence of power achieved through invisible surveillance recalls Plato's fable of the ring of Gyges (*Drone Warfare*, pp109-12). As Rancière reminds us, Plato modifies the fable originally told by Herodotus: in that version, Gyges was a captain of the guard who was invited by a king to spy on his beautiful wife as she undressed (*Aesthetics*, p92). The wife revenged herself on her husband by seducing Gyges and arming him against the sovereign. In the case of drone operations, there is so far little evidence, unfortunately, that their intimacy with their objects will lead US military crews to rebellion. But the fear that intimate surveillance might destroy the viewer is implicit in the mythologisation of drones.

ARTEMIS AND THE MEDUSA

Like the ring of Gyges, drones convey an almost magical power and aggrandise the egos of those who operate them. In some cases the technological advantage they represent makes men think of themselves as gods. Operators call the laser used to guide ground and local air support to a target 'the light of God'. Former JSOC commander Gen. Stanley McChrystal observed that victims are 'being shot at like thunderbolts from the sky by an entity that is acting as though they have omniscience and omnipotence' (*Death by Drone*, p7).

58. Elisabeth Bumiller, 'A Day Job Waiting for a Kill Shot a World Away', *New York Times*, 29 July 2012.

Another pilot described himself as a quasi-divine figure:

> I *knew* people down there. Each day through my camera I snooped around and came to recognise the faces and figures of our soldiers and marines, unbeknownst to most of them... I truly felt a bit like an omnipotent god with a god's seat above it all.[59]

Complementing the self-proclaimed divinity of drone visuality, the military has consistently drawn on mythology to advertise its technical innovations. An early precedent for drone warfare was Project Aphrodite, 'a scheme to fly remote-controlled B24 bombers packed with explosives into German submarine pens' during World War Two (*Kill Chain*, p24). The name invokes the goddess of love, who is trapped by her husband - the god of technology - in a net, while she trysts with Ares, the god of war.

Another myth which is well suited to the iconography of drone warfare is that of Actaeon and Diana. Artemis is a favoured icon for developers: there is the Artemis Drone Worx Project, 'a conglomeration of two Corporations who want to make a difference' who have developed aviation technology for the US Army, Air Force and Marines and the Ministry of the Interior of Saudi Arabia;[60] Airbus's Shadow M2 drone was rebaptised 'Artemis' when it was sold to the French military;[61] and there are various personal and agricultural drones also by that name. According to J-P Vernant, the myth of Artemis was invoked in initiation rituals which patrolled the boundaries between civic territory and wild or uncultivated lands.[62] The myth has powerful resonances with drone operations: Actaeon's secret surveillance of the goddess leads to his transformation into an animal which can be hunted down and destroyed; Artemis patrols the boundaries between the American imperium and the *ilaqa ghair*. Drone warfare is explicitly described as a form of hunting: in 2004 the US Air Force's commissioned new 'hunter/killer remotely operated aircraft' - terms adopted and still used today for its unmanned aerial systems programme.[63] Hunting is also implicit in an aide's disturbing comment about Obama, who oversaw two drone strikes just days after his inauguration: 'He's been blooded, just like you would a hunting dog' (*Kill Chain*, p225).

However, whereas in the myth it is the voyeur who is transformed into an animal and hunted down by the female goddess, drone mythology justifies watching *and* reclaims hunting as a masculine prerogative. It is the seductive other, simultaneously desired and castrated by the phallic aggression of the drone, who is destroyed by the gaze, not the viewer. Drone hunting also has the asymmetrical character of colonial warfare in which, Mbembe argues, '*savage life* is just another form of *animal life*, a horrifying experience, something alien beyond imagination or comprehension' (p24). Drone victims are referred to as 'slants', bugs ('bugsplat'; 'It really is like swatting flies. We can do it forever easily and you feel nothing'[64]; 'they infest urban areas and hide among the civilian populations' [cited in *Kill Chain*, p170]), and rats (*Predator*, p49). This

59. Matt J. Martin with Charles W. Sasser, *Predator, The Remote-Control Air War over Iraq and Afghanistan, A Pilot's Story*, Minneapolis, Zenith, 2010, p121.

60. http://www.artemisdroneworx.com/about.html.

61. http://forcesoperations.com/en/frances-sdt-programme-update/

62. J-P Vernant, 'Death in the Eyes' and 'In the Mirror of Medusa', 1985, trans. Thomas Curley and Froma I. Zeitlin, *The Medusa Reader*, ed. Marjorie Garber and Nancy Vickers, New York and London, Routledge, 2003, p211. (Hereafter *Medusa Reader*).

63. Rich Tuttle, 'Fleet of "hunter/killer" planes would see initial use in FY '07', Aerospace Daily & Defense Report, *Aviation Week*, 29 Jul 2004

64. Micah Zenko, 'Institutionalising America's Targeted Killing Program', *Council on Foreign Relations* blog, 24 October 2012, http://blogs.cfr.org/zenko/2012/10/24/institutionalizing-americas-targeted-killing-program/

military demotic also works to undercut the intimacy with the object which is an operational risk of drone surveillance.

The Medusa is another scopic myth which has been invoked by a high-profile drone project. Gorgon's Stare is a system of long-durational drone surveillance designed to overcome the problems of 'blinking'. It promises comprehensive coverage of entire towns (though early tests have not been promising), constructing a panopticon in which 'there will be no way for the adversary to know what we're looking at, and we can see everything'.[65] The Medusa, the only mortal sister among the Gorgons, turned people to stone with her gaze, and was defeated by Perseus who only looked at her through a reflection in his shield. Vernant contrasts the Gorgon with Artemis. While Artemis is a figure who presides over the horizontal boundaries of the wild and the cultivated, the Gorgon incarnates an opposing form of alterity which 'operates according to a *vertical* axis' (emphasis mine) within the city and 'wrenches humans away from their lives and themselves, [...] to cast them down into the confusion and horror of chaos' (*Medusa Reader*, p211). Noting that the Gorgon is always depicted frontally, Vernant argues that confronting the power of death which she represents entails a risk of becoming fascinated: 'To see the Gorgon is to look her in the eyes and, in the exchange of gazes, to cease to be oneself, a living being, and to become like her, a Power of death' (p220). This mythic reading of the 'violent separation from the self' initiated by a face-to-face confrontation with radical alterity which produces 'an utter disorientation in the midst of intimacy and contact' is also a consequence of drone operations, in which the operator becomes part of a prosthesis of death.

Freud famously interpreted the Medusa as a castrating figure whose face and snaky locks represented the female genitals. It was an interpretation he owed to Ferenczi, who argued that the serpents signified the absence of the penis (castration), and the 'fearful and alarming staring eyes of the Medusa head have also the secondary meaning of erection'.[66] Within the Oedipal dynamic, Freud argues, a glimpse of the maternal genitals turns the boy to stone - either paralysing him or eliciting an erection. Freud describes the erection as a 'consolation', an emblem of defiance which assures the spectator that 'he is still in possession of a penis'. To look at the Gorgon is to be petrified, but petrification in Freud's reading is not destruction, but rather the defiant assertion of masculinity. Of course, in the myth Perseus is not castrated, but triumphs over the Medusa by decapitating her. The boy's Oedipal violence and castration anxiety conclude with the splitting not of his psyche but of her body from her head, which the hero then weaponises.

Freud's reading of the Gorgon, despites its disturbing characterisation of the female genitals as horrifying (and its ludicrous erectile defiance), readily suits the drone contexts I have set out: the ambivalence of scopophilia, the fear that prosthetic violence implies a kind of castration, the libidinal attachment to the object of the gaze and the need to reassert a violent

65. Ellen Nakashima and Craig Whitlock, 'With Air Force's Gorgon Drone 'we can see everything', *Washington Post* 2 January 2011: http://www.washingtonpost.com/wp-dyn/content/article/2011/01/01/AR2011010102690.html

66. Sigmund Freud, 'Medusa's Head', *Writings on Art and Literature*, in *The Standard Edition of the Complete Psychological Works of Sigmund Freud*, ed. James Strachey, Stanford, Stanford University Press, 1997, pp264-5. (Hereafter *Medusa*).

phallic dominance of that object. But its scopic elements require further elaboration. Drawing on Merleau-Ponty and Callois' *Meduse et compagnie*, Lacan distinguishes between the eye and the gaze.[67] Like Freud, Lacan notes that the Medusa's face was taken as an apotropaic symbol of conquest to cover the shield, deflecting blows and gazes from 'the eye filled with voracity, the evil eye'.[68] In typically Hegelian terms (but also drawing on Sartre's keyhole paradigm), he also depicts the dialectic of lordship and bondage as a visual contest, in which the struggle produces recognition of those aspects of the self which are materialised in the other, or those aspects of the other which are introjected into the self. Lacan argues that 'in the scopic field, everything is articulated between two terms that act in an antinomic way—on the side of things, there is the gaze, that is to say, things look at me, and yet I see them' (*Four*, p109). In these late essays Lacan returns to the grounds of his theory of the mirror stage, but emphasises the importance of the gaze which institutes us as 'beings that are looked at' (p75), by another, but also by the big Other and things. This gaze paradoxically entails not the creation of the subject, but his disappearance: 'From the moment that this gaze appears, the subject tries to adapt himself to it, he becomes that punctiform object, that point of vanishing being with which the subject confuses his own failure' (p83). Vanishing is not a consolation, but the initiation of the subject into the Symbolic as a castrated object, driven by desire for the *objet a*, the lack which constitutes him. Thus the gaze reproduces the split in the subject, drawing him into a violent visual conflict which for Lacan is signified by the evil eye, 'that which has the effect of arresting movement and, literally, of killing life' (p118).

In terms of this discussion, the fear of castration which many drone pilots associate with the loss of their status as fighters (and the potential struggle to the death of combat missions) is already implicit in their act of viewing - and being viewed by the military big Other, on Kill TV. Drone surveillance is a literalisation of the evil eye, the gaze which kills. It splits the subject into a person attempting to live honourably at home, and an operator of prosthetic violence abroad. He dwells simultaneously in two worlds: the world of the local military order, and the distant landscape peopled by pure aggression and desire. At the same time, the attempt to know the target through visual surveillance produces a false intimacy from which the object - the Afghani, Yemeni, or Pakistani person targeted, often for arbitrary reasons - constantly disappears, either through their inaccessibility as witness to their own trauma, or their obliteration by a Hellfire missile.

CONCLUSION: DRONE POETICS

The six phenomenological particularities of drone operations which I have drawn out are intended to prompt a consideration of what the new cynegetic and carceral technology of the drone reveals about the committed lyric. They

67. An account of these topics is given in Martin Jay, *Downcast Eyes: The Denigration of Vision in Twentieth-Century Thought*, Berkeley and Los Angeles, University of California Press, 1993, pp329-70.

68. Jacques Lacan, *The Four Fundamental Concepts of Psycho-Analysis*, ed. Jacques-Alain Miller, (trans) Alan Sheridan, London, Penguin, 1977, p115. (Hereafter *Four*).

urge us to confront the possibility that our lyric poems are kill boxes: mobile spaces of predation in which relations of intimate force can be arbitrarily established while ensuring minimal damage to other friendlies; miniaturised states of exception which can be opened and closed at will. Lyric gives the impression that it can collapse spatial and temporal distances. The lyric allows us to zoom in on opportunistically selected objects from the safe containers of a 'radical' aesthetic. This liberatory power is both real, and a part of an economy of globalised domination by those nations which, according to Hegel, have achieved a certain stage of historical development, freeing their poets to 'accept the principle of particularisation and individualisation'.[69] Particularisation and individualisation are not just basic human rights, but also tactical concepts imposed on people who have the misfortune to become military 'Objects'. If we take our individuation for granted, we might reflect on how sheltering in the corporate identity of 'poetry' prevents us from being held accountable for how we use these objects. But the targets on which we alight in order to write our poems are not accidental and arbitrarily chosen, or rather, the right accidentally to choose an object is not arbitrary. If committed lyric attempts to make its critiques of capitalism and militarisation through the appropriation of objects who cannot see us, and who cannot assert their own identity against our projections of poetic power, then the relation we are establishing is not one of commonality but of domination.

Drone poetics tricks us into believing that we are omniscient beings, diviners, foreseers, and prophets, freely ranging within the zodiac of our own wits. It transgresses the conventional boundaries of space and time, filling history with the imminence of its 'now' and mapping every terrain as an opportunity for intervention. It presumes that a top-down perspective allows us to know everything: foreign cultures, personal interactions, internal spaces, and the whole of the past, present and future. At the same time, it privileges the notions of intimacy, immersion in daily life and erotic attachment so intensely that it projects these subjective experiences deep into spaces with which it has no actual familiarity. This is a regime of visuality, not immersion. From the ground, the drone is experienced not as an intimate participant in social life, but as a constant noise.

In military, pornographic or poetic contexts, the fantasy that we dominate the objects of our gaze actually recoils against us, revealing the emptiness or petrification of our subject positions. That recoil is existential and operational: a consequence of 'blinking', the failure to gather testimony, the latency of signal and trauma, and the capacity of the object to look at and derange the viewer. But these limits to the hypervisibility of the subaltern should also encompass what Édouard Glissant refers to as the 'right to opacity', 'the opacity of the diverse animating the imagined transparency of Relation'.[70] Transgressing against that right in the interests of a critique of capitalism or imperialism, the committed lyric produces its universalism by risking contributing to a regime which recognises others not as political

69. G. W. F. Hegel, *Hegel's Aesthetics: Lectures on Fine Art*, (trans) T. M. Knox, 2 vols., Oxford, Clarendon, 1975 [1988], vol. 2, p1132.

70. Édouard Glissant, *Poetics of Relation*, (trans) Betsy Wing, Ann Arbor, University of Michigan Press, 1997, pp190, 192.

agents but as beings whose mouths only emit cries of pain (and so whose sounds will benefit from being translated into the language of the poem). Attempts to co-ordinate our lamentations only at the level of content, while using forms of observance and address which reproduce the I-thou structure in which lyric has historically held its objects as erotic others whose absence or silence enables the production of the poem, of course do nothing to derange that regime.

Drone visuality interpellates its objects as criminals and animals in order to destroy them, and to hold at bay the fear that this regime of surveillance and domination also threatens to destroy the viewer the minute we stop 'mowing the lawn': or at the very least, that the little hole in the eye shows more than the fused heat signatures of others, that it 'Has exposed us naked / To the world', as one Grumman employee wrote.[71] This threat of destruction or castration urges us to obliterate the other before he can turn us to stone. But apart from a capacity to empathise, it is only the fact of this perpetual ability to destroy which tells us that we are not already ossified. We fear that our poems are nothing more than epitaphs. Finally the lyric poet who claims a heroic capacity to confront the gods of militarisation must recognise her empathy for the other also includes her symmetry with the power of death. The best she can do is not to attempt to police the boundary of civility and wilderness, but to demonstrate the confusion and horror which permeates her own city, a reality which the exercise of prosthetic violence brings out of virtuality into proximity and which contradicts the imperialist ideology which seeks to compartmentalise geographies and psyches, or to contain them in lethal boxes.

Andrea Brady is Professor of Modern and Contemporary Poetry at Queen Mary University of London. Her publications include *English Funerary Elegy in the Seventeenth Century* (Palgrave Macmillan, 2006), *The Uses of the Future in Early Modern Europe* (co-edited with Emily Butterworth, Routledge, 2009), and several books of poetry, including *Cut from the Rushes* (Reality Street, 2013), *Mutability: Scripts for Infancy* (Seagull, 2012), and *Wildfire: A Verse Essay on Obscurity and Illumination* (Krupskaya, 2010), as well as many articles on early modern and contemporary poetry, especially ritual, the intersection between poetry and politics, mourning, and women's writing.

---

71. George Oppen, *New Collected Poems*, Michael Davidson (ed.), New York, New Directions 2002, p101.

Dying for Sex: Cultural and Forensic Narratives of Autoerotic Death

Lisa Downing

Abstract This article explores representations of autoerotic death in a range of discursive fields: the media, forensic pathology, the psy sciences, literary fiction, and internet humour. It adopts a broadly Foucauldian approach to the study of the topic; i.e., rather than interrogating what sexual practices leading to autoerotic death *mean*, or what motivates people to experiment with these 'extreme' practices, it explores instead what attitudes towards autoerotic death tell us about normative cultural understandings of sexuality and gender. The article interrogates the ways in which gender norms and roles are at play in the apprehension of autoerotic fatalities, marking some of the men who die in this way as effeminate, failed men; while others are represented as hypermasculine misadventurers. It also discusses why the rare female autoerotic fatality troubles assumptions about the nature and role of women. The biases guiding definitions of 'normal' and 'abnormal' sexuality and gender are thus revealed in particularly striking ways by moving the focus of interrogation away from the pathologised practices and the bodies they produce, and onto the discourses that pronounce about them.

Keywords autoerotic death, erotic asphyxiation, gender, sexuality, perversion, Foucault

---

> Vladimir: What do we do now?
> Estragon: Wait.
> Vladimir: Yes, but while waiting.
> Estragon: What about hanging ourselves?
> Vladimir: Hmm. It'd give us an erection.
> Estragon: (highly excited) An erection! [...] Let's hang ourselves immediately!
>   Samuel Beckett, *Waiting for Godot*

> It has been my experience that people learning of erotic asphyxia and autoerotic fatalities through a lecture or reading respond with initial disbelief and, as belief takes hold, wonder how it is that there could be such an aspect of human behaviour that they had previously not known.
>   Park Elliot Dietz, 'Recurrent Discovery of Autoerotic Asphyxia'

The practice of erotic asphyxiation (oxygen deprivation leading to heightened sexual arousal, with the concomitant potential of resulting death) has a history of being described and depicted as an example of the most irrational and bizarre manifestation of non-normative human sexuality. This may account for Beckett's decision to have Estragon suggest it as means of killing time whilst 'waiting for Godot' in his absurdist classic of that name, from 1954, cited above. And, relatedly, novelist of excess William Burroughs's *Naked Lunch* (1959) and *Cities of the Red Night* (1981) contain so many descriptions of eroticised hangings that one critic, in a review entitled 'Pleasures of Hanging', described them as displays of Burroughs's 'curious id capering and making faces and confessing to bizarre inclinations'.[1] Indeed, the word 'bizarre' features so frequently as a descriptor of these practices in texts of all kinds that it becomes something of a *cliché*. For example, in a paper on 'erotized repetitive hangings', Resnik writes: 'although they are bizarre, these deaths are not medical rarities or forensic curiosities';[2] while another medical doctor and criminologist, Cordner, describes the conditions of autoerotic death as being of a 'bizarre nature'.[3] The terms used by medical professionals to describe the phenomenon differ in no appreciable measure from the lexicon chosen by journalists and headline-writers. Reporting in 1994 on the autoerotic fatality of Stephen Milligan, the UK Tory MP and Parliamentary Private Secretary to Jonathan Aitken, headlines proclaimed: 'Bizarre death of Lawmaker Shakes Tories' (*Los Angeles Times*, USA, 9 Feb 1994) and 'MP's bizarre death jolts Tories: Body of rising star discovered dressed only in stockings and suspenders' (*The Independent*, UK, 8 Feb 1994). Incredulity, the distancing of the writer from the practice/practitioners, and an insistence on the 'otherness' of autoerotic death characterise all the above examples.

In this article, I will explore representations of erotic asphyxiation and erotic fatalities taken from a range of discursive fields including forensic pathology, the psy sciences, media coverage of celebrity deaths, humorous internet 'ecards', and, finally, literary fiction in the form of a reading of the novel *Breath* (2008) by Tim Winton. *Breath* offers a rare depiction of a female practitioner of erotic asphyxiation, allowing me to evaluate how gender norms and expectations shape cultural understandings of this practice. Given the relative shortage of forensic accounts of female erotic fatalities in comparison to cases of males, the use of a work of imaginative literature is justified. In each case, my analysis of these cultural products will aim to ask what assumptions have to be in place about the nature of 'normal' sexuality, and also about gendered behaviour, to account for the repeated characterisation of this sexual practice as 'bizarre' and as so other to comprehensibility.

In examining diverse discursive representations of this bodily practice, a broadly Foucauldian approach to the history and theory of sexuality and biopolitics will be adopted. Foucault pointed out in 1976, in the first volume of the *History of Sexuality*, that sexuality is not an ahistorical or natural phenomenon. Rather, it describes a field of knowledge and interpretation that could only be produced thanks to the influence and historical coincidence of the medico-legal institutions that gained traction as shapers of meaning in the

1. T. M. Disch, 'Pleasures of Hanging', book review, *New York Times*, March 15, 1981, 14-15, p15.

2. H. L. P. Resnik, 'Erotized Repetitive Hangings: A Form of Self-Destructive Behavior', *American Journal of Psychotherapy*, vol. 26, 1972, 4-21, p4. (Hereafter *Eroticized Repetitive Hangings*.)

3. S. M. Cordner, 'An Unusual Case of Sudden Death Associated with Masturbation', *Medicine, Science and the Law*, vol 23, no. 1, 1983, 54-56, p56.

modern West, finding their apotheosis in the mid-to-late nineteenth century. Within this epistemological framework 'kinds' of sexual practice were named and classified, to be understood as natural or unnatural, normal or abnormal, according to the workings of normative power. The personages of the 'sexual pervert' and the 'homosexual' were simultaneously produced as categories to describe modern individuals whose sexual practices were understood in sexology - and especially psychoanalysis - not simply as bodily acts, but as clues to reading the essential identity or ontology of the practitioner. This is what Foucault describes as a 'specification of individuals'.[4]

It is with this history of the naming and categorising of sexuality and sexual subjects in mind, that I turn to the topic of erotic asphyxiation and autoerotic death. Rather than interrogating what sexual practices leading to autoerotic death may say about the practitioner, or identifying factors that might psychologically motivate people to experiment with these 'extreme' death-risking practices, in what follows I will explore instead how looking at discourses produced about erotic asphyxiation and autoerotic death, sexual modalities that lie on the margins of comprehension and acceptability, might elucidate precisely how cultural norms of sexuality and gender more generally are established and inscribed. The assumptions and biases guiding definitions of normal and abnormal sexuality are revealed in particularly striking ways by moving the focus of interrogation away from the pathologised practices and the bodies that they produce and are produced by, and onto the interests of those who pronounce on normal and abnormal sexuality, according to the Foucauldian logic that classifying sex is a matter of the exercise of (normalising rather than interdictive) power. Finally, the analysis will reveal the extent to which media, fiction, the internet, and popular culture, along with the more readily recognised 'authority discourses' of sexual science and the medico-legal institutions, are complicit in contributing to the creation of sexual norms and drawing limits regarding acceptable and unacceptable degrees of risk of bodily harm, which are in line with normative socio-cultural agendas. In using erotic asphyxiation as a limit case of the workings of normativity, I reveal the extent to which the Foucauldian method is pertinent still today for thinking about cultural expectations as a form of power. Secondly, I extend beyond the remit of Foucault's own work by considering the precise interaction between gender norms and sexual norms in the example of this limit case, where the former are often minimised or ignored in Foucault's somewhat male-centric works.

Throughout, I will use the deliberately broad term 'erotic asphyxiation' to encompass a number of disparate bodily practices whereby the practitioner is deprived of oxygen for erotic pleasure (usually in a solitary, autoerotic setting, but sometimes with a partner). This umbrella term is deliberately intended to be descriptive and non-judgmental and to encompass the variations in practice and context reported in the literature (from manual or ligature-based strangulation, through suffocation, hanging, and the use of chemicals

4. Michel Foucault, *The Will to Knowledge, The History of Sexuality 1*, (trans) Robert Hurley, Harmondsworth, Penguin 1990, pp.42-3.

such as aerosol propellants). In cases where a solo practitioner of asphyxia dies, the phenomenon is usually described as an 'autoerotic fatality'; whereas a person who dies as a result of a partnered or group activity of this kind would be an 'erotic fatality'. Those are the terms I shall use here. There is relatively little existing literature on (auto)erotic asphyxiation, erotic fatalities, and autoerotic fatalities. In particular, with a few notable exceptions, there is a dearth of cultural, humanities-based scholarship that explores the social and gender-political implications of the practices and deaths; such that this article may provide a cultural analytical paradigm for further work of this kind.[5] Existing works on erotic asphyxiation tend instead to issue from the fields of abnormal psychology and other psy science perspectives. In the case of autoerotic fatalities, most work comes from the discipline of forensic pathology, notably Hazelwood, Dietz and Burgess's massive tome, *Autoerotic Fatalities* (1983), often considered the key forensic pathology text of fatal erotic asphyxiation, which I will discuss below.[6]

The broad association between hanging and ecstasy, on which Beckett has Vladimir and Estragon draw in the epigraph to this article, has a long history that pre-dates the eighteenth and nineteenth-century sexological fashion for naming 'the perversions'. It is instructive to note how this history is treated by Dietz, who provides a chapter for *Autoerotic Fatalities* (from which I drew for the second epigraph of this article) that sets out to chart the chronology of reported practices of self-asphyxiation. He comments on the existence of found Mayan artefacts that bear witness to this link, including a stone sculpture of a naked man with a rope around his neck and an erect penis, found in Mexico City and believed to originate from the late classic (c. 250-900 AD) or early post-classic (c. 950-1539 AD) period. According to the religious belief system of the Maya, 'the souls of individuals who hang themselves go directly to paradise, where they are received by Ixtab, Goddess of the hanged' (*Autoerotic Fatalities*, p14). Dietz goes on: 'Whether the ancient Maya had discovered autoerotic asphyxia, as the sculpture so strongly suggests, will perhaps never be known with certainty' (p14). The set of assumptions underlying the forensic author's pondering is telling, and illustrates neatly the problem that the current article sets out to explore. The contention that a people with a wholly different way of understanding bodily practices, and lacking the modern classificatory system of sexuality with which we are familiar, might have 'discovered' erotic asphyxiation per se makes no sense if we adopt a framework that understands sexual practices, acts, and identities, not only as culturally and historically situated, but as gaining their meaning and status as a *direct result* of dominant local epistemic conditions. Seemingly identical behaviours can thereby 'mean' radically different things according to cultural and historical context. What was considered sexually deviant in Vienna in 1890 may have been understood as divinely mystic in Chichen Itza in 950 AD. So, it is because of the predominance of the classificatory model of sexual knowledge, as described by Foucault, in the modern Western episteme,

5. Exceptions include my own previously published works on erotic asphyxiation: Lisa Downing and Dany Nobus, 'The Iconography of Asphyxiophilia: From Fantasmatic Fetish to Forensic Fact', *Paragraph*, 27(3) (2004): 1-15 and Lisa Downing, 'Beyond Safety: Erotic Asphyxiation and the Limits of S/M Discourse' from *Safe, Sane and Consensual: Contemporary Perspectives on Sadomasochism*, Darren Langridge and Meg Barker (eds), Basingstoke, Palgrave Macmillan, 2007, pp119-32. Another exception is a recent article on celebrity autoerotic fatalities, on which I will draw in this article: Darren Kerr and Donna Peberdy, 'Playing with the Self: Celebrity Autoerotic Asphyxiation', *Celebrity Studies*, 4(1) (2013), pp58-70 (Hereafter *Playing with the Self*).

6. Robert H. Hazelwood, Park Elliott Dietz and Ann Wolbert Burgess, *Autoerotic Fatalities*, Lexington, Massachusetts and Toronto: Lexington Books 1983. (Hereafter *Autoerotic Fatalities*).

that voluntary self-asphyxiation is understood as a sexual perversion rather than, for example, as a spiritual practice. The ancient Mayans simply could not 'discover' something that had yet to be discursively constructed.

In fact, history tells us precisely *when* the practice was written into modern medico-legal discourse *as a sexual perversion*. This occurred at the end of the eighteenth century, with the case of the Czech composer František Koczwara (frequently anglicised to Francis Kotzwarra). In 1791, Kotzwarra employed the services of a prostitute, Susannah Hill, whom he instructed to have intercourse with him while a noose was placed around his neck and attached to a door handle, in order that he could strain against it and experience the heightened effects of asphyxiation. When the act of sexual intercourse was completed, Kotzwarra was found to be deceased and Hill was put on trial for his murder. Ultimately, she was found guilty of the lesser crime of accidental manslaughter and was released. The anonymous pamphlet, *Modern Propensities, or, An Essay on the Art of Strangling*, which includes excerpts from the trial transcript and Hill's own memoir, helped to inscribe the case - and the sexual practice - in the public consciousness.[7] Dietz discusses this case in a chronological, but historically un-nuanced, way; that is he treats it as if it is part of a seamless trajectory both with the producers and consumers of the Mayan artefact described above and with cases of autoerotic fatality described by pathologists and psychiatrists in the late-twentieth century. However, Dietz himself is a player in the discursive process of the production of modern sexuality as a system of classification. In a 1978 paper,[8] he had proposed the adoption of the term 'Kotzwarraism' for the practice of erotic asphyxiation (following the model set down by Richard von Krafft-Ebing in naming 'sadism' after the Marquis de Sade and 'masochism' after Leopold von Sacher-Masoch). In fact, Dietz's suggestion was not much taken up in psychiatry and sexology, since sexologist John Money's coining 'asphyxiophilia' would instead be used in the American Psychiatric Association's *Diagnostic and Statistical Manual of Mental Disorders* in the early 1980s.[9]

One of the most striking features of discourses of erotic asphyxiation, which separates it from the way in which other sexual perversions are discussed in historical and contemporary psy science literature, is that most of the information and commonly-circulating ideas about it have been drawn from the evidence of death scenes, rather than from the reports of living practitioners as told to doctors, psychoanalysts, or sexologists. It is featured most commonly in case studies in journals and manuals of forensic pathology, such as the one discussed above, or as news stories when celebrity deaths are at stake. This means that estimates of the frequency of the practice (among those who do not die from it) are likely to be partial and skewed.

In a psychoanalytic paper of 1997 about autoerotic asphyxiation, Julien Quackelbeen, Dany Nobus and Karin Temmerman write:

> In our opinion, the 'uncommonness' that is often ascribed to such cases

7. Anonymous, *Modern propensities, or, An essay on the art of strangling, &c.: illustrated with several anecdotes: with memoirs of Susannah Hill, and a summary of her trial at the Old-Bailey, on Friday, September 16, 1791, on the charge of hanging Francis Kotzwarra, at her lodgings in Vine Street, on September 2*, London, J. Dawson, nd (Hereafter *Modern Propensities*).

8. Park Dietz, 'Kotzwarraism: Sexual Induction of Cerebral Hypoxia', Medical Criminological Research Center, McLean Hospital, Belmont, Massachusetts, unpublished ms, 1978.

9. See Lisa Downing, Iain Morland and Nikki Sullivan, *Fuckology: Critical Essays on John Money's Diagnostic Concepts*, Chicago, University of Chicago Press 2015, p46.

refers to their clandestinity, i.e, to the rareness with which they come to the attention of medical practitioners, sexologists, rather than to the low frequency of AEA [autoerotic asphyxiation] itself.[10]

10. Julien Quackelbeen, Dany Nobus and Karin Temmerman, 'Autoerotic Asphyxiation: A Sexual Praxis in Neurosis and Perversion', *Clinical Studies: International Journal of Psychoanalysis*, 3(1) (1997): pp31-54, p31.

Two reasons these authors suggest to explain the scarcity of self-reporting are that: 'manifestations of [abnormal] human sexuality do not de facto lead to a demand for help' and 'relatives of those who died from autoerotic asphyxiation, in refusing the disgrace, do the utmost to have the case recognised and registered as suicide' (p31). This points up that the 'sexually sick' may not themselves suffer at all from their 'sickness', however, they may go to great lengths to preserve their secret (in order to be able to keep practising their preferred sexual act without interference, or to protect loved ones from shock and shame). That the relatives of those who are involved in, or die from, erotic asphyxiation practices, should feel primarily *shame* tells a story of the normalising power of discourses about sex in society. It tells that sexuality is a very serious game with rules, and that those who die in this way are deemed to have *failed* at sex, at successful sexual subjectivity, and, ultimately, at life. A pervasive set of modern beliefs shore up the ideology of what sexuality *is* and *is for*.

In her classic essay on the politics of sex, 'Thinking Sex' (1984), Gayle Rubin argued that 'popular culture is permeated with ideas that erotic variety is dangerous, unhealthy, depraved, and a menace to everything from small children to national security'.[11] Her diagram of 'The sex hierarchy: the charmed circle vs. the outer limits' illustrates this point by showing how sex that is 'heterosexual', 'procreative', 'coupled', 'married', or 'vanilla' is placed closest to the centre of the circle, whilst sex that is 'non-procreative' and carried out 'alone or in groups', as well as being 'homosexual' or 'S/M', are found at the outer limits (p13). A fatal autoerotic practice is, logically, the furthest from the healthy ideal of sex that one could imagine in this model of social norms. This is because it *literalises*, and thereby lends credence to, the cultural fantasy of non-reproductive sex as socially dangerous, as spelling the decline of morality and the death of the natural order, that Rubin identifies in her essay. In turn, assumptions about the nature of sexuality rely on notions of the stability of binary sex and of masculinity and femininity as adducible attributes of maleness and femaleness. Our contemporary cultural understanding of gender is key to the ways in which narratives of erotic asphyxiation and autoerotic death are deployed and interpreted.

11. Gayle Rubin, 'Thinking Sex: Notes for a Radical Theory of the Politics of Sexuality', in Henry Abelove and Michele Aina Barale (ed), *The Lesbian and Gay Studies Reader*, New York & London, Routledge 1993, pp3-43, p12.

One of the major available sources of such narratives, given the perceived scarcity of clinical information about these practices, as attested to by Temmerman et al, is media reporting on high-profile autoerotic fatalities. In their recent article 'Playing with the Self', Darren Kerr and Donna Perbedy have explored how three reported cases of celebrity fatalities from the past few decades (either ruled by coroners to be the result of erotic asphyxiation, or strongly suspected of so being despite official rulings) reveal considerable differences between the pre-mortem reputations of these men's personae. Stephen Milligan, whose case from 1994 I referenced at the start of this article, died as a result of an act of erotic asphyxiation, while cross-dressed and with an amyl-nitrate-injected orange segment in his mouth. He had been respected as a financial talent and hailed as one of the 'rising stars' of John Major's Tory government, such that the manner of his death constituted a shaming for both the individual and his political party. By contrast, Australian singer Michael Hutchence, who hanged himself in 1997, was associated in life with a strong sex drive, 'rock 'n' roll' extravagance, and a taste for extreme experiences (as seen in the nickname given to him by one journalist: 'Mr Sexcess').[12] Widespread disbelief among Hutchence's family, friends and fans followed news that the verdict of suicide, rather than of death by misadventure, had been returned by the coroner.[13] Thirdly, cult actor David Carradine, star of *Kung Fu* and later of Quentin Tarantino's film trilogy *Kill Bill*, enjoyed a star persona that depicted him as an eccentric personality, obsessed with risk and danger and who liked to keep a loaded gun by his side at all times. He died of accidental (i.e. erotic) asphyxiation in 2009. Kerr and Perbedy detail how, following the death of a high-profile individual by autoerotic asphyxiation, it is common for reporters to try to find augurs of the practitioner-victim's endings in the evidence of their lives. This is a phenomenon that is explicable in terms of Foucault's premise that, in modernity, an individual's sexuality is seen as revelatory of the very essence of their identity; it is a secret that needs to be uncovered. Thus the celebrity is retroactively constructed in light of their death by erotic asphyxiation as shamed and unmanly (Milligan), as thrill-seeking (Hutchence), or as just plain strange (Carradine).

From these brief sketches, it is straight away noticeable that at least two distinct and apparently contradictory stories about Western masculinity (and its failings) are adumbrated, showing up, perhaps, the lack of coherence inherent in the idea of a gender norm (an incoherence which does not, it should be added, render such a norm any less subtly coercive or obligatory. Instead, it renders it only more anxiety-provoking, as it suggests the difficulty, if not impossibility, of the achievement of 'real manliness').

A number of comic ecards, which appear on the website www.someecards.com, feature erotic asphyxiation in ways that reveal much about how the practice and its relationship to gender are viewed. In one such card, which is reminiscent of a public health poster, or a 'Your Country Needs You'-style patriotic appeal to duty, we are told that: 'Real men say no to autoerotic asphyxiation'.[14] As Freud (1905) and others have famously told us, jokes are never *just* jokes, but rather they are barometers of cultural values, common fears, and unconscious anxieties. One aim of a joke is to turn fear into humour, and thereby to displace anxiety. By means of the Freudian mechanism of displacement, jokes also often used to target 'others' - those outside the hegemonic norm, who are perceived to be strange or lacking; in short those who are 'bizarre'. (The category of jokes Freud terms 'tendentious' always

12. Miranda Sawyer, 'Mr Sexcess: An Interview with Michael Hutchence', *The Advertiser*, 19 April 1997.

13. Katrina Jaworski, *The Gender of Suicide: Production, Theory and Suicidology*, London & New York, Routledge, p118.

14. See: https://www.someecards.com/usercards/viewcard/ad27c4e592b105e4c70758a19a76daeb/

entail lust, or hostility, or both.) And, moreover, commonly shared fears of falling short of the standards of the gendered norm can be projected onto 'those others', those perverts, those who are not 'real men', through the passive-aggressive hostility underpinning the architecture of such jokes. From a jointly Freudian and Foucauldian perspective, we can read jokes as discursive artefacts that tell us what it is that is valued in a given cultural context.

Consider two further humorous ecards, both of which exploit the idea of autoerotic asphyxiation as a secret. The first[15] shows a group of people talking and laughing over drinks. The caption reads: 'Sorry I brought up my erotic asphyxiation fetish during the holiday party'. The other[16] depicts one portly Victorian gentleman informing another that 'If you ever die from auto-erotic asphyxiation I promise to rearrange your corpse before it's discovered by your loved ones.' These two cards use the idea of shame in different ways. The first works by juxtaposing a pair of apparent opposites: autoerotic asphyxiation and what is presumably an office holiday party. A shameful, squalid, solitary, secret practice is shown to have no business erupting discursively as a Freudian slip amidst the codified conformity of an organised social gathering. If this scenario demonstrates the shock of shame involved in this lapsus, the other joke card does something else with the secret and its attendant shame: it shares and thereby enshrines them. The assurance on the part of the gentleman that, should his friend ever die from autoerotic asphyxiation, he would be sure to rearrange his corpse before it were discovered by his family, makes the dark and dirty sexual secret into a gesture of male bonding. While, at one level, the disparity between the gentlemen's formal appearance and the subject matter of their conversation works to provoke humour via simple incongruity, this joke also turns solitary shame into the stuff of friendship and solidarity, into something almost heroic or noble.

The two different ways in which masculinity, shame, and a non-normative sexual practice are seen to intersect in the humour of these two ecards offer us a guide to understanding how Milligan's story on the one hand and Hutchence's and Carradine's on the other, may function as recognisable narratives of non-normative masculinity, and, moreover how they fit with prescriptive historical discourses about the correct behaviour of men and the nature of male sexuality. The notable feature of the joke involving the office party is the way in which a secret has been leaked, the truth has slipped out, the male figure who accidentally brought up his fetish is no longer in control: he is unmanned. A primary meaning of an autoerotic fatality, then, is as the *revelation of lack of continence* on the part of a subject.

In the modern Western imaginary control and rationality are anchored to masculinity, such that the spectre of loss of control signifies effeminacy and provokes shame. Stephen Milligan's body was found in his London residence, on the kitchen table, wearing a pair of stockings, with a black bin liner over his head, a length of electrical flex around his neck and a segment of an orange in his mouth. The manner of his dress during his erotic asphyxiation

15. See: https://www.someecards.com/usercards/viewcard/6b636aa59d4c224f557dbd5aa64de53d0d/

16. See: https://www.someecards.com/usercards/viewcard/eea3c10dfaeb6ef8c6eb386707343c36/

ritual compounded the sense of unmanliness created by the shameful fact of drug-and-asphyxiation-enhanced onanism that had gone too far. Forensic accounts of autoerotic fatalities reveal that the presence of cross-dressing or the wearing of stylised garments or uniforms during the ritual are relatively often found at such death scenes. In his paper on 'erotised repetitive hangings', Resnik describes a syndrome, most commonly found in young adult males, involving 'compression of the neck' coupled with masturbation, in which 'binding of the body [....] and female attire may be present' (*Erotized Repetitive Hangings*, p6). This has led some more pathologising commentators to posit an intrinsic psychological link in practitioners of these acts between erotic asphyxiation on the one hand, and, variously, on the other: masochism, psychic hermaphroditism (Robert Brittain's term), and, for psychoanalysts, separation anxiety and castration complex. My aim here, as I have already stated, is not to attempt to understand the meaning of erotic asphyxiation for its participants, nor to analyse the participants psychologically or psychoanalytically through their practices. I am interested, rather, on this point, in the cultural association made between effeminacy and shame that finds articulation in such cases of autoerotic fatality. It is unsurprising that non-normative practices, desires, identities, and gender performances that bring cultural ridicule on subjects, and risk producing shame in them and in those who love them, should find expression in the *same* ritualistic scene and space (since they are close neighbours in the outer reaches of Rubin's hierarchy diagram).

Worrying about effeminacy, which is linked precisely to weakness and to incontinence (to slipping up), has been a feature of sexological and other psy scientific writing about male sexuality and male masturbation since its earliest days. In the eighteenth century, the Swiss physician Samuel-Auguste Tissot co-opted for medicine a discourse previously belonging to the Church, when he warned of the danger that excessive ejaculation through masturbation could both physically and mentally enfeeble men, and consequently feminise them.[17] The threat described by Tissot resurfaced in a slightly different form in the second half of the nineteenth century in the strange phenomenon of 'spermatorrhoea' panics, in which seepage of sperm from the body was seen to lead to weakness and emasculation in men and, as Elizabeth Stephens points out, in which men's bodies were pathologised as leaky and incontinent for the first time, a form of body-shaming previously reserved for female corporeal functions.[18] In many ways, male masturbation involving erotic asphyxiation seems to thematise and take further the older fear of male weakness through onanism and other forms of bodily loss of control. Not only is the seed lost and the vital spark killed, but, in the case of erotic asphyxiation, the man himself may die in the paroxysm of a non-productive, non-*re*productive loss of continence and consciousness.

To turn now to the alternative narrative of masculinity suggested by the ecard featuring the two Victorian gentlemen, we see here also the

17. Samuel-Auguste Tissot, *Onanism: A Treatise on the Diseases Produced by Masturbation*, trans. A. Hume [1723]; New York, Garland 1985.

18. See: Elizabeth Stephens, 'Pathologising Leaky Male Bodies: Spermatorrhea in Nineteenth-Century British Medicine and Popular Anatomical Museums', *Journal of the History of Sexuality*, Vol. 17, No. 3 (Sept, 2008), pp421-438, p. 442.

suggestion that male sexuality hides a secret, the revelation of which could do harm. The secret of male sexuality alluded to is the idea of the excessive, potentially out-of-control, and dangerous force that is male libido itself. While similarly marking a potential loss of control in the spectre of the autoerotic death, in contradistinction to the leaky slipperiness of the loose-tongued figure at the party (whose lack of control equates to effeminacy), the presence of male solidarity and brotherhood - the homosocial relationship built around the secret - lends something grandiose and hyper-masculine to the notion of a desire so strong that it cannot be controlled. And, indeed, a fantasy of mastery that outlives accidental death is suggested here, since the secret will be preserved and will die with the subject of the autoerotic fatality.

Reminiscent of this desire for mastery of experience, Michael Hutchence stated in an interview with Australian *News* in 1997 that: 'I'm always on the look-out for the ultimate sex-kick ... I want to experience these extreme things myself and not just read about them like everyone else' (cited in *Playing with the Self*, p62). Kerr and Perbedy liken this to a statement by David Carradine in an interview from 2004, that 'there's a Zen thing of [...] "if you want to learn to fly, jump off a cliff", right? And either you'll fly or it won't matter. One or the other' (p62). While Hutchence's statement refers explicitly to sexual kicks, and Carradine's to a more existential ambition, both statements contribute to construct the autoerotic decedents as reckless physical risk-takers, playing, Russian-Roulette style, with their sexuality, while mastering fear of loss of control.

The kinds of fantasy and sophistry woven around experiences of sexual excess discussed above echo a trope that is central to nineteenth-century sexological writing on masculinity and male sexual desire, and that survives long beyond that period. Richard von Krafft-Ebing in the opening pages of *Psychopathia Sexualis* (1886) describes male sex drive as: 'a natural instinct which, with all-conquering force and might, demands fulfilment'.[19] He goes on 'in course, sensual love, in the lustful impulse to satisfy this natural instinct, man stands on a level with the animal' (p1). An ambivalent picture of the male sex drive emerges as magnificently dominant and powerful, on the one hand, and yet, on the other, as threatening to overwhelm the individual rational, moral man, who would stand above 'the animal'. Krafft-Ebing's argument for the danger of male libido unchecked by the social institutions of morality, echoes the language used at Kotzwarra's trial regarding the existence of 'men who, to gratify the most unwarranted species of lust, resorted to methods at which reason and morality revolted' (*Modern Propensities*, p41). Autoerotic asphyxiation stands in, metonymically, for the secret that is the strength of male desire and its compulsiveness.

Within Krafft-Ebing's sexological system, two potentially contradictory theories of sexual perversion uneasily co-exist. The first identifies it as a degenerate, 'fixated' behaviour, repetitively and obsessively carried out in

19. Richard von Krafft-Ebing, *Psychopathia Sexualis, with especial reference to Contrary Sexual Instinct: A Medico-Legal Study*, translation by Charles Gilbert Chaddock of the seventh enlarged and revised German edition, Philadelphia and London, F. A. Davis 1893, p.1.

ritualistic fashion by the deviant few, who are likely also to be mentally and physically enfeebled. The second argues instead that male sexual appetite, as floridly depicted by Krafft-Ebing, is so voracious in and of itself that it tempts *all* men to perverse experimentation. And a man, having once strayed from the path of sexual health, may be tempted to try ever more extreme practices in order to sate his libido. Marriage, family and capitalistic production are offered by Krafft-Ebing as the proper means of taming or tempering this errant drive and keeping the individual and the population safe from sexual sickness. This is the 'sliding scale' model of perversion.

This idea of the sliding scale evokes the trope of 'jaded' male sexuality that is often linked to practices such as erotic asphyxiation. This is seen in the sexual persona that risk-taking Michael Hutchence embodied. There is a common discourse, and an accompanying set of moral panics, about the danger of that quality of male sexuality that lends itself to jadedness (its 'almightiness' as described by Krafft-Ebing). This is seen in worries about the availability of pornography and its corrupting influence on men that have featured throughout modernity in sexological writing and feminist writing alike, and have adapted and proliferated in response to the birth of the internet and its capacity to deliver instant gratification in the form of ever more diverse (and 'extreme') images. And, it is as the endpoint of this logic that we find one interpretation of what erotic asphyxiation culturally signifies: male libido so saturated with sexual options, and so bored with its more mundane exercises, that it turns eventually to its own annihilation for kicks. Like many perceived sexual and gender deviations, then, erotic asphyxiation is used both to recall the idea of failed masculinity on the one hand and yet, on the other, to suggest that this act is merely the final step, the furthest extreme potential of all masculinity - the nature of which is to be sexually rapacious, experimental and curious. The cultural narrative of male erotic asphyxiation is schismatic and contradictory precisely because the cultural narrative of masculinity is and has been so since the earliest texts of modernity. The question thereby arises: what of female erotic asphyxiation?

Consider a further asphyxiation-themed ecard.[20] The humour here works by refusing the expected disjuncture between the demure, conventionally feminine-looking woman in the drawing and her confession in the caption: 'I'm into auto-erotic asphyxia. What about you?' As we have seen, autoerotic asphyxiation is commonly perceived to be something that men do (and something that they must be ashamed of). And it takes historical (religiously inflected, albeit scientifically appropriated) shame over male masturbation - wasting the seed, being self-indulgent - a step further. The ideology that makes wasted seed a problem, namely the notion that sexuality is *for* reproduction, brings us directly to the question of female sexuality. For, in hetero-patriarchy, reproduction is what women, who are often synonymous with sex, are understood to be *for,* too.

20. See: https://www.someecards.com/usercards/viewcard/MjAxMi02ODIxMzJkYTMwYzZkYjkw

All celebrity cases of autoerotic death recorded in recent years have been of male decedents. This does not, however, mean that (non-celebrity) women do not die in this way. Indeed, the available forensic literature reveals that some do, as in the case described in *The Handbook of Forensic Pathology* by Abdullah Fatteh (1973), and excerpted as 'Sex Hanging in a Female' in the *Amok Journal*'s special issue on erotic fatalities (1995). The case describes a 19-year-old female decedent by autoerotic hanging, who was found with her body bound with rope and dressed, in the words of the pathologist, in 'the attire of an Oriental "harem girl"'.[21] A paperback copy of an erotic novel, open at pages that contained scenes describing how women would be hanged around the walls on hooks, after being sexually used in a harem, was found near the body. This case echoes the incidence of 'cross'-dressing/ dressing up, bondage, and stylised costume that has been remarked upon as a prominent feature in the male cases examined. But there are so few reported cases of this type featuring women, and so little written on them, that no syndrome of specifically female psychopathologies linked to this type of death scene, such as those theorised by Resnik and Brittain for male autoerotic fatalities, has been formulated.

However, if it is the case that there are *fewer* female autoerotic deaths, this does not necessarily mean that fewer women engage in erotic asphyxiation practices than men. It may instead mean that women are better at ensuring they do not accidentally die, it may suggest that they practise it to less extreme degrees than men, or that they do it with a partner so that any fatalities that do occur are more likely to figure in the statistics of manslaughter/ murder victims than in the woolly hinterland between suicide by hanging and erotic fatality figures. Psychoanalysts Temmerman and Quackelbeen make this argument in their paper 'Autoerotic Asphyxia from Phenomenology to Psychoanalysis' as a direct redress to Hazelwood, Burgess and Groth's gender-stereotypical assertions in *Autoerotic Fatalities* that autoerotic asphyxiation is mainly found among men because men 'participate to a greater extent in unconventional sexual practices than do women'.[22] This is a necessarily unsubstantiated claim, as there is no reliable way of proving the extent of a phenomenon that is largely based on self-reporting.

Given the lack of media coverage of autoerotic deaths in women, we are forced to turn instead to fictional representation if we wish to explore cultural attitudes to this phenomenon when the practitioner is female. Australian novelist Tim Winton's *Breath* (2008) offers an exemplary case study of cultural attitudes towards gendered asphyxiation, by juxtaposing the activities of surf-obsessed, breath-holding male youth, Bruce Pike, and those of his older, married lover, Eva Sanderson, a devotee of erotic asphyxiation. The novel is constructed from the point of view of Bruce's first-person narrative. The scene is set by describing how he and his best friend Ivan Loon or 'Loonie', who 'liked anything with an edge on it', challenge each other to ever more dangerous water-bound adventures.[23] The following quotation is a typical description of their behaviour:

21. 'Sex Hanging in a Female', *Amok Journal, Sensurround Edition: A Compendium of Psycho-Physiological Investigations*, ed. Stuart Sweezy, Los Angeles, Amok 1995, 58-59, p58.

22. Karin Temmerman and Julien Quackelbeen, 'Autoerotic Asphyxia from Phenomenology to Psychoanalysis', *The Letter: Lacanian Perspectives on Psychoanalysis*, Autumn 1996, 49-70, p56.

23. Tim Winton, *Breath*, London, Picador 2008, p31. (Hereafter *Breath*).

Loonie and I acted out the impulse [...] We held our breath and counted. We timed ourselves in the river and the ocean, in the old man's shed or in the broken autumn light of the forest floor. It takes quite some concentration and will power to defy the logic of your own body, to take yourself to the shimmering edge. It seems bizarre, looking back, to realise just how hard we worked at this. We were good at it and in our own minds it's what set us apart from everyone else. (*Breath*, pp41-42)

Reviewer Cathleen Schine describes Winton's novel as valorising the 'Macho Romanticism' and 'Heroic Sensibility' that it portrays.[24] Indeed, obsessive risk-taking as a form of heroism is legitimised throughout the fictional narrative by means of the intimate identification the reader is invited to engage in with Winton's colloquially-voiced male narrator, and the sympathy that it is designed to engender.

By contrast, the treatment of Eva is more ambivalent and considerably less sympathetic. Much of the second half of the book details Bruce's sexual affair with Eva, who is viewed wholly from the boy's (and, by extension, the male author's) heteronormative point of view: 'She wasn't quite the stuff of my erotic imaginings. True, she was blonde and confident in that special American way, but there was nothing *Playboy* or Hollywood about her' (*Breath*, p164). Consider the scene in which Eva reveals her preferred sexual practice to Bruce and asks him to watch while she hangs herself. Bruce recounts:

> I looked at the padded collar and the brass ring that did the work of a slipknot. From where I lay I could smell the sweat and perfume in the leather.
> You *hang* yourself?
> Sure, sometimes.
> Why?
> Because I like it. [...]
> So how do you know when to stop?
> Practice, I guess. You should know.
> Me? Gimme a break.
> Come on, Pikelet, she said soothingly. I've heard you guys talk. Spots, stars, tunnel vision. (*Breath*, p181)

Eva insists on the similarity between her erotic practice and the boys' sporting adventures, and asks that Bruce stay and watch her for safety, to act like a 'dive buddy' (p181). The narrator's refusal to see the similarity between the phenomenological and bodily experiences they both practise recalls at once the misogyny which dictates that the young male narrator should *objectify* this not-quite-*Playboy* blonde rather than *identify with* her, and the cultural insistence on separating out bodily activities categorised as 'sexual' from all others, however similar in kind they may physiologically and/ or experientially be.

24. Cathleen Schine, 'Walking on Water: *Breath* by Tim Winton', *New York Review of Books*, August 14, 2008, http://www.nybooks.com/articles/2008/08/14/walking-on-water/ last accessed 31/05/2016. (Upper case letters Schine's own).

As might be expected from what is essentially a gender-conservative narrative, Eva is punished in a very conventional way for her unconventional behaviour. Firstly, she falls pregnant - that time-honoured plot device for correcting female deviance and straightening out the lovemap of a wayward female character. And she announces the news of her gravid condition to her young lover in telling terms, bespeaking the end of pleasure: 'Go home [...] The fun's over now' (p192). Secondly, her narrative is concluded by autoerotic death, while the male characters, who had been taking equally reckless physical risks in the water, live to surf another day: 'Eva was found hanging naked from the back of a bathroom door in Portland, Oregon. A Salvadorean hotel employee found her with a belt around her neck. The deceased had been the sole occupant of her five-star room, the cause of death cardiac arrest as a result of asphyxiation' (p206). The description of her death signals a shift in register from Bruce's colloquial first person to the impersonal reportage style of police report or 'Reuters column' (p206), marking the official inscription of Eva as an autoerotic fatality statistic.

In summary, then, *Breath* teaches us several lessons about cultural attitudes to gender and to death-related sexual practices that are similar to those found in descriptions and reports of non-fictional erotic asphyxiation. Firstly, it conveys that what may be seen as brave and noble in one context (such as sporting feats performed by virile youths) is perceived to be shameful, stupid, and base in the realm of the erotic, where it is codified as a 'sexual perversion'. (Bruce describes Eva's appearance mid-asphyxiation as 'squalid beyond imagining' (*Breath*, p190).) Secondly, what may be a quasi-admirable form of 'risk-taking' by a 'manly man' (e.g. Hutchence) would become bizarre or shameful when found in an 'unmanly' man (e.g. Milligan) and, of course, in a woman, since misogyny is the very stuff from which the pejorative discourse of male effeminacy is made in the first place. Thirdly, we note that Eva in *Breath* is portrayed as selfish and adolescent; fifteen-year-old Bruce observes: 'Yes we had some things in common, Eva and I. At twenty-five, she was as solipsistic as any teenager' (p171). This is a familiar discourse: the practitioner of sexual perversion, who writes an alternative narrative for sexuality in which the outcome of the exercise of desire is something other than reproduction, is dismissed as 'immature'. And the non-reproductive woman, who resists fulfilling woman's 'proper' role and purpose, is perceived as the most selfish of sexual personages. (That Eva compounds the perversion of resisting motherhood with that of erotic asphyxiation, carried out by an underage, adulterous partner makes her eventual punishment all the more inevitable.) Finally, while the male 'breath-players' of Winton's book have no harm come to them, despite their risk-taking antics, the dissident sexual female is corrected with pregnancy and then punished with death. I describe her death as 'punishment' from *within* the logic of the novel because it, like the rest of the book, is narrated from a heteronormative mainstream perspective (the very perspective from which Rubin's charmed circle is constructed). Whether a death that occurs during an act of autoerotic asphyxiation would be viewed as a punishment and failure, or as a triumph and success (or as something else entirely) *by the practitioner* is a question that is rarely, if ever, asked in cultural narratives of erotic asphyxiation, owing to the shortage of practitioners volunteering to discuss their sexual behaviour, and guided by the overwhelming assumption that life must be the desired outcome of sex and that dying for sex is never a risk that is worth taking.

We have seen that mainstream media discourses use fatal erotic asphyxiation to label male public figures who die from it as either examples of failed and weak masculinity *or* of excessive, risk-taking hyper-masculinity, echoing established ideas from foundational texts of sexual science about the problematic nature of male sex drive. But, in either case, what is at stake is a delicate balance between non-normativity and gender conformity: being either *not enough* or *too much* of a man. Yet, if erotic asphyxiation is linked to failed masculinity, to not 'being a real man', how much more reviled and pathological does it appear when the practitioner is a woman. This is because women are decidedly not supposed to be perverts and are not allowed to seek the expression of excessive sexual desire to the detriment of social duty (rather, in the role of wife and mother, they were traditionally seen as the gatekeepers of the wild, beastly male libido of their sons and husbands). And - crucially - women are supposed to be reproductively-driven, primarily motivated by the desire for a child, the perpetuation of life, rather than the search for selfish, erotic pleasure. The female autoerotic fatality, embodied in Tim Winton's fictitious Eva, is thus a doubly othered, doubly pathologised subject.

Finally, erotic asphyxiation, in coupling the ideational thrill of proximity to death with the risk of actual bodily death, is the ultimate non-reproductive sexual practice. It is a practice that literalises the deathliness that has, from the very inception of sexology and psychiatry, been associated with the sterility of homosexuality and with the danger of the so-called sexual perversions or paraphilias. Therefore, we can go so far as to state that it represents both an individual example of a non-normative sexual practice *and* a limit case that risks destabilising the field of 'sexuality' itself, where this is an ideological category that presupposes utilitarian and normative aims motivating bodily behaviours. Acts of erotic asphyxiation, especially in their autoerotic forms, are statements that the pursuit of ecstatic bodily sensations and/ or altered psychological states may be ends in themselves - even as they risk constituting literal ends for their practitioners.

Lisa Downing is Professor of French Discourses of Sexuality at the University of Birmingham, UK. She has published widely on sexuality and gender studies, death studies, and cultural studies. In particular, she is the author of several major books, including: *The Subject of Murder: Gender,*

Exceptionality, and the Modern Killer (Chicago: University of Chicago Press, 2013); *Desiring the Dead: Necrophilia and Nineteenth-Century French Literature* (Oxford: Legenda, EHRC, 2003), *The Cambridge Introduction to Michel Foucault* (Cambridge: Cambridge University Press, 2008), *The Subject of Murder: Gender, Exceptionality and the Modern Killer* (University of Chicago Press, 2013) and, forthcoming in 2014, *Fuckology: Critical Essays on John Money's Diagnostic Concepts* (co-authored with Iain Morland and Nikki Sulllivan, University of Chicago Press).

The Violations of Empathy

Jennifer Cooke

Abstract This article questions the assumption that empathy is a positive, politically beneficial emotion through two examples of poetry about deaths with sensitive political dimensions. I begin by returning to the origins of 'empathy' in English, as written about by Vernon Lee in the early-twentieth-century, to show how far the word has drifted from Lee's sense of it as an embodied aesthetic response to an artwork. Rob Halpern's book of poems *Common Room* refuses imaginative empathy with its subject, a dead Guantánamo Bay detainee, and yet, I show, surprisingly aligns with Lee's sense of empathy through the author's erotic and imaginative response to the man's autopsy report. What results in this revivification of Lee's empathy is a violation of the religious beliefs of the detainee. In contrast, Andrea Brady's poem 'Song for Florida 2' takes up a more contemporary sense of empathy in its focus upon the killing of the unarmed teen Trayvon Martin by George Zimmerman in 2012. Brady's poem presents several possibilities for empathising with Martin's mother - by imagining being her, or imagining similarly losing a son - but eventually draws back from this as a limit. Empathy here risks erasing the specificity of the racialized context which led to Martin's unjust death. The white poet's son cannot 'replace', even imaginatively, the black mother's son without effacing the difference which saw Martin targeted in the first place. Brady's poem, I argue, marks how empathy can violate through supplanting the grief and political context for that grief of the person to whom empathy is extended. What is needed instead of empathy is a commitment to political change.

Keywords empathy, Trayvon Martin, Black Lives Matter, Guantánamo Bay, Vernon Lee, autopsy, imagination, poetry.

Empathy is a young word: it first arrived in English in 1909 as a translation of the German term *Einfühlung*, 'feeling into', in a text by the American psychologist Edward Titchener.[1] *Einfühlung* itself was a technical neologism, coined earlier by Robert Vischer in his 1873 discussion of the psychological dimension of aesthetics, and then expanded upon by the psychologist Theodor Lipps.[2] It is to this German tradition and its Anglophone proponents that Vernon Lee refers when she makes empathy the crucial component of her psychological aesthetics in her co-authored book of 1912, *Beauty and Ugliness and Other Studies in Psychological Aesthetics*.[3] From these specialised and technical beginnings in a branch of German-inflected thinking that combined ideas

1. Edward Bradford Titchener, *Lectures on the Experimental Psychology of Thought-Processes*, New York, The Macmillan Company 1909, p21.

2. A useful overview of Lee's thought and its influences is provided in Carolyn Burdett, '"The subjective insider us can turn into the object outside": Vernon Lee's Psychological Aesthetics', *19: Interdisciplinary Studies in the Long Nineteenth Century* 12 (2011), pp 1-31. (Hereafter *Subjective Insider*).

3. Vernon Lee and C. Anstruther-Thomson, *Beauty and Ugliness and Other Studies in Psychological Aesthetics*, London, John Lane Company 1912. (Hereafter *Beauty and Ugliness*).

from psychology and aesthetics to discover how we relate to artworks, empathy has since migrated to name interpersonal states and affects which align closely with non-aesthetic terms, especially its more ancient cousin, sympathy, the rather later psychoanalytic concept, identification, and more recent theories from psychology such as Theory of Mind. In what follows, I examine literary and critical theory accounts of empathy and read two poems to question the usual assumption that empathy is benign. Rob Halpern's *Common Place* has a surprising alignment with Lee's earlier aesthetic theory of empathy but rejects the later sense of the term, and in so doing creates a disturbing, and, I argue, violating, sexual fantasy out of a corpse. Andrea Brady's 'Song for Florida 2' explores a different way in which empathy violates by colonising the emotions of the other and erasing the specificity - and, indeed, masking the injustice - of their experience. Halpern's *Common Place* and Brady's 'Song for Florida 2' respond to the suicide of a Guantánamo detainee and the killing of Trayvon Martin, respectively. These are deaths with public and political significance and the poems contribute to and comment upon the public sentiment surrounding them and, in Brady's words, work to 'unsettle our sense of moral priority or certitude'.[4]

In questioning empathy, I am not alone. Most recently, Paul Bloom's work, culminating in his book *Against Empathy: The Case for Rational Compassion*, has highlighted how 'empathy is narrow in its focus, rendering it innumerate and subject to bias' because we tend to focus on the individual rather than the group, the one child in need rather than the whole suffering community. It can even, he argues, 'motivate cruelty and aggression and lead to burn out and exhaustion', the first because empathy tends to be directed towards the like and the proximate at the expense of others further away or different, and the latter because those who empathise too much render themselves less helpful to others: for instance, the social worker who over-empathises with his clients will be less effective at his job because he is emotionally depleted.[5] While Bloom accepts that empathy can motivate prosocial behaviour, he warns that it 'is often used by those who wish to generate animus toward outgroups'(p27). Bloom's work - and the title of his book - is preceded by an article by the philosopher Jesse Prinz, who had made many of the same arguments first. For Prinz, like Bloom, empathy is not 'desirable as a *moral* emotion' because it clouds our rational judgements.[6] Instead of compassion, which is what Bloom argues we should cultivate as a better emotion than empathy, Prinz suggests concern, but the reasons both give for not trusting empathy are very similar (*Against Empathy*, p230-1). In both arguments, it is not the one who we empathise with who suffers from our empathy, but those who are obscured from view by what Bloom calls empathy's 'spotlight', whereas in the poems I will read it is those empathised with who are displaced by the attempt to imagine them and their situation (*Rational Compassion*, p25).

A further problem with empathy is its lack of definitional clarity, resulting in a proliferation of overlapping terms. There is projection (imagining

---

4. Andrea Brady and Sarah Howe, 'Interview', *Prac Crit* 1 (July 2014). Available online: http://www.praccrit.com/poems/song-for-florida-2/. Accessed 24 March 2016. (Hereafter *Interview*).

5. Paul Bloom, 'Empathy and Its Discontents', *Trends in Cognitive Science* 21:1 (2017), p 24. See also: Paul Bloom, *Against Empathy: The Case for Rational Compassion*, New York, Harper Collins 2016. (Hereafter *Rational Compassion*).

6. Jesse Prinz, 'Against Empathy', *The Southern Journal of Philosophy*, 49 (2011), p 214. (Hereafter *Against Empathy*).

7. Meghan Marie Hammond and Sue J. Kim, eds., *Rethinking Empathy Through Literature*, New York and London, Routledge 2014, pp7-8 (Hereafter *Rethinking Empathy*); Julinna C. Oxley, *The Moral Dimensions of Empathy: Limits and Applications in Ethical Theory and Practice*, Basingstoke, Palgrave Macmillan 2011, p26. (Hereafter *Moral Dimensions*).

8. Steve Vincent, *Being Empathic: A Companion for Counsellors and Therapists*, Oxford, Radcliffe 2005. Martha Nussbaum, *Cultivating Humanity: A Classical Defense of Reform in Liberal Education*, Cambridge, Mass., and London, Harvard University

yourself in someone else's place), perspective-taking (imagining what the world looks like from another's position), and cognitive empathy or theory of mind (anticipating how someone else will react); there are distinctions between self-, other- and dual-focused empathy (imagining myself in someone's place, myself as someone else, or imagining both of these).[7] Often, when empathy is used, imagination is meant. Yet in all contemporary accounts of empathy, whether therapeutic, pedagogic, literary, moral, or psychological, the idea of the other is central.[8] The most prevalent definitions of empathy stress either the importance of imagination in projecting oneself into the position of the other and thus trying to see and feel as they do or, alternatively, the importance of imagining how we would be affected were the same set of circumstances to befall us.[9] Thus, Suzanne Keen describes empathy as 'I feel what you feel', in contrast to sympathy as only 'a supportive emotion about your feelings', a distinction which is commonly used (*Rethinking Empathy*, p7).[10] For others, such as philosopher Julinna Oxley, a more specific set of definitions is required: empathy, she argues, is 'feeling a congruent emotion with another person, in virtue of perceiving her emotion with some mental process such as imitation, simulation, projection, or imagination' (*Moral Dimensions*, p32). Tellingly, here, rather than being one of several, imagination is necessary for all the mental processes Oxley lists.

This concentration upon empathy as an activation of imagination explains why literary theorists have been especially drawn to consider empathy in explanations of how readers of narrative relate to characters and their scenarios. Unlike for Bloom and Prinz, literary empathy is usually extolled, whether for the representation of empathy within literary works or the encouragement of a reader's empathy. A focus on how literature imaginatively extends its readers' emotional range and knowledge through encounters with new contexts and experiences is the foundation of Rick Rylance's final chapter on empathy in his book-length defence of literature as a public good.[11] Rylance's argument is germane for what it omits: he does not proffer a definition of empathy - in fact, the word is only used twice in this long final chapter, apart from in the chapter's title, 'The Power of Empathy'. Instead, Rylance concentrates on how literature beneficially exposes readers to new experiences and emotional nuances: in a memorable formulation, he writes, 'In reading literature, we are being "you"'(p194).

In other literary conceptions, such as those collected in *Rethinking Empathy Through Literature*, Eleonore de Felip has argued that lyric poetry 'speaking from non-human points of views' can 'help readers to imagine moments of exceptional empathy' with animals, while Mary-Catherine Harrison has argued that the social problem novels of the nineteenth century allowed readers to 'empathise with individual fictional characters' in a manner which introduced them to people 'from social groups who would otherwise be understood as an undifferentiated mass'.[12] In the same volume, Eric Leake uses the example of Bret Easton Ellis's protagonist in *American Psycho* to

Press 1997, pp 90-91 (Hereafter *Cultivating Humanity*); Tim Gauthier, *9/11 Fiction, Empathy, and Otherness*, Lanham, Lexington Books 2015 (Hereafter *9/11 Fiction*); Michael C. Corballis, *The Recursive Mind: The Origins of Human Language, Thought, and Civilization*, Princeton and Oxford, Princeton University Press 2011.

9. Rajini Srikanth, *Constructing the Enemy: Empathy/Antipathy in U.S. Literature and Law*, Philadelphia, Temple University Press 2012, p2 (Hereafter *Constructing the Enemy*). Steven Pinker, *The Better Angels of Our Nature: The Decline of Violence in History and Its Causes*, London and New York, Penguin 2011, pp571-575. Pinker proclaims, 'We live in an age of empathy', p571.

10. Suzanne Keen, *Empathy and the Novel*, Oxford, Oxford University Press 2007, p5. (Hereafter *Empathy and the Novel*).

11. Rick Rylance, *Literature and the Public Good*, Oxford, Oxford University Press 2016, pp 163-203. (Hereafter *Literature and the Public Good*).

12. Eleonore de Felip, 'Hearing the Speechless: Empathy with Animals in Contemporary German Lyric Poetry', p102, and Mary-Catherine Harrison, 'The

argue how 'difficult empathy', activated by representations of challengingly unpleasant literary characters with whom 'we might not otherwise wish contact or association', is 'of particular use in novels of critique'.[13] In all such accounts, imagining the world differently through reading literature entails empathy.

Most of the theoretical literature on empathy, unless investigating those claimed to lack it, tends to assume that people find it easier to empathise with others who are like themselves and therefore the more imaginative challenge is cultivating empathy for 'the other who is different'.[14] In several accounts, including Rylance's, this is celebrated as a route to developing a richer understanding of people from different cultures and countries.[15] Yet even this invocation of 'the other who is different' can be problematic if it assumes that there is an identifiable or easily-imagined 'us' against whom that other is measured. The writings of Martha Nussbaum and Tim Gauthier can serve here by way of example: both use 'we' as a convenient placeholder in books that argue for more empathetic relations towards people from different countries to improve cosmopolitanism and combat U.S. insularity.[16] Neither Nussbaum nor Gauthier believe that North Americans are the sole standard against which all otherness needs to be measured; even so, in such accounts the other is conceived as culturally, nationally, racially or religiously different (or a combination of these factors) to U.S. citizens, who are implicitly bequeathed an inaccurate homogeneity secured by nationality. A keener sense of the diverse ethnicities and cultural heritages that comprise the north American population would arguably be a more advantageous start for those arguing for the importance of imagining otherness. Theorising empathy, it appears, is hard work, full of unimagined pitfalls, but has nevertheless continued to attract theorists and thinkers. Even while the 'we and them' or 'us and others' rhetorical binary upon which empathy frequently rests appears divisive, it is simultaneously the case that empathy, like its far older cousin, sympathy, testifies to an impetus towards human connectedness and a recognition of our dependency upon others. Because of this, in the work of Nussbaum and others it has been hailed as a cosmopolitan sentiment in need of further attention and development post-9/11, commended as a key component in effective education for global citizenship, and, as Carolyn Pedwell has identified, been understood as instrumental in political movements calling for greater social justice, including feminism and anti-racism.[17]

The list of the benefits to be derived from encouraging an empathetic stance towards others is, despite Bloom and Prinz, predominately laudatory but, as we shall see, it is at a considerable distance from the original sense of empathy brought into English that Lee employed. Lee was keen to distinguish empathy (*Einfühlung*) from the more usual German sense of the term *sich einfühlen*, which she translates as '*to feel oneself into something or someone*', a definition much closer to how empathy has continued to be understood (*Beauty and Ugliness*, p54). She worries, moreover, that Lipps, whose work

---

Great Sum of Human Anguish: Statistical Empathy in Victorian Social-Problem Novels', p136 in Meghan Marie Hammond and Sue J. Kim, eds., *Rethinking Empathy Through Literature*, New York and London, Routledge 2014

13. Eric Leake, 'Humanising the Inhumane: The Value of Difficult Empathy', p184, in Meghan Marie Hammond and Sue J. Kim, eds., *Rethinking Empathy Through Literature*. New York and London: Routledge 2014.

14. For a discussion of those lacking empathy, see Simon Baron-Cohen, *The Science of Evil: On Empathy and the Origins of Cruelty*. New York, Basic Books 2011. Baron-Cohen has worked extensively on autism.

15. See: Nussbaum, *Cultivating Humanity*; Rylance, *Literature and the Public Good*; Gauthier, *9/11 Fiction*; and James Brassett, 'Cosmopolitan Sentiments After 9/11? Trauma and the Politics of Vulnerability', *Journal of Critical Globalisation Studies* 2 (2010), pp12-29.

16. Albeit a cosmopolitanism firmly anchored in liberal Western values, e.g. Nussbaum, *Cultivating Humanity*, p88.

her theories of aesthetics built upon, has yielded at points to this common definition and so fallen into 'a little metaphysical mythology'(p55). The ego cannot project itself into something else, she argues. Instead, it can only understand something else through its experience of itself. Furthermore, in Lee's account, empathy is not felt for others but is an internal reaction (*Einfühlung* as literally 'in-feeling') to an artwork or object of natural beauty. Her slightly later text, *The Beautiful: An Introduction to Psychological Aesthetics* (1913), concentrates on the empathy involved in seeing a mountain rising before us.[18] Crucial to Lee's conception of how we understand the mountain as rising - even while it is not, of course, growing in size - is that we lift our gaze, even perhaps incline our heads upwards to see it better, so the body moves to match the metaphor. At the same time, in rather tangled prose, Lee explains that 'our awareness of raising or lifting or *rising*':

> ...coalesces with the shape we are looking at; in short that the *rising* continuing to be thought, but no longer to be thought of with reference to ourselves (since we aren't thinking of ourselves), is thought of in reference to what we *are* thinking about, namely the mountain, or rather the mountain's shape, which is, so to speak, responsible for any thought of rising, since it obliges us to lift, raise or rise ourselves in order to take stock of it.[19]

The observer's psychological and physical reactions 'coalesce' with the mountain's form so it seems to be rising: this is what Lee calls empathy. Moreover, this rising is an accretion of past, present and future risings, both real and imagined, that we have experienced or witnessed:

> ...and it is this general idea of rising, i.e. of *upward movement*, which gets transferred to the mountain, along with our own particular present activity of raising some part of us, and which thickens and enriches that poor little thought of a definite raising with the interest, the emotional fullness gathered and stored up in its long manifold existence (p65).

Empathy is coalescence, transference, a simultaneity of action (my eyes rise) and reaction (I attribute this to the mountain) in which verbs of mixing dominate within prose that is performatively muddling.

ROB HALPERN AND THE GUANTÁNAMO DETAINEE

It is not surprising, as Caroyln Burdett notes, that reviewers occasionally complained of Lee's convoluted prose, attributable in some instances to her attempts to refute similar concepts in use by other theoreticians (*Subjective Insider*, p1). Notwithstanding, Lee provides a remarkable description of aesthetic responsiveness, and it is a wonder contemporary affect theory has

17. See, respectively, James Brassett, 'Cosmopolitan Sentiments After 9/11?'; Nussbaum, *Cultivating Humanity*; Carolyn Pedwell, *Affective Relations: The Transnational Politics of Empathy*, Basingstoke and New York, Palgrave Macmillan 2014, pp 46-50.

18. One of the difficulties of glossing Lee on empathy is that her ideas develop and alter with her reading. There is first the essay, 'Beauty and Ugliness', *Contemporary Review*, October-November 1897, then the book, *Beauty and Ugliness* (1912) and *The Beautiful* (1913), all of which show a progression of ideas.

19. Vernon Lee, *The Beautiful: An Introduction to Psychological Aesthetics*, Cambridge, University Press 1913, p 63. (Hereafter *The Beautiful*).

not made her more central to its theorisations, or, indeed, if we attend to the accidental innuendos Lee manages to wring out of rising, why her work is not more used in characterisations of pornography or erotic writing. In turning now to the poetry of Rob Halpern, an unexpected contemporary resonance with Lee's theorisations will become apparent. Halpern's 2015 book *Common Place* is a complex and disturbingly eroticised elegy for a Guantánamo Bay detainee who committed suicide while incarcerated in 2009.[20] The man's autopsy report was subsequently made public, first by the American Civil Liberties Union, under a Freedom of Information request, and later by the international press; this is how Halpern came to read it. The detainee's Guantánamo file has since been published by Wikileaks.[21] While the U.S. government accused him of fighting for Al-Qaeda, the detainee maintained he only ever fought for the Taliban. He never saw a lawyer in the seven years he was detained at the camp and his death has been seen by some as suspicious or a result of negligence.[22] In the year before he died he had been on hunger strike and subjected to force-feeding while strapped into a restraint chair. The autopsy, which concludes that he committed suicide using the elastic from his underwear as a ligature around his neck, mentions that he had made several suicide attempts in the weeks before and was suffering from 'stressors of confinement', noting that lesions on his face were likely the result of banging his head against walls. The extremity of the conditions under which this detainee suffered and the little we know of him are considerable challenges to attempts to extend towards him or his situation empathy in the contemporary sense of the word. However, as we shall see, Halpern's treatment of the dead detainee has some intriguing and potentially disturbing parallels with Lee's conception of empathy.

Common Place is composed of lyric, prose, and transcription poetry, as well as a kind of poetic essay at the end. Halpern is a skilled writer and his poems are tight and dense, often employing provocative enjambment to keep a restless sense of how contemporary global events have local and personal implications. *Common Place* can be tender and elegiac, even in a poem entitled 'False Communiqué':

And so I sing this body on a table
For since the war I've read reports i
-magined events studied pro

-cedures assisting incarceration
W/ coroners who must know
Something and whose language

Rushes like unfettered streams on
-ly half-knowing the work I mean
Check out this wonder of a guy

---

20. Halpern names the detainee in *Common Place*; here, I shall not in the main body of my text, and the argument that follows will clarify why. However, I do provide references to files which name him.

21. The autopsy is one of the many files published on the University of California, Davis's Center for the Study of Human Rights in the Americas Project. See: http://humanrights.ucdavis.edu/projects/the-guantanamo-testimonials-project/testimonies/prisoner-testimonies/. The Guantánamo file is available on the Wikileaks website. See: https://wikileaks.org/gitmo/prisoner/78.html. Accessed 25th March 2016.

22. Jeffrey Kaye, 'Recently Released Autopsy Reports Heighten Guantánamo "Suicides" Mystery', *Truth Will Out* 29 Feb 2012. Accessed 1 June 2016.

A spectacle withdrawn & covered
With my latinate phrases issue
Displace so gorgeous a figure again[23]

In his determination to pay attention to the dead man, 'this wonder of a guy', 'so gorgeous a figure', Halpern attempts to imaginatively rescue the detainee from the only way the public can know him: through the formal medical prose of his autopsy report. The counter-language Halpern uses to describe this 'guy' is casual, colloquial, and sensually admiring. Yet, if the coroners are deemed complicit in the system that fettered the men they dissect, the language they use is still spoken by the poet, so Halpern renders it *'my* latinate phrases' (emphasis mine), aware that he too is reconstructing the dead man. It is unusual for Halpern to use 'this body', with its overtones here of the Eucharist, instead of his more usual appellation 'my detainee', a designation echoing how in his previous book, *Music for Porn*, he claimed the figure of the dead U.S. soldier also as his (*Common Place*, p41). In both books, the logic of Halpern's imagination is primarily erotic and so in *Common Place* there are frequent repetitions of how the reading and physical transcription of the autopsy report produce the erectile rising of desire or a set of sexual physiological reactions in the poet-speaker, who is then galvanised into a fantasy, that merges and transfers his physical sensations onto the figure of the detainee performing or responding to sexual acts. It is the erotic uses to which Halpern puts the detainee, resurrected into fantasy that is the most disquieting aspect of *Common Place* because of its poetic violation of the dead Islamic man.[24]

Before analysing Halpern's imaginative responses to the autopsy report, it is worth considering what the Guantánamo detainee has symbolised in public discourse. As Rajini Srikanth, in her chapter on relations between Guantánamo detainees and their lawyers, describes:

> The construction of detainees as 'the worst of the worst'…and as incapable of suffering (i.e. their suicides are not really evidence of a deep pain but rather are publicity stunts in asymmetric warfare) has precluded the emergence of a publically embraced politics of feeling with regard to their captivity. The detainees are denied subjecthood of any kind - being consigned to the category of potentially lethal weapons (*Constructing the Enemy*, p136).

Srikanth highlights how the public's sympathy requires evidence of suffering, which is not part of the narrative of these men as terrorist enemies of the state and potential suicide bombers.[25] For Halpern, rather differently, the detainee represents a form of unavowable excess because of his role as a pawn in a larger political and military context:

> The detainee's body realises a singularity whose radical specificity arouses

23. Rob Halpern, *Common Place*, New York, Ugly Duckling Presse 2015, p50. (Hereafter *Common Place*).

24. The final section of *Common Place*, 'Postscript: On Devotional Kink', discusses different objections raised to the poem by friends and people at readings. See also the review by Stephen Boyer in *The Poetry Project Newsletter*, #247 (April-May 2016), p30.

25. This narrative is starting to shift as more and more detainees are released without charge and then testify to what occurred within *Guantánamo*. One such account is the remarkable autobiography of a detainee, written from within Guantánamo and published while he was still incarcerated. See: Mohamedou Ould Slahi, *Guantánamo Diary*, ed. Larry Siems, Edinburgh and London, Canongate 2015. Ould Slahi was freed without charge in the autumn of 2016.

precisely what is uncontainable in it: a quality that can't be absorbed by circuits of exchange, a use that may paradoxically be characterised as the embodiment of uselessness under the militarised conditions of our contemporary life world.[26]

Outside of the law since their containment is extrajudicial, and incarcerated outside of the socius or its sympathies, the detainee's use lies only in his uselessness in confinement. They are kept at the level of 'bare life', in Agamben's philosophical conceptualisation of the term as 'that whose exclusion founds the city of men' but also in a very concrete material sense for the many detainees who have had, for instance, their sole bed sheet confiscated indefinitely, or been shackled naked, or force fed and left in their own faeces.[27] For Halpern, the body of the detainee 'is what the system must render invisible in order to reproduce the visible' (Useless Commodities, p153). *Common Place* deliberately raises - to invoke a term from Lee - the detainee into imaginative focus.

An example from the section of *Common Place* entitled 'Funeral Rites' illustrates how Lee's early conception of empathy applies to Halpern's poetry. 'Funeral Rites' gestures to a legacy of gay French writers such as Jean Genet and Pierre Guyotat, whose sexuality spills over into their writing, and to a similar, if more coded, history of American queer erotics discussed by Sam Ladkin as Halpern's 'poetics of masturbation'.[28] In this scene, Halpern is in the corner of the library, writing: 'my hand around my cock concealed inside the pocket whose lining I've conveniently torn' (*Common Place*, p81). He informs us that 'the glands between my thighs work intensely, generating all the familiar symptoms my Propranolol otherwise subdues, exasperating sweat, swollen tongue & quickened pulse. Even my perineum feels enlarged…' (p80-81). He is transcribing the autopsy report:

> But the stylisation of his [the detainee's] body's poses creates a series of persistent gestures that animate my form *head thrown back like Hecuba mourning on the beach* each of which works like a screen to deflect the meanings it appears most to resemble, or a mirror behind which value withdraws, unavailable for use. With torso bent forward, well-built though emaciated, his flesh fills my frame as though a slight change in pressure sucked it all thru an orifice *this fault in my syntax* whose limit limns a ligature when there's no hope of healing or becoming someone else, a fantasy wherein I raise my head to the level of his knees and in supplication beg for his prick before wiping his forehead so drenched with sweat, the disfigured face relieved by darkness out of which his two black eyes go shining (p81-82).

The body responds to the work of transcription; words from the autopsy literally 'animate' the poet, exciting him into a sexual fantasy which merges

---

26. Rob Halpern, 'Useless Commodities, Disposable Bodies: An Essay on Value and Waste' in Sam Ladkin, Robert Mackay, and Emile Bojesen, eds., *Against Value in the Arts and Education*, London, Rowman and Littlefield 2016, pp150-1. (Hereafter *Useless Commodities*).

27. Giorgio Agamben, *Homo Sacer: Sovereign Power and Bare Life*. Trans. Daniel Heller-Roazen. Standford, C.A.: Sanford University Press, 1998, p 7. Halpern engages with Agamben's theory in *Common Place*, p149, and in *Useless Commodities*, pp153-5. The story of the detainee whose bed sheet had been taken away without explanation is told by a lawyer in *Constructing the Enemy*. The detainee suspected that his case had caused the removal of his bed sheet, which was making it incredibly uncomfortable at night. He tried to drop his case as a response, causing the lawyer to think 'I'm part of this totally ridiculous worthless system that isn't even worth a bed sheet', (p151).

28. Sam Ladkin, 'The "Onanism of Poetry": Walt Whitman, Rob Halpern, and the Deconstruction of Masturbation', *Angelaki* 20:4 (2015), p3.

the bodily upheaval of the poet-speaker with the bodily responses (bending forward, sweating) he imagines for the detainee. The object he is responding to - the autopsy report - presents a bodily shape which will not remain inert, and appears to grow until 'his flesh fills my frame', an ambiguous phrase which suggests both a bodily coalescence and penetration. This is not the *'projection of the ego'* which Lee decries and which contemporary versions of empathy tend towards when they suggest one imagines what the other is feeling, for the other, in this case, is dead (*The Beautiful*, p67). And while I am sure that Lee would not deem this as clean - in all senses of the word - an example of what she means by empathy as she provides with her rising mountain, the two constitute provocatively parallel examples of aesthetic and imaginative responses. Halpern's somatic reaction to the autopsy report reanimates the detainee's corpse, violating cultural codes that demand respect for the dead. As the poet's flesh rises, the scene becomes a full-blown sexual fantasy.

It is thus possible to use Halpern's work here to plot an obscene route through Lee's aesthetics, a use of her work she might have deemed a violation, in fact. Lee insists that empathy 'tends to exist throughout our mental life' (p68):

> ...entering into what is called imagination, sympathy, and also into that inference from our own inner experience which has shaped our own conceptions of an outer world, and given to the intermittent and heterogeneous sensations received from without the framework of our constant and highly unified inner experience, that is to say, of our own activities and aims (p68).

Halpern's imagination, his inner experience, as well as his own activities are sexual, as far as are communicated in *Music for Porn* and *Common Place*. Halpern's desire in pursuing such a necrotic poetry is explained more fully in 'Postscript: Devotional Kink', where, marking out a distinction between his own work and the more computational motivation for much of conceptual writing's electronic copying of source material, he claims:

> ...I wanted to return transcription to its roots in somatic practice, to bring my body into contact with the linguistic remains of extraordinary rendition and state-sponsored death, like a scribe reproducing Torah or a monk labouring over illuminated books unable to restrain himself from spilling into the text. How would my writing *prosthetic of nerve & bone* metabolise such language in an effort to perceive my body's relation to a detainee's occulted corpse? (*Common Place*, p155).

Halpern's relation to the corpse is sexual, prompted by the autopsy's focus on the body. Lee's experiments with aesthetic empathy also had a queer dimension: for years, her and her partner, Clementina (Kit) Anstruther-

Thomson, looked at artworks together and recorded their reactions, testing out various hypotheses and relating their results to the continental theories of aesthetics and psychology they were reading. Anstruther-Thomson's body was more receptive than Lee's own, she eventually concluded, and had therefore been the focus of their investigations, a fact read by some later commentators as a form of sublimated desire. Even in contemporary understandings of empathy, mostly quiet on matters erotic, there is at least one theorist who comments that empathy can be sexual (*Empathy and the Novel*, p40). It makes sense that Halpern's poetry brings out the untheorised queer implications in Lee's conception of empathy.

Halpern refuses to 'presume to recognise [the detainee's] suffering': *Common Place* deliberately does not try to imagine it (*Common Place*, p162). He declares that in this situation 'there can be no compassionate identification with the other' (*Useless Commodities*, p155). This cauterises the potential for empathy in its contemporary sense, too, since empathy, compassion, and identification all require an engagement with the other that responds to their context. The poems of *Common Place* refuse to imagine the detainee as the detainee, raising him instead into a sexual fantasy, in what Halpern calls 'the reinvention of use' but which can also be read as a violation (*Useless Commodities*, p156). Halpern's refusals of empathy and imagination are the ethical stakes of *Common Place*. Thus Lee's empathy is the only kind of empathy we can identify in the poetry. Halpern recognises the sexual scandal of his poems and knows they might be read as violations, admitting that 'to sexualise *exploit* the body of a hunger-striking detainee crosses a line…to make the body of the detainee's body the common place of my devotional kink is like ripping a hole in his corpse in order to go on fucking it' (p160). The grisly simile he reaches for unapologetically consolidates that violation.

Halpern's poems search for the basis of a new form of community by confronting what is currently excluded. But, as fellow poet Andrea Brady has recently argued in a lengthy discussion of *Common Place*, this 'instrumentalisation of the body' of the detainee, 'is not unlike capitalism in forcing the ' disposable body' to work, to create the surplus value which is its theory of the commons'.[29] This rapaciousness is a sexual violation of the memory of a man whose religion, Islam, forbids same-sex relations, as Brady also notes, and is the reason why I have withheld his name from this article (p43). Imaginative, transgressive, and in many ways, ethically complex and committed as Halpern's *Common Place* is, it fails to imagine how the detainee's family might feel about the sexual use to which his corpse is put, and fails to imagine that the detainee, before his death, would likely have interpreted such a use as yet another U.S. violation committed against him. In being against empathy as we know it today, yet through that embodying Lee's conception of empathy instead, the very problem *Common Place* performs is its imaginative recursivity: it cannot get beyond the self of the poet, and the poet's desire is violating, as Halpern acknowledges.

29. Andrea Brady, 'Poetry and Bondage: Halpern to Wyatt', talk delivered at New York University on 1 April 216 and Yale University 4 April 2016, p 44. My thanks to Andrea Brady for sharing this unpublished essay with me.

30. See the following two collections of essays for work on how policing, the courts, and the general population are racially biased in the United States: Devon Johnson, Patricia Y. Warren and Amy Farrell, eds., *Deadly Injustice: Trayvon Martin, Race, and the Criminal Justice System*, New York and London, New York University Press 2015; George Yancy and Janine Jones, eds., *Pursuing Trayvon Martin: Historical Contexts and Contemporary Manifestations of Racial Dynamics*,

ANDREA BRADY AND TRAYVON MARTIN

Halpern and Brady are poets committed to confronting the political and its uncomfortable ramifications. My second example of a poem that points to the limitations of understandings of empathy is Brady's 'Song for Florida 2', about the shooting of unarmed black teenager Trayvon Martin in Sanford, Florida in 2012 and the subsequent trial and acquittal of his killer, George Zimmerman. From its outset, this work responds to violations of justice: first, Martin's shooting, and then the lack of conviction for his killer. Brady's poem incorporates facts and found material from the trial and its reporting, including quotes from Zimmerman's much-discussed call to 911. The poem is a condemnation of racial bias and violence in the United States' population and justice system and, in Brady's words, 'a kind of elegy' for Martin (*Interview*).[30] In the final third of the poem, Brady explores what she calls, in an accompanying interview, 'the possibility of sympathising with Trayvon Martin's parents' experience - the possibility or impossibility of that empathetic identification'. Brady's resultant exploration of how empathy might violate is considerably more nuanced than the violations of *Common Place*. In the interview, she employs sympathy and empathy as loose synonyms together with identification, which, despite its complex psychoanalytic connotations, is used here with 'empathetic' in a more colloquial sense that addresses the reactions to Martin's death. In the immediate aftermath of Zimmerman's acquittal, people across the U.S. took to the streets, and social media sites were flooded with images of black people holding hand-made signs proclaiming 'I am Trayvon Martin'. Criticisms and denunciations of the court's ruling were accompanied with the hashtag #BlackLivesMatter, popularised by Patrisse Cullors, Opal Tomesti, and Alicia Garza, who now lead what has mushroomed into an international organisation.[31] Martin, who was wearing a hoodie at the time he was shot, was described by Zimmerman in his call to the police as black and 'a real suspicious guy' who 'looks like he is up to no good, or on drugs or something' because '[i]t is raining and he is just walking around, looking about'.[32] The 'I am Trayvon Martin' signs and the Tumblr created in his name, inviting people to send in photographs of themselves 'looking suspicious' in hoodies, underline the racist assumptions that immediately deem young black men suspicious and dangerous even when involved in everyday activities, as Martin was in popping to the shop to buy candy.[33] It is to the outpouring of identification with Martin that Brady is referring in the interview.

While the urge to identify with Martin through a shared black vulnerability to white violence is understandable and undoubtedly political, there are theorists who are wary of political solidarities built in such ways or based upon empathy between those who have been hurt and traumatised. The two strongest arguments made in this vein are put forward by Lauren Berlant and Wendy Brown and concern particularly what they call respectively 'subaltern

Lanham, Lexington Books 2013. (Hereafter *Pursuing Trayvon*).

31. Within 26 hours of the verdict, 4.9 million tweets had disseminated this information. These were predominantly without comment, but a notable 31 per cent expressed opposition and only 7 per cent support. See: Chenelle A. Jones and Mia Ortiz, 'The Zimmerman Verdict: Media, Political Reaction, and Public Response in the Age of Social Networking' in Johnson, Warren and Farrell, eds., *Deadly Injustice: Trayvon Martin, Race, and the Criminal Justice System*, New York and London, New York University Press 2015 pp 275-297.

32. The transcript was published online by the news website, *Mother Jones*. See: http://www.motherjones.com/documents/326700-full-transcript-zimmerman. Accessed 26 May 2016.

33. For a discussion of how black men are rendered invisible as individual citizens but highly visible as a dangerous group, see Jacqueline Anderson, Sarah Lucia Hoagland, and Anne Leighton, 'Now You See It, Now You Don't: Magic Tricks of White Supremacy in the United States' in *Pursuing Trayvon*, pp 25-32.

pain' and 'politicised identity'.³⁴ Berlant's argument, put simply, is that solidarity built through empathising with the pain of oppression does not, ipso facto, make for an effective political imaginary for structural change. Berlant fears a politics founded in feeling not because injustice is not real or fails to pain its victims, but because those feelings do not necessarily tell us what a just world or a more just conception of the good life might look like (*The Subject*, p128). Brown's complementary point, although it does not directly condemn empathy, analyses how political opposition originating from oppressed minorities tends to measure injustice as unequal treatment before the law, which implicitly agitates to be included within a system built around the privileges of a white liberalism instead of 'conjuring an imagined future of power to make itself'(*States of Injury*, p66). In these critiques, empathy, or what Brady calls 'empathetic identification', foreshortens capacities for imagining an alternative future by tethering people too closely to their traumas and wounded sensibilities. Additionally, Berlant is justifiably wary of understanding 'the social world as an affective space where people ought to be legitimated because they have feelings'.³⁵ It is easy to see an injustice was committed in the Zimmerman case and reasonable for anger to be the response, but that does not necessarily mean that the perception of injustice and the anger that follows it are always and in all cases justified; and nor is a beneficent and other-inclusive emotion, as empathy is supposed to be, sufficient as the foundation for an ethical politics, as Bloom and Prinz would no doubt agree.³⁶

An alternative stance, one which also abandons empathy and the site of specific trauma as political unifiers but seeks instead a more generalised and factual shared similarity, is offered by Judith Butler in her book *Precarious Life*. She suggests we experience a 'primal vulnerability', initially as dependent infants exposed to others, their care, and perhaps their violence.³⁷ Butler asks us to imagine a community wherein 'we are alike only in having this condition [of vulnerability] separately and so hav[e] in common a condition that cannot be thought without difference' (p27). Vulnerability is common to us all, but different for each according to their context and circumstance. Butler advocates nurturing our acknowledgement of this vulnerability in both ourselves and others, especially in the wake of 9/11, a time period which 'offers a chance to start to imagine a world in which that violence might be minimised, in which an inevitable interdependency becomes acknowledged as the basis for global political community'(pxii-xiii). *Precarious Life* is part of the 'process of that imagining', she hopes (pxiii). As with Berlant and Brown, for Butler imagination creates new political ways of being in the world. However, it is not empathy that we need to appreciate another's vulnerability, but, in line with the trajectory of Butler's work, a reconfigured Hegelian recognition of difference. Empathy and vulnerability may sound the same, since both bridge differences and reach towards understanding similarities between people, but

---

34. Lauren Berlant, 'The Subject of True Feeling: Pain, Privacy, and Politics' in Wendy Brown and Janet Halley, eds., *Left Legalism / Left Critique*, Durham and London, Duke University Press, 2002, p122. (Hereafter *The Subject*). Wendy Brown, *States of Injury: Power and Freedom in Late Modernity*, Princeton, N.J., Princeton University Press 1995, p54. (Hereafter *States of Injury*).

35. Lauren Berlant, *The Female Complaint: The Unfinished Business of Sentimentality in American Culture*, Durham and London, Duke University Press 2008, p2.

36. See Philip Fisher, *The Vehement Passions*, Princeton and Oxford, Princeton University Press 2002.

37. Judith Butler, *Precarious Life: The Powers of Mourning and Violence*, London and New York, Verso Books 2004, p31. (Hereafter *Precarious Life*).

38. Harrison also discusses the phenomenon of statistical empathy, whereby the greater the numbers of people involved in a tragedy the harder it is for people to empathise in *Rethinking Empathy*, pp135-149.

39. Zimmerman's killing of Martin

they are not. Vulnerability, for Butler, is a constitutive state of being human, whereas empathy is an emotion not everyone experiences.[38]

The 'I am Trayvon Martin' signs recognise black vulnerability to racist misinterpretation by whites and the potentially life-threatening consequences.[39] As protesters and critics of the verdict pointed out, Zimmerman's descriptions of Martin were heavy with the stereotyping of young black men as urban delinquents, which, in the words of Cathy J. Cohen, is 'yet another trope that [has] helped to create and solidify an 'other' that whites and middle-class people of color could rally against', contributing to an atmosphere of 'white fear'.[40] White fear is thus a perception of white vulnerability to black violence that in fact makes most vulnerable the black people who are feared. The stakes in whose vulnerability is recognised as legitimate are high, and sometimes, as in Martin's case, fatally unjust. Butler argues that the recognition of another's vulnerability is a performative act, changing the nature of that vulnerability, and it is this that the 'I am Trayvon Martin' signs hope to achieve in highlighting a shared vulnerability to racism (p43).

Brady's poem marks white fear and black vulnerability from the start:

> You may be called upon
> to testify   to your worst fears
> it was a dark and rainy
> (setting the scene)
> was dark and
> (set)
> and mangling the apparition can't be
> gated, dog whistles, blocks
> these assholes always get the specter of
>   the elevator, shadow of
>   grass and graven recess down
> ever-hooded sea.[41]

The worst white fears, of dark and shadowy, hooded 'assholes' threatening their gated communities like apparitions or spectres, mix here in a halting, fragmentary manner with extracts from Zimmerman's 911 call after he saw Martin in his neighbourhood.[42] Much of the case hinged upon Zimmerman's memory, his interpretation of the scene and of the young man Martin. In the poem, 'Dark' first refers to the weather conditions of that night, but echoes the pathetic fallacy in setting the scene for what will come. The next iteration, 'was dark and', leaves an unspoken indent where Martin's name could go, had he not been killed, or had Zimmerman admitted that the teen's skin colour had inspired the conclusion that he was suspicious. Finishing on 'and' the line suggests that skin colour has ramifications which might be 'set' insofar as there is little that can be done to alter pre-determined negative views.

---

has generally been seen as an act of white racist violence. However, Zimmerman's mother is Peruvian and his father of German ancestry so he is mixed-race Hispanic or what has been referred to by some as 'white Hispanic'. See Nicole Akoukou Thompson, 'George Zimmerman's Ethnicity: Is He White, Latino, or 'White Hispanic'?', *Latin Post*, 24 October 2013.

40. Cathy J. Cohen, 'Afterword: When Will Black Lives Matter? Neoliberalism, Democracy, and the Queering of American Activism in the Post-Obama Era' in Travis L. Gosa and Erik Nielson, eds., *The Hip Hop and Obama Reader*, New York and Oxford, Oxford University Press 2015, p282.

41. Andrea Brady, 'Song for Florida 2', *Prac Crit* 1 (July 2014). Available online: http://www.praccrit.com/poems/song-for-florida-2/. Accessed 24 March 2016. All references refer to this online page.

42. Zimmerman had a history of calling the police about black men. See http://www.motherjones.com/documents/327330-george-zimmerrman-911-call-history. Accessed 24th March 2016. He recently sold the gun which killed Martin for $250,000, donating some

^{proceeds to 'fight [Black Lives Matter] violence against law enforcement officers'. See: 'Gun that Killed Trayvon Martin Makes $250,000 for Zimmerman', *BBC News*, 22 May 2016.}

^{43. For an exploration of this last point, see: Devonya N. Havis, '"Seeing Black" through Michel Foucault's Eyes: "Stand Your Ground" Laws as an Anchorage Point for State-Sponsored Racism' in *Pursuing Trayvon*, pp 117-228.}

While they initially sound like references to elements of a neighbourhood, 'gated, dog whistles, blocks' can all be read as manifestations of racism: the gated communities that protect rich whites from the poor, often black communities they keep out; the political 'dog whistle' is a racist slur readable only to those who catch its undertones; 'blocks' compounds the containment and restraint carried by the three previous words, adding the physical sense of stoppage embodied in the Stand Your Ground laws in Florida and running on into the next line, which is from Zimmerman.[43] 'These assholes they always get away', he said in the police call, but Brady here replaces the final word, for Martin did not get away; instead, he got the spectre of white fear in fatal form. In Brady's poem, Zimmerman's regurgitated words indict him in a manner they did not manage to achieve in court. 'Song for Florida 2' opens by intimating that we are all implicated in this scene - with its opening addressed to 'you' - and the final line quoted above, repurposed from Wallace's Stevens' 'The Idea of Order at Key West', is the start of the poem's engagement with what Brady calls, in interview, his '*chiaroscuro* poetics, and its divisive *visual imagery*' which repeatedly pits whiteness against blackness or darkness. The fact that racism is embedded within language, in poetry as much as in calls to the police, is one of 'Song for Florida 2''s most implacably made points.

It is in the third and final section of the poem that Brady begins to experiment with what she has called 'empathetic identification'. The poem returns to the scene of death, firstly through Zimmerman's words from the 911 tape, then by tenderly describing Martin's dead body on the grass, and finally by failing to fully imagine the death of Brady's own son. Remarkable in this section is the address to Martin himself:

> I can be your mother, your friend, your victim, your
> juror I can't be you I can't be so quickly and inevitably dead

^{44. For an article which summarises these criticisms, see: Jelani Cobb, 'Rachel Jeantel On Trial', *The New Yorker* (27 June 2013). Available at: http://www.newyorker.com/news/news-desk/rachel-jeantel-on-trial. Accessed: 8 April 2016.}

The poet cycles through the positions of people affected or involved in Martin's death and the trial, a classic example of perspective-taking, as the language of empathy might class it, but treated too swiftly to be convincing. What looks like empathy can be dispensed fast from the position of white privilege. Yet, these lines can also be read as venturing a disquieting displacement of the black people who cared deeply for the teen, Martin's own mother and his friend, Rachel Jeantel, whose diction during her trial evidence was commented upon unfavourably in certain news reports.[44] The violating effect of this usurpation is amplified by including in the list the women who failed to convict Zimmerman, and even the suggestion that Zimmerman is Martin's victim, a potential that the poem has not until now countenanced. This kaleidoscopic position-taking, levelling all the participants to interchangeable parts of an imaginative thought experiment that ends in death, indicts empathy as empty, a form which looks good on the surface but lacks moral content and thus leads to violation.

Instead of dwelling here, though, the poem attends to the scene of death, noting, 'That is the cross of your ankles / they are tender to each other and to the hands that washed them'. But Brady quickly pulls herself out of imagining this scene, admitting, 'That is not my son. It is someone else's. / I perjure myself'. Here is a further violation, a further cuckoo intrusion into the other's family. Is Brady imagining herself as Martin's mother or imagining that Martin is her son? It could be either, and the poem marks these violations as the ethical limit to imagination, beyond which would be a transgression into bearing false witness. Empathy is shown to end in falsehood here, even in a kind of child appropriation, until the poet refuses to continue. Empathetic identification, Brady intimates, can be almost seductive, drawing the empathiser into gestures that over-step propriety. There is another option, in the lexicon of empathy's positions, however, and Brady exhausts it in the poem's final few lines by attempting and failing to imagine the death of her own son, in the place of Sybrina Fulton's:

> my son unhoods himself
> for the summer his hair is white
> his head is so dear and so expansively loved
> then he flashes invisibly and safely
> into the grass we own.
> Oh Florida, protect his dear head forever
> from the likes of *YOU* I kiss him into life
> I go with the majority if the majority
> never bleeds I have to hold out
> my hand to catch his blood if I'm
> to get any

Brady's son's safety is emphasised in the clarity of the lyrical lines dedicated to describing him: unlike Martin, he is invisibly white, unhooded, and safely surrounded by his parents' private property. While Florida - and by implication, its Stand Your Ground exemptions and their racist implementation in the law - is condemned directly, with the famous Uncle Sam capitalised interpolation, the poet too indicts herself, in going with the majority. The last four lines of the poem are complex, bracketed with two conditionals that double-layer the imaginative contingencies at stake. 'I go with the majority if the majority' goes against the principles of majority rulings, which structure both democracy and justice in the U.S.A., since it suggests that one can impose conditions on a situation which does not allow for them. In the U.S.A., as the poem has repeatedly explored, the majority is white and potentially racist, so the line's run-on syntax suggests the poet plays it safe, going with the majority if it precludes pain and death. '[I]f the majority / never bleeds' seeps into the necessity of reaching for the blood of the son who does. In the final conditional, blood can only be caught - stopped? - through a supplicatory hand, that universal gesture to ask for aid.

In the poem, Brady's son does bleed, though not necessarily to death. Imagining the death of one's child Brady deems a kind of violation in itself, calling it, in the interview, 'the black hole of thought', and thereby reproducing the same linguistic error for which she upbraids Stevens (*Interview*). In the poem, the bleeding son - hers, but also, of course, Martin - leaves the poet potentially with blood on her hands. Brady is implicated in the racism that killed Martin, not just because she is American and alludes to memories of childhood racism in the poem, but precisely because her white son is safe while a black son dies at the hands of a racist. Brady does not quite put herself in Fulton's position or imagine for her own son the fate that befell Martin. That would be the violation the poem wants to mark as the imaginative limit. Such a violation might fulfil the demands of empathy but would miss the intersectional point: Brady's white son is highly unlikely to have been treated in the same way by Zimmerman and the poem's reluctance to empathise underlines how the dynamics of race, class, and nationality dictate our lives and life chances. The ethics of such an imaginative refusal of empathy lie in recognising the differences between people caused by their structural positions in a socio-economic order that is still disastrously racist, misogynistic, and economically uneven and unjust.

In *Beauty and Ugliness*, Vernon Lee upbraids Theodor Lipps for 'the dangerous advantage of using an already existing expression for a new idea' in his coining of *Einfühlung*, which became empathy (*Beauty and Ugliness*, p46). We can only wonder today what might be the name for trying to imagine another's situation or how circumstances look from their perspective if Lee and others interested in psychological aesthetics had not brought empathy into English. As it is, empathy is repeatedly subdivided and redefined in the critical, philosophical, and psychological literature. In Halpern's *Common Place*, Lee's original conception of empathy as an aesthetic affect is evident and leads to violation. The poem lacks empathy in its contemporary sense because Halpern deliberately refuses what he sees as an impossibility. Within this poetics, any attempt to empathise with the detainee would be a violation, even while the alternative violates the dead man's religion. In Brady's 'Song for Florida 2' empathy is shown to be an inadequate concept: putting ourselves in the place of the other supplants and erases them and their grief; and imagining what we might feel if their fate belonged to us or our beloveds results in the erasure of the differences which make the other's world unlike our own, when we need instead to acknowledge the injustices of those differences. These poetic works on political deaths echo the distrust of Bloom, Prinz and Berlant for empathy, which proves to be not simply an insufficient concept for imagining how to build a more just world but, through the imaginative violations it can entice us to, a dangerous way of obliterating the differences to which we need to urgently attend for that imagining to take place.

I would like to thank the two anonymous reviewers of this article and Jill Richards for their illuminating comments upon the first draft.

Jennifer Cooke is a Senior Lecturer at the Centre for Life-Writing at Wolfson College, University of Oxford and a Senior Lecturer in English at Loughborough University. She's editor of the book of essays *Scenes of Intimacy: Reading, Writing and Theorizing Contemporary Literature* (Bloomsbury Academic, 2013), and a special issue of *Textual Practice* on challenging intimacies and psychoanalysis (September 2013). Previous publications include *Legacies of Plague in Literature, Theory and Film* (Palgrave Macmillan, 2009). Her research interests lies in theories of intimacy; the affective turn and theories of the emotions; queer and feminist theories; and experimental literature of the twentieth and twenty-first centuries. She is currently working on a monograph, *The New Audacity: Contemporary Feminist Life-Writing*.

Imaginary Intimacies: Death and New Temporalities in the Work of Denise Riley and Nicholas Royle

Georgina Colby

Abstract In *The Severed Head: Capital Visions* (2014), Julia Kristeva understands there to be two forms of relation to death in contemporary culture. The 'imaginary intimacy with death, which transforms melancholy or desire into representation and thought' is opposed in Kristeva's work to 'the rational realization' of the act of capital punishment, the former epitomizing 'vision' in contrast to the 'action' of the latter. This essay proposes that Kristeva's idea of an 'imaginary intimacy' with death can be read in the context of contemporary literary responses to the death of a loved one by Denise Riley and Nicholas Royle. In particular, this essay addresses the relationship between death and new temporalities in Riley's essay *Time Lived, Without Its Flow* (2012), her recent collection of poems *Say Something Back* (2016), and Royle's *Quilt* (2010). The non-linear models of time found in Riley's and Royle's works are contextualised via the attempts in phenomenology to theorise the relations between temporality and finitude, as well as via Stephen J Gould's work on geological time. For Riley, the experience of the death of her son brings with it an 'altered condition of life' in which time takes the form of 'a-temporality.' Questioning the limits of the sentence, and collapsing the narrative boundaries between the living narrator and the deceased father, *Quilt* traverses the boundaries between experience lived and an experience impossible to claim. Through such an analysis the essay explores the capacity of experimental works to harbour new non-linear temporalities that reflect on the relation between temporality and finitude in the contemporary.

Keywords temporality, death, experimental writing

1. Julia Kristeva, *The Severed Head: Capital Visions*, translated by Jody Gladding, New York: Columbia University Press, 2012, p91. (Hereafter *Severed Head*).

In 1998, Julia Kristeva curated an exhibit for the Louvre titled 'Capital Visions'. The exhibition formed part of the gallery's *parti pris*, or 'biased view' series. In *The Severed Head: Capital Visions* (2014), the book that emerged from her exhibition, Kristeva understands there to be two forms of relation to death in contemporary culture. There is the 'imaginary intimacy with death, which transforms melancholy or desire into representation and thought'.[1] Such imaginary intimacy is opposed in Kristeva's work to 'the rational realisation' of the act of capital punishment, the former epitomising 'vision' in contrast to the 'action' of the latter. This essay positions Kristeva's idea of an imaginary intimacy with death in relation to two contemporary literary responses to experiencing the death of a loved one: Denise Riley's essay *Time Lived, Without Its Flow* (2012) and her recent volume of poetry *Say Something Back* (2016), and Nicholas Royle's experimental novel, *Quilt* (2010). Riley's works and Royle's work share a meditation on the impossibility of representing death within conventional narrative form. Both too offer insights into new temporalities that emerge in writing about death. By the term 'experimental writing', I refer to writing that disrupts conventional relations between word and referent and thereby obstructs conventional meaning. This essay argues that experimental writing has a unique capacity to inscribe death and create the textual conditions for the attendant non-linear temporalities that accompany the experience of bereavement.

The vital question of the representation of death has been at the forefront of a number of studies.[2] For Kristeva death is the 'fundamental invisible' (*Severed Head*, p4). She compares modern painting, which copies objects from the external world in acts of representation with the Byzantine icon, which 'inscribes the presence of a religious experience'. An icon, Kristeva argues, does not represent, rather 'it is taken in, it is absorbed, it is experienced: it translates an invisible world into its visible lines' (p41-2). In his 1984 book *Death Sentence: Styles of Dying in British Fiction*, Garrett Stewart takes up the paradox that writers meet when attempting to render the experience of death in language and literature. For Stewart, death is 'treacherous, excessive, the occasion of terror' but 'without being a renderable object of it'. This denotative absence inherent to death is such that 'the notion in the name of death, waiting untamed beyond any representation, remains, for all its attendant anxiety, unthinkable; for all its tenacity, in the root sense *untenable* - refusing containment either of content or by form - becoming in itself just a form or figure of speech'.[3] Death brings an intractable absence to literature for Stewart: 'it is the intransigent abstraction death that persists across literary history as a semantically unoccupied zone of utterance, at once linguistic horizon and void' (*Death Sentence*, p4-5). In his rigorous work on the representation of death and absence in modern French poetry, Richard Stamelman calls attention to the relation between writing and loss. Citing Robert Hass he states: 'a word is an elegy to what it signifies'.[4] The dispossession at the core of representation, in Stamelman's view, 'makes possible the creation of images, and, negatively as embodied in absence, death and loss animate the quest of writing and other forms of figuration'(*Lost Beyond Telling*, p21). This essay explores the ways in which Riley's work, in its engagement with a-temporality and abstraction, and Royle's work, in its engagement with deep time and etymological layering, offer new forms of figuration of death through experimental textual practice. Experimental writing is able to represent denotative absence and the 'dispossession at the core of representation' of which Stamelman writes.

Denise Riley's essay *Time Lived, Without its Flow*, and her collection of poetry *Say Something Back* are works written after the death of her son. Riley proposes

2. For example Sarah Goodwin and Elisabeth Bronfen (eds), *Death and Representation*, Baltimore and London, The John Hopkins University Press 1993.

3. Garrett Stewart, *Death Sentence: Styles of Dying in British Fiction*, Cambridge Mass, Harvard University Press 1984, p4. (Hereafter *Death Sentence*).

4. Richard Stamelman, *Lost Beyond Telling: Representations of Death and Absence in Modern French Poetry*, Cornell University Press 1990, p.ix. (Hereafter *Lost Beyond Telling*).

that there is an intimate alliance between the possibilities for describing and the temporalities we inhabit. Within contemporary culture she understands responses to death to be either silence or the 'sweetened overlay' of highly conventional expressions of sentiment, each of which is a consequence of the 'impassable structural barriers to telling'.[5] Riley's and Royle's works offer depictions of the relation between death and temporality that are historically specific to the contemporary moment. This essay explores the way in which experiment with language and form is able to harbour the new temporalities experienced by, in Riley's work, the bereaved parent, and in Royle's work, the bereaved child, and to move beyond the ' structural barriers to telling' that Riley understands to be present in contemporary culture in the twenty-first century. In each of the three works discussed here, the engagement with the new experienced temporalities through experimental inscription gives rise to an imaginary intimacy with the deceased.

The phenomenological tradition has sought to think through the relationships between temporality and finitude. In *Being and Time* (1927), Heidegger offers a theory of temporality aligned with his theory of existence as being-towards-death. Heidegger understands death to be a 'phenomenon of life'.[6] For Heidegger: 'If indeed death belongs in a distinctive sense to the Being of Dasein, then death (or Being-towards-the-end) must be defined in terms of these characteristics' (p293). Finitude is the prerequisite for authentic life and, in relation to this imbrication of finitude with authentic life, mortality is the condition for freedom. The basic structure of temporality for Heidegger is being-towards-death, in which, as Bruce Baugh has observed 'the future illuminates, determines and so is "prior" to the past and present'.[7]

In each of the texts examined here two temporalities operate: the time of the lived world (linear time) and the time of death and mourning (non-linear time). These two narrative temporalities position experimental writing in a certain dialogue with Stephen J Gould's work on geological time. When depicting death, Riley alludes to the natural world and physical law. Royle specifically refers to the concept of deep time and uses the metaphor of the ray to signify death's vast temporality. The unrepresentability of death can be brought into dialogue with the incomprehensibility of deep time. Each presents a temporality impossible to cognitively grasp. Gould remarks: 'Deep time is so alien that we can really only understand it as a metaphor'.[8] Gould articulates a well-worn dichotomy of the nature of history in terms of two temporal concepts: 'time's arrow', that is the idea that 'history is an irreversible sequence of unrepeatable events' in which '[e]ach moment occupies its own distinct position in a temporal series, and all moments, considered in proper sequence, tell a story of linked events moving in a direction'; and 'time's cycle' - events that have no meaning as distinct episodes with causal impact upon a contingent history. Fundamental states are immanent within time, always present and never changing. Apparent motions are parts of repeating cycles, and differences of the past will be realities of the future. Time has no

5. Denise Riley, *Time Lived, Without Its Flow*, London, Capsule Editions 2012, p58. (Hereafter *Time Lived*).

6. Martin Heidegger, *Being and Time*, (trans) John Macquarrie and Edward Robinson, Oxford, Blackwell Publishing 2015, p290.

7. Bruce Baugh, 'Death and Temporality in Deleuze and Derrida', *Anglelaki, Journal of the theoretical humanities*, 5:2, August 2000; pp73-83, p73.

8. Stephen Jay Gould, *Time's Arrow, Time's Cycle: Myth and Metaphor in the Geological Discovery of Deep Time*, Harvard, Harvard University Press 1987, p3. (Hereafter *Time's Arrow*).

direction' (*Time's Arrow*, p11). The experimental text holds the capacity to represent non-linear forms of time through experimentalism, and to thus offer unconventional narrative temporalities that are more akin to cyclical time and non-historical temporality than linear time, the time of history, and the time of conventional narrative.

The alignment of the time of death with geological time in Riley's and Royle's works renegotiates the relation between temporality and finitude. Deep time, as Gould observes, imposes a 'great temporal limitation ... upon human importance' (p2). The idea of an earth that has its origins at the onset of human rule, Gould points out, is compatible with human domination. Geological time is, conversely, threatening, putting forth 'the notion of an almost incomprehensible immensity, with human habitation restricted to a millimicrosecond at the very end' (p2). By aligning the deceased and the temporality of death with geological time, Riley and Royle offer a counterpart to the finitude of human death, opening the text into a different temporality that runs counter to the irreversible events of linear time that are documented in the texts.

Riley's and Royle's works are works of mourning centred upon the deceased. Each text constitutes a loss of self in the process of mourning the other. Such a positioning can be read in a certain counter relation to Heidegger's idea bound to 'being-toward-death' in *Being and Time* that only one's own death is authentic death. In a 2002 article, Simon Critchley challenges Heidegger's non-relational notion of death with 'the thought of the fundamentally relational character of finitude, namely that death is first and foremost experienced as a relation to the death and dying of the other and others, in being-with the dying in a caring way, and in grieving after they are dead'.[9] This is a position taken by Derrida. Derrida maintains the Heideggerian relation between temporality and finitude in *The Gift of Death* (1995). However, for Derrida it is the gift of death that 'puts me into relation with the transcendence of the other' and which 'gives me a new experience of death'.[10] For Derrida, it is the 'concern for death', it is 'this conscience that looks death in the face' that is freedom (p16). The relational idea of death as Derrida and Critchley conceive it is present in Riley's and Royle's works. Riley and Royle write about the undoing of the self, and the loss of the self in the process of grief and mourning. This symbiosis with the deceased involves a movement out of linear time and a movement into new temporalities associated with death.

9. Simon Critchley, 'Enigma Variations: An Interpretation of Heidegger's Sein und Zeit', *Ratio: An International Journal of Analytic Philosophy*, Vol 15, Issue 2, June 2002: pp154-175.

10. Jacques Derrida, *The Gift of Death*, (trans) David Wills, Chicago and London, University of Chicago Press 1995, p6.

A-TEMPORALITY AND NARRATION: TIME LIVED, WITHOUT ITS FLOW

In the opening lines of her essay, Riley explains: 'I'll not be writing about death, but about an altered condition of life' (*Time Lived*, p7). Riley contends that the death of a child causes a pluralising of temporality for the mother who outlives the child. The experience Riley found herself confronted with after the death of her son was 'of suddenly living in arrested time: that acute sense of being cut off from any temporal flow' (p7). This condition Riley terms 'a-temporality'. The curtailing of linear temporality, and the recognition of plural temporalities within a lived condition, opposes every assumption Riley had of lived time. Riley's allusion to her inherent apprehension of time as linear is characteristic, in Gould's view, of Western thought. He cites Richard Morris, in his work *Time's Arrow*, who observed the belief of ancient peoples that time was cyclic, whereas in the contemporary Western world people, in Morris's words 'habitually think of time as something that stretches in a straight line into the past and future' (*Time's Arrow*, p12).[11] Importantly, for Riley as a writer her experience of a-temporality 'is also a question of what is describable, and what are the linguistic limits of what can be conveyed' (*Time Lived*, p9). Conventional narrative is imbricated with linear time. A-temporality cannot be expressed within a language that assumes a past and a future. The very act of writing was impossible for Riley for two years after her son's death because of the relation to past and future that inheres in the act of narrating. 'Describing', she explains, 'would involve some notion of the passage of time. Narrating would imply at least a hint of 'and then' and 'after that'. Any written or spoken sentence would naturally lean forward towards its development and conclusion, unlike my own paralysed time' (p10). To live on in paralysed time is to live on 'without inhabiting any tense yourself' (p57). Narration becomes 'structurally impossible', because, for Riley, as the movement of time stops for the bereaved person 'so do all the customary 'befores' and 'afters' that underpin narration' (p57). In this condition any comprehension of sequence is taken away, and this has obvious linguistic implications: 'A sentence slopes forward into its own future, as had your former intuition of a mobile time. But now your newly stopped time is stripped of that direction. Or, rather the notion of directedness is gone' (p58). A-temporality brings with it then a cessation of narrative time.

The experience of a-temporality is closely connected to an imaginary intimacy with the deceased. The suspended state of a-temporality is for Riley the temporality of her son's death. In a journal entry six months after the death she articulates her son's death as a 'vicarious death'. She writes: 'If a sheet of blackness fell on him, it has fallen on me too. As if I also know that blankness after his loss of consciousness' (p21). The experience and perception of a-temporality ushers in a revelation of the conflation of time with the self: 'You *are* time. You are saturated with it, rather than standing apart from it as a previously completed being who was free to move in it'(p59). Taking up Merleau-Ponty's work on the relation of time to the self in *Phenomenology of Perception* (1945), Riley draws the relation between linear time and self-presence. She cites Merleau-Ponty's idea that 'the explosion or dehiscence of the present towards a future is the archetype of *the relationship of self to self*, and it traces out an interiority or an ipseity' (p60).[12] The relation between the sequence of time and self-presence is intricately related to the perception

11. Here Gould is citing Richard Morris, *Time's Cycle*, New York, Simon and Schuster 1984, p11.

12. Here Riley is citing Maurice Merleau-Ponty, *Phenomenology of Perception*, (trans) Colin Smith, London, Routledge, Kegan & Paul 1962, p410.

of a future. By contrast, the experience of a-temporality brings a loss of any sense of interiority and the experience of self-absence, a lived absence that is an intimate relation with the deceased. The inability to narrate parallels this absence. Throughout the essay Riley refers to 'the death' when speaking of the death of her son. This use of the definite article in place of the possessive pronoun 'his' is a way of voicing the failure of grammar when confronted with the task of inscribing death. 'The very grammar of death,' Riley observes, 'falters in its conviction in the same breath that the focus of talk, the formerly living person, himself disintegrates'. She states: 'Even the plainest "he died" is a strange sentence, since there's no longer a human subject to sustain that "he"' (p54). Any death, in Riley's understanding, seems to cause 'the collapse of the simplest referring language': 'As if the grammatical subject of the sentence and the human subject have been felled together by the one blow' (p55). This crisis of the referent that death engenders is a feature of the experimentalism of Riley's and Royle's works. The paradox of language, for Riley, is that the 'continuing possibilities for discussing the no longer existing person' persist so that 'a curious linguistic quasi-resurrection' emerges within language itself. This tension between the absence of the subject and the presence implicated in the structures of language when writing of the deceased pervades Riley's work. Within language, Riley notes, '[n]o subject can easily be conceived as extinguished. Language doesn't want to allow that thought; its trajectory is always to lean forward into life, to push it along, to propel the dead onward among the living' (p56). It is precisely for this reason that conventional language structures cannot accommodate death.

Philosophies of time and narrative alike fail to account for the new a-temporal condition. For example, the idea of time and narrative being imbricated with interiority is fundamental to William James's idea of the stream of thought and the 'specious present' set out in the fifteenth chapter of *The Principles of Psychology* (1890). Riley remarks that whilst philosophies of time understand 'how atomised instants of perception may be felt as an extended streaming,' the experience of a-temporality, 'this other feeling of a literal timelessness' remains unrecognized (*Time Lived*, p58). Riley does not specify which philosophies of time she is alluding to but it is pertinent to think through Riley's comments on a-temporality in relation to James's stream of thought and Henri Bergson's duration (*la durèe*). The idea of the 'specious present', whilst it rejects conventional notions of time, implicates temporal sequence within the present moment. James defines the specious present as 'the original paragon and prototype of all conceived times, the short duration of which we are immediately and incessantly aware'.[13] It is for James 'all my *direct experiences*, whether subjective or objective' (p638). As Gerald E Myers remarks: 'The fact that one word or note precedes the other is recognised during the enduring *now*, and thus the before-after relation is given in the present moment'.[14] Perception within the specious present is characterised by this simultaneity. This is a touchstone of modernist thought and experiment.

13. William James, *The Principles of Psychology: Volume One*, New York, Dover Publications 1950, p631.

14. Gerald E. Myers, *William James: His Life and Thought*, London and New Haven, Yale University Press 2001, p146. (Hereafter *William James*).

A paradigmatic visual illustration is Marcel Duchamp's *Nude Descending the Staircase* (1912) in which the multiple variations of the nude are held on one present temporal plane simultaneously. Myers observes that the Jamesian concept of the specious present 'not only allows but requires that the initial and final phases of the specious present be perceived simultaneously, and the intervening temporal relations are made noticeable within and because of those temporal boundaries' (*William James*, p146). Riley's a-temporal perception is dispossessed of any before-after relations. It is a state of exteriority rather than interiority, and therefore does not share the temporal boundaries of the stream of consciousness; nor does Riley's a-temporal condition share the phenomenological relation between temporality and finitude that is ascribed to the living in Heidegger's thought.

Riley's intent in *Time Lived, Without Its Flow* is to document this experience of arrested time. The death of a child brings for the bereaved mother an experiential form of temporal defamiliarisation, which is matched in Riley's work with a literary form of temporal defamiliarisation. The Russian formalist critic Viktor Shklovsky claimed that when the general laws of perception are examined it becomes evident that 'as perception becomes habitual, it becomes automatic'.[15] For Shklovsky:

15. Viktor Shklovsky, 'Art as Technique' in *Russian Formalist Criticism: Four Essays*, (trans) Lee T. Lemon and Marion J. Reis, Nebraska, University of Nebraska Press 2012, pp 3-25, this citation, p11. First published in 1965.

> art exists that one may recover the sensation of life; it exists to make one feel things, to make the stone stony. The purpose of art is to impart the sensation of things as they are perceived and not as they are known. The technique of art is to make objects 'unfamiliar', to make forms difficult, to increase the difficulty and length of perception because the process of perception is an aesthetic end in itself and must be prolonged (p12).

The experience of a-temporality brings with it a form of temporal defamiliarisation, which is accompanied by 'a vividly physical perception' (*Time Lived*. p51). The pluralising of temporality in this new condition is such that 'multiple possible temporal perceptions' become apparent to Riley (p50). At work in Riley's essay and poetry is a form of defamiliarisation that takes Riley out of the perceptual habits of time, and, through literary abstraction, offers an inscription of a-temporality as it is perceived and experienced by the bereaved parent.

A-CHRONICITY AND ABSTRACTION

Riley differentiates a state of 'a-chronicity' from the familiar idea that bereavement brings about a distortion of time. The feeling of 'a-chronicity' arises from the halting of sequence, a state in which there is 'no impression of any succession in events, there is no linkage and no cause' (p50). Unlike the distortion of time, a-chronicity has 'no traces of old temporal shapes, and it resists intelligible description'. Instead, the experience of a-temporality involves 'violently new and hitherto unsuspected states of temporal perception' (p48). Riley articulates herself as inhabiting 'this sharply distinctive life inside a new temporal dimension' (p52). The struggle to convey this state within language is realised in Riley's linguistic abstraction both in the series of journal entries in her essay, and in the volume of poems *Say Something Back*.

In Riley's works, imaginary intimacy works on two levels. It is the intimacy between mother and deceased child within the shared condition of a-temporality, and an empathetical relation between the reader of the text and the author of the work. Prefacing her journal entries, Riley takes up the problem with the typical response to her experience of outliving her child. She draws attention to the paradox inherent to the typical statement of sympathy 'I cannot imagine what you are feeling'. This is at once an expression of sympathy but also 'a disavowal of the possibility of empathy'. In response, Riley states her aim to convey 'this curious sense of being pulled right outside of time' (p12). The experience of the new a-temporal perception ushers in new modes of empathy. Riley states that she would like people to '*try* to imagine' what she is experiencing, rather than to renounce the possibility of grasping her condition, and thus relegating those with dead children into the realms of the 'unimaginable'.

Riley's attempt to articulate the sudden transition into a state of a-temporality, a form of non-relational time, explains her repeated use of simile throughout her essay. Thus, for example, Riley describes herself being pulled outside of time 'as if beached in a clear light' (p12). In his short essay on the text, Peter Riley comments on the way in which Denise Riley makes her experience known through the 'discourse of simile'.[16] Simile is able to inscribe the inexpressible condition of a-temporality through the comparison of the condition with often abstract yet renderable states. In simile the inexpressible condition of death is only ever articulated in terms of its approximation to something else, it is never directly represented, rather it is both gestured towards and shielded through analogy. Simile enables both inscription and abstraction, offering a form of figuration of a-temporality, whilst harbouring the impossibility of representing death. In her essay on abstract art, Catherine de Zegher notes that dictionaries derive the adjective 'abstract' from '*abstrahere*' 'meaning "to draw from, to remove, to separate," and define the noun "abstraction" as "the act or process of abstracting: the state of being abstracted."'[17] Zegher observes: 'Inherent to these definitions in art is the notion that preceding the abstraction there is something from which the form has been drawn'. This could, Zegher remarks, be an object in the phenomenal world but it could equally be comprehended as 'the formation of an idea apart from any perceivable object, understood that is, as thought itself' (*Abstract*, p23). Abstraction offers a form of nonrepresentational writing. Riley's form of figuration of arrested time linguistically resembles the aesthetic practices of abstract artists such as Hillma af Klint and Agnes Martin. Klint's *Parcitai Series, Group 2, Section 4: The Convolute of the Physical Plane, Backwards, November 1916* (watercolour on paper) is part of a series

16. Peter Riley, 'Denise Riley and the Force of Bereavement'. *The Fortnightly Review*, 21 March, 2012. http://fortnightlyreview.co.uk/2012/03/denise-riley-force-bereavement/

17. Catherine de Zegher (ed.), 'Abstract' in *3x and Abstraction: New Methods of Drawing by Hilma Af Klint, Emma Kunz and Agnes Martin*, New Haven, Yale University Press 2005, p23. (Hereafter *Abstract*)

of six monochrome watercolours. Group 2 section 4 is a yellow square with the word 'backwards' written in the margin of the painting. The stark yellow paint floods the canvas, at once illuminating and glaring in its brightness. Riley's use of visual abstraction, using light and colour as denotative of her objectless state, is comparable to Klint's practice. For her part, Agnes Martin achieved timeless form through abstraction. Martin understood painting to have the capacity to resist representation. Works such as *Morning* (1965) gesture to something beyond representation, which remains unrepresented yet acknowledged through the abstract work. In contrast to Riley's essay, Martin's work points to blissful states of mind. Yet the rectangular system of co-ordinates that resists any notion of sequence and before-after relations offers an illuminating comparison with Riley's notion of a-temporality and aesthetic temporal suspension. As Zegher notes, for af Klint, abstract figuration is a mode of visualising the 'ineffable and the super sensible in a metaphysical cosmology that deals with the universe as an orderly system and has its space-time relationships rooted in science and theosophy' (p23-24). In this work, the condition of a-temporality is an abstracted state of temporality.

Riley's similes are modes of verbalising the ineffable and stand in contrast to the crisis of expression encountered in normal time in twenty-first century culture. A passage in which Riley recalls her inability to enunciate the word 'ashes' a day after Jacob's death takes up the issue of simile:

> In how many ways this folded-together state appears. You already share the 'timeless time' of the dead child. As if you'd died too, or had lost the greater part of your own life. As if a new ether of no-time stands still in your veins. That's the over-arching 'as if'. Then there's an 'as if' of uttering, when the speech of the one left behind can turn staccato. That first day afterward, speaking by phone to the funeral director, I needed to yet could not get the word 'ashes' out of my mouth without a strenuous physical struggle. 'Ah-aassh-aashhes', came a dry stammer. As if uttered through sawdust (*Time Lived*, p38-39).

In the opening lines the simile gestures towards a shared experience with the deceased child in a concrete unambiguous relation of empathy and intimacy: 'As if you died too, or had lost the greater part of your own life'. Here 'you' addresses both Riley and the reader. In doing so, it very precisely invites the reader to imagine what Riley is experiencing. However, the experience of a-temporality then demands a further movement into abstracted language and imagery: 'As if a new ether of no-time stands still in your veins'. This use of simile is a movement outside of conventional language use to invite empathetic engagement with an experience outside of the everyday. It stands in contrast to the 'as if' of uttering, where 'as if' denotes incomprehensibility and impossibility, a state attached to living in the ordinary world. Riley's recollection of her failure to enunciate the word 'ashes', as part of a necessary social exchange, registers a sense of the gap between her experience and ordinary language: 'That first day afterward, speaking by the phone to the funeral director, I needed to yet could not get the word 'ashes' out of my mouth without a strenuous physical struggle'. At this point, the perspective of the writing, distanced through a first-person factual account, removes the reader from the experience of a-temporality. The perspective then shifts back again and strives to close the distance between narrative voice and reader with the simile: 'As if uttered through sawdust'. What cannot be enunciated in the factual account, which positions the reader as a bystander to Riley's struggle, is inscribed through the use of simile. The simile moves the narrative back into a-temporality and the folded-together state of the narrator and her deceased child.

Riley continues to reflect on her struggle with expression. Of her inability to enunciate the word 'ashes' she uses a vivid, abstract statement: 'A cut fell between the thought and its voicing' (p38-39). The phrase gives materiality to the word 'cut' through the use of the verb 'fell', as if the cut were a physical object. The similes that follow voice the folded-together state of Riley and her deceased son. Once again, it is simile that has the capacity to inscribe a-temporality. Such expression is not possible in the given world that witnesses only Riley's stammering. Riley's physical incapacity to speak the words 'disposal of his ashes' in the social context is counteracted in this text through the use of simile. 'As if' the mouth 'had itself become sifted up thickly with ashes'. Ashes are not disposed of but rather the body of the mother is folded-in with the body of the child in an imaginary intimacy inscribed through simile. This for Riley, is a 'transfer of affect', which she compares to the 'blurring of the physical edges that happens between lovers'. It is an intimacy and a form of symbiosis made possible as inscription through the use of simile, and stands in contrast to the cut experienced between thought and voicing that the demand to enunciate precipitates.

The notes that Riley reproduces in *Time Lived, Without Its Flow*, a series of journal entries written after the death of her son, reveal the emergence of literary abstraction as a means to inscribe her experience of a-temporality. At the outset she explains that her notes are 'condemned to walk around only the rim of this experience' (p13). The use of the word 'rim' again materialises the incomprehensible experience and once more offers a clear, tangible physicality to the impossible experience. Simile and metaphoric, physical language, defamiliarises Riley's experience to offer a non-denotative yet vivid depiction of her states of perception in the condition of a-temporality. The simile embodies the idea of ontological disjunction - 'as if'; where metaphor insists on ontological parity. Thus, in her first entry two weeks after the death she writes: 'In these first days I see how rapidly the surface of the world, like a sheet of water that's briefly agitated, will close silently and smoothly over a death. His, everyone's, mine. I see, as if I am myself dead. This perception makes me curiously light-hearted' (p14). The ontological disjunction of simile marks the separation between the indifferent world and the a-temporality of the narrator's state. It is the indifferent world that is the subject of the passage, yet the abstract aesthetics of the passage locate the narrative in the a-temporal condition. The distance between the narrator and the world is unfathomable and, within the framework of the inscription, immeasurable. The vastness of the planetary conception of the earth is brought into relation with, and is a means to achieve, abstraction. The allusion to the natural world brings together the state of a-temporality and geological deep time. The colossal perspective implicated in the 'surface of the world' indicates the spatial relation that accords to a-temporality and exteriority. The voice is far removed from what is being seen and perceived. The paradoxical state of the bereaved who has in part died, but in part is invigorated by the spirit of the child is evidenced in the clear juxtaposition of the two states in the line: 'You are cut down, and yet you burn with life'. Abstraction and simile pervade the entries and give breath to the expressionless, objectless state. Thus, one month after the death Riley writes:

> At the death of your child, you see how the edge of the living world gives onto burning whiteness. This edge is a clean strip of celluloid film. First came the intact negative full of blackened life in shaded patches, then abruptly, this milkiness. This candid whiteness, where a life stopped. Nothing 'poetic', not the white radiance of an eternity - but sheer non-being, which is brilliantly plain (p16).

Inexistence, non-being, is rendered a perceivable state through the objectless colour white. Any possible religious associations of the whiteness perceived by Riley are stripped away and brought into abstract visual radiance by the words 'brilliantly plain'. The transparency of celluloid gives a tangible apprehension to the parameters of Riley's perception of the world, which remains non-denotative and non-concrete. There is no object yet the objectless non-relational state is clear, and conceivable through abstraction.

The pervasive instances of simile are antithetical to the encounters with language in the everyday world that have no bearing on the condition of a-temporality yet persist in the structures of conventional language. Riley observes:

> Unanticipated death does such violence to your ordinary suppositions, as if the whole faculty of induction by which you'd previously lived has crumbled. Its textbook illustration was always, 'Will the sun rise tomorrow?' But now that induction is no more, the sun can't any longer be relied on to rise. And my son does not rise. This silly pun alone can reliably work its mechanical work' (p27).

The 'mechanical work' of the pun parallels the mechanical conventions of language and the outside world in Riley's work. In contrast to the work of simile, the pun's only motility is within the bounds of definitive everyday meanings. Grappling with the absence of her child the pun is deficient in grasping the ineffable: 'It stills seems ludicrous to decide, finally, that I shall not see that face on earth [...] More limp puns abound. You conceived the child, but you can't conceive of its death' (p33). By contrast, in simile, the evasion of fixed meaning opens up space for the inscription of a-temporality. Five months after the death Riley writes:

> Wandering around in an empty plain, as if an enormous drained landscape lying behind your eyes had turned itself outward. Or you find yourself camped on a threshold between inside and out. The slight contact of your senses with the outer world, and your interior only thinly separated from it, like a membrane resonating on the verge between silence and noise. If it were to tear through, there's so little behind your skin that you would fall out towards the side of sheer exteriority (p19).

Simile is able to articulate the void here: 'an enormous drained landscape' is not directly conceivable, yet it voices a mode of perception, as does the abstract idea of being 'camped on a threshold between inside and out'. 'A membrane resonating on the verge between silence and noise' can be apprehended as a mode of perception. These geological, abstract images vividly render the inconceivable state of a-temporality.

There is arguably more of struggle to represent the timeless time of death in the poetry. The physical language and abstraction found in the diary entries is not as present in the poetry, in which Riley wrestles with the conventions of poetry and elegy, as well as with the conventions of mourning in the lived world. Riley's 'A Part Song', first published in the *London Review of Books* in 2012, is a sequence of twenty poems often read as a companion piece to her essay. The sequential form of the body of work stands in tension with the non-sequential nature of Riley's notion of a-chronicity. The formal tension between sequence and a-chronicity mirrors the temporal demands of telling in *Time Lived, Without Its Flow* that strain and constrain the writer's narration of a-temporality. A later poem, published after 'A Part Song', titled 'Death Makes Dead Metaphor Revive', takes up the relation between death and what she terms 'dead metaphor':

> Death makes dead metaphor revive,
> Turn stiffly bright and strong.
> Time that is felt as 'stopped' will freeze
> Its to-fro, fro-to song
>
> I parrot under feldspar rock
> Sunk into chambered ice.
> Language, the spirit of the dead,
> May mouth each utterance twice.

> Spirit as echo clowns around
> In punning repartee
> Since each word overhears itself
> Laid bare, clairaudiently.
>
> An orphic engine revs but floods
> Choked on its ardent weight.
> Disjointed anthems dip and bob
> Down time's defrosted spate.
>
> Over its pools of greeney melt
> The rearing ice will tilt.
> To make *rhyme* chime again with *time*
> I sound a curious lilt.[18]

18. Denise Riley, *Say Something Back*, London, Picador 2016, p62.

The poem voices in poetic form the tensions between normal temporal flow and the a-temporality in which the poet finds herself existing. Riley's ironic choice of the 'hymn meter' for the poem is an aural analogue to the revival of dead metaphor that death brings. The poet repeats, parrots language under the feldspar, a transparent rock-forming mineral. Here, as in *Time Lived Without Its Flow*, the poet's existence in the stasis of a-temporality and removal from the world is brought into relation with motility and natural law. Time in the final lines is geological, measured by the thawing ice. At the same time the final lines foreground the artifice in the use of rhyme and conventional poetic forms of elegy and hymn, while pointing to the poet's own struggle to bring atemporal experience into language.

The abstract clarity in expression and imagery found in Riley's journal entries is present in the shorter poems in 'A Part Song', placed toward the end of the sequence. These poems address neither the poet nor the son:

> xvi
> Dead, keep me company
> That sear like titanium
> Compacted in the pale
> Blaze of living on alone (p12).

Here the use of simile, as in *Time Lived, Without Its Flow*, offers a mode of inscribing the ineffable. The image of burning titanium and the 'pale blaze / of living on alone' inscribe the objectless state and non-relative time of a-temporality, abstracted form the ordinary world. In the following poem Riley reaches an abstract harmony whereby the state of a-temporality is rendered in tetrameter with no recourse to the constraints of poetic convention:

xvii
Suspended in unsparing light
The sloping gull arrests its curl
The glassy sea is hardened waves
Its waters lean through shining air
Yet never crash but hold their arc
Hung rigidly in glaucous ropes
Muscled and gleaming. All that
Should flow is sealed, is poised
In implacable stillness. Joined in
Non-time and halted in free-fall (p13).

The sea that holds the deceased child's ashes is brought here into dialogue with the abstract physicality that Riley understands to be characteristic of a-temporality. This poem offers a site of imaginary intimacy through abstraction and contemplation of the natural world and physical law. There is no past or future in the lines, nor is there a subject. Mother and son are both present, 'Joined in non-time', yet absent as subjects in the poem. Time is frozen through the verbs 'suspended', 'arrests', 'hold', 'hung', 'sealed', 'poised', and 'halted'. Water is 'hardened', solidified, so that it does not move. The use of sea imagery creates an abstract sublimity, imbricated with geological time, which inscribes the state of non-time and pure exteriority.

DEATH AND DEEP TIME: NICHOLAS ROYLE'S *QUILT*

Nicholas Royle's *Quilt* confronts the impossibility of conventional narrative to accommodate the experience of death. Questioning the limits of the sentence, and collapsing narrative boundaries between the living narrator and the deceased father, *Quilt* traverses the boundaries between experience lived and an experience impossible to claim. In content and form, Royle brings the experience of death into relation with deep time. The novel is divided into three parts. The first part documents the father's death and the funeral of the father. In this part there is the collapsing of the language of the narrator with the language of the father and frequent instances of experimentation with inflection and word play. In the second part, the narrator clears the house and builds a ray pool. Here the experiment moves to infiltrating the prose with the language of the environment. In the third part the narrator detaches from reality and shifts to an obsession with the rays and language. Royle offers a mode of imaginary intimacy with death through bringing deep time into relation with experiment with form and language. In *Quilt* the work centres on the bereavement of a son after the death of his father. As in *Time Lived, Without Its Flow*, there is a disparity between the time lived in the world and the time of the bereaved. The work opens with the lines: 'In the middle of the night the phone rings, over and over, but I don't hear it. First it is the hospital, then the police'.[19] These lines of the text are separated from the subsequent passage that moves back in time to the days before the narrator's father's death by an omega, the final letter of the Greek alphabet. The omega marks the end in the secular sense of the series of letters that form the alphabet, and, in Christianity is associated with the Book of Revelations, and the apocalypse. In Royle's novel it is often used to separate sections of the narrative. The implication is that the writing that follows is positioned after the end, which is recurring.

The opening statement is repeated throughout the book, creating a circular structure to the text. In his Afterword titled 'Reality Literature' Royle comments on the distance between the reader and the narrator: 'The reader hears what the narrator doesn't hear. It is the novel calling. The novel is a kind of weird telephone exchange'. That which Royle terms 'reality literature' is 'writing that acknowledges this weirdness and goes somewhere that's not foreseeable, either for the author or for the reader' (*Quilt*, p157). The first omega is followed by the words 'these things happen from time to time'. As with the opening recollection, the phrase is repeated throughout the book. Yet rather than folding the narrative back into one moment of linear time, the saying, spoken by the father and repeated by the son, gestures to a plurality of temporalities. In a later section the narrator draws on the phrase to suggest that a new temporality emerges from the experience of bereavement:

> There is time given. It is a time that never existed before. It is as if your father's phrase 'from time to time', apparently so casual, opens up like a cuckoo clock, intimating a time in between the one and the other, a mad gift. Even your employer proves unexpectedly benign, granting you compassionate leave (officially described as 'sick'), for as long as, so long as, what does the voice say? You try to recall the manager's exact words: three months, is it? What does it matter? (p82).

This new temporality, a liminal time in between one and the other, is non-conventional and non-linear, and clearly positioned in contrast to established measurements of time ('three months, is it? What does it matter?'). It is a new temporality that is ingrained in the father's words that are repeated in the text. Here the use of the father's words brings the text into a certain relation with Derrida's *The Work of Mourning*, a literary paean to the philosopher's deceased friends. Of his chapter on Levinas, Pascale-Anne Brault and Michael Naas remark that citation in the text is being used 'as a form of interiorisation'. They observe that 'the words of the dead are being incorporated not merely to become part of the text, to be 'in it,' but to act as a point of infinite alterity 'within' the text, to act as its law'. The editors continue: 'It would seem that Derrida's 'rhetoric of mourning' is borrowing from the schema of interiorisation in order to convert citation from a gesture simply dictated by the genre into another consequence of the metonymic force of mourning'.[20] The father's words in *Quilt* operate too as a law that drives the text and open

19. Nicholas Royle, *Quilt*, Brighton, Myriad Editions 2010, p3. (Hereafter *Quilt*).

20. Pascale Anne-Brault and Michael Naas, 'Introduction' to Jacque Derrida, *The Work of Mourning*, (eds) Pascale Anne-Brault and Michael Naas, Chicago and London, Chicago University Press 2001, p21.

up a new temporality, which is the time of death and mourning.

The novel occupies the two differing modes of time, through shifting from conventional prose, which tells of the days and events before and after the death of the narrator's father, into linguistic experiment. The catalyst for the new language occurs in the opening pages when the narrator is helping his father to dress to go to the hospital: 'He's lying on the bed and he is my flesh, so simple, his body mine, and so difficult so com-pli-cated he'll say shortly in a portmanteau coming apart at the seams, just when it will have come to my mind most straightforward, so deluded' (*Quilt*, p4). There is a 'transfer of affect' here from father to son. This intimacy precipitates the renunciation of conventional grammar: 'Give up the thought of the sentence, he seems to tell me, and I am in his grip, he mine'. Experiment with language is imbricated with the father's body: 'My father needs some new underwear and pyjamas. His incontinence, lack of time to get any washing done before coming to hospital. Sentences stop, leak, caught, soil themselves short' (p9). Experiment with language halts the linear time of the writing, opening up a new temporal and spatial dimension:

> Yesterday I called the doctor in, he asked my father if it would be possible to go upstairs so that he could examine him on the bed and we all went up together, one by one, three bears, each of us holding onto the handrail as we went, the doctor remarking with admiration on its crafting, smooth but knotty trunk of a young pine fallen in the garden years ago meticulously bolted to the stairway wall by my father. Solid *silva*, yes, *silva silvam silvae*, the way words twinkle to other's uses, other to her, solid flesh, melting into dew, slivering into you. My father makes to lie down on his bed but the doctor asks him to lie down on the *other* bed, because it is closer to the window and he'll be able to see better (p5).

Here and elsewhere, the sequence of words that occurs in between sections of linear narrative transforms from word to word through inflection. The word solid folds into the Latin, 'silva' meaning forest, or woods. The familiar wood of the handrail is expanded through the Latin inflections of the same word, 'silva' (nominative, ablative, vocative), 'silvam' (accusative), 'silvae' (genitive, dative). The intimacy between the words generates the intimacy of the lines 'other to her, solid flesh, melting into dew, slivering into you'. 'Silva' does not denote handrail or the simple wood of a tree in Latin but forest, woods. The domestic handrail expands through the Latin to encompass the environment, a vastness of wood. A few lines later the narrator remarks 'we seem to be embarked on some new phase of language'.

The experimental writing in the novel is a form of 'environmental writing', a term Royle takes up in his work *Veering: a Theory of Literature* (2011). Royle's theory of 'veering' 'is concerned to interrogate and displace all thinking of an environment in straightforwardly anthropocentric terms'. 'If an environment *environs*,' Royle states referring to the definition of 'environ' to 'surround' or 'enclose', 'it does not merely environ the human'. Importantly, at the core of Royle's idea of 'veering' is a rejection of anthropocentrism in the recognition that '[t]he human animal is not at the centre of the world'.[21] Referring to Timothy Clark's work as exemplary, Royle argues 'nowhere is the need for rigour and inventiveness more urgently demanded than in the experimentations of environmental writing' (*Veering*, p63). Environmental writing in *Quilt* offers a form of writing about death. The narrator directly invokes John McPhee's geological idea of 'deep time'.[22] After a recollection of his father's time in Tibet the narrator states: 'To follow this yarn you have to go back into what is called deep time (as if there were any means of doing so)'. As is intimated by Royle, deep time, like death, lies beyond human comprehension, as it is outside the sphere of human experience, and, more specifically, exceeds human conceptions of temporality and finitude. At the end of a passage detailing a brief history of the ray the narrator reminds the reader: 'All of this keep in mind, took place in deep time (as if there were any other)' (*Quilt*, p22). Two comparable forms of temporality are present in *Quilt* that can be formulated in relation to Gould's idea of time's arrow and time's cycle. Ordinary sequential time that tells of the father's final days, the funeral, the clearing of the house, and the building of the ray pool can be compared to Gould's notion of 'time's arrow'. The sections of experimental writing, the metaphor of the ray and divergent passages into philosophy and geology are comparable with 'time's cycle'. It is a non-linear form of narrative time that interrupts sequential time and holds the narrative in a new temporality that has no direction.

UNCONFORMITIES

Layering is fundamental to the concept of deep time. In geology such layering is termed 'unconformity'. A recent exhibition 'Imagining the Unimaginable: Deep Time Through the Lens of Art', held at the National Academy of Sciences in Washington DC from August 28, 2014 to January 2015, explored the ways in which art has the capacity to represent deep time. In his essay, the curator of the exhibition J.D. Talasek discusses engravings of unconformities, in particular John Clerk's celebrated engraving of Hutton's unconformity at Jedburgh, Scotland:

> Added to the imagery constructed by geology is that of strata often visualised as a layered cross section of the earth's depths. Geologic cross section views often reveal unconformities that are vast gaps in time of up to hundreds of millions of years where no rock exists to represent that time period. Unconformities depicted in cross sections have long been considered compelling field evidence for the vastness of time. John Playfair elegantly articulated the idea of unconformity in his 1802 *Illustration of the Huttonian Theory of the Earth*. Unconformity was depicted in John Clerk of Eldin's celebrated engraving *Hutton's Unconformity at Jedburgh, Scotland*.

21. Nicholas Royle, *Veering: A Theory of Literature*, Edinburgh, Edinburgh University Press 2012, p3. (Hereafter *Veering*).

22. John McPhee was the first geologist to coin the phrase in his seminal work *Basin and Range*, New York, Farrar, Straus and Giroux 1981.

The engraving is a slice of earth made visible, a perspective that reveals strata and unconformity as, in Gould's words, '…the complex panorama of history that can be inferred from the simple geometry of horizontal above the vertical'.[23]

The layering in unconformities inscribes the enormity of the temporality of deep time. As Talasek remarks: 'This visualisation of the earth is so powerful that it has become a metaphor of the vastness of time'. He refers to the work of geologist and photographer Jonathan Wells whose photograph *Boston Basin* (2005) illustrates a 16-mile-wide by four-mile-deep perspective of the Boston Basin, 'looking west towards downtown as if the viewer were positioned in the harbour'. Talasek observes: 'The large city seems minuscule in comparison to what lies beneath' (*Imagining the Unimaginable*).

Etymological erosion and layering in *Quilt* create a comparable perspective whereby the surface linear narrative is thrown into a diminishing relief by the environmental writing. Royle creates etymological layering through literary experiment. The title of the book *Quilt* is a singular example of such layering. In the final part of the novel the narrator reveals the etymological layering of the word 'quilt'. Earlier in the novel digressions occur into the history of the ray, and the discussion of the ray in Plato's *Meno* (offering intertextual as well as etymological layering). The ray is given its Latin name *Potamotyrgon motoro*. This assigns a temporality to the ray that exceeds the ordinary language in the text. In the third part it emerges that 'quilt' is a word that had been used throughout history interchangeably with 'ray'. The ray, the narrator states, 'is at the origin' (*Quilt*, p118). The figure of the ray is linked by Royle to the Gothic: 'It's the ordinary spook. Plato was already onto that, in the ray haunting Socrates and Meno'. The Gothic here is defined here as 'a kind of anamorphic manifestation of the effects of the ray'. Drawing on the plethora of cloaks and shrouds in Gothic literature, the narrator states: 'It is necessary, however, to realise how integrally, how inextricably, this motif is folded into the figure or the property of the ray, the living blanket or quilt'. Comparing the ray to the bat, the narrator suggests that in the ray: 'What haunts is of greater scope, more minatory and dangerous, all enfolding, from another element' (p118). The etymological history of the ray is then offered, *'manta'* first emerged at the beginning of the eighteenth century and was used interchangeably with the word 'quilt'. The narrative expands on the ray and its appearance in literature and philosophy. Royle's etymological expansion of the word 'ray' is a means of shifting thinking about the Gothic to a secular platform through environmental writing. The narrator states: 'It is a question of a new imaginary, not a regression of into the vagary of animistic belief, a restituted primitivism, but a thinking of the ray as a force, a trace, whether buried or dancing, in quite a different understanding of the spectre and the wake'(p119-120). Royle employs archaeological and anthropological terms to articulate the idea of the ray: 'Like a dream of excarnation without any possible fossilisation, dream

23. J D Talasek, *Imagining the Unimaginable*. Catalogue for the exhibition 'Imagining the Unimaginable: Deep Time Through the Lens of Art', held at the National Academy of Sciences in Washington DC from August 28, 2014 to January 2015. Unpaginated. http://www.cpnas.org/exhibitions/imagining-deep-time-catalogue.pdf. (Hereafter *Imagining the Unimaginable*).

as impossible fossil, there is a naked cape and it is alive. Rays to the ground: starting off in the substrate. It is a matter of a new teratology, an enantiodromic animism that is radically non-theological, nanothinking through the ray' (p120). Excarnation, the practice of removing the flesh from the bones before burial, is here attributed to an impossible fossil. Elsewhere it is ascribed to literature: 'Excarnation is literature. Its music strips you. Literature is excarnation' (p62). The new teratology, a scientific mythology, is brought into relation with the idea of an 'enantiodromic animism'. The term enantiodromia (ἐναντιοδρομίας) is a Greek compound word that translates as 'a conflict of opposites' and was used by Diogenes Laërtius in his précis of the philosophy of Heraclitus. The word has an extensive history and was taken up by Carl Jung who used the term to designate 'the emergence of the unconscious in the course of time'.[24] Royle's use of the figure of the ray is a means to offer a secular non-theological perspective on death. Deep time functions in the novel as a replacement for religious time and etymological layering emerges as a form of textual nonconformity.

Deep time is registered in the imagery, the conflation of the father with the ray, and in the inflections and transformation of meaning in the play of words. As the father is collapsed through language with the figure of the ray, the father is given presence through the text after his death. For Royle there is a reciprocal conflict in the ray's relation to language. 'Language wrecks the ray', the narrator asserts, and a few lines later, 'The ray wrecks language' (*Quilt*, p33). Literary experiment is imbued with the ray and associatively with deep time. Intimacy with the father is created through the figure of the ray. In an early passage detailing the father's preparations for hospital, the father is merged with the figure of the ray:

> A miner yes, that thought is never far away. Underground, he carries it with him, for three years during the Second World War a coalminer day after day deep down in the dark and apparently relishing it, sheer subterranean strength, coming up for air at the end of the day face blackened, hot shower then tea at his digs, a couple of pints at the local, and bed, then before dawn down again into the earth, mole of my life. It's as I help him now I have this searing sensation, smell and feel the look of his body mine, mined out, to have to hold, every article exhausting and he has to rest, catch or fall back seeking breath, respite resources from somewhere unrecognizable. He insists on a vest and two pullovers even though it is the end of July, a hot summer's day. We get to the socks, he is lying down and his feet swollen, one of them worryingly red, a rash that runs up over his right foot to his ankle (p6).

Here deep time is evoked and conflated with the father's history through the phrase 'sheer subterranean strength'. Like the ray, the father is portrayed as 'coming up for air at the end of the day' from the mines. His father has resources 'somewhere unrecognizable'. The father and son merge in the play

---

24. Jung, C.G. 'Symbols of Transformation,' *Collected Works*, 5, 2nd ed,. Princeton, Princeton University Press, p709.

on words 'mine, mined out'. This intimate temporality runs beneath the surface narrative of the son helping his father get dressed. At other points in the text the idea of nanothinking, slownesses and spectralities that Royle associates with a 'new literature' and the working of the ray emerge through erosion and the creation of neologisms, a double play of erosion and the appearance of new linguistic forms. When clearing the house the narrative takes up the smell of the house: 'Uncapturable but ubiquitous, on every surface, on every object are the residues, the residutiful, residentical odour that he recognises as not the father's but that of the house itself' (p43). Here the uncapturable nature of the odour plays out in the transformation of 'residues' to 'residutiful' and 'residentical', neologisms that have no meaning. The pervasive nature of the smell is held in the continuation of the word residue into the neologisms that follow.

The new temporality in *Quilt* is not a-temporality in Riley's sense of the term. Rather it is a folding of the past into the present (the father into son), and the simultaneous alienation from linear time. At the outset the narrator states: 'That is where living backwards begins' (p4). In the house after the narrator's father's death the 'past' embeds the word 'post' so that past and future ('post') become embedded in the present: '*post*, post saying past all post past past the post. The room is almost knee-deep in junk mail, a choked sea of pointless post' (p26). The merger of post and past generates a diversion that merges the narrator's visiting lover with experiment with language: 'The post is past. Words come away. Letters capsize. She is digression, syncopation, asyndeton, ontradiction. Her 'c' curls off invisibly, leaving the shoreline of a new language: *ontra*' (p27). The lover's word 'contradiction' is truncated, eroded to produce 'ontradiction' a neologism with no definition but one that nevertheless implies a relation with 'ontic', real rather than phenomenal existence. Literary experiment is tied to the inability to comprehend linear time after the death of the father. 'The order' of the outside world and the demands of convention and bureaucracy are 'impossible to disentangle' for the narrator. By contrast, there is 'the incredible world of the cottage, dead and surviving, stuffed with the past now present, the present now past, in a convulsion of lunatic tranquility (p37). The narrator apprehends perception to resemble 'a strange mimosa' in which 'Everything seems shadowed, shadowing something else' (p34). The mimosa is a sensitive plant with compound leaves that are sensitive to touch. Once again the natural world provides the metaphor through which the experience of the father's death is expressed. The environmental language and metaphor in the novel functions both to inscribe that which cannot be directly represented and to throw death into bas-relief. Deep time and environmental language emerge as a way of negating death. The narrator states 'life and time in truth never die' and this infinity is bound to deep time (p42). In the second part of the novel the narrator recalls a nightmare of 'unimaginable length and intensity'. He attributes this to his 'marine correspondence' with his lover, H. The latter part of the novel moves further away from the everyday happenings. Recalling the process of excarnation, the narrator states: 'Everything is being stripped away. I can't express it. It's a kind of magical sharpness, as if shadows have light […] It has to do with that mimosa thing I told you about. It's a kind of upside-down space of coincidence, a portal' (p95).

The expansion of time that is signified by the ray pool functions as an inversion of the common 'anthropomorphic ego-projective perception of everything' that the narrator understands to be prevalent in contemporary culture. 'You come to experience this quite different thing,' he remarks, 'the murky registration that, in terms of deep time, in terms of the actual timeframe of life on the planet, half a hiccup ago, you were a lungfish yourself'. This results in a reversal: 'you dimly sense a sort of vast retelling, a turning shadow cast out over the waters in the flickering light of which the projection actually goes *the other way*'. The 'refractively aleatory antics' of the rays in the ray pool are 'no different now from how they would have been a couple of hundred million years ago,' and for the narrator, 'show us frankly what or who we are' (p107). Time is measured in time akin to deep time in the third part of the novel. The final part of the novel opens: 'It is scarcely seven weeks, still less than two months since the funeral. A week, a month, whizzing in an hour'. Objects are given the brief lifespan of a mayfly: 'Every noun is another ephemeroid' (p111). The narrator has switched to H. She describes the three days that she does not hear from him as '[t]hree oceans'. The narrator embarks on a writing projects in the final part of the novel, 'a work of lexicography devoted to the buried life of anagrams and homophones, each word with its own idiosyncratic definition […] a verbal laboratory, a dictionary testamentary to the way the ray leaves its mark in everyday language, a vocabulary that might constitute a new species of bestiary, and generate an altogether estuary English'(p121). This emergence of a new language each word of which contains the 'ray' coincides with the birth of a giant ray in the father's study. The transformation into the ray at the close of the novel is, as the narrator points to elsewhere, an allegory. It is at once an allegory through which the narrator is able to confront his father's death, and a political allegory that tells of the need to move away from thinking about the environment in anthropocentric terms. The displacement of anthropocentrism enables the consideration of the father's death in deep time, a temporality that has no end.

NEW FIGURATIONS

To return to Kristeva, and her distinction between representation and inscription, what Riley and Royle offer in their contemporary works are two inscriptions. Death, impossible to represent, is inscribed through experimental practice. In each of the works addressed in this essay, the writer or poet offers literature as a space of compassion in response to living on in the world after the loss of a loved one. This space is bound to the experience of a new non-linear temporality. Riley understands her work to be part of what she terms a 'literature of consolation'. For Riley this is a literature of solidarity, offering a way for mothers who have lost their child to access a shared experience. We might think of the implications of Riley's work in terms of the contemporary political climate in which thousands of parents are experiencing bereavement, forced displacement, and seeking asylum, as a result of war and conflict in Syria and elsewhere. One month after the death of her son, Riley writes in her notes:

> This instant enlargement of human sympathy. It's arrived in me at once. His death had put me in mind of all those millions whose children were and are lost in natural disasters, or accidentally killed, or systematically obliterated; no wonder that bitterness and loss of hope has filtered down the generations, and then the disengagement. Millions disorientated, perhaps, but this quiet feeling of living only just this near side of the cut (*Time Lived*, p15).

A literature of consolation might have the capacity to generate Riley's felt 'enlargement of human sympathy' in the reader. In both Riley's and Royle's work imaginary intimacy with death has a close relation to the transpersonal. Embodying the timeless time of the dead, and inhabiting also the time of the living, Riley asks: 'How to think historically about all those myriad lived temporalities that find themselves increasingly resonant and densely layered because they've come to include the time of others?'(p73) Riley asserts that 'As these temporalities are intermingled with each person, they'll also run across and between people, so to speak, become transpersonal' (p74). Riley's reference to transpersonal individuality here is Marx's *Theses on Feuerbach* (1888). She draws the connection between the idea of transpersonal identity and a 'de-centred being'. Royle's *Quilt* takes up this idea through environmental writing in his reversal of anthropomorphism. A new politics of experimental writing emerges in Riley's and Royle's works, which through linguistic innovation, offer sites of imaginary intimacy. The experience of the death of the loved one in Riley's and Royle's work is the catalyst for transpersonal individuality that goes beyond cultural boundaries through an imaginary intimacy with death.

Georgina Colby is Lecturer in Contemporary Literature at the University of Westminster. She is author of *Kathy Acker: Writing the Impossible* (Edinburgh University Press, 2016), and *Bret Easton Ellis: Underwriting the Contemporary* (Palgrave Macmillan, 2011). She has published widely on contemporary literature, in particular experimental writing, in journals such as *Textual Practice*, *Comparative Critical Studies*, *Contemporary Literature*, and *Women: A Cultural Review*. From 2012 to 2013 she was co-organizer with the artist Anthony Luvera of the Arts Council funded project 'Death and the Contemporary'. She is currently working on a collection of essays, *Reading Experimental Writing*.

BLIND SEEING: DEATHWRITING FROM DICKINSON TO THE CONTEMPORARY

Peter Boxall

Abstract The essay traces a tradition of what is here called 'deathwriting' as it stretches from Emily Dickinson, to Franz Kafka, to Samuel Beckett, to Cormac McCarthy. The work of all these writers, the essay argues, is driven by the urge to give a poetic form to the experience of death, to make death thinkable and narratable. Alongside this tradition of deathwriting, and interwoven with it, one can discern too, a fascination with 'blind seeing', an attempt to make darkness visible, or to overcome the distinction between the light and the dark, the visible and the invisible. In reading the connection between deathwriting and blind seeing as it runs from Dickinson to the contemporary, the essay argues that these writers allow us to glimpse a differently constituted relationship between the living and the dead, and between the perceptible and the imperceptible. At a contemporary moment when it has become urgent to rethink our apparatuses for world picturing, with the emergence of the Anthropocene as a critical context for all of our imaginings, the essay offers this history of deathwriting as a radically different way of seeing, without the aid of human light.

Keywords Emily Dickinson, Samuel Beckett, Cormac McCarthy, deathwriting, blind seeing, Heidegger, Agamben

---

I

LIGHT AND SHADOW IN THE WORLD PICTURE

I want in this essay to explore the possibility that, in our time, a set of distinctions that have helped us to frame and understand being have entered into a state of quite profound transition. Our understanding of the relationship between the living and the dead, between the human and the nonhuman, and between the visible and the invisible has come under a certain amount of pressure, I will argue, as we enter into a contemporary period dominated on the one hand by the imminence of eco-catastrophe, and on the other hand by info-technological revolutions that have transformed the place of the human in the world. The traditions of thought that have allowed us to associate the human with life and with light, in opposition to a world of animals and things which do not share our world view, and which come to visibility and thinkability through reflected human light - these traditions, I suggest, look precarious or exhausted, as humanism itself enters into a crisis, and as our wasted environment is flung clear of its alignment with any given human world picture. As these traditions of thought, philosophical as well as theological, enter into crisis, it is possible, I will further suggest, to discern latent counter traditions, other ways of thinking about the relation between the enlightened and the benighted, between the human and the non-human, that have stretched through our literary and intellectual histories, but that have remained thus far difficult to articulate. More specifically, I will argue, one can trace a thread of what I will call 'blind seeing' running through the poetic and literary tradition, a way of thinking and seeing that recasts the relationship between the visible and the invisible, and that can allow for a shifted relationship between life and death, one which does not conform to the demands of the humanist tradition, and which allows us to glimpse the possibility of a differently configured life world.

The writer whose work might most immediately come to mind, when thinking about the possibilities of a literature which brings death into the sphere of the thinkable, is Franz Kafka. Take, for example, the diary entry of the 9 December 1914, in which Kafka speculates that his own death might afford him a certain happiness, and further that it is this welcoming relationship with death that enables him to write. 'On the way home', he writes,

> told Max that I shall lie very contentedly on my deathbed, provided the pain isn't too great. I forgot - and later purposely omitted - to add that the best things I have written have their basis in this capacity of mine to meet death with contentment.[1]

In an inversion of Woody Allen's famous witticism ('I don't want to achieve immortality through my work, I want to achieve it through not dying'), Kafka imagines a fundamental connection between the capacity to write, and the capacity to die; his work grants him not immortality, but the very possibility of dying.[2] As Maurice Blanchot puts it, in his discussion of that same diary entry, Kafka's work is propelled by a peculiarly circuitous and contradictory relationship with the death that enables it - 'write to be able to die - die to be able to write'.[3] Kafka's protagonists, Blanchot writes, 'carry out their actions in death's space, and [...] it is to the indefinite time of 'dying' that they belong' (p92).

In his discussion of Kafka's deathwriting, from 1955, Blanchot suggests that there is something anomalous about this discovery of a kind of generative principle in the experience of death. 'Naturally', Blanchot writes, Kafka's thinking here is 'in conflict with generally accepted ideas about art and the work of art'. 'To write in order not to die', Blanchot goes on, 'to entrust oneself to the survival of the work: this motive is apparently what keeps the artist at his task' (p94). It is a mark of Kafka's singularity that he should

1. Franz Kafka, *Diaries, 1910-1923*, New York, Schocken 1948, p321.

2. Eric Lax, *On Being Funny: Woody Allen and Comedy*, New York, Manor Books 1975, p232.

3. Maurice Blanchot, *The Space of Literature*, (trans) Ann Smock, Lincoln, The University of Nebraska Press 1982, p94.

refuse such a fundamental principle or motive, that he should so effortlessly evacuate the weighty idea that art is about the prolongation or affirmation or consecration of life. This may be so; but what I want to explore in this essay is the possibility that Kafka's work, whatever its singularity, belongs to a literary tradition which has found in the approach to realised death not only a form of negation, but also a means of producing a new kind of possibility, a means, as Emily Dickinson puts it in 1862, of inventing 'another way - to see'.[4]

This shadowy tradition may stretch as far back as writing itself, may simply be a darkling version of Harold Bloom's 'western canon' or Erich Auerbach's 'western literature'; but I will trace it here only as far back as the beautifully deathbound verse of Emily Dickinson. There is, I will suggest, a line of influence or affinity, reaching from Dickinson to Beckett to a body of contemporary deathwriting, that evokes this counter-tradition, and that allows us to imagine a way of thinking about death, and its relationship to life, that might work against the 'generally accepted ideas' that Blanchot talks of in 1955; that might allow us to picture a different kind of life world, in which the 'survival of the work' rests not on the eradication of the dark and the deathly, but on a radically reconceived relation between the dark and the luminous, between the quick and the dead. At a time when our conception of the life world is in an unprecedentedly deep crisis, when our capacity to picture the world as an environment in harmony with human modes of life is most attenuated, it is perhaps an urgent task to read for such a counter-tradition, to find new ways to see without the aid of human light.

Indeed, I shall start by addressing the question of our picture of the world in terms of the relation between the visible and the invisible, between light and dark. For Martin Heidegger, famously, what marks the birth of what he calls the 'modern age' is the transformation of the world into a picture. He writes, in his essay 'The Age of the World Picture' (first delivered as a lecture in 1938), that 'the fundamental event of the modern age is the conquest of the world as a picture'.[5] In contradistinction to the medieval and ancient conceptions of the world, the 'modern age' is characterised by its conception of the world as pictorial representation, and what is more by human representation. 'The essence of the modern age', Heidegger writes, is that the world becomes a picture which is projected by 'man'. With the arrival of the world picture, he writes, 'man becomes that being upon which all that is, is grounded as regards the manner of its being and its truth' (p128). When world becomes picture, 'Man becomes the relational centre of that which is as such'. In casting the world as a picture, 'man sets himself up as the setting in which whatever is must henceforth set itself forth [....] Man becomes the representative of that which is' (p132). It is for this reason that the rise of humanism, for Heidegger, coincides with the modern age, and with the age of the world picture. 'It is no wonder,' he writes, 'that humanism first arises where the world becomes picture':

---

4. Emily Dickinson, 'The Tint I cannot take - is best -', in Emily Dickinson, *The Poems of Emily Dickinson*, (ed) R.W. Franklin, Cambridge, Harvard University Press 1998, p310, l. 24. All further references to Dickinson's poetry will be to this edition, and will include the number of the poem, and line number.

5. Martin Heidegger, 'The Age of the World Picture' in Martin Heidegger, *The Question Concerning Technology and Other Essays*, (trans) William Lovitt, New York, Harper 1977, p134. (Hereafter *The Age of the World*).

It would have been just as impossible for a humanism to have gained currency in the great age of the Greeks as it would have been impossible to have had anything like a world picture in that age. (p133)

For Heidegger, the conquest of the world by the human is intricately bound up with the emergence of a form of pictorial representation which allows us to shape the world that we inhabit, the world which 'is normative and binding for us' (p129).

Now, it is easy to see that this conjunction between the human and the very conditions of seeing, the very conditions of 'worlding', rests on a quite radical anthropocentrism. Heidegger's correlation between man and world is part of what Giorgio Agamben, in his 2002 work *The Open*, calls the 'anthropological machine' - the organising of the world around a human centre that has been, he argues, at the heart of western metaphysics, and that has provided 'the motor for man's becoming historical'.[6] To produce a picture of the world, Agamben's work suggests, we have been required to banish the nonhuman from the sphere of the human, to banish darkness from the light, to banish death from life. This exclusion, this banishment, is what has allowed us to make a picture of the world. Ontology, anthropogenesis, the 'becoming human of the living being', has required us, repeatedly, to enforce distinctions between 'the human and the animal, between nature and history, between life and death' (p79). If this is so, however, it is central to Agamben's project to recognise that our own age sees the winding down of the anthropological machine. 'The end of philosophy', Agamben writes in *The Open*, and 'the completion of the epochal destinations of being mean that today the machine is idling' (p80). To think about the world now might require us to adapt a different kind of seeing, one that is not structured by Heidegger's world picture, and that does not posit the human as the 'relational centre of that which is as such'. It might require us to learn to see with the eyes of what Agamben calls, in 2009, the 'true contemporary'. To rise to the challenge of the contemporary, Agamben writes in his essay 'What is the Contemporary', requires us to see not only the world picture, to see not only what is made visible and brought into the light, but also to see what is banished from the visible, what is excluded from representation. 'The contemporary', he writes, is 'he who firmly holds his gaze on his own time so as to perceive not its light but rather its darkness'.[7] 'The ones who can call themselves contemporary', Agamben goes on:

> are only those who do not allow themselves to be blinded by the lights of the century and so manage to get a glimpse of the shadows in those lights, of their intimate obscurity [....] The contemporary is the person who perceives the darkness of his time as something that concerns him, as something that never ceases to engage him. Darkness is something that - more than any light - turns directly and singularly toward him (*Contemporary*, p14).

6. Giorgio Agamben, *The Open: Man and Animal*, (trans) Kevin Attell, Stanford, Stanford University Press 2004, p80. (Hereafter *The Open*).

7. Giorgio Agamben, 'What is the Contemporary?' in Giorgio Agamben, *Nudities*, (trans) David Kishik and Stefan Pedatella, Stanford, Stanford University Press 2011, p13. (Hereafter *Contemporary*).

Our own contemporary moment, Agamben suggests, requires us to overcome those distinctions that have separated life from death, human from animal. It requires us, perhaps, to conceive a different way of thinking about how death relates to life, how the pictured relates to the unpictured. But, if we are to glean a connection here between this contemporary requirement, and the tradition of deathwriting I am proposing here, we have to address a paradox that is at work in Agamben's understanding of contemporaneity, and that complicates any perception that Agamben's project is involved in simply dismantling or overcoming a Heideggerian anthropocentrism, or in discomposing Heidegger's world picture. This paradox lies in the perception that the experience of contemporaneity has *always* involved the discerning of a darkness within the sphere of the visible, a deathliness within the province of the living. 'All eras', Agamben writes, 'for those who experience contemporariness, are obscure. The contemporary is precisely the person who knows how to see this obscurity, who is able to write by dipping his pen into the obscurity of the present' (p13). Indeed, the no doubt correct idea that Agamben's project, in *The Open*, is devoted to overcoming the distinctions that have separated human from animal, is troubled by the possibility that, in Heidegger's own work, in his exercising of his own contemporaneity, these distinctions are already under a certain kind of erasure. Agamben writes in 2009 that 'the contemporary is the one whose eyes are struck by the beam of darkness that comes from his own time' - that seeing one's own time requires one to see outside the precincts of the word picture, of the world as it is made visible to us, as it binds and normalises us. But Heidegger, even as he outlines the conditions of world picturing in 1938, is already cognisant of the conjunction between light and dark which is part of the picture itself. The picture of the world includes a glimmer of what Heidegger calls the 'incalculable' - the latent possibility of world picturing itself that cannot be contained within any given picture of the world. 'This becoming incalculable', he writes, 'remains the invisible shadow that is cast around all things everywhere' when the world has been 'transformed into a picture' (p135). To know our historical moment, to 'safeguard into its truth', requires us, Heidegger writes, to see into this shadow, as it is 'by means of this shadow' that 'the modern world extends itself out into a space withdrawn from representation' (p136). 'Everyday opinion', Heidegger writes, 'sees in the shadow only the lack of light, if not light's complete denial. In truth, however, the shadow is a manifest, though impenetrable, testimony to the concealed emitting of light' (p154). To look only at that which is illuminated or pictured - to be, in Agamben's terms, 'blinded by the lights' of one's own time - Heidegger writes in 1938, 'can bring about nothing in itself other than self-deception and blindness in relation to the historical moment' (p136).

II

BLIND SEEING AND DEATHWRITING IN EMILY DICKINSON

So, the tradition that I am seeking to trace here is one that has grounded itself in this peculiar fusion between the light and the dark - in this conjunction between the living and the dead that has been at work within the very forms that have allowed us to conceive of the human, and to conspire in the rise of humanism. And I have chosen to locate the beginning of this tradition in the writing of Emily Dickinson because it is in her verse, I think, that the aesthetic embrace of death comes closer than in any other writing to the obsessive tracing of a failed distinction between the visible and the invisible, between blindness and sight. Across the range of her poetry, it is possible to see that her chief literary and philosophical preoccupation - the aesthetic encounter with death, the conjunction between death and writing that Kafka describes in 1914 - is thought through a repeated, obsessive concern with what we might call a blind seeing. It is as light itself darkens and darkness glows, as seeing shades into and mingles with unseeing, that Dickinson's poetry reaches towards a conception of death as possibility. As Dickinson most famously puts it in 1862, she is committed not to picturing the world, but to a particular kind of unpicturing, a kind of ungraven poetics, what Harold Bloom calls a 'passion for unnaming'.[8] 'I would not paint - a picture' (348, l. 1), she writes, dedicating herself to what she calls 'bright impossibility' (l. 3), to a writing which can only illuminate a failure of the possibility of vison or luminosity - a kindling of the impossible which remains unthought, even as it comes forth into brightness. It is through this unpicturing, through the dismantling of the mechanics of vision, that her poetry penetrates the shadows in which Heidegger discovers the 'concealed emitting of light', and in which she approaches Blanchot's 'death's space'.

To read Dickinson now, I think, is to attend newly to this unpicturing, and to acknowledge the challenge that her poetry presents to reading and to seeing - a challenge that is perhaps not met, in Paul de Man's resonant phrase, by any existing 'rhetoric of blindness'.[9] It is to recognise that de Man's own deconstructive approach to the conjunction between blindness and insight - in which, he writes, 'critics' moments of greatest blindness with regard to their own critical assumptions are also the moments at which they achieve their greatest insight'(p109) - cannot bring the visual and epistemological terrain of Dickinson's poetry into focus. Where for de Man, as for Derrida and for Blanchot, blindness is the empty content of any act of seeing or thinking - the 'negative movement that animates the critic's thought', the 'unstated principle that leads his language away from its asserted stand'(p103) - the poetic tradition I am trying to trace here suggests that the relation between blindness sight opens onto something less epistemologically evacuated, something like new kind of ground to being, one which can only glimmer forth

8. Harold Bloom, *The Western Canon: The Books and School of the Ages*, London, Papermac 1996, p295.

9. See Paul de Man, 'The Rhetoric of Blindness' in *Blindness and Insight: Essays in the Rhetoric of Contemporary Criticism*, second edition, London, Routledge 1983, pp102-141. (Hereafter *Blindness*). There are a number of different rhetorical forms in which the relation between blindness and sight has been couched. Paul de Man's work is part of a deconstructive rhetoric of blindness; for a recent book which addresses the question from a disability studies perspective, see Georgina Kleege, *Sight Unseen*, New Haven, Yale University Press 1999.

under intense poetic pressure, and which does not yet have a vocabulary in which to express itself. Paul De Man writes that 'a certain degree of blindness is part of the specificity of all literature'(p141), as Derrida suggests that a certain 'invisibility [...] inhabit[s] the visible', or 'come[s] to haunt it to the point of being confused with it'.[10] To gain access to the ways in which blindness is attached to sight in Dickinson, and in which the invisible is attached to the visible, requires us, I think, to develop a new mode of critical reading, one that is not contained within the rhetoric of deconstruction.

To gather a sense of this conjunction between deathwriting and blind seeing in Dickinson's verse, one can draw on examples from across her oeuvre. Take, for example, the opening of poem 869:

> What I see not, I better see -
> Through Faith - My Hazel Eye
> Has periods of shutting -
> But, No lid has Memory - (869, ll. 1-4).

As readers of Dickinson have pointed out, this reads as a response to William Shakespeare's Sonnet 43.[11] Dickinson's speaker finds that seeing well involves the failure of sight, as Shakespeare writes that 'When most I wink, then do my eyes best see'. 'For all the day', Shakespeare's sonnet continues:

> They view things unrespected;
> But when I sleep, in dreams they look on thee,
> And, darkly bright, are bright in dark directed.[12]

Shakespeare's sonnet continues to play with this paradox to its end. The effect of looking on beauty is to make shadows bright, and to make brightness shadowy so that, in the concluding couplet:

> All days are nights till I see thee,
> And nights bright days when dreams do show thee me (ll. 13-14).

There is a light play of oppositions in Shakespeare's sonnet, in which the overcoming of the limits of daylight can only be expressed in terms of the conditions of seeing which the poet is seeking to supersede. To see the object of this poem is to stage a reversal between bright and dark; but as bright becomes dark, and dark becomes bright, the very opposition that drives the poem is peculiarly cancelled, and the difference between 'winking' and 'seeing', the difference upon which the poem depends, yields to a kind of unity, a poetic fusion between seeing and unseeing. The poet looks upon his loved one here with 'unseeing eyes' (l. 8), with 'sightless eyes' (l. 12), and the collapsing play between opposition and identity that the poem enacts allows for a kind of looking which can at once maintain and overcome this

---

10. Jacques Derrida, *Memoirs of the Blind: The Self-Portrait and Other Ruins*, (trans) Pascale-Anne Brault and Michael Naas, Chicago, University of Chicago Press 1993, p51.

11. See Páraic Finnerty, *Dickinson's Shakespeare*, Amherst, University of Massachusetts Press 2006, pp118-19.

12. William Shakespeare, 'Sonnet 43', in William Shakespeare, *The Complete Works*, eds. Stanley Wells and Gary Taylor, Oxford, Clarendon Press 1988, p756.

difference between blindness and sight.

Dickinson's poem performs a similar operation, and moves in step with Shakespeare's sonnet, towards a climax in which Dickinson's poet, like Shakespeare's, suggests that the seeing demanded by the loved one involves a more perfect kind of light, a brighter kind of brightness, than that which allows for conventional seeing. She beholds the 'Features so beloved' (l. 8), in the light of 'Faith' (l. 2) and 'Memory' (l. 4), she writes at the poem's close, 'Till jealous Daylight interrupt -/ And mar thy perfectness' (ll. 11-12). Normal daylight, in Dickinson and in Shakespeare, seems like night, like dimness, in comparison with the pristine light by which the loved one is beheld. But if there is a close accord between Dickinson and Shakespeare here, there is also a deep chasm between them, one which opens around the way that the two writers understand the oppositions that drive their verse. Shakespeare balances the opposition between bright and dark against their apparent sameness; but Dickinson's verse, here and always, produces a bottomless gulf between seeing and unseeing, a borderless zone of non-knowing, that is the signature of her thinking and of her poetics, and which opens onto a kind of deathly writing that is uniquely her own. The first line, 'What I see not, I better see -', forces a schism within the idea of seeing itself - that 'internal difference', as Dickinson puts it in poem 320, 'Where the Meanings, are' (320, ll. 7-8). She sees well when she is not seeing, so seeing, at its best, contains and emerges from unseeing; and the poem can do nothing to sustain or overcome this contradiction, this internal difference. It is only in a kind of living death - only, she writes, with 'all my sense obscured' (869, l. 5) - that she is able to achieve her blind seeing, because the gap that opens, within seeing itself, between seeing and not seeing, can only find itself thought, or poetically realised, in the space of Dickinsonian death - the space of the dash, when words are gone, when thinking outlives itself.

This relation between deathwriting and blind seeing emerges repeatedly in Dickinson's verse - so much so that it becomes the motor and the medium of her thinking. Take poem 428, in which death is imagined as a process by which 'We grow accustomed to the Dark', and learn to see in the night of nonbeing. 'The Bravest', she writes, 'grope a little',

But as they learn to see -

Either the Darkness alters -
Or something in the sight
Adjusts itself to Midnight -
And Life steps almost straight (428, ll. 16-20).

Death is here imagined as an alteration of the dark, an alteration in which life itself impossibly persists, learning to hold itself 'almost straight' in the province of a poetically lit dark. Or take poem 484, 'From Blank to Blank -':

From Blank to Blank -
A Threadless Way
I pushed Mechanic feet -
To stop - or perish - or advance -
Alike indifferent -

If end I gained
It ends beyond
Indefinite disclosed -
I shut my eyes - and groped as well
'Twas lighter - to be Blind -

Here, the groping encounter with not being - with the blank that stretches before the beginning of existence and after its end - takes place, as in 'We grow accustomed to the Dark', in the precinct of a lit or altered dark. The poem is impelled by the impossible recognition that blankness, as the unthinkable origin and destination of all being, can only come to us in the form of a sign, a sign which immediately and unerringly betrays the blankness that it seeks to represent, either in the form of a word or in the form of a dash. The metrical feet of the poem, and the bodily feet of the groping poet, can only crank out a mechanical testimony to the blankness that both being and poetry are - and by staging such testimony, deny it. The figure of blind seeing upon which the poem rests - 'Twas lighter - to be Blind -' - is the apotheosis of this irresolvable antinomy. The phrase might suggest a response to the indifference that the poet feels; it is easier (lighter) just to stop trying to see one's being or make sense of one's condition, as the heaviness of those trudging feet can only be lightened by a kind of careless resignation to unthinking. But it also suggests that the impossible combination of living and dying that being in time is - a being which is generated by nothingness and leads to nothingness and is continually giving way to nothingness, even as it finds itself impossibly persisting, pushing itself forward - can only be seen by inventing a looking which is also an aversion of the gaze, by learning to see in a dark which remains dark, even as it alters, even as it adjusts itself to the conditions of visibility.

The poem which perhaps captures this assemblage of dying and blind seeing most sharply is poem 591, 'I heard a Fly buzz - when I died -':

I heard a fly buzz - when I died -
The Stillness in the Room
Was like the Stillness in the Air -
Between the Heaves of Storm -

The Eyes around - had wrung them dry -
And Breaths were gathering firm

> For that last Onset - when the King
> Be witnessed - in the Room -
>
> I willed my Keepsakes - Signed away
> What portion of me be
> Assignable - and then it was
> There interposed a Fly -
>
> With Blue - uncertain - stumbling Buzz -
> Between the light - and me -
> And then the Windows failed - and then
> I could not see to see -

The task of this poem is to open a blind space within seeing, in which the event of death might be allowed, against all the rules of life, to take place. The first line - 'I heard a fly buzz - when I died -' - makes the impossible claim, common to all posthumous narration, that one's own death has been achieved, that one has been able to experience and outlive one's own dying. The following stanzas seem in part to fall back from this claim, recasting the poet's death as the future moment towards which the poem is moving, as the mourners in still room prepare for their grief, and as the poet herself manages her final affairs. But as the poem moves towards its climax, it comes ever closer to the rent in being that is torn by that opening line, working its way back into the crevasse between life and death, before and after, that has already swallowed it. The opening line inaugurates a shattering difference within the I itself; the I who hears the fly's buzz cannot be quite the same as the I who has died, as the buzzing is surely a prelude to the death that the dead I has already achieved. This difference within the speaking voice can be heard again in the third stanza as the poet 'Signed away / What portion of me be /Assignable' (ll. 9-12). Just as the poet of 'From Blank to Blank' experiences a difference from herself, as she 'pushed' her 'mechanic feet' along her threadless way, so here the poet feels a vast distance from herself in the very signs she has for herself - the signs with which she gives a portion of herself away. And then, as we reach the extraordinary ending of the poem, as the fly 'interposes' between the dead I and the living I, or between the I and the signs by which it knows itself, this difference flies wide open, leading to one of the most intense figures of blind seeing in Dickinson's verse. The fly buzzes at the window, which marks the threshold between 'the light' and 'me' (l. 14); perhaps, as the uncertain, stumbling buzz begins its buzzing, the window marks the boundary between a celestial light outside or beyond, and the living 'me' who lies still on her deathbed, in her still room, on this side of death. But 'then', as the 'Windows failed', the distinctions that have held the poem in place suddenly give way, returning us to an impossible naked gulf between living self and dead self, a gulf in which the visible and the invisible, seeing and unseeing, reach an awful, utterly disjunct identity. As the poet finds that 'I could not see to see' (l. 16), she understands that she is already beyond the horizons of the room, already in the death that has happened in the poem's first line. As the windows fail, the dead I can no longer see into the room, into the body and the mind in which she carries out her last act of seeing, can no longer see into herself in order to see out of the window towards her dying light. But even as this failure offers itself as the final act of the poem (the poem is driven by those urgent markers of temporal progression, 'and then' (l. 11), 'and then' (l. 15), 'and then' (l. 15)), the poem tells us that it is also its opening impulse, and the very condition of seeing itself. To see is to conjure some conjunction between the I who lives in sequential time and the I who is already and always in the blank province of death; and the light by which we achieve such seeing is always riven by the darkness of dying, always dimmed by its connection with the shadowy 'portion' of the self which is not 'assignable', which cannot find itself illuminated by any kind of light.

III

THE TOTAL OBJECT, COMPLETE WITH MISSING PARTS.

It is this kind of seeing, I think, that both Heidegger and Agamben have in mind, when they talk of a darkness which contains a 'light that, while directed towards us, infinitely distances itself from us'(*Contemporary*, pp14-15), or when they see shadows as a 'concealed emitting of light'(*The Age of the World*, p154). Picturing, for Dickinson, as for Agamben and for Heidegger, *involves* a kind of unpicturing, is shot through or bound up with unpicturing. To find 'another way to see' is to learn to see this hidden communication between light and dark. As Dickinson puts it in 'The Tint I cannot take - is best', this kind of picturing requires us to understand that a 'portion' of the life world is resistant to visibility, to apportioning or assigning, and cannot take any representative or material tint, so that one can only picture the world, can only 'see it', when the 'Cheated eye/ Shuts arrogantly - in the Grave' (696, ll. 22-23). To see by this dark light is to see in the grave, to see in the space of death that Dickinson's verse so singularly, so miraculously summons to thought. And, if one can see a shared vocabulary of blind seeing, in this dialogue between Dickinson, Heidegger and Agamben, so too it is possible to see a submerged or minor literary heritage that has its roots in Dickinson, and that stretches this relation between death and 'bright impossibility' (348, l. 3) beyond Dickinson's own time, into the twentieth century, and on into our own contemporary moment.

Take the work of Samuel Beckett, which is, I think, engaged throughout in a certain kind of slantwise dialogue with Dickinson's poetry - a dialogue which has so far largely eluded critical expression. There is I think a buried affinity between these two writers, a shared mood and sensibility that causes a certain shock of recognition when reading from one to the other, as if, in Beckett's words, they emerge from the same 'profounds of mind. Of mindlessness'.[13] Think, for example, of Beckett's 1946 French language poem La Mouche (which I give here also in Steven Connor's translation):

> entre la scène et moi
> la vitre
> vide sauf elle
>
> ventre à terre
> sanglée dans ses boyaux noirs
> antennes affolées ailes liées
> pattes crochues bouche suçant à vide
> sabrant l'azur s'écrasant contre l'invisible
> sous mon pouce impuissant elle fait chavirer
> la mer et le ciel serein
>
> between the vista and me
> the pane
> void save it
>
> belly down
> strapped in its black guts
> crazed antennae, bound wings
> legs crooked mouthparts sucking on void
> slashing the blue crushing itself against the invisible
> under my helpless thumb it convulses
> sea and quiet sky [14]

The image here, in Beckett's poem, of a fly pressed against a window pane calls irresistibly to Dickinson's 'I heard a fly buzz - when I died'. 'La Mouche' reads almost as an anagram of Dickinson's poem, with the 'blue' of the 'Blue - uncertain - stumbling Buzz' reframed in the phrase '*sabrant l'azure*', with the failure of sight that ends Dickinson's poem rendered as a 'crushing' 'against the invisible' ('*s'écrasant contre l'invisible*'), and with the interposing of the window between 'the light - and me' in Dickinson cast here as the installing of a 'pane' ('vitre') between 'la scène' and 'moi'.

Such a recreation of the elements of Dickinson's poem in 'La Mouche', of course, is no proof of 'influence', and indeed I have no interest in claiming that Beckett is knowingly referencing Dickinson here. I do not seek to reveal that Beckett has an active interest in Dickinson that has so far been missed by his critics, but rather to suggest that Beckett's literary thinking has a rich resonance with Dickinson's, one which underlies their manifest differences in cultural attitude and religious conviction. What the Dickinsonian cast to

13. Samuel Beckett, *Ohio Impromptu*, in Samuel Beckett, *The Complete Dramatic Works*, London, Faber and Faber 2006, p448. (Hereafter *Complete Dramatic Works*).

14. Samuel Beckett, 'La Mouche', in Samuel Beckett, *Collected Poems*, London, Calder 1986, p45. (Hereafter *Collected Poems*).

Beckett's poem does allow us to see is a kind of shared sensibility, a shared visual vocabulary, that is evident in a particular way in 'La Mouche', but which turns and glimmers throughout Beckett's oeuvre, from 'Serena 1' and *More Pricks than Kicks* in the early 1930s to *Worstward Ho* and *Stirrings Still* in the 1980s. As Steven Connor and others have demonstrated, the image of the fly pressed against the window pane recurs through Beckett's oeuvre, and each time it does it brings with it associations that evoke a Dickinsonian undertow to Beckett's writing, a pull towards a kind of blind seeing that he shares with her, and that opens onto the space of an instantiated, imagined death.[15] *Watt*, written in 1944, contains an image of flies seeking the warmth and light that has a Dickinsonian pulse:

> The flies, of skeleton thinness, excited to new efforts by yet another dawn, left the walls, and the ceiling, and even the floor, and hastened in great numbers to the window. Here, pressed against the impenetrable panes, they would enjoy the light and warmth of the long summer's day.[16]

The fly pressed against the impenetrable pane here carries something from the fly crushed against the invisible in 'La Mouche', and prepares the ground for Beckett's later houseflies - in *Company*, for example, which focuses sharply on a 'live fly' that might provide some company to the lone protagonist of the novella, a 'live fly mistaking him for dead';[17] or in *All Strange Away*, where the narrator commands himself to imagine, to 'lodge a second in that glare', a 'dying common house or dying window fly'.[18]

Now, there is nothing in particular to suggest that this recurrence of the 'window fly' in Beckett is associated with Dickinson's death fly (although one of the few essays to extend a comparison between Beckett and Dickinson reads the fly in *Company* as a cousin of the fly in 'I heard a fly Buzz - when I died').[19] But the associations that gather around the fly in these recurring passages are woven into a particular kind of thinking about death, about visibility, and about the requirement that one brings death to visibility and perception as part of any attempt to picture the world - a kind of thinking that Beckett and Dickinson deeply share. Dickinson's fly, in interposing between the dead and living 'I', between 'the light' and 'me', and in marking that gap that opens up in seeing as the poet 'could not see to see', stumbles into the limit space that her entire work strains to make thinkable, the space underlying being, in which the oppositions that make being possible are both revealed and overcome. There is, there has to be, a space between darkness and brightness, between being alive and being dead, where these two conditions meet and separate; to think is to approach this zone of mingling and separation, to find oneself at once annulled and brought to being within it. Both Dickinson and Beckett know this, and for both the task of writing is to enter this zone, to enter the indefinition, the indifference, that it confers upon the thinker, while making of such indefinition, such indifference, the very difference and

---

15. See Steven Connor, 'Making Flies Mean Something', in S.Connor, *Beckett, Modernism and the Material Imagination*, Cambridge, Cambridge University Press 2014, pp48-62.

16. Samuel Beckett, *Watt*, London, Calder 1976, p236.

17. Samuel Beckett, *Company*, in Samuel Beckett, *Nohow On*, London, Calder 1992, p22. (Hereafter *Company*)

18. Samuel Beckett, *All Strange Away*, in Samuel Beckett, *The Complete Short Prose 1929-1989*, New York, Grove Press 1995, p172. (Hereafter *Complete Short Prose*).

19. Mary F. Cantanzaro, 'More Than a Common Pest: The Fly as Non-human Companion in Emily Dickinson's "I Heard a Fly Buzz When I Died" and Samuel Beckett's *Company*', in Anna-Teresa Tymieniecka, ed., *From Sky and Earth to Metaphysics*, New York, Springer 2015, pp157-162.

definition that allows us to maintain a subject position, and allows us to cast a picture of the world. Sharon Cameron, in what remains one of the most incisive readings of 'I heard a Fly buzz - when I died' remarks on just this attention in Dickinson to the commingling of dark and bright, of life and death, in terms which make the continuity between Dickinson and Beckett palpable. Dickinson's lyrics, Cameron writes, 'attempt to cross boundaries, to blur distinctions between life and death, time and timelessness, figure and its fulfilment, or to put it more accurately, to wear a passage between them';[20] and the force that allows her to cross such boundaries, to wear such a passage, is that of imagined, perceived death, an imagining of death that manages to conjure a continuity between bright and dark, between blindness and seeing. The last two lines of Dickinson's poem ('And then the windows failed - and then / I could not see to see'), Cameron writes, forge a space in which 'death is survived by perception', and in which the poem 'penetrates to the invisible imagination which strengthens in response to the loss of visible sight' (p115).

20. Sharon Cameron, *Lyric Time: Dickinson and the Limits of Genre*, Baltimore, The Johns Hopkins Press 1979, p135.

For any reader of Beckett's work, this description of Dickinson's blind seeing is eerily prescient of the passage that Beckett's own writing wears from blank to blank, 'on', as he puts it, from 'nought anew'(*Company*, p12), from the 'unthinkable first to the no less unthinkable last'.[21] If for Dickinson, death is survived by perception, so for Beckett, the imagination continually outlives its own death. 'I don't know when I died', the narrator of *The Calmative* says at the opening of his narrative, in an impossible posthumous gambit which mirrors the opening of Dickinson's poem;[22] and Beckett's writing career, from the *Unnamable* on, is nothing more than an extended attempt to imagine the death of the imagination, to conjure a kind of seeing that continues, after the difference between seeing and unseeing, between living and dying, has been cancelled. As the narrator of *All Strange Away* imagines that Dickinsonian fly, pressed against the window pane in the bright glare of a death that has already been died, the narrator summons this requirement, this demand that the Beckettian imagination lives on in the throes of its own death. 'Imagination dead imagine', the narrator says: 'Imagination dead imagine to lodge a second in that glare a dying common house or dying window fly, then fall the five feet to the dust and die or die and fall' (p172).

21. Samuel Beckett, *How It Is*, London, Calder 1996, p153.

22. Samuel Beckett, *The Calmative*, in Samuel Beckett, *The Expelled and Other Novellas*, London, Penguin 1980, p51.

The light that shines in Beckett's work, from the 'darkness visible' of 'A wet night' to the 'unfading light' of 'Neither',[23] is drawn from this encounter with a perceived death, this capacity to open a glaring second in which the imagination imagines its own dying. In all of the 'rotunda texts' of the sixties and seventies, in *Imagination Dead Imagine*, *All Strange Away*, and then in *The Lost Ones*, *Company*, *Ill seen Ill Said*, and *Worstward Ho*, the undifferentiated storyscapes are lit by a peculiar light, which is made of the shadows that it seems to vanquish, and which is won by an imagination that is working at and beyond the limits of its own conditions of possibility. The scene in *Company*, in which the protagonist lies 'on his back in the

23. Samuel Beckett, 'Neither', in (*Complete Short Prose*, p258).

dark' in a placeless cylinder, listening to a 'voice' which tells him of his life, is periodically lit by precisely this light. The light, the narrator says, has 'no source', 'as if faintly luminous all his little void' (p15) - in the same way that the light in the rotunda of *Imagination Dead Imagine* comes from 'no visible source' (p182). The light in these works appears to saturate the space - so that in the rotunda of *Imagination Dead Imagine* 'all shines with the same white shine' (p182), and in the cylinder of *The Lost Ones* the light 'appears to emanate from all sides and to permeate the entire space as though this were uniformly luminous down to its least particle of ambient air'.[24] This lends these works a kind of brilliance, a shadowless quality, like the relentless illumination of a shopping mall, or of a rubber cell. But even as these works bask in omnipresent light, it is clear at all times that the light here is only another kind of darkness, that brightness is, as in Dickinson's 'We grow accustomed to the Dark -', simply an alteration of the dark. The brilliant light of Beckett's late works always holds a darkness within it, always trembles on the brink of revealing an identity with the dark that it opposes - this, the narrator of *Company* suggests, is a 'shadowy light' (p15), a light which simply makes the 'darkness visible' (p15).

To learn to see in this light requires one to develop a particular kind of blind seeing, one that we are taught too in reading Dickinson's verse, as she stumbles from blank to blank. When Beckett seeks to picture a world, when he reaches for what the narrator of *The Lost Ones* calls 'a perfect mental image of the whole system' (p204), he seeks to imagine a space in which everything is included, in which death is included in the sphere of life, in which dark is included in the sphere of light. As a young Beckett puts it, he seeks to imagine the art work as a 'total object, complete with missing parts'.[25] And this requires him to understand that the picture of the world, in its fullness, includes those shadows that are concealed within Heideggerian light, just as any attempt to imagine being requires us to apprehend the thought that nonbeing is one of its constituent parts. Beckett's late works seek to produce pictures of completion, pictures of the totality. But what Beckett finds is that the harder we try to imagine the world in its blankness or in its completeness, in its fullness or in its emptiness, we find that there exists always a remainder, some deathly element or ingredient of life, some dark element of light, that cannot quite come to thought or expression; some difference from self that is a feature of the very grammar of being. The narrator of *Worstward Ho* - Beckett's most excruciating experiment in blind seeing - finds that the attempt to 'see all' produces not simply omnipresent light, but a kind of Dickinsonian blank, a flaw in being, in thinking, that runs right through its very fabric. To try to say everything, Beckett's narrator writes, produces only a kind of Dickinson unsaying, in which we are cast into unthought, into 'profounds of mindlessness' which are marked only by those 'Blanks for when words gone'.[26]

24. Samuel Beckett, *The Lost Ones*, in (*Complete Short Prose*, p215).

25. Samuel Beckett, *Proust and Three Dialogues with Georges Duthuit*, London, Calder 1965), p101.

26. Samuel Beckett, *Worstward Ho*, in Beckett, *Nohow On*, London, Calder 1992, p124.

IV

THE PONDEROUS SPECTACLE OF THINGS CEASING TO BE

It is perhaps in the lit darkness of our own contemporary moment that this fugitive affinity between Beckett and Dickinson, this latent tradition of blind seeing, comes to a kind of oblique perceptibility. There is, I think, a recognition, across a wide range of contemporary writers, that the task of making a picture of the world today involves us in the apprehension of a kind of darkness that is woven into the picturing mechanism itself - just as there is a growing sense that to think about life now, under contemporary conditions, requires us to re-see the junction between the living and the dead. As Jane Bennett argues in her 2010 book *Vibrant Matter*, there is an urgent imperative now to rethink the means by which life is distributed in matter, beyond the forms prescribed by humanist traditions - a rethinking which requires us to 'dissipate the onto-theological binaries of life/matter, human/animal'.[27] Our current predicament both allows and requires us to produce a new material account of the terrain that opens up between life and death, to overcome our habit, as Bennett puts it, of 'parsing the world into dull matter (it, things) and vibrant life (us, beings)'(*Vibrant Matter*,pvii), and in doing so, we are led too to resee the difficult boundary between the blind and the sighted, between the visible and the invisible.

This articulation of world picturing, with blind seeing, with a new kind of inclusive disjunction between life and death, can be found, as I have said, across the range of contemporary imaginings. But I am going to focus here on one example - Cormac McCarthy's novel of global death *The Road* - a novel which owes an explicit debt to Beckett, and perhaps an implicit one to Dickinson, as the originator of the mode of deathwriting I am seeking here to articulate. McCarthy's novel sets out to offer a picture of the world, as an environment given over in its entirety to death. The man at the heart of the story is afforded, at one moment in the novel, a vision of this kind of planetary death. 'He walked out in the grey light', the narrator says,

> and stood and he saw for a brief moment the absolute truth of the world. The cold relentless circling of the intestate earth. Darkness implacable. The blind dogs of the sun in their running. The crushing black vacuum of the universe.[28]

This is a moment of blind seeing of some intensity. The grey light in which the man stands is cast by a blind sun; the absolute seeing that he is granted - his sudden grasping of the mechanical turning of a cosmic machine - is a vision that emerges from and takes place in implacable darkness. The moment of seeing itself is peculiarly annulled or proleptically cancelled, as it belongs to a model of looking and observing that, in the wake of whatever disaster

27. Jane Bennett, *Vibrant Matter: A Political Ecology of Things*, Durham, Duke University Press 2010), p.x. (Hereafter *Vibrant Matter*).

28. Cormac McCarthy, *The Road*, London, Picador 2006, p138.

has befallen the world, is now defunct. As the man puts it later in the novel, whatever world picture is granted here is one that no longer organises itself around the human as a relational centre. It is only 'in the world's destruction' that it is 'possible at last to see how it was made' (p293).

McCarthy's novel sets out to produce this picture of borderless death; but in doing so, in setting out to imagine the process by which the human extinguishes itself entirely, McCarthy produces that same kind of remainder, that same possibility of new modes of seeing, new ways of understanding the relation between the dead and the living, that we find in Beckett, and in Dickinson. McCarthy's novel is drenched in Beckettian rhythms and allusions - it conducts itself throughout as an exercise in Beckettian thinking. Beckett's *Imagination Dead Imagine*, with which McCarthy's novel is in constant dialogue, opens with the declaration that, in whatever space the narrator is imagining, there is 'No trace anywhere of life',[29] and this phrase comes back repeatedly in *The Road*, like a mantra or an undertone. In this world, the narrator says, there is 'no sign of life' (p11); 'The roadside hedges were gone to rows of black and twisted brambles. No sign of life' (p20); there are 'No tracks in the road, nothing living anywhere' (p29); there is 'no smoke, no movement of life' (p82); there is 'No sign of life anywhere' (p216). As the man and the boy walk the road, as they push their mechanic feet along the 'black shape' of the road, 'running from dark to dark' (p279), they walk in the footsteps of all those tramping figures in Beckett, who in turn walk mechanically along that threadless way that Dickinson strings between blank and blank. In a rare moment of humour, McCarthy's boy asks his father 'What are our long term goals?' (p170), and in the question we can hear Beckett's grim dismantling of the Christian mechanics of hope, Dickinson's disclosure of the indefinition of the end. But, in reanimating these Beckettian, Dickinsonian rhythms, McCarthy's novel also produces that same furtive duplication, that same opening of wriggling difference within the static picture of the self-same, that moves in Beckett's imagination, that animates Dickinson's deathwriting. The boy asks his father at one point, perhaps as an adjunct to the question of 'long term goals', whether there is any other world, whether the world that they inhabit, in the last throes of its destruction, is the only world available to thought or to life. 'There could be people alive someplace else', the boy suggests:

> Whereplace else?
> I dont know. Anywhere.
> You mean besides on earth?
> Yes.
> I dont think so. They couldnt live anyplace else.
> Not even if they could get there?
> No. (pp260-261)

This question is at the heart of McCarthy's imagination, as it is central to

29. Samuel Beckett, *Imagination Dead Imagine*, in (*Complete Short Prose*, p182).

Beckett's thinking, and to Dickinson's. It calls, perhaps faintly, to Dickinson's assertion that 'the Brain - is wider than the sky -' (598) ('put them side by side', she says, 'The one the other will contain / With ease' (598, ll. 2-4)), and much more loudly to that moment in Beckett's *Endgame* when another love-crazed father seeks some kind of escape from the world that contains us. In the post apocalyptic wastes of *Endgame*, where the 'earth is extinguished',[30] where the 'waves' are 'lead' and the 'sun is zero' (p107), a desperate father asks Hamm for some bread, to keep his child alive for another day, and Hamm refuses him, pointing out that survival in this world is only a prolongation of a time that has already died. 'Use your head', Hamm tells the pleading man, 'I give you some corn':

> the colours come back into his little cheeks - perhaps. And then? [*Pause.*] I lost patience. [*Violently.*] Use your head, can't you, use your head, you're on earth, there's no cure for that! (p118)

For Beckett's Hamm, as for McCarthy's father, the world is all there is. The vision that McCarthy's father is granted of the 'absolute truth of the world' is a monologic vision, a 'total object', like the 'mental image of the entire system' that lies at the heart of Beckett's *The Lost Ones*. There is no place 'besides on earth', there is no cure for our worldedness. But what McCarthy's world picture discovers, like Beckett's, like Dickinson's, is that picturing itself contains always a kind of darkness, a kind of countersight that is woven into seeing, and that offers a death that is also, as in Dickinson, 'Another way - to see'. The light that shines in McCarthy's novel is, like that in Beckett and in Dickinson, a dark kind of light, a light made of 'implacable darkness'. In another of those breath-taking seams, in which McCarthy's world folds into Beckett's, the light in *The Road* is describes as 'sourceless' - the 'faint light all about, quivering and sourceless, refracted in the rain of drifting soot' (pp13-14). This is the light that is cast when the sun is 'zero', and in both Beckett and McCarthy there is an echo here of the possibility of seeing that emerges from the dark light cast in Dickinson's verse. But, in the halflight of the tradition I am sketching here, this sourceless light, this light compounded of the darkness it withstands, is not the result of a theology, but instead the fugitive corollary to seeing and thinking itself, the obscurity that inhabits the act of picturing, and that carries a latent, unthought, ungraven future. McCarthy's father equates world seeing with world destruction. It is only 'in the world's destruction' that it might be 'possible to see how it was made'; but the kind of world seeing that McCarthy reaches for, the kind of seeing that we find in Beckett, and in Dickinson, is one that unearths a junction between the destruction of the world, and its very possibility, the motor of its becoming. The father sees before him 'the sweeping waste, hydrotopic and coldly secular', but he sees also 'The ponderous counterspectacle of things ceasing to be' (p293) - the counterspectacle that accompanies all instances

30. Samuel Beckett, *Endgame*, in (*Complete Dramatic Works*, p132).

of the spectacle, and that harbours that Heideggerian 'shadow that is cast around all things everywhere' (p135).

V

ANOTHER WAY - TO SEE

I have talked throughout this essay of a tradition, a tradition of 'blind seeing', one to which we have to tune ourselves if we are to conceive of the world picture today, in the wake of the human project, and under the conditions of the Anthropocene. I have used this word, because I cannot find another that names the kind of work that I am suggesting that we need to do, or that could be equal to the kind of history that might address the future that awaits us. But I hope that it is clear that a tradition of blind seeing is hardly a tradition at all, and that it resists just the kind of lucidity it calls for, as Susan Howe recognises when she traces the 'ambiguous paths of kinship' that connect her to Emily Dickinson, or as Deleuze and Guattari recognise when they try to conscript Kafka into a 'minor literature'.[31] Harold Bloom declares, in *The Western Canon*, that the operation of recruiting Dickinson's slantwise thinking for the great tradition is unproblematic. 'Her canonicity', he writes, 'results from her achieved strangeness, her uncanny relation to the tradition' (p308). Her 'Sublime', he goes on, 'is founded upon her unnaming of all our certitudes into so many blanks; and it gives her, and her authentic readers, another way to see, almost into the dark' (p309). That Bloom can rehearse the jargon of authenticity, while blithely laying claim to Dickinson's poetics of unnaming, indicates, I think, how weak this gesture of incorporation is, how it fails to respond to the kind of thinking that Dickinson's poetry demands, or to see in the kind of light that it casts. Seeing 'almost into the dark' is not, I would suggest, what Dickinson's poetry does; rather, it opens a buried junction between blindness and sight, an impossible meeting ground which sets the conditions for seeing itself, for being itself.

To imagine a tradition to which such seeing belongs requires us to rethink the tradition itself, to suspend the cultural forms that have bound us and normalised us. Heidegger argues as much, when he offers a proleptic rebuke to Bloom's canon, and to the work of tradition more generally. The shadow which accompanies the world picture, which is in fact a 'concealed emitting of light' points, Heidegger writes, 'to something else, which it is denied to us of today to know' (*The Age of the World*, p136). To 'experience' and 'ponder' this counterspectacle, requires us, Heidegger writes, to resist the 'flight into tradition' which 'can bring about nothing in itself other than self-deception and blindness in relation to the historical moment' (p136). If we are to see by the light of Dickinsonian darkness, or by the light that shines in Beckett's shade, then we need to learn to think a tradition, while resisting the flight into tradition - while recognising that world seeing today requires us to think

31. See Susan Howe, *My Emily Dickinson* (Berkeley: North Atlantic Books, 1985), p1, and Gilles Deleuze and Félix Guattari, *Kafka: Toward a Minor Literature*, Minneapolis, University of Minnesota Press 1986.

beyond the human forms that have bound us. 'Reflection', Heidegger writes, 'transports the man of the future into that "between" in which he belongs to Being and yet remains a stranger amid that which is' (p136). To reflect on the world picture today requires us to achieve just this between-ness, and just this estrangement. To see with the eyes of the blind, as McCarthy and Beckett and Dickinson asks us to do, is to accustom ourselves to a Dickinsonian dark, in which 'something in the sight/ Adjusts itself' (428, ll. 18-19). It is this adjusted sight that will allow us to behold the 'larger - Darknesses' (l. 9) of today.

Peter Boxall is Professor of English at University of Sussex. He is author of *The Value of the Novel* (Cambridge University Press, 2015); *Twenty-First Century Fiction: A Critical Introduction* (Cambridge University Press, 2013), *Since Beckett: Contemporary Writing in the Wake of Modernism* (Continuum, 2009), and *Don DeLillo: The Possibility of Fiction* (Routledge, 2006).

SITES OF DEATH IN SOME RECENT BRITISH FICTION

Robert Hampson

Abstract We generally think that death has retreated from contemporary everyday life, withdrawn to the non-places of nursing homes, hospitals, hospices, funeral parlours, crematoria. Graham Swift's *Last Orders*, with its journey from technologised hospital death to the scattering of the ashes, occupies precisely these non-places of death. J. G. Ballard's *Crash*, however, provides a counter-example: *Crash* takes place in the non-places of motorway slip-roads, airport access roads, police-pounds and reservoirs. At the same time, it registers how these spaces and non-spaces are overwritten by various pre-existing scripts of violent death by films, television and newspaper photographs. The essay then demonstrates the ubiquity of death in contemporary life by exploring Tom McCarthy's engagement with accident, trauma and re-enactment in *Remainder*; Gordon Burns's depiction of tabloid journalism and modern improvised rituals of death in *fullalove*; the psychogeographic identification of particular sites of death in the work of Iain Sinclair and Peter Ackroyd; and the recognition, in detective fiction, that anywhere can be a site of death. The essay concludes by considering the popularity of forensic-science series and how *Silent Witness*, *Waking the Dead*, *Cold Case*, and *CSI* present death in its multiple forms for peak-time viewing.

Keywords non-places, death, dying, simulcra, forensics, post-human

In *The Birth of the Clinic*, an extended engagement with medical science and its institutions in eighteenth-century France, Michel Foucault argued that an epistemic shift took place at the end of the eighteenth century, a major component of which was the rediscovery of the idea that death provided 'the absolute point of view over life and opening ... on its truth'.[1] For Foucault, the development of pathological anatomy in this period was the most vital expression of the new medicine. Through the dissection of the dead body came the discovery that 'it is at death that disease and life speak their truth' (*BoC*, p145). From this perspective, disease breaks away from the metaphysic of evil and becomes, instead, 'life undergoing modification in an inflected functioning' (p153). More importantly, the anatomical gaze revealed 'the forbidden imminent secret: the knowledge of the individual' (p170). Accordingly, Foucault concluded that 'the experience of individuality in modern culture is bound up with that of death' (p197).

Elisabeth Bronfen made productive use of this re-emergence of the idea that death is 'that moment in a person's life where individuality ... could

1. Michel Foucault, *The Birth of the Clinic*, New York, Vintage 1973, p155. (Hereafter *BoC*).

2. Elisabeth Bronfen, *Over Her Dead Body: Death, femininity and the aesthetic*, Manchester,

finally be attained' and 'an otherwise incommunicable secret could be made visible' in her reading of nineteenth-century literature and art.² She cites, as one example, Nell's death in *The Old Curiosity Shop*, where death 'recreates the body into a perfect version of its former self' (*Over her dead body*, p89). She notes also the nineteenth-century literary convention in which the deathbed scene involves not only the farewell greetings from friends and kin but also the dying person's last minute vision of the after-life (p77). While death remains an untransmissable experience, the deathbed spectators watch the dying person hovering on the threshold and through them hope to gain a glimpse into 'the Beyond'.

This new conception of 'death's presence in life' which Foucault delineates, Bronfen suggests, gave a new power to the dying person and led to 'elaborate stagings' of death (p77). Death certainly seems to have been a regular part of everyday Victorian life, from high infant mortality rates to the death of women in childbirth, from public executions to familial death-beds, from elaborate rituals of mourning to commemorative photographs of the dead.³ Victorian fiction bears eloquent testimony to 'death's presence in life' in a rich variety of forms. If we confine ourselves to the works of Dickens, in addition to Nell's long journey to death in *The Old Curiosity Shop*, there is Oliver Twist's morally-improving final meeting with Fagin in the death-cell; the 'Resurrection Men' in *The Tale of Two Cities*; the unhealthy graveyards of *Bleak House*; the death-house of *Our Mutual Friend*; and Pip's meditations over the tombstones of his parents and five little brothers at the start of *Great Expectations*.

By contrast, we generally think that dying and death have retreated from contemporary everyday life, withdrawn to the non-places of nursing homes, hospitals, hospices, funeral parlours, crematoria. Thus Ruth Richardson, in her pioneering work on the history of attitudes towards death in the early Victorian period, observes that nowadays 'preparation of the dead for disposal is regarded as a sanitary problem, dealt with professionally by hospitals and undertakers'.⁴ Roger Luckhurst makes a wider claim: 'In advanced capitalist societies, encounters with extremity are suppressed: birth, death, insanity are all removed from the everyday and placed under technical and institutional command'.⁵ In Marc Augé's words, this is 'a world where people are born in the clinic and die in hospital'.⁶

In this essay, I will argue that while the process of dying has been removed to these non-places, death itself (in mediated and unmediated forms) has become ubiquitous in contemporary life. I will approach this through the engagement with death in a range of recent novels arguing that, if 'death's presence in life' was linked with the attainment of individuality for the Victorians, death in recent fiction is rather associated with an alienation and a randomness that de-emphasise individual identity. In the first section, I will explore this through the analysis of three very different takes on death in two important literary novels (*Last Orders* by Graham Swift and *Remainder*

Manchester University Press 1992, p77. (Hereafter *Over her dead body*).

3. See, for example, Pat Jalland, *Death in the Victorian Family*, Oxford, Oxford University Press 1996, for an account of how the high infant- and child-mortality rate and short life-expectancy in the Victorian period produced a deep pre-occupation with death; Julie-Marie Strange, *Death, Grief and Poverty in Britain, 1870-1914*, Cambridge, Cambridge University Press 2006, for an account of grief and mourning among the Victorian and Edwardian working class; and Mary Elizabeth Hotz, *Literary Remains: Representations of Death and Burial in Victorian England*, New York, SUNY 2009, for the centrality of death and burial for various Victorian discourses, including law, medicine and social planning.

4. Ruth Richardson, *Death, Dissection and the Destitute*, Harmondsworth, Penguin Books 1988, p15. (Hereafter *Death,Dissection*).

5. Roger Luckhurst, *The Trauma Question*, London, Routledge 2008, pp128-9.

6. Marc Augé, *Non-Places: Introduction to an Anthropology of Supermodernity*, London, Verso 1995, p78.

by Tom McCarthy) and the counter-cultural fiction of J.G. Ballard.

While Swift's novel explores the non-places of death and dying in contemporary society through low-mimetic realism, the central figure of Ballard's high-concept, techno-pornographic novel dreams of an erotic encounter with death. This dream might be read in relation to Foucault's suggestion that 'in that perception of death ... the individual finds himself escaping from a monotonous average life' (*BoC*, p172). However, his death actually returns him to the regime of the simulacrum, the circulation of mediated and remediated images of violent deaths which prompted his dream. McCarthy's novel also focusses on re-enactment and simulacra, but its peripheral vision registers the threat of arbitrary, violent death that is part of our contemporary reality not just in the form of traffic accidents and urban crime, but also through acts of terrorism.

In the second section, I will consider the very different project of the counter-cultural, psychogeographic novels of Iain Sinclair and Peter Ackroyd, which cultivate particular sites of death as part of a process of self-transformation. I will approach this through Gordon Burn's novel, *fullalove*, with its tabloid journalist narrator, which presents both the mediation of death in popular journalism and the improvisation of rituals in the face of death. Where Foucault argued for an epistemic change in the medical discourses of death, Ruth Richardson's account of the context for the Anatomy Act of 1832 foregrounds the length of popular memory and the survival in popular belief of a strong tie between the body and the personality that produced both 'solicitude towards the corpse and fear of it' (*Death, Dissection*, p7). In the final section, accordingly, I will consider popular fiction in the form of the detective novel. In the contemporary context, however, 'popular' refers not to survivals of an earlier culture within folk memory and practice, but rather to an imposition of ideas from above through popular media. I will suggest that the ubiquity of death in mediated forms, particularly through the staging of the dead body in recent popular culture, is characterised, not by a focus on the self and the revelation of individuality, but rather by the performance of the 'medical gaze' that carefully separates the body from identity. In particular, in certain contemporary forms of popular culture, individual identity is subordinated to a technologised and militarised version of the collective aligned with the governmental agenda of state security and with the post-human.

Alienation and inauthenticity

Graham Swift's prize-winning novel *Last Orders* (1996) occupies precisely the non-places of death to which Augé refers: through Jack's medicalised hospital dying, his body disappearing behind the technology that keeps it alive, and through Vic's work as an undertaker, the narrative repeatedly returns to the contemporary non-places of death.[7] Swift's novel, which takes off from

7. Graham Swift, *Last Orders*, London, Picador 1996. (Hereafter *Last Orders*).

Faulkner's *As I Lay Dying*, is the account of a journey from Bermondsey to Margate, undertaken by four men (Vic, Vince, Lenny and Ray) to scatter the ashes of their friend Jack. The novel consists of their thoughts and memories during the course of this drive. Vic, the undertaker, sums up the non-places of contemporary death in the alliterative phrase 'Homes, Hospitals and Hospices, where people hexpire' (*Last Orders*, p211), and the novel initially focusses, through Jack, on the middle term here: it presents the medicalised treatment of dying, where dying and death take place in the non-place of the hospital removed from the course of daily life. Thus Jack is introduced into the text in his hospital bed: 'His hands lying there on the bedclothes, the fingers half-curled, the tapes and stuff further up on his wrist where the tubes go in' (p33). As Jack's condition deteriorates, his body disappears behind the technology that keeps him alive. At first he is remembered 'sitting up there in that little white smock thing, with the extra tubes going in', but then 'it seemed like every day they rigged up another tube' with the prospect that he will reach the condition of those 'others in there that were all tubes, tubes and wires and bottles and apparatus, complete chemistry sets' so that you had to look close to see 'a human component still there somewhere' (p152). This is hardly death as the revelation of individuality, but rather the human ceases to be fully human and is reduced to a 'component' in a complicated machine for dying.

There is, of course, no death-bed scene with family and friends gathered around. Instead, through Vic, *Last Orders* also presents two other non-places of contemporary death: the funeral parlour and the crematorium. Vic's place of work is mentioned early on with its 'wax flowers and the marble slabs and the angel with its head bowed in the window' (*Last Orders*, p4). The narrative repeatedly returns to this place with its customers, its 'lodgers', and the relations visiting to view the body. Vic also recalls Jack's cremation (and the numerous others in which he has been involved) and the modern embarrassment 'in the face of death': 'When those curtains come across and the music plays nobody knows when to turn round and go' (p79). In addition to this lack of recognised ritual in the face of death, Ray registers another of the sources of this unease: he recalls the 'velvet curtains, the flowers, the amens, the music', but also his feeling that 'none of it had to do with [Jack], none of it' (p201). Where the deathbed scenes of Victorian literature were both rituals of farewell and affirmations of continuity, the crematorium, like the funeral parlour, with the anonymity of the space and its furnishings, is markedly discontinuous with the life of the deceased. Where the hospital presents the medicalised process of dying, Jack's profession produces two further sites of contemporary death, non-places which serve only to confirm the absence of the dead, the removal of the dead from the living.

Daniel Lea describes *Last Orders* as 'Swift's elegiac contemplation of mortality in a secularised community'.[8] As he notes, Swift 'mimics Faulkner's progressive disentanglement of family secrets' through his narrative

8. Daniel Lea, *Graham Swift*, Manchester, Manchester University Press 2005, p161. (Hereafter *Lea*).

exploration of 'individual registers of debts incurred and paid' (*Lea*, p162). One of those debts, what Lea calls the 'ethical debt' of the living to the dead, motivates the narrative and is expressed through the characters' implicit search for 'a suitable symbolic protocol to enact their leave-taking' (p163, 167). In Lenny's words, this is the concern to have 'done our duty by Jack here' (*Last Orders*, p209). That contextually ambiguous word 'here' is a reminder that, although the characters' sense of 'duty' is plain, Jack is unambiguously not 'here'. Indeed, *Last Orders* repeatedly explores the place of death in relation to the absence of the most important person: the deceased. Ray, for example, looks at Jack's body in the hospital bed and thinks 'Everyone has their own space and no one else can step in it, then one day it's unoccupied' (p183). The dead body is not a threshold 'to the Beyond', but rather a mirror in which the spectator sees themselves (*Over her dead body*, p84). Instead, the novel confronts the passage from being to non-being from the perspective of the witnesses or survivors and their meditation on the difference between the embodied person and the lifeless body. Thus, when Vince views Jack's corpse in the 'Chapel of Rest', he ponders the mystery of embodiment: how 'nobody ain't more than just a body, than just their own body, which ain't nobody' (*Last Orders*, p199). The body is, ultimately, not the person - just a place-holder for them. The narrative explores the gap left in other people's lives by a death - and probes the mystery of life and death, not in relation to any hypothesised 'after-life', but as revealed in the difference between the living and the dead body.

Cremation adds a further twist since it produces the uncanny return of the dead body in another form. The fact that the four characters are carrying Jack's ashes in an urn, which is passed between them during the drive, emphasises both the materiality of the body and the difference between the remains and the person. If Jack is a thought-provoking absence, the urn is insistently and awkwardly present. At the start of the novel, when the party gathers in the bar of the *Coach and Horses*, the urn is already causing problems: 'Vic takes the jar and starts to ease it back in the box but it's a tricky business and the box slides from his lap onto the floor' (p10). The urn also begins the first of its many transformations: as Vic solves the problem of holding the urn, by placing it on the bar, he thinks 'it's about the same size as a pint glass' (p10). Later, Vic is described as carrying the urn 'like it might be his lunch' (p21), a motif that reappears, when the urn is slipped into a Rochester Food Fayre bag along with a jar of coffee (p109). Another kind of transformation is suggested, when Ray tries to move the urn onto the car seat next to Lenny, and Lenny quips 'Jack in a box, eh' (p49). The attention to the funeral urn and the ashes of the dead in numerous comic scenes from Edward Bond's *The Sea* (1973) onwards testifies to the embarrassed fascination with this awkward relic, the urn and the ashes, resulting from the increased use of cremation in modern times. At the end of the novel, as the funeral party come to throw Jack's ashes into the sea from Margate Pier, attention shifts from the urn to its contents. When Ray unscrews the cap and holds out the jar 'like I'm holding out a tin of sweets', Vic is concerned that the ashes will get 'stuck to our hands' (p293), while Ray is worried that he will have to bang the jar 'like you do when you get to the bottom of a box of cornflakes' (p294). The abject physicality of the residue stands in contrast to the absence of Jack himself, as the soft sift 'slipping through' Lenny's fingers gives way to the last of the ash 'carried away by the wind ... whirled away by the wind till the ash becomes wind and the wind becomes Jack what we're made of' (p295). This takes us back to Ray's thoughts at the crematorium: 'nothing ain't got to do with Jack, not even his own ashes. Because Jack's nothing' (p201).

Last Orders thus presents a series of sites of contemporary death - hospitals, funeral parlours, graveyards and crematoria - and in this way echoes the common conception that contemporary dying and death are removed from everyday life.[9] However, the journey that provides the frame to this narrative also points towards another perspective - one from which death is not so far removed from daily life after all; indeed, where death is literally ubiquitous in the sense that its sites are everywhere about us. Early in *Last Orders*, Vince offers a peon to the motor car: 'A good motor is a comfort and companion and an asset to a man' (*Last Orders*, p71). J.G. Ballard offers a much darker vision of our relationship with cars: in Ballard's counter-cultural work, the companionable vehicle of Swift's narrative brings death into everyone's daily life. Ballard's *Crash* (1973) thus provides a counter-example to Swift's *Last Orders*. *Crash* takes place in the non-spaces of motorway slip-roads, airport access roads, police-pounds and reservoirs. At the same time, however, it registers how these spaces and non-spaces are over-written by various pre-existing scripts and fictions: 'desires encoded by media circuits ... compulsions instigated by television trauma'.[10] Jean Baudrillard described *Crash* as 'a work of death that is never a work of mourning; and called it 'the first great novel of the universe of simulation'.[11] As Ballard said in his Introduction to the 1995 re-issue: 'The fiction is already there. The writer's task is to invent the reality'.[12]

Crash tells the story of a character called Ballard, his wife Catherine, and Vaughan, who is, in effect, their sex guru or life trainer. It begins with the announcement of Vaughan's death in 'his last car-crash' and with the unfulfilled sexual fantasy that lay behind it - of death in a collision with the film star Elizabeth Taylor off the Heathrow airport flyover:

> In his vision of a car-crash with the actress, Vaughan was obsessed by many wounds and impacts - by the dying chromium and collapsing bulkheads of their two cars meeting head-on in complex collisions endlessly repeated in slow-motion films, by the identical wounds inflicted on their bodies, by the image of windshield glass frosting around her face as she broke its tinted surface like a death-born Aphrodite ... (*Crash*, p8)

Instead of this desired consummation, however, Vaughan's car 'plunged

9. Lea convincingly argues that the novel involves the 'enforced recognition' by the narrators of the provisionality of their own existence (*Lea*, p164). From this, he concludes that death is 'ordinary' and, indeed, ubiquitous (p187). However, this is using 'ubiquitous' in a more metaphysical sense, rather than with a focus on the sites of death.

10. Roger Luckhurst on T-cell, the precursor of Vaughan in Ballard's *The Atrocity Exhibition*. Luckhurst, 'The Angle Between Two Walls': The Fiction of J. G. Ballard, Liverpool, Liverpool University Press 1997, p95. (Hereafter *The Angle*).

11. Jean Baudrillard, *Simulacra and Simulations*, (trans) Sheila Faria Glaser, Ann Arbor, Michigan University Press 1994.

12. J. G. Ballard, *Crash*, London, Vintage 1995, p4. (Hereafter *Crash*).

through the roof of a bus filled with airline passengers', and 'his body lay under the police arc-lights at the foot of the flyover' in a 'broken posture' of legs and arms that 'seemed to parody the photographs of crash injuries that covered the walls of his apartment' (p9). Instead of being an orgasmic escape from the circuit of images, Vaughan's death is marked as an anticlimactic return to the regime of the simulacrum.

The banality of the airport flyover is re-narrativised in his fantasy by an imagination full of 'slow-motion films' of accidents and 'photographs of crash injuries'. As Luckhurst observes, the media 'have released irresolvable traumatic material which can only induce repetition of the trauma, in a futile attempt at mastery' (*The Angle*, p95). For Luckhurst, this is 'the media as the embodiment of the death drive' (p95). In this media context, Vaughan's imagination is, unsurprisingly, heavily invested in celebrity: in addition to his supreme fantasy of dying in a collision with Elizabeth Taylor, Vaughan 'dreamed endlessly of the deaths of the famous', inventing 'imaginary crashes for them'. It is an imagination fed by the real deaths of high-profile figures: 'Around the deaths of James Dean and Albert Camus, Jayne Mansfield and John Kennedy he had woven elaborate fantasies' (*Crash*, p15). Vaughan remediates this mediated reality through his photographs and films, his filmed reconstructions of accidents. Indeed, Jeannette Baxter has suggested that Vaughan can be seen as a performance artist 'whose life is a theatrical exhibition of his own death', staging and re-staging the human body in abject displays of pain.[13] However, the engagement with death that provides the basis for this work is familiar to the reader, too, through news media: newspaper photographs and newsreel footage. The black-and-white photos of Dean's smashed-up Porsche Spyder, Camus's Facel Vega piled against a tree, and Jayne Mansfield's Buick Electra after it ran under a trailer (not to mention Abraham Zapruder's silent, colour movie footage of Kennedy's assassination) are part of collective memory, which is also now readily accessible through the internet. Such images are also familiar as part of a photographic tradition that includes the 1930s US photographer Weegee and through Andy Warhol's 1960s 'Death in America' series, which reworked images of electric chairs and car accidents. In this case, we might say, using Robert Smithson's terms, that the site of death is the non-site of the newspaper photograph or television image.[14]

As with the hospital death mentioned earlier, the car crash is a technologised death, but the conjunction of technology and death is seized upon in Ballard's novel as the basis for a new (and problematic) sexuality.[15] In the second chapter, the narrator describes his own first crash 'below the entrance to the Western Avenue flyover'. His account initially foregrounds the aesthetics of the crash, 'the stylisation of violence and rescue' (*Crash*, p23). He soon links this experience to 'all those scenes of pain and violence that illuminated the margins of our lives … that real world of violence calmed and tamed within our television programmes and the pages of news magazines'

13. Jeannette Baxter, *J.G. Ballard's Surrealist Imagination: Spectacular Authorship* (Ashgate, 2009), p101. (Hereafter *Ballard*).

14. See Robert Smithson, 'A Provisional theory of Non-Sites'. https://www.robertsmithson.com/essays/provisional.htm

15. As Luckhurst notes, *Crash* is 'obsessively phallic' (*The Angle*, 112), and what is desublimated, as in *The Atrocity Exhibition*, is not simply desire within a phallic economy, but violence towards the female body (p109).

(p37). The technological shift in this sentence from illuminated letters in medieval manuscripts to contemporary news media marks also a shift from the marginal to the sublimated, but pervasive, violence of the world of the simulacrum. In this context, the narrator realises that the 'crash was the only *real* experience I had been through for years' (p39), and he sets about a 'remaking of the commonplace' (p52) through 'the erotic delirium of the car-crash' (p16). As Luckhurst argues, this 'logic of the accident, of the orgasmic transgression of death,' can be seen as a strategy aimed at 'breaching the endless circulation of traffic', an attempt to break out of the order of simulation (*The Angle*, p127) through a moment of recognition produced by the conscious experience of transgression; however, if Baudrillard is right, death is pre-programmed and simply 'reinscribes transgression as perfect confirmation of a system that can have no outside' (p127). This is the issue on which *Crash* hinges.

Tom McCarthy's more recent literary novel, *Remainder* (2005), described by Zadie Smith as 'one of the great English novels of the last ten years', is also engaged with accident, trauma and re-enactment.[16] The narrator has suffered brain damage in a traumatic accident ('Something falling from the sky', [*Remainder*, p5]), an event which he cannot recall. To recover lost motor functions, he has to engage in 'rerouting', laying new circuits in the brain through a process of visualising actions. As a result of this process, with its conscious attention to bodily movement, a visit to the cinema leads him to the paradoxical conclusion that the actors are more authentic, more natural, than he is: 'if I'd been walking down the street like De Niro... I'd still be thinking: *Here I am walking down the street* .... Second-hand' (p24). This, in turn, alerts him to the 'second-hand', inauthentic behaviour of those around him: 'performing - to the on-lookers, each other, themselves' (p51). The media-types in the café remind him of an advert: 'not a particular one, but just some ad with beautiful young people in it having fun ...they acted out the roles of the ad's characters' (p23). In this context, he recalls a moment when or, more accurately, a place, where his movements had been 'fluent and unforced': 'They'd been *real*; I'd been real' (p62). This is when he makes the decision 'to reconstruct that space and enter it so that I could feel real again' (p62). In pursuit of this impossible dream, in the central part of the novel, he oversees the construction of this replica of the remembered place and moment. He consciously enters the world of the simulacrum, the hyper-real. In the second part of the novel, he undertakes further 're-enactments' in search of 'the real'. The re-enactment of a Brixton shooting eventually leads him to the re-enactment of a bank robbery in a real bank: 'lifting the re-enactment out of its demarcated zone and slotting it back into the world' (p244). In this final re-enactment, life imitates the copy; the routines of everyday are exposed; and re-enactment and the everyday gradually merge. McCarthy's focus is on re-enactment, but various sites of death are implied: the small-scale shooting; the bank robbery; and, finally, the blowing up

16. Tom McCarthy, *Remainder*, London, Alma Books 2005. (Hereafter *Remainder*). Zadie Smith, 'Two Paths for the Novel', *New York Review of Books* (20 November 2008).

of passenger planes. In the background to the novel are the events of 11 September 2001, and the way in which terrorism - and the mediated and remediated images of terrorist attacks - now brings the possibility of death into everybody's everyday life.

RITUALS AND SELF-TRANSFORMATION

As this suggests, for Ballard and McCarthy, through traffic accidents and acts of terrorism, the place of death is everywhere. Jeannette Baxter describes accident sites as 'public spectacles of private exposure' and calls Vaughan 'the cartographer of wound culture' (*Ballard*, p130).[17] She describes his photographic project as an attempt 'to reintroduce memory to the amnesic pathologic public sphere' (p131). McCarthy's narrator's engagement with memory and amnesia is on a more personal level, but his re-enactments, too, increasingly move towards the public spectacle of private exposure: from 'the black man dying beside his bicycle outside the phonebox' (*Remainder*, p171) on Coldharbour Lane, through another Brixton shooting of a man in a car (p205) and a third shooting off Brixton Hill (p206), to the real shootings in the 're-enacted' bank robbery and the blowing up of passenger planes. In *Remainder*, violent death is an everyday occurrence: both in acts of urban violence at street level and through acts of terrorism. In *Crash*, not only is the site of death anywhere along the network of roads - with specific sites of death marked out with improvised shrines of flowers and soft toys - but it is everywhere present, in mediated form, through film, television news, and the pages of newspapers and magazines. This is the area that Gordon Burn explores in his literary novel *fullalove* (1995).[18] The protagonist of this novel, Norman Miller, introduces himself at the start as 'a hack, a scribbler, a fully-benefited and BUPA-ed pen performer' (*fullalove*, p1). To be more precise, he works for a tabloid newspaper at the 'wall-shining, nose-poking, leg-in-the-door end of the trade' (p1) with the role of the 'victim's ... friend' as his speciality.

The novel begins with a dying television personality, the victim of an assault, and the hospital as the site of death:

> McGovern is dying of an acute haematoma and lacerations of the skull - an unstill package, ventilated, evacuated, fibrillated, palpated, catheterised in his polyurethane plastic tent ... A modern death in a tiled hospital room. (p23)

This, again, is the technologised death of *Last Orders*: the dying man is the passive object of various procedures that take care of breathing, excretion, urination and the beating of his heart. With all these functions technologised, he is dehumanised, reduced to 'an unstill package' in the non-place of a tiled room. Against this background image of 'modern death', Miller's story lays

17. For 'wound culture', see Mark Selter, *Serial Killers: Death and Life in America's Wound Culture*, London, Routledge 1989.

18. Gordon Burn, *fullalove*, London, Sacker & Warburg 1995. (Hereafter *fullalove*). Burn's first novel, *Alma Cogan*, won the 1991 Whitbread Prize. He has also written two books on serial killers, *Somebody's Husband, Somebody's Son* (1984) on Peter Sutcliffe and *Happy Like Murderers: The Story of Fred and Rosemary West* (1986), and published a book of interviews with Damien Hirst, *On the Way to Work* (2001).

bare 'the daily reported spectacles of death and destruction' of newspaper journalism (p34) and the conversion of events into the formulae of journalism ('Friends are still stunned ..Parents are deeply shocked ...Park officials are still visibly affected ...' [p63]). His story traces the removal of the event from experience to spectacle, from the real-world site to the non-site of the newspaper or television report.

In this context, Burn is particularly interested in modern, improvised rituals of death: 'the impromptu pavement shrines marking the site of the latest nail-bomb or child-snatch or brutal sex-death' (p4). He draws particular attention to the contrast between their 'peaceful, pastoral, consolatory' air and the 'raw modern city' that provides their setting: 'the railway-embankments, playing-field perimeters, tower-block entrances '(p4). These are the marginal spaces, the in-betweens, the non-places of the modern city that Ballard's fiction also occupies.[19] However, as in the fiction of Ballard and McCarthy, death is really everywhere - both as random, real-life visitations and in mediated form as part of Burn's depiction of a world where 'experience' is overwhelmed by 'information' (p73). Thus, in Miller's information-soaked, media-marinated consciousness, a drive through London becomes a glide past 'rape sites and murder sites, scenes of hit-and-runs, child snatches, vendetta assassinations, car-jackings, care-in-the-community neck stabbings, and their commemorative shrines in varying conditions of completion' (p135). This is the super-modern city of dystopian landscapes over-written by popular newspaper culture and what Miller calls 'post-literate paganism' (p178).

Burn's narrative comes to focus on 'maps of places where news has suddenly erupted' (p77), places that have become part of the newspaper repertoire. First, however, in an echo of 'Heart of Darkness', it addresses 'a blank on the chart' - in this case, a place that is not marked on the public plan of the hospital. This blank space is occupied by 'the morgue and the post-mortem room, a sluice room, a furnace room' - in short, 'the place where death is' (p139). The places of death with which the narrative increasingly concerns itself, however, are the sites where policemen and policewomen have been killed - including, perhaps most famously, 'the exact spot where WPC Yvonne Fletcher was mowed down' in St James's Square outside the Libyan Embassy (p80). These memorials are presented as 'sources of negative energy', sites of 'bad juju' (p78), as evidenced by further acts of violence attracted to them. In this context, the novel introduces the fictional Veorah Batcheller, first seen cleaning the memorial for Yvonne Fletcher, and follows her 'voyage in the symbolic realms of death' (p175). On her living-room wall, Miller sees 'a map of the pilgrimage route round the Buddhist temples on the Japanese island of Shikoku' juxtaposed to 'maps showing Irish holy places, medieval, Marian and twentieth-century shrines':

> ...the Kop, Kent State, the Texas Schoolbook Depository, the Dakota Building, Graceland ... the shapes traced and laid over one another in - I

19. See Ballard's other 1973 novel, *Concrete Island*, where the protagonist, Robert Maitland, goes off the Westway interchange after a tyre blows out at speed and finds himself stranded 'in the waste ground between three converging motorway routes'. This in-between space becomes the island setting for Ballard's modern, urban version of *Robinson Crusoe*.

> guessed - the search for correspondences ... with the nine-sided, roughly kite-shaped figure you get ... by linking the police memorial sites in a chain ... (p178)

Veorah Batcheller's super-imposition of maps and her psychogeographic quest for occult correspondences recalls, respectively, parts of Allen Fisher's 1970's *Place* project and Iain Sinclair's *Lud Heat*.[20] In the closing chapters, after the novel's thanatological journey, she sets out, in Sinclair mode, 'to walk the route which connects all the London police memorials' in 'a ritual of cleansing and reclaiming, of undoing harm' (p205).[21] She proposes to escape being situated as a victim through 'acting in the world, stepping out into the blankness of motorways, loopways and roundabouts' (p206), undertaking her own pilgrimage, a 'rite projected in space' (p215), through these non-places.

Sinclair's long poem *Lud Heat* (1975) involves the creation of precisely such private rituals and takes off from just such a psychogeographical linking of Hawksmoor's London churches. The accompanying map traces the triangles and pentacles they form, while the text explores their linkage to 'sources of occult power'.[22] The initial account of Nicholas Hawksmoor and his churches announces that the eight churches, built after the Great Fire of London, 'give us the enclosure, the shape of fear ... erected over a fen of undisclosed horrors' (*Lud Heat*, p4). As a result of their construction, Sinclair claims, 'certain hungers were activated that have yet to be pacified' (p4). The triangle formed between Christ Church, St George-in-the-East and St Anne, Limehouse, each of which has 'a close connection with burial sites, Roman and pre-Roman' (p16), is thus presented as a source of latent power: 'the frustration mounts on a current of animal magnetism, & victims are still claimed' (p5), while the pentacle formed by the remaining churches serves to 'guard or mark', 'two major sources of occult power', the British Museum and Greenwich Observatory, a power that is also evidenced in the closeness of these churches to the sites of the Ratcliffe Highway murders and the later Ripper murders through to the murder of Abraham Cohen in the summer of 1974. Sinclair links these modern sites of death to an occult 'system of energies' (p10), so that the Whitechapel Murders, for example, become part of a 'karmic programme' (p11). As Robert Sheppard notes, the sub-title, 'a book of the dead hamlets', 'should not obscure the fact that death does not imply inertia, but potential'.[23] Hawksmoor's 'rewriting of the city' after the Fire of London through his building of a series of churches is seen as creating a series of sites of negative energy, 'funnels of power for the gods', emerging in acts of murder, which are linked to ideas of ritual killing and human sacrifice (*Sinclair*, p30).

The third section of *Lud Heat*, 'Rites of Autopsy', engages with the films of Stan Brakhage, including 'The Dead', filmed in Père Lechaisse Cemetery, and, in particular, 'Acts of Seeing', filmed in the Alleghany Coroner's Office

---

20. Allen Fisher, *Place*, Hastings, Reality Street 2005, written during the 1970s and published in parts during the 1970s and 1980s, and Iain Sinclair, *Lud Heat: a book of the dead hamlets*, London, Albion Village Press 1975.

21. Compare Iain Sinclair's walk around the M25 which he recounts in *London Orbital: A Walk around the M25*, London, Granta Books 2002.

22. Iain Sinclair, *Lud Heat*, London, Albion Village Press 1975, p5; (Hereafter *Lud Heat*).

23. Robert Sheppard, *Iain Sinclair*, Tavistock, Northcote House 2007, p25. (Hereafter *Sinclair*).

in Pittsburgh, two institutional sites of death. 'Acts of Seeing' shows the 'secret operation' of the autopsy, which Sinclair describes in detail. He begins by describing how Brakhage is 'granted access to the theatres of life and death' (LH, p40). However, it is theatres of death rather than life which particularly interest Sinclair. Thus he notes Brakhage's fliming of open-heart hospital surgery ('Deus Ex Machina') and the coroner's office ('Acts of Seeing'), but he focusses on the autopsy: 'this awful revelation of meat' (*Lud Heat*, p40). For him the filming of the autopsy, this probing and disassemblage of the human body, involves 'a confrontation of the body's most deeply held fears', and the filming is presented as an act of initiation, being granted access to 'secret rites' and rituals (p43).[24] In Sinclair's narration, the scientific operations of surgeon and coroner are ghosted by 'hieratic ritual', 'Egyptian autoptic rites' (p43). As in his account of Brian Catling's work later in *Lud Heat*, which acts as a subject rhyme with this account of Brakhage, the artist is presented as a priestly or shamanic figure, exploring dark forces, working 'in fear & expectation of death', but also working with 'an understanding of the mutualities & relevances in Siberian, Egyptian, Meroean, Sumerian & Mayan cultures' (p65). In Sinclair's account of Catling's exhibition at the Royal College of Art, Egyptian tombs are aligned with megalithic chambers and the crypts of Hawksmoor churches, as the account comes to foreground two particular pieces, a raft and a sledge: the raft is 'made ready for the great voyage that is death' while the sledge, an object 'made for extreme margins', contains 'the idea of kneeling, prayer', but also recalls 'the urban hurdle of execution ceremonies' (p66).[25] Sites of death and the process of dying are the focus of Catling's exhibition and Sinclair's narrative. In Sinclair's reading of the exhibition, through his engagement with death and dying, the sculptor (like Brakhage) places himself at risk and opens himself to 'divine or demonic possession' (p68). By implication, Sinclair's own work exposes him, too, to the same risk. In the final section, Sinclair records an act of 'total body exhaustion' (p108), that involves him in running to 'the oracle' and back, not so much as a ritualistic act of healing, but as an attempt 'to empty the body of all resistance' in a quest for transformation (p109) . The 'oracle', a former machine-gun bunker, is described as the 'epicentre of energies' (p108), a 'crossing place' where the route of the Northern Sewage Outflow passes over the River Lea. It is identified subsequently, through casual browsing, as the place where a huge stone coffin of unknown origin was found in 1867. Sinclair seizes on this chance discovery as confirmation of his intuitive decision: 'So again we service the dead, complete the stifled gesture, grasp at the arm raised in salute from the choked ground' (p111). Sinclair's exploration of the 'archetypal expression of common needs' (p20) concludes with this reaching back into the past, which also anticipates the conclusion of Brian de Palma's 1976 film *Carrie*, with its graphic assertion of the continuing life of the dead.[26]

In Sinclair's first novel, *White Chappell, Scarlet Tracings* (1987), he returns to 'the sites of the Jack the Ripper murders', those urban sites of death made

24. Sinclair might also have in mind Allen Ginsberg's visits to cremations at the Nimtallah burning ghats in Kolkatta, which he recorded in his *Indian Journals*, San Francisco, City Lights Books 1970, pp56-7, p59, p67. See Iain Sinclair, *The Kodak Mantra Diaries*, London, Albion Village Press 1971, for Sinclair's record of Ginsberg's various visits to London between 1966 and 1971.

25. The raft also suggests depictions of the Egyptian sun-god Ra on the solar boat.

26. *Carrie* (1976) was based on Stephen King's novel *Carrie* (1974).

familiar by this narrative: 'all the courtyards, doorways, factory gates' of a specific area of east London.[27] In this context of an obsessively retold story, Sinclair's narrative explicitly picks up on Stephen Knight's interpretation of the murders that attributes them to a triumvirate engaged in an Establishment cover-up: 'Sickert the painter, Netley the coachman, Gull the doctor' (*WCST*, p54).[28] In addition, while the title alludes to Conan Doyle's *A Study in Scarlet* and the discovery by a trio of book-dealers of 'the first printing of the first appearance' of Conan Doyle's story (p25) forms part of a second contemporary narrative strand, Sinclair consciously sets out to 'reverse the conventions of detective fiction, where a given crime is unravelled, piece by piece, until a murderer is denounced whose act is the starting point of the narration' (p61).[29] Instead, Sinclair's narrative 'starts everywhere' and assembles 'all the incomplete movements' until the point is reached 'where the crime can commit itself' (p61). Beginning where *Lud Heat* ended, *White Chappell, Scarlet Tracings*, as its third narrative strand, follows two characters, Sinclair and Joblard (based on Catling) in 1970s' London.[30] In this strand, Joblard describes how 'you lay yourself open to a form of occult possession': 'You complete the other man's work … The job doesn't end with death' (*WCST*, p65). Thus, in the Victorian strand of the narrative, Gull completes Hinton's 'work', but that act of completion reflects back upon the work of Sinclair and Joblard. Brian Baker has commented on how, picking up on the triumvirate of Sickert, Netley and Gull, 'tripartite male relationships' are used to structure the text.[31] The novel also produces a proliferation of doubles and splits: Sherlock Holmes and Dr Moriarty, John Merrick (the Elephant Man) and Dr Frederick Treves, Dr Jekyll and Mr Hyde. The pairing of Sinclair and Joblard, which at times playfully echoes that of Holmes and Dr Watson, also explores the dangers of laying yourself open 'to a form of occult possession' in the pursuit of self-transformation. Thus, after the account of the contemporary murder of 'Hymie Beaker', reference is made to the 'identikit portrait of a man seen lurking' that accompanies the newspaper report: 'horror hybrid, the features of myself and Joblard blended … Gone out of the human range' (p97). The novel has already suggested that 'When two men meet a third is always present, stranger to both' (p36). Here, as Baker suggests, that third is 'a malignant entity … seemingly let loose to rampage across the city, brought forth by occult forces' (*Iain Sinclair*, p72). In his letter to Sinclair, which begins Book Three, the poet Doug Oliver comments approvingly on the novel's 'recognition that the self and its phantasmic forms and ghosts must be recognised before the self-as-self-healing or self-"disappearing' can enter the simultaneity of true knowing' (*WCST*, p163). However, what Sinclair also confronts is how this project might have less benign effects.

Peter Ackroyd had already made fictional use of the psychogeographic materials of *Lud Heat* in *Hawksmoor* (1985).[32] In Ackroyd's novel, the historical Hawksmoor becomes the fictional Nicholas Dyer in the eighteenth-century strand of the novel, while Hawksmoor's name is given to a detective in

27. Iain Sinclair, *White Chappell, Scarlet Tracings*, London, Paladin 1987, p35. (Hereafter *WCST*).

28. Stephen Knight, *Jack the Ripper: The Final Solution*, London, Bounty Books 1976.

29. As the novel's title suggests, and as Sinclair makes clear at various points in the narrative, Arthur Conan Doyle's 'A Study in Scarlet' (1887), which introduced the characters of Sherlock Holmes and Dr Watson, is an important intertext.

30. *White Chappell, Scarlet Tracings* is, in fact, the third part of a trilogy: a second extended poetic work, *Suicide Bridge*, was published in 1979. For discussion of this work, see Robert Sheppard, *Iain Sinclair*, Tavistock, Northcote House 2007, pp33-41.

31. Brian Baker, *Iain Sinclair*, Manchester, Manchester University Press 2007, p71. (Hereafter *Iain Sinclair*).

32. Peter Ackroyd, *Hawksmoor*, London, Abacus 1986; all references are to this edition. (Hereafter *Hawksmoor*).

contemporary London for the modern strand. Dyer's churches, the churches built by the historic Hawksmoor, are sites of death in both narratives. In the first part of the novel, the 'new church of Spittle-Fields' is 'built near a Pitte' and 'there are so vast a Number of Corses that the Pews will allwaies be Rotten and Damp' (*Hawksmoor*, p7). Similarly, the 'Church at Limehouse' is built upon 'a burying-place of Saxon times, with Graves lined with chalkstones and beneath them earlier Tombs' (p62). Dyer records that the site was 'a massive Necropolis', and it has 'Power still withinne it' (p62). These are sites of death in so far as they are sites of burial, and they are associated in the novel with demonic powers. As Dyer's narration subsequently reveals, however, this plague-pit has a particular significance for him, since his parents died from the plague and were buried in this very pit. He recalls their death and burial, and presents his building of the church as a compensation for the tears he was unable to weep at the time. The siting of this church is not a coincidence, but a deliberate plan: 'in that place of Memory will I fashion a Labyrinth where the Dead can once more give Voice' (p16). In addition, these churches are sites of death in that they are associated with foundational acts of child sacrifice. Dyer is 'no Puritan nor Caviller, nor Reformed, nor Catholick, nor Jew', but 'of that older Faith' (p20). In his creed, 'He who made the world is also author of Death' (p20), and he looks back to the pre-Christian temples of Britain: 'my own Churches will rise to join them, and Darknesse will call out for more Darknesse' (p22). As this suggests, as in *Lud Heat*, the churches are also sites of death in that they are associated with acts of violence and murder; indeed, they are seen to prompt and provoke such acts. Thus Dyer describes the building of his third church in Wapping and reports: 'Here all corrupcion and infection has its Centre' (p92). Accordingly, he recalls the serial murder of children by Mary Crompton in Rope Walk, the murders committed by Abraham Thornton in Crab Walk, and the brutal murder of Mr Barwick in Angell Rents as associated with the location of the church (p63). In Part Two, Hawksmoor is investigating a series of murders being committed at the sites of Dyer's churches. At the start of Part Two, there have been three murders: at Spitalfields, Limehouse, and Wapping. He speculates that murderers 'were drawn to those places where murders had occurred before'; he ponders various ritual murders in his east London patch; and, after thinking about murders besides St Georges-in-the-East and 'in the streets and alleys around Christ Church, Spitalfields', he even articulates a theory 'that certain streets or patches of ground provoked a malevolence which generally seemed to be quite without motive' (p116). Hawksmoor's theory is clearly the mirror to Dyer's creed, and Hawksmoor seems to be set up to be the detective who will find the solution to the murders. However, Dyer is presented as an irrational alternative to the rationalism of his time, and Ackroyd is careful to advance the cause of irrationality over rationality. Accordingly, Hawksmoor is increasingly positioned as a potential victim or perpetrator of the murders as the novel's snake of time swallows its own tail.

Ackroyd's work and Sinclair's subsequent fictions bear witness to the continuing life of the dead as they revisit the sites of death of Sinclair's first psychogeographic work, *Lud Heat*. However, where Burn's novel primarily engages with the media landscape of crime reports and newspaper campaigns to commemorate murdered police-officers, Ackroyd and Sinclair go back to literary sources and earlier cultures to revive the metaphysic of evil.

TECHNOLOGY, THE INDIVIDUAL AND THE COLLECTIVE

The psychogeographical works of Sinclair and Ackroyd identify particular sites as sites of death and cultivate these sites as special sites of self-transformation. As we have seen, however, Burn's novel, *fullalove*, leads to a very different conclusion: that the site of death is potentially anywhere. Accidents and random acts of violence have an entirely arbitrary relation to place; at the same time, our consciousnesses are over-loaded with representations of death, and we carry those images with us wherever we go. The potential for the site of death to be anywhere is also the basis of another fictional genre, a genre that is dedicated to death, which has already been invoked - namely, the crime novel. For example, Patricia Cornwell's detective, Dr Kay Scarpetta, is a forensic scientist, whose work involves two of the specialised, institutional sites of death - the morgue and the forensic laboratory - but also the arbitrary sites of the murder. *Body of Evidence* (1991) begins with Dr Scarpetta with 'a packet of surgical gloves' tucked into her 'black medical bag', as she takes the lift down to the morgue and the body of a murdered woman.[33] The murder scene, by contrast with the morgue, is not a specialised site of death: indeed, it is described as 'not the sort of neighbourhood where one would expect anything so hideous to happen' (*BE*, p8). It is an international-style detached house, 'large and set back from the street' on an 'impeccably landscaped' lot (p8). The victim had moved back there from Key West precisely because Key West had become a site of everyday death: she had written, in a letter to a friend, 'AIDS is a holocaust consuming the offerings of this small island' (p2). In attempting to escape one form of death, she relocates to what becomes the site of another. Similarly, in *Cruel and Unusual* (1993), the narrative begins with two institutional sites of death, the electric chair and the morgue, where the autopsy on the still-warm prisoner is described in some detail, but the first murder scene is behind a convenience store, where the victim had gone to buy a can of cream of mushroom soup. A banal everyday action and location become re-visioned through murder. In crime fiction on this side of the Atlantic, there is the same sense that the site of death can be anywhere. Thus, the scene of crime in Denise Mina's Glasgow-based *The Dead Hour* (2006) is a Victorian villa 'in Bearsden, a wealthy suburb to the north of the city, all leafy roads and large houses with grass moats to keep the neighbours distant'.[34] In Ian Rankin's Edinburgh-based Rebus novels, the sites of death are located all over the city. In *Set in Darkness* (2000), the bodies are found where the new Scottish parliament building is being erected 'on

33. Patricia Cornwell, *Body of Evidence*, London, Warner Books 1992, p5; all references are to this edition. (Hereafter *BE*).

34. Denise Mina, *The Dead Hour*, London, Bantam Books 2006, p11.

the cleared site, directly across the road from Holyrood House, the Queen's Edinburgh residence'.[35] By contrast, *Exit Music* (2007) begins with a body found at the foot of Raeburn Wynd in the Old Town, 'a multistoreycar park on one side, Caste Rock and a cemetery on the other'.[36] In detective fiction, the narrative moves between official, institutional sites of death (the hospital, the morgue, the forensic laboratory), the varied sites of murder and the various sites where bodies are found. These can be anywhere from closed rooms on the Rue Morgue to compartments on the Orient Express, from city side-streets to university departments.

As we have seen, recent British fiction (as represented here by the novels of Burn and McCarthy) is remarkable for its sense of the ubiquity of death - or, at least, the potential for death to take place anywhere. The places of death include the sites of traffic accidents and the sites of death from violent crime: terrorist attacks, murder, police action. These novels also pick up on those other places of death: the neo-pagan commemoration of sites of death in amateur shrines, alongside official memorials. They also engage with the non-sites of death which make it all-pervasive: the mediation of death through newspaper photographs, through newsreels, through other media. Over the last twenty years, popular culture has added to this rich, dense mix through the popularity of forensic-science series: *Silent Witness*, *Waking the Dead* and the *CSI* series present death in its multiple forms for peak-time viewing. In such series, the human body is staged as spectacle through incidents of violent death; the disposal of bodies; the processes of decomposition, dismemberment and autopsy. At a time when dying has largely been moved out of daily life to the specialist sites of the hospital ward and the hospice, both the dissolution of the body and the forensic penetration and disassemblage of the body become part of the ambient mediascape, the mediated environment we inhabit. In contrast to the representation of death in nineteenth-century fiction, however, this is not a staging of the corpse as an approach to the mystery of the afterlife, but the presentation of the corpse as the carrier of the legible signs of an event, as the bearer of traces that are readable genetically, medically, forensically by the trained observer. This is precisely the 'medical gaze' that separates the body from identity, and the viewer is educated into sharing this gaze. While death and dying are removed from immediate everyday experience, they return in the displaced, mediated form of the dead body, but they also return on specific terms: this is the dead body as the object of various technologies and scientific discourses rather than as the summation of an individual life. Thus death and dying are conceptually excluded, but return through the representational ubiquity of the dead body which is recuperated into the culturally symbolic order through the scientific gaze.

These series also foreground the institutional setting as the most important site of death. Thus, *Silent Witness* (1996 -), from its title, announces its engagement with forensic pathology and foregrounds the dead body as the subject of post-mortem analysis: it is a body that will be made to speak through

35. Ian Rankin, *Set in Darkness*, London, Orion 2000, p4.

36. Ian Rankin, *Exit Music*, London, Orion 2007, p3.

the forensic skills of specialists. Attention is shifted from the site where death took place to the forensic laboratory, although where the death took place may be read or reconstructed through the forensic skills of the laboratory. The series began with a private morgue in Cambridge as its primary location, but, by series three, it had shifted to the institutional context of a university in London (using framing shots of the portico and corridors of UCL). In both cases the institutional context was independent from police and government, and, indeed, both police and government agendas might be challenged by forensic findings. Originally, the focus was on Dr Sam Ryan (Amanda Burton), but when she was replaced by Dr Leo Dalton (William Gaminara), the focus became a team of forensic scientists: although Dr Harry Cunningham (Tom Ward) and Dr Nikki Alexander (Emilia Fox), for example, were technically subordinate to Professor Dalton, the drama depended on the dynamics between them. *Waking the Dead* (2000-2011), a police procedural series based on a fictional 'cold case unit' within the Metropolitan Police, similarly involves a combination of new evidence and contemporary technologies to make the dead speak (though with more attention to exhumation rather than immediate post-mortem analysis). It, too, focusses on team work (involving CID police officers, psychological profilers and forensic scientists) rather than the exceptional individual of classic detective fiction. Detective Superintendent Boyd (Trevor Eve) has some of the characteristics of this figure, but his maverick, transgressive tendencies are counter-balanced within the dynamics of the team by the ethical and professional concerns of the profiler, Dr Grace Foley (Sue Johnston), and the forensic scientist, Dr Frankie Wharton (Holly Aird).

In the United States, *CSI: Crime Scene Investigation* (2000-2015) was the source of a number of popular spin-off series.[37] In the original *CSI: Crime Scene Investigation*, Gil Grissom (William Petersen), a forensic entomologist with various eccentricities, was positioned by these eccentricities (and a tendency to gnomic utterances) as the exceptional individual leading a team. In *CSI: Miami* (2002-2012) and *CSI: New York* (2004-2013), this role of the exceptional individual is gradually reduced and replaced by what Samantha Walton calls 'an integrated network of technologies and human investigators'.[38] The team leaders, Lieutenant Horatio Caine (David Caruso) and Detective Mac Taylor (Gary Sinise), establish the ethos of their team, but are dependent on the specific skills of other team members and a range of technologies: from dissection, sampling, chemical analysis through to databases and surveillance technologies. In the case of Caine, that ethos is one of care; in the case of Taylor, much is made of his past as a marine, and, as Walton shows, the gap between military and civilian elements of state security is erased and the team becomes a militarised collective. It is also significant that Taylor lost his wife in the events of 9/11. As Walton argues, *CSI: New York* is shaped by the changing relations of the individual and the state in the wake of 9/11 and the government response to perceived threat, the 2001 Patriot Act (*Detection*, p103). The series effectively promotes state surveillance and the 'exploitation of comprehensive databases',

37. The series was a CBS co-production with G.S. Capital Partners (an affiliate of Goldman Sachs); it was originally shot at Rye Canyon, a corporate campus owned by Lockheed Martin.

38. Samantha Walton, 'Detection in a Complex Age: Collective Control in CSI: New York', *Concentric: Literary and Cultural Studies*, 38.1 (March 2012), pp103-23, p103. (Hereafter *Detection*).

which it does, in part, by presenting the CSI team as motivated by 'selfless commitment to protecting the security of the collective' (p103). Repeated references to the marines' motto 'Semper Fidelis' cement this message.

Episodes in all three CSI series involve graphically detailed autopsies and the full gamut of violent death. Forensic attention to crime scenes, which the title promises, reconstructs a range of sites of death. However, one of the distinctive and controversial features of CSI was its close attention to the invasive procedures of the autopsy and its reconstruction of killings through depicting in slow motion the movement of bullets through the body. The reduction of human lives to materials for forensic analysis and this fetishistic pleasure in damage to the body - together with what Walton demonstrates as the series's promotion of 'anti-individualistic teamwork on a military model' (p105) - are part of the series's diminishing of the individual and promotion of a militarised collective.

Where Swift's *Last Orders* focussed on the removal of the process of dying from everyday life and presented the non-places of death, Ballard, McCarthy and Burn show the ubiquity of death - in the immediate form of accidents and street crime and in the mediated form of newspaper and television reportage. Where Ballard and McCarthy present the sites of death as arbitrary, the psychogeographic fiction of Ackroyd and Sinclair identify specific sites of death, sites which draw violence towards them, which they focus on as part of an individual's process of self-transformation. The focus on special sites of death, self-transformation and the return to a metaphysics of evil places this fiction at odds with the other literary fiction discussed here. Detective fiction is the genre *par excellence* where the arbitrariness of the site of death is asserted. In the classic detective novel, however, rather than death signifying the deceased's attainment of individuality, the dead body is used to present the individuality of the detective at the expense of the individuality of the deceased. In recent American police procedural television series, this diminishing of the individual takes what Walton identifies as a post-human turn: not only is the dead body reduced to matter to be processed, but the investigator is no longer an exceptional individual, just part of a team, and the team is presented as simply the operators of various technologies engaged in 'self-abnegating mediation between the disorder of the crime scene and the ordering capacity of the computer' (p106).

Robert Hampson is Professor of English and Distinguished Research and Teaching Fellow at Royal Holloway, University of London. He has published extensively in the fields of Joseph Conrad studies and modern and contemporary poetry and had edited numerous collections and editions. He is author of *Clasp: Late Modernist Poetry in London in the 1970s* (Bristol: Shearsman, 2016); *Conrad's Secrets* (Basingstoke: Palgrave Macmillan, 2012); *Cross-Cultural Encounters in Joseph Conrad's Malay Fiction* (Palgrave: Basingstoke, 2000); and *Joseph Conrad: Betrayal and Identity* (Basingstoke: Palgrave Macmillan, 1992).

CAR THOUGHTS

Janet Wolff

Lynne Pearce, *Drivetime: Literary Excursions in Automotive Consciousness*
Edinburgh, Edinburgh University Press, 2016, 216pp; £70.00 hardback

In 2000, Lynne Pearce published a striking and original essay, 'Driving north, driving south: reflections on the spatial/temporal co-ordinates of home'. This was an extended account of her driving experience, travelling regularly from Lancaster to Scotland, and from Lancaster to Cornwall, an early attempt at a phenomenology of being on the road. Twelve years later she returned to the theme, initially with a couple of new essays and eventually in the larger project that resulted in this book. As she records in her preface, in the intervening years the new field of 'mobilities research' has emerged and thrived, much of the work being done by her colleagues at the University of Lancaster. But where others have explored the 'car system', or the history of motoring, or car cultures, Pearce has continued to examine the question of what she refers to as 'automotive consciousness' - or 'what we're thinking when we're driving'. Her approach is phenomenological, but of an impure type: that is, it is grounded in a phenomenology that recognises the crucial role of memory and of cultural context. Her intention is to render explicit the cognitive and affective aspects of driving (and, to a lesser extent, of being a passenger in a car).

The main body of the book consists of readings of a variety of literary texts, written across the twentieth century ('the motoring century'), and organised into four thematic chapters: Searching, Fleeing, Cruising and Flying. These are preceded by a substantial theoretical introductory chapter, situating the study in a complex philosophical and interdisciplinary framework and offering preliminary thoughts on writing about driving. A little disconcertingly, this chapter begins by asserting the parallels between driving and thinking. Pearce opens with this statement:

> It is my aim, in the first chapter of this book, to demonstrate how driving is paradigmatic as well as formative of the way we think. By this I am suggesting that the way in which the mind travels through time and space on its everyday cognitive journeys ... is figuratively similar to the way in which cars and their drivers engage with the temporal and spatial environments through which they pass (p1).

It is a somewhat misleading opening, since it soon becomes clear that the main focus of the book is the driving experience itself - not driving as something *like* thinking, or driving as a model for thinking. It is 'the rapid succession of thoughts that present themselves to a driver's consciousness - directed now towards the past, now towards the future, and prompted, in both cases, by a perceptual encounter with the present' (p1). This is a daunting project - how can one grasp these swiftly passing ideas, some perhaps barely conscious, and how can they possibly be captured in words? Lynne Pearce does an impressive job of showing some of the ways in which the mind works in the very particular circumstances of an enclosed space and a constantly moving state - which is to say a constantly changing parade of impressions outside the car. For the most part this is done through a dazzling, if eclectic, choice of texts. But the literary exploration of her theme, which takes up a good three-quarters of the book, is prefaced by a kind of re-run of her essay of 2000, in which she sets out again in her own car - this time in March 2015, and once again driving south and driving north. The following short extract gives a flavour of how well she takes hold of the experience in words.

> The unfamiliar business of the road notwithstanding, I am still unable to suppress my excitement as I make the final sweep west. The sun is getting low in the sky and sunglasses are essential. It seems a long time since this morning's eclipse and, because of the distance I have travelled subsequently, what I witnessed already feels like a part of history; I could be remembering it from another fifteen years hence rather than as something that happened today...
>
> From here it is only a couple of miles to where my parents are buried, half a mile more to the family home, and less than another mile to my friend's house. From this point on, the 'memory flags' are so dense that it is no longer possible to see or respond to them individually and, interestingly, I don't even try. Instead, all my attention is focused, once again, on the visible, physical landscape: what's changed, what's not (pp53-4).

(I did find myself wondering when - presumably in the absence of a dictaphone - the impressions are recorded, and how they can be recalled so precisely in retrospect. This applies, too, to the non-fiction texts she goes on to recruit to her project.)

Each of the four thematic chapters focuses on two or three specific texts. Under the title of 'searching', Pearce looks at two British writers of the late 1920s and early 1930s, writing about driving as tourism (H.V. Morton and Edwin Muir). As examples of 'fleeing', she turns to 1950s fiction, focusing in particular on Patricia Highsmith's novel *Carol* and Jack Kerouac's *On the Road*. The next chapter, on 'cruising', moves on another twenty years to 1970s California, mixing memoir, fiction and city history in a discussion of texts by Neil Young, Joan Didion and Rayner Banham (though Young writes about the 1970s in retrospect, so in that sense his is not exactly a 'period piece').

Finally, the chapter on 'flying' returns to the 1930s, taking its examples of driving events from novels by the British writers Elizabeth Bowen, Rosamund Lehmann and Elizabeth Taylor. Pearce foresees various potential criticisms of her choice of texts, insisting that she writes as a cultural critic and not as a literary critic, and mentioning more than once that she is aware that fiction cannot be read in the same way as non-fiction. Nevertheless, the reader may begin to feel that the mix of genres and periods (and countries) is a little too random. Not only that, in the end, the thematic division turns out to be rather schematic. The chapter on 'flying' really barely sticks with that theme. And more than once an author re-appears in a later chapter (Kerouac is discussed in the final chapter as well as earlier on, for example). A rather strange diagrammed matrix of cognitive-affective states devised in the final chapter does not seem to have much pay-off. By the time we read that the car both protects the driver's delusion and can expose it, we might wonder whether it has, in the end, proved impossible to generalise about any aspects of the experience of driving (p185).

I think, though, that this may not be the point. The categories may be provisional, the selection of texts in some ways arbitrary, but in the end this does not really matter. The great achievement of the book is to immerse the reader in aspects of the automotive consciousness. In the judicious and suggestive choice of authors, and in the succession of fiction and non-fiction quotations, Lynne Pearce has allowed us to understand something about what we are thinking when we are driving, about how the mind works under the influence of motion, speed and the proliferation of sensory impressions. She concludes with some thoughts on the (possible) end of the driving culture, with the twenty-first-century promise of driverless cars and other forms of transport - a prospect she does not look forward to. As far as the motoring century is concerned, however, she has produced a wonderful account of something very familiar but - until now - also quite mysterious.

A note about the disastrous journey. Reading the book, I wondered why, from quite early on - perhaps at the first mention of driving at speed - I detected a low-level anxiety in myself. It was clearly the fear of the car accident. For some reason, I kept recalling the final scene in Jules Dassin's 1962 film, *Phaedra*, and Anthony Perkins' last shocking drive (accompanied by music by Bach). I put this down to personal angst. But then Pearce too refers to what can so easily go wrong. She talks about 'safe skills' (pp136-7). She eventually broaches the possibility of road accidents (p163). She mentions the death drive, though only in passing. She even admits, almost at the end (p191), that she never gets into her car without the thought of the possibility of a fatal accident. With nearly 2000 road deaths a year in Britain, and more than ten times that number of serious injuries, the dark side of driving is always present. Perhaps there is more to say, with a different selection of texts, about the psycho-pathology of the road.

Finally, I must acknowledge a personal interest in the publication of this book. As Pearce says, her return to the subject of driving consciousness after a break of some years was to write a chapter for a collection I co-edited with Jackie Stacey in 2013 - *Writing Otherwise*. It was a lovely essay, and a wonderful contribution to the volume, and I have looked forward to seeing the finished book since them. Its publication more than fulfils the promise of that essay.

Janet Wolff is Professor Emerita of Cultural Sociology at the University of Manchester and the author of seven books on the aesthetics and the sociology of art. Her family history, *Austerity Baby*, is published by Manchester University Press in June 2017.

Capacious aesthetics

Ben Highmore

Ben Anderson, *Encountering Affect: Capacities, Apparatuses, Conditions*, Farnham, Ashgate, 2014, 194pp, £65.00 hardback

Maurizia Boscagli, *Stuff Theory: Everyday Objects, Radical Materialism*, New York and London, Bloomsbury, 2014, 279pp, £16.99 paperback

Elizabeth Chin, *My Life with Things: The Consumer Diaries*, Duke University Press, 2016, 239pp, £19.99 paperback

Tonino Griffero, *Atmospheres: Aesthetics of Emotional Spaces*, translated by Sarah de Sanctis, Farnham, Ashgate, 2014, 174pp, £65.00 hardback

Anyone with half an eye on trends in research and publishing in the theoretically-inclined humanities and social sciences might have noticed two particular orientations emerging over the last decade or so. One orientation is concerned with the material world of things, of objects and stuff. The other is attentive to affects, atmospheres and moods. A casual observer might see a degree of conflict or bifurcation in the way that these concerns have emerged simultaneously. On one hand they would be right: a good deal of the writing around affect, for instance, stresses intangible forces and ineffable eruptions of affective energy; most of the writing around 'things' is keen to apprehend a world of solidities on which we can, potentially at least, stub our toes. A less casual observer (or at least an observer who has been doing their observing for a while) might want to notice some similarities and overlaps between the two themes. Both might invoke a form of 'new materialism', both are attentive to bodies (as a scene of affect, as a quasi-object), both draw on a diverse range of historical and disciplinary sources.

Seen as part of a non-linear unfolding of theoretical sensitivities since the 1950s we could see this theoretical moment as something like a time of 'post-post-structuralism'. It is an ungainly term, and might not be particularly helpful in capturing the range of enthusiasms and concerns at work across thing-work and affect-work, but it does, I hope, make vivid the fading of one theoretical proclivity and the rise of another. Seen from the perspective of post-post-structuralism, post-structuralism's inordinate interest in theorising subjectivity as radically disjointed, explosively divided and dynamically unfinished, can look like a form of 'wholeness' that is unavailable to the thing theorist or the affect mapper. What would be the point of such an attention towards human subjectivity if it ignored the hordes of creaturely and non-creaturely objects, devices, and systems that are clamouring at the doors of history? What would be the point in unsettling the world of consciousness by investigating the disruptive powers of the unconscious if it meant being unresponsive to all those other pulsations and propulsions floating around bodies and environments?

One way of characterising the move from post-structuralism to post-post-structuralism is a move from the split and fragmented to the scattered and diffuse. Like most shifts and turns in theory there are gains and losses along the way. What might have been lost is the idea of a central problematic around which (and against which) a debate can be focused, and concepts can be tested ('how do you conceive the subject?'). One of the first gains, though, has got to be the way that this emphasis on a scattered set of atmospheric conditions and material environments can allow for a new understanding of collective experience. If post-structuralism decentred the subject as an agent of history, post-post-structuralism seems to provide a wildly capacious aesthetic attention that can re-find the subject, as a subject-amongst-subjects and an object-amongst-objects. It is this potential to see human subjectivity as already entangled in all sorts of other realms (environmental, biological, animal, technical, and so on) and to see it as simultaneously articulated and disarticulated by a vitalism that is distributed across the human-non-human continuum, that offers the potential for a worldlier engagement with culture. And I think that this engagement can fruitfully be termed as aesthetic in its concern with trying to describe sensations, perceptions, energies, and qualities of the world. That this aesthetic approach is particularly capacious is, I think, demonstrated by a field that can incorporate an attention both to a world of things and a world of affects and atmospheres.

Elizabeth Chin's *My Life with Things: The Consumer Diaries*, is a fantastic book. I can't imagine anyone reading it and not wanting to become an anthropologist. It is also one of the funniest books I've read in a long time, with actual laugh-out-loud moments. One of the overarching themes of the book is that theory, the sort of theory 'we' automatically reach for to explain something like consumption, is nearly always ethnocentric, and quite often deeply racist. So, for instance, the decision that Marx made to describe the commodity form as fetishistic would have been recognised at the time for what it was: a racialised slur. But her solution to this state of affairs is brilliant: rather than vigilantly denouncing the ethnocentrism of theory at every available moment (which would be exhausting for all concerned), she localises it. In this she follows anthropologists like Joanne Kealiinohomoku who write about ballet as a form of ethnic dance, as well as acting on Dipesh Chakrabarty's invitation to 'provincialise Europe'.

It is worth following how she does this in some detail. The book, as the title suggests, has an autoethnographic component at its centre. As is usual in books about 'things', especially ones that encourage autobiographical description, one of the first 'things' to be named is her childhood comforter or security blanket; a piece of cotton material (pink and white) with a picture of two teddy bears on it. This piece of cloth she names Banky. After describing how she used it and how she lost it, she launches into a theoretical 'digression' (her term) by turning her attention to D. W. Winnicott's famous account of 'transitional objects' (which is a psychoanalytic investigation of objects like Banky). But rather than buying (or not) Winnicott's account she works to reveal its cultural circumstance. Using the estrangement techniques famously deployed by Horace Miner in the 1950s in his description of the Nacirema tribe (which is 'American' spelt backwards) she shows how the Nacirema ('us' in other words) are a culture who put an inordinate value on getting children to sleep alone, in their own special places, separated from others. This is a characteristic that the Nacirema people share with none of the other great cultures (hunter-gathers, or agricultural peoples), and it marks them out. Rather than offering their children the warmth and softness of their own bodies for comfort they buy them soft toys, give them brushed-cotton blankets and make them drink warm soothing drinks. Thus insisting that they, right from the get-go, make meaningful social relationships with things rather than rely on the comforts of other members of the culture.

What we are witnessing, with Banky and the young Betsy (Chin), is not a 'universal' child searching out for their first 'not-me' object, but a distinct child rearing practice that privileges thing relations as an inauguration into a culture of possessive individualism (for Winnicott, Banky-like objects are an important first 'possession'). In this, psychology stops being a spuriously over-reaching account of universal verities, and instead becomes a local explanation. And it has to be said that in doing this (provincialising him) she makes Winnicott much more useful in explaining the world (provincialising is not reductive critique but is both generative and generous in its effects). Now Winnicott can be recruited as an explainer of something that is perpetually underexplored: how do we learn commodity fetishism? Or as Chin asks: 'How does one *learn* to mesh self and sneakers, identity and eye shadow?' (p48). 'In the end, then, Winnicott's notion of the transitional object' writes Chin, 'is incredibly useful because it helps us understand the social processes through which the imperatives of capitalism shape our most fundamental being, the way we experience ourselves, naturalising our alienation to the point where we experience it as proper parenting, as citizenship, as patriotism, as love' (p55).

All those instructions on how to get your child to go to sleep on their own turn out to be a foundational lesson in modern capitalist object relations. But people don't always stick to instructions (Chin, herself, happily slept with her child against the dire warnings of the child rearing manuals). And so it turns out that the Nacirema people's entanglement in capitalist materialism is never straightforward. People surprise you with what they do with things: 'One girl I talked with while doing research on children and consumption told me she had at least ten Barbies. 'What do you do with them?' I asked, imagining faux beauty contests and fashion shows. 'I take their heads off,' she replied, 'and go bowling with them!' (p10). The answer to the question posed by the abstractions of social theory (or psychology recoded as vernacular social theory) is always fieldwork: 'our own imaginations are not nearly rich enough to come up with all the possibilities that others have explored' (p10). *My Life with Things* is fieldwork conducted as autoethnography. What unfolds is a relationship with things that is never simply free of capitalist object relations, but can't be reduced to a blind capitulation to it either. Her love for beautiful Oriental rugs and intricate antique lace, for instance, isn't accomplished by simply ignoring the social relations that produced them, as if they arrived in her world 'heaven sent'. She knows the child labour practices that ruined eyesight and bent spines and which went into making nineteenth-century Bedfordshire lace. In this her appreciation of things (which is often simultaneously absurdist, joyous and deeply melancholic) has to reconcile itself with Walter Benjamin's sense that every 'document' is indelibly tainted by barbarism.

The book's final section is a piece of narrative fiction, which she describes as a 'surreal autoethnography of what might have happened' (p203). It concerns the found diary of an anonymous academic who has, in an extreme version of Benjamin's collector, learnt to reverse the procedures of commodification, but in doing so has become a hoarder who can't even let go of her pets' excrement. But this story doesn't end with a tragi-comic overwhelming by the proliferation of things; instead the anonymous academic becomes involved in a siege at an ethnography museum. In this the process of de-commodification is the explicit recognition of the barbarism of all forms of commodification, including museological commodification. Objects speak to her by revealing the social relations that fashioned them and that conspire to keep them as mute historical witnesses, and these objects call upon her to be the spokesperson for a slave revolt of things. Let's just say that the siege doesn't end particularly well for her or for the artefacts in the museum, though it does suggest the possibility of another, more sensitive way of living with things.

In light of Chin's critical anthropology, Maurizia Boscagli's *Stuff Theory: Everyday Objects, Radical Materialism* could be seen as an example of an ethnically specific materialism. I don't think Boscagli would object to such a designation. The names that congregate in the index to this book will be familiar to most people who have studied European modernism across the twentieth century: James Joyce, Virginia Woolf, Marcel Proust, Surrealism, Henri Bergson, Georges Bataille, and so on. A late modernism is also present in the attention given to writers and filmmakers such as Georges Perec, Agnes Varda, Peter Greenway, Elfriede Jelinek and Jean-Luc Godard, as well as to theorists such as Roland Barthes, Henri Lefebvre, and Jean Baudrillard. The chapters of *Stuff Theory* are thematic rather than chronological but they all gather together constellations of different items that tend to be drawn from periods of financial and material crises (the 1920s and 30s, the 1970s and 80s). So, for instance, in a chapter on 'the unnatural use of clothes' Boscagli moves between Joyce's *Ulysses* (1922) and Jelinek's *The Piano Teacher* (1983) to show shifts and continuities in the recalcitrant possibilities of dress and gender performance across the century. Other chapters are concerned with memory, garbage and space.

Stuff Theory attempts to systematically reconfigure a tradition of modernist materialism by submitting it to the concerns of a putative 'new materialism'. The 'hinge' between these two worlds is supplied by the endlessly suggestive writing of Walter Benjamin who acts as the richest example of what can be gleaned when these two worlds are entangled. 'Stuff', for Boscagli 'refers to those objects that have enjoyed their moment of consumer allure, but have now shed their commodity glamour - without yet being quite cast aside' (p6). You can see immediately why Benjamin would loom large over a project with such a central concern. Benjamin's interest in the recently outmoded (last year's fashion, last century's architecture), in kitsch objects (snow globes and taxidermy) and in depictions of the good life promised by a previous generation's advertising, makes him the ideal candidate for rescuing 'stuff' from landfill. And rescuing 'stuff', for Boscagli, will require attending to stuff's 'willingness not to be contemplated but to be touched' so 'that we may find, in their complex concreteness, a template of a materiality to come' (p6). The fact that this 'materiality to come' was announced (or at least presaged) ninety years ago by Benjamin might make you wonder if the realisation of a new materiality will be a constantly delayed and deferred promise.

Boscagli both follows Benjamin and pushes his work into new arenas. Initially he operates as a spirit guide demonstrating a range of critical procedures for attending to stuff. Benjamin's attitude towards commodification isn't to demystify it and return it to the world of labour. In many ways he works to increase the magical properties of the commodity by giving it a life beyond the moment of its promotion. This dynamism reveals 'the unpredictability of the object' which 'stands as a form of chance capable of unsettling the system of use and exchange value with which the fetish is saddled in modernity' (p43). While this loosens one aspect of the commodity's fetish character (it cancels its promissory note, so to say) it does little to unshackle it from the fate that capitalism has bestowed on it. What is needed is *more*, rather than less, fetishism: 'Through a play of disenchantment *and* re-enchantment the commodity is transformed from an object carrying the inscription of capital, that is, an object whose materiality has been irreversibly disembodied and abstracted, to a fetish which carries traces of a collective dream' (p47). The collective dream is the planetary memory of a classless society that can be glimpsed when the object is seen from the perspective of eternity. But what Boscagli also insists on is that 'stuff theory' doesn't just reveal an obdurate materiality in objects, it undoes the identity values that are inscribed across subjects too, making it an essential tool for feminists.

Stuff Theory's engagement with 'new materialism' is wide ranging (Jane Bennett, Donna Haraway, Catherine Malabou, etc.), but at its heart lies the idea of the 'quasi-subject quasi-object' that Michel Serres first introduced in 1980 in his book *The Parasite* and which was then adopted by Bruno Latour. Serres' classic example of a quasi-object is a football, which, when in play, is the centre of the action - a sun around which players circulate. 'Playing' writes Serres, 'is nothing else but making oneself the attribute of the ball as a substance'.[1] It is this ability of objects, as 'stuff', to invoke human subjects as attributes, as materials in accord or discord with other materials, that is at the heart of Boscagli's book. To this end it isn't Benjamin who is the exemplary stuff theorist of the book but the filmmaker Agnes Varda, who in her documentary film *The Gleaners and I*, a film about people who forage for farmers' leftovers, demonstrates the aesthetic capacities of stuff as 'quasi-subject, quasi-object'. Varda films 'stuff', she films people who forage for stuff (be they hungry and in search of food, or artists in search of 'finds') and she films images of people foraging for stuff (in famous and not-so-famous paintings of gleaners). Sometimes the stuff she films is her hand holding a potato or trying to 'grasp' the image of passing truck with her hand. Her hand reveals her age, her stuff-ness, her creaturely-ness. When she picks an over-ripe and discarded fig, she declares it beautiful, she opens it up, bites into it, consumes the fruit and throws the skin into the trees.

1. Michel Serres, *The Parasite*, Minneapolis, University of Minnesota Press 2007, p226.

'Stuff theory', with its foregrounding of 'quasi-objects, quasi-subjects', disrupts the stable organisations of subjects and objects. They (objects, subjects) fail to stay in their proper places, they wander, bleed into one another, collide and merge. The undoing of subject and object stabilities is something that is shared by affect theorists, where affect is precisely that which is pre-individual and unmoored from material supports (though it may still be reliant on them in some form). As Ben Anderson suggests, affect theorists have been inordinately interested in affects' capacities to disrupt equilibriums, to rain chaos down on order. But 'what is needed', writes Anderson 'is an account of how affective life is organised and mediated that sits alongside the emphasis of the excess of affective life over and above existing determinations' (p17). This, then, is the project of *Encountering Affect: Capacities, Apparatuses, Conditions*, and it is a generative and necessary one.

Unusually for current work on affect, Anderson's most significant theoretical resource is Michel Foucault. In one sense what Anderson proposes is an approach to affect (and its cognates such as mood, atmosphere and feeling) that wants to see how it is managed and mobilised. So while affect is never simply a property of an object or subject, and is always wayward in its affections and attachments, it can become regulated and predictable in certain historical and geographical circumstances. Or at least this is what all sorts of agencies (from advertising to psychology, from interior designers to government departments) expend energy on attempting. And this is where Foucault provides the foundational perception. It is the notion of the '*dispositif*', a French term that is often translated as apparatus but can refer to physical devices, legal provisions, systems and plans, and so on, that is crucial for Anderson's book. The heterogeneity and intermeshing of an apparatus was what was important for Foucault: for instance, a visit to a doctor's surgery involves a vast array of arrangements, which include the physical circumstances of 'waiting', the archive of your medical records, the vast array of medical statements, the training of the doctor, the dog-eared magazines and the décor and notices in the waiting room, and so on. And it is this that provides the theoretical perspective for attending to some of the regularities of affect. For instance, in an evocative case study based around a company the produces various smells for businesses it isn't the scent on its own that is the apparatus, but the ensemble of environment, scent delivery system, the scent, the consumers, the idea of branding, and so on. A smell might be used to manage the anxiety of a patient undergoing an MRI scan (and 'beach-themed' scent has been used to such an end) but there is no direct correspondence between seaside smells and calming affects: rather it is the encounter within an apparatus or ensemble that is the scene of affect.

Encountering Affect is often primarily concerned with theoretical discussions of affect, aesthetics, emotions, sense (and so on) and with the political and cultural outcomes of different ways of understanding affect, but it is also laced with some memorable case studies. Some of these are historical; for instance, there is fascinating discussion of the way that morale was discussed and managed during World War Two. As part of a discussion of Raymond Williams' understanding of 'structures of feeling' Anderson explores the popular historical practice of naming a period (often a decade, or similar chunk of time) as an 'age' of anxiety (or some such affective descriptor). Crucially, he recognises that such designations don't belong to the past but are a product of a particular encounter with its documents, memories and material traces: 'it would be' he writes, 'very easy, for example, to characterise liberal-democratic societies in terms of an age of rage, an age of boredom, and age of a vague feeling of being connected, an age of pleasure in the suffering of others, and so on' (p109). And yet while it is easy to critique designating a period with one overarching feeling, it does offer a perspective for doing heuristic 'meso-level' work connecting large scale accounts of social organisation with the patterns of experience that are often felt by those caught up in the dominant forces of change. Anderson provides a very useful analysis of how designating our contemporary moment as an 'age of precarity' allows all sorts of phenomena to be connected as a 'generalised affective condition' (p126) where instability is normalised and where premonitions of catastrophe are part of a general mood.

Other case studies are ethnographic and include some powerful accounts of how music can reconfigure an emotional situation in surprising as well as predicted ways (and in today's world of portable music systems, a personal soundtrack is often an everyday form of mood management). One particular ethnographic case study describes the author taking part (but as an observer) in an exercise simulating a disaster (a nuclear strike, a biological attack, or some other catastrophic event). It is an intriguing case study partly because it has been anonymised (as a condition of being allowed access to such planning) so we have no idea what arm of state is simulating this particular disaster scenario and planning exercise. In this ethnographic case study, the author explores affect as a particular atmospheric arrangement that attunes and orients bodies to events as a form of attention. It is in describing this ability to gather and focus, to dissipate and scatter, that draws out and reveals the general orchestrating capacities (of sense, perception, emotion and so on) of the affective apparatus. And it is this which is the substantial achievement of *Encountering Affect*.

Atmospheres: Aesthetics of Emotional Space continues the exploration of the vague 'air' of material environments and affective situations. If atmospheres name a situation that we all comment on ('you could cut the atmosphere with a knife', 'you should have been there, what an atmosphere') but find hard to pin down in any great detail (beyond the evaluation of them being conducive or not, comfortable or not, and so on), then how should we go about attending to them? Does the elusive vagueness of an atmosphere require a mode of investigation that will need sidelong glances, rather than being met face on? Just as you need to record the sound of wind by registering its ability to make leaves rustle or telephone wires whistle, atmospheres might best be registered as they exert their effects on bodies and situations. This is partly the way that the Italian philosopher of aesthetics Tonino Griffero approaches atmospheres in his book on the topic.

Atmospheres pursues its vague 'object' through a sustained dialogue with a tradition of existential phenomenology, to which it also contributes. The great benefit of treating atmospheres from the perspective of phenomenology is that phenomenology, particularly when it is informed by Heideggerian sensitivities, is particularly adept at drawing attention to ambient orientations *as ambient orientations* (rather than as meaningful entities that should be named, located and evaluated). Thus in Heidegger ideas of 'care' or 'mood' or 'attunement' become both foundational and constitutional of our being-in-the-world without losing their phenomenal form as ambient and organisational. The phenomenological tradition that Griffero is in dialogue with consists of both familiar names (Heidegger, Husserl and Merleau-Ponty) and less-familiar phenomenologists such as Ludwig Klages, Herbertus Tellenbach, and Hermann Schmitz. Indeed, it is in relation to the latter, who conducted investigations into atmospheres as part of a programmatic 'new phenomenology' in the 1960s and 70s, that Griffero orients his work. If Schmitz used atmospheres to produce an objectivist and externalist phenomenology, Griffero sees atmospheres as phenomena that function as sensorial ambiance (often registered through a general synaesthesia) that requires sentimentally attuned subjects. For Griffero atmospheres are a form of 'emotional weather' that objectively exists but only for us as sensitive barometers.

Atmospheres exist as 'a spatialised feeling', as 'a something-more, a *je-ne-sais-quoi* perceived by the felt-body in a given space, but never fully attributable to the objectual set of that space' (p6). But this 'something-more' isn't just something to name as a quality or as qualia (the way that the world seems to us): it also requires a taxonomical approach - its own 'atmospherology'. The atmospherology undertaken here is often directed by an attention to the sensual and sensorial environment - to qualities of light, to the climates of space (vastness, urbanity, and so on) and to the peculiar qualities of materials. For instance, wood has its own atmosphere 'for being a material whose stiffness is not at the expense of its 'warmth' and its certain rustic authenticity' (p97). As Griffero notes this might well be culturally specific. After all, for wood to function in this way might well require a society that also has steel, concrete and glass. The historicity (and therefore the cultural politics) of atmospheres is not, here, developed. In the end *Atmospheres* reads as establishing the foundations for an approach to our ambient and sentimental being-in-the-world, that intervenes at the level of theoretical orientation rather than offering an approach that could grasp the particular qualities of significant atmospheres that are being mobilised today by political rallies, by media assemblages, and by institutional settings.

These books represent a diverse range of work. It would be unfair to see them together as representative of a condition of 'post-post-structuralism', and as a symptom of our academic climate. They do, however, seem to point to the capaciousness of an aesthetic approach to the world, where the object of aesthetics is neither the artwork, nor the 'art-ification' of life, but where aesthetics instead attends to the whole gamut of sensual and affectual life, to the pulsions and propulsions of our material and sentimental world. And in that they also reveal the capaciousness of the aesthetic realms of life in things and stuff, in affects and atmospheres.

Ben Highmore is on the *New Formations* editorial board.

Un-learning to see Palestine

Ruth Preser

Gil Z. Hochberg, *Visual Occupations: Violence and Visibility in a Conflict Zone*, Durham, Duke UP, 2015

Adi Kuntsman and Rebecca L. Stein, *Digital Militarism: Israel's Occupation in the Social Media Age*, Stanford University Press, 2015

Sometime during the summer of the First Lebanon War, my father, then a reserve soldier on a short leave, brought home three war souvenirs: a miniature radio-tape, a stray puppy and a huge machete-like knife. These were the only visual evidence of a combat taking place far from sight (at least for those who did not reside near Israel's northern border) and far from today's battlefield in which 'digital natives' post, rather than 'bring home', their military souvenirs, often in the form of a militarised 'selfie' (Kuntsman and Stein 2015, p77). Yet as *Visual Occupation*, by Gil Hochberg, and *Digital Militarism*, by Adi Kuntsman and Rebecca L. Stein, demonstrate, seeing does not always already translate into knowing, and knowledge does not always already entail seeing. The question - how is it possible that in spite of the circulation of representations of Israeli military brutality and Palestinian suffering, the situation in fact is deteriorating - becomes even more poignant as one reads these books in tandem. That cameras carried by Israeli soldiers might serve as a conscience-cleansing device while maintaining the very condition that provokes a bad conscience, has been noted previously (Nathansohn 2010). Hochberg's and Kuntsman and Stein's books aim at a different project. The questions that inform their work explore the organisation of the Israeli-Palestinian conflict's visual field and the conditions of seeing and knowing that underlie it. Using different (and sometimes overlapping) theoretical trajectories, data and periodisation, they ask what it means when a people fails to appear from the perspective of the coloniser even when the colonisation is palpable and its images are viral.

Visual Occupation and *Digital Militarism*, both published in 2015, offer a comprehensive and complementary study of the Israeli-Palestinian conflict through its visual arrangements, from artistic (Hochberg) and digital (Kuntsman and Stein) perspectives. Coinciding with (and sometimes overlapping) the conflict's timeline, the books provide a fascinating discussion based on different visual archives, beginning with the Palestinian Nakba and the establishment of the state of Israel. They go on to cover the major milestones such as the occupation of the West Bank, Gaza and the Golan Heights, the Second Intifada, the 2006 invasion of Lebanon, the colonial regime in the West Bank and the assaults on Gaza from 2008 through 2014.

Focusing on the political importance of various artistic interventions, Hochberg explores literature, painting, photography, video and film while reworking the relationship between power and vision and engaging not only with the colonised's failure to appear but also with the coloniser's failure to erase. Through attentive reading of Jewish and Palestinian cultural work, Hochberg demonstrates how empowerment and transformation, which are commonly taken as dependent on seeing and being seen, may equally depend on opacity, blindness and the ability to disappear, thereby disrupting the logic of forensics and testimony. Kuntsman and Stein focus on Israeli archives of social media such as Facebook, Instagram and Twitter, unearthing the process by which the state as well as Israeli Jewish citizens develop digital literacy and adopt it as a strategic tool in the war over public opinion. Kuntsman and Stein also move beyond the prevailing dichotomous analysis of exposure of the military violence versus its concealment, and demonstrate how various normalising mechanisms such as public secrets and exceptionalism come into play in justifying militarism and colonialism.

The books resonate with the same concern that the growing circulation of images of Palestinian suffering, which contributes to its visibility, does not necessarily translate into political change. This is evident in Hochberg's discussion of visible invisibility and in Kuntsman and Stein's analysis of public scandals. These scandals display the everyday abuse of Palestinians, yet fail to engage the Israeli public in any ethical process of accountability. In that sense, the two books present a complementary and sobering discussion of the crisis of witnessing and the limits of visual proofs in contributing to the protection of Palestinians' human rights.

Hochberg's book is divided into three parts, each with two chapters. The first part, 'Concealment', discusses the centrality of erasure of the Palestinian past in the Israeli cultural and political imagination. Here the aim is not simply to represent the invisible and the unrepresentable but to elaborate on the cultural practices of erasure. Indeed, throughout the book Hochberg is not interested in mere restoration, although she does elaborate on subtle acts of Palestinian resistance. The second part, 'Surveillance', concerns the domination of the Israeli military gaze, and acts of artistic transgression which destabilise the demarcation between the owner of the gaze, namely the Israeli soldier, and the gazed-at Palestinians. Through a reading of Sharif Waked's campy video, 'Chic Point: Fashion for Israeli Checkpoints', Hochberg brings to light the checkpoints' practices, 'unearthing their performative nature as a theatrical display of power' (p84), and emphasises 'the queerness of the exchange between the Israeli soldiers and the Palestinian men' (p87). Rula Halawani and Khaled Jarrar's photographic projects are employed to inquire into photography's capacity to intervene in the visual field and the political order that sustains the uneven distribution of visual rights. For example, Hochberg reads Halawani's focus on hands in her photography as a perverse intimacy which existed at checkpoints prior to their 'modernisation' and transformation into 'new terminals' which minimise and annul direct contact. A refusal of the gaze is also discussed in her reading of Jarrar's work which documents soldiers and Palestinians gazing at a series of photos taken by him at various checkpoints and then hung on a checkpoint's fence. Here too the gaze is refused, if not reversed altogether, as 'Usually ... [Palestinians] don't do the looking' (p111). While she perceives these works as attempts to articulate Palestinian political agency, Hochberg does not mobilise a redemptive reading. The third part, 'Witnessing', seeks to problematise the act of witnessing by discussing the failure to speak truth to power in an age saturated with visual proofs of Palestinian suffering. While the analysis demonstrates the limitations of rendering visibility to suffering, it also elaborates on the process of rendering visible one's failure to witness, namely the process by which one learns and acknowledges one's failure to see.

While *Visual Occupation* covers the artistic manifestations of the conflict's visual regime between the 1948 establishment of the state of Israel and the Palestinian Nakba, through the military assault on Gaza in 2008, *Digital Militarism* focuses on digital media between 2008 and 2014, and discusses the means by which social media are militarised and co-opted into hegemonic discourses. Kuntsman and Stein's analysis points to the ordinariness of the forgetting of the most explicit representations of Israeli military action, both by state and civilian users who agree not-to-know the violence. *Digital Militarism* is coined by the authors to conceptualise the centrality of global networking conventions as shaped in the past two decades within the Israeli militarist political landscape. Kuntsman and Stein's objects of analysis include the Israeli soldier with a smartphone, official military bodies' use of digital media, and the ordinary Jewish-Israeli civilian user. Comprised of five chapters, the book tackles viral events, 'that were spectacularly visible on Israeli social networks [...] [but whose] virality often worked to obfuscate rather than to expose' (pp16-17). In addition to tracking its gradual development and transformation from a hackers' subculture to a military PR policy, the book provides a fascinating discussion of the digital context of a militarised society, where 'everyday Israel Social media users would gradually become conscripts [...] within the state's occupation project' (p23). Such a process is explored in chapter three, where the authors discuss a Facebook album of Eden Abergil, a former soldier, which contains snapshots of her, posing playfully against the background of handcuffed and blindfolded Palestinian men. While the Israeli public was shocked, the debate spun around Abergil's individual and exceptional vulgarity, describing her as 'one bad apple' (p45), and lamenting Israel's and the IDF's damaged reputation. This storyline, argue the authors, emphasises a common practice of inverting the violence, turning Israel rather than the Palestinians into the scandal's victim, while the soldier is found guilty of inappropriate exposure, and the public discourse is busy with concerns about fragile confidentiality, blaming Facebook. Here, the chief offender is not the Israeli army but social media, which emphasise the Israeli public discourse's agreement both not to see the violence as well as to see the violence as something else. Such refusals are also elaborated in chapters four and five. Chapter four explores digital suspicion as a weapon to divert public debate from war crimes to a technical discussion on image manipulation of images of dead Palestinians. Chapter five analyses the scripted response to such scandals, namely the IDF's insistence on the exceptional nature of recorded abuse of Palestinians by soldiers, employing IDF's 'spirit and values' discourse (p73) as an opposition to the misconduct exposed in social media (chapter 5).

Reading these books next to each other offers a fascinating and comprehensive discussion of hegemonic modes of visibility in archives which reside both in the margins (Hochberg) and at the heart (Kuntsman and Stein) of dominant fields of vision. Against the backdrop of current modes of unseeing and un-knowing, these books urge us to question conventional reliance on familiar images and strategies which might blind us, and instead, as Hochberg asserts, to replace it with alternative configurations, in order to *un-learn* to *see* Palestine.

Ruth Preser is an affiliated fellow at the ICI Berlin Institute for Cultural Inquiry and a founding associate of the Haifa Feminist Institute.

ARTs AND THE UNCONSCIOUS

Karín Lesnik-Oberstein

Review of Katie Gentile (ed.), *The Business of Being Made. The Temporalities of Reproductive Technologies in Psychoanalysis and Culture*, London and New York: Routledge, 2016, 253pp; £24.99 paperback

As Katie Gentile, the editor of *The Business of Being Made* rightly points out, reproductive technologies and attendant ideas of parenthood, motherhood, science, gender, bodies and babies remain topics of fascination in American (and other) culture and much remains to be thought and understood about this. The volume asserts that it is 'the first book to critically analyse assisted reproductive technologies (ARTs) from a transdisciplinary perspective integrating psychoanalytical and cultural theories' (blurb), and one of its key claims and aims, as reflected in its subtitle, is that:

> creating links to the world at large requires a new theory of relational subjectivity, where emergence occurs through a process of coming into being within the vast world of human and nonhuman objects upon which we are dependent, and thus, where the human is not at the centre. In this new theory of subjectivity detailed here, temporality - the generation of time and space - is conceptualized as *the* linking capacity. (p4)

Gentile argues that the importance of this is that:

> While queer theorists have deconstructed the temporal normativity conveyed through reprofuturity, psychoanalysts, often steeped in the Oedipal and other canonical developmental trajectories, have held firm to reifying linear temporal development and maturity through reproduction as the sign of psychological health. (p16)

Both Gentile and all her contributors are practising clinical psychologists or psychoanalysts and the volume is the first of a series, 'Genders and Sexualities in Minds and Cultures' (edited by Gentile and Muriel Dimen) which argues that:

> Several academic presses have created book series specifically examining genders and sexualities from different theoretical and disciplinary perspectives. Whilst many take psychoanalytic theory as a foundational form of inquiry, few are edited or written by trained analysts or clinicians. What is missed are the unique contributions that advances in

psychoanalytic theory and clinical work have to offer (prefatory matter, no page number).

In order to explore these issues, the volume offers first four chapters by Gentile herself, arguing the theoretical frameworks, then a section with chapters on 'Filling in the Gaps of ARTs', which includes discussion of what are here claimed to be less considered aspects, such as the politics and kinship formations of egg donation, male infertility, and ART babies and parents in the neo-natal intensive care unit, then a section with chapters on 'Looking Closely: a Case Study of Egg Donation' and, finally, a concluding theoretical epilogue by the editor.

As the quote above on psychoanalytical allegiance to 'canonical developmental trajectories' might already have revealed, these clinicians' version of psychoanalysis unfortunately relies on a rather unquestioned and vague mix of American ego-psychology and trauma-and affect-theory inspired reformulations. As a result the book, even where it does acknowledge prior theoretically relevant work (usually, tellingly perhaps, only through minimal reference), never seems to understand or work-through implications for psychoanalysis *itself*. Remarkably, in a book claiming to be part of a series that uses 'psychoanalysis as the fulcrum that complicates and deepens our conceptualizations of genders and sexualities' (series blurb) the term I missed most was 'unconscious'. A psychoanalysis effectively deprived of the unconscious is not psychoanalysis but something other, and this is apparent throughout in the ways that certain classic psychoanalytic concepts and ideas are deployed: for instance, with respect to the 'temporality' claimed as key to this volume, nowhere is the unconscious as *timeless* considered; nowhere are the implications of psychoanalysis as necessarily *retroactive* (*nachträglichkeit*) ever mentioned; nowhere are conscious choice, knowledge and feeling not the underpinnings of the entire discussion of ARTs and those engaged with them one way or another. It might well be the case that many psychoanalysts do in practice rely on such 'common sense' ideas, but work such as this claiming to be using temporality as not just a key focus, but innovatively so in terms of theory, needs to be able to demonstrate above all an understanding of how prior theoretical work has a bearing on what it claims to be setting out to do. Compare, for instance, Gentile's formulations about temporality and 'this new theory of subjectivity' she and her contributors set out to offer, to Juliet Mitchell's classic arguments in *Psychoanalysis and Feminism* (1974), where Mitchell writes of:

> [Freud's] increasing stress on moving from a chronological, 'time'-dependent notion of 'stages' of development to a theory of imbrications, parallels, simultaneity, and diachronology; […] Freud's later works […] posit a fluidity, a multifariousness, a complex 'time' of space, not a simple 'time' of place, an awareness verbally expressed, that every moment is a historical one - a summation of a person's life. (p22)

Similarly, with respect specifically to ARTs, Rachel Bowlby's *Freudian Mythologies: Greek Tragedy and Modern Identities* (2007) asks whether and how ideas about the family and gender can change (can 'identities' be 'modern'?), referring particularly to questions to do with the ways new reproductive technologies are often thought of as changing the family. Central to Bowlby's focus are ideas of timelessness (the unconscious) and timeliness (consciousness, history and society).

An understanding of the issues worked-through in *Freudian Mythologies* and related works might also have helped to address the struggle in this volume around the Oedipus complex, where it is understood in a very 'literal' sense, long since much critiqued within psychoanalysis itself by Mitchell and many others:

> ARTs then simultaneously stretch and challenge the Oedipal structure while enabling this structure to spread and enfold even more diverse configurations of couples, families, singles. After all, the Oedipal functions to structure the hierarchy of generations, as Leowald (1980) observed, such that parents cede authority to the adult children. This generational temporality can be both challenged and spread through ARTs. (p6)

In a similarly 'literal' way, Adam Kaplan's personally courageous discussion of male infertility in his chapter is seen to be relevant to Gentile because it demonstrates

> just how enmeshed the penis and testes are with the phallus as a symbol of power. Male infertility is so taboo and unthinkable that the culture collapses masculinity into the penis. Physical function is equated with heterosexuality and gender expression (p17).

Mitchell explains how and why the Oedipus complex, gender and the body ('physical function') might be read differently than this in psychoanalytic terms:

> In its absence [of what is needed], need changes to demand (articulation), and if unsatisfied or unreciprocated, to desire. It is in expressing symbolically this essential 'lack' that the phallus features. The phallus is not identical with the actual penis, for it is what it signifies that is important. So, for example, the mother who herself in her infancy has envied the penis that she lacked will find a substitute for it in the child to which she gives birth; in a sense then, she will want her child to represent her phallus (p396)

In other words, unlike for Gentile and her contributors, in Mitchell's (and of course many other psychoanalytical and gender theorists') understanding of psychoanalysis the penis is not known to be a 'neutral' body part which merely has 'physical function' and onto which 'culture collapses masculinity', but instead, the phallus is what the penis 'signifies', and it is this which is 'important'.

Finally, all of this has a bearing too on the product the ARTs have all been invented to produce: the 'biological child'. As I wrote in my own book *On Having an Own Child: Reproductive Technologies and the Cultural Construction of Childhood* (2008):

> fundamental questions to do with reproductive technologies appear to continue to be supremely difficult to discuss, and these are to do with why people should want to have 'own' or 'biological' children *at all*, and what those children are defined to be (pxii).

Although Gentile's volume points towards questions about the child and futurity - typically only minimally referencing Lee Edelman's famous *No Future* (2004) without considering its use of psychoanalysis - and asks 'How do cultural ideals shape desire for children?' (p219), her volume cannot be in any doubt that

> Babies born through ART are anything but fantasy. They are true, live, in-reality babies that psychic reality may have trouble coming to terms with. (p203)

This retention of the child as the undisputed, finally knowable 'real', outside of 'psychic reality', rests, as Jacqueline Rose seminally argued in *The Case of Peter Pan or the Impossibility of Children's Fiction* (1984), on a rejection of the psychoanalytic unconscious.

Gentile's book thus does itself no favours by from the start considerably over-stating its aims and achievements: both on the blurb and in Gentile's first, introductory, chapter, there are also repeated, wider, claims that the book is the 'first inter- and transdisciplinary exploration of ARTs' (p4) and that it is 'unique because it does examine ARTs from a variety of different perspectives and disciplines' (p9). Not only is it not true that it is the 'first' or 'unique' in these ways, but these are remarkable assertions to make with respect to what might be argued to be *the* area where interdisciplinary and transdisciplinary thought and enquiry have burgeoned and flourished in the past half century -- in my view *par excellence* -- following on from, for instance, the classic work of Michel Foucault on biopower to the foundational arguments on gender, the body and reproduction of feminist theorists such as Rayna Rapp, Donna Haraway, Ludmilla Jordanova and Judith Butler, to the brilliant analyses of the 'new kinships' of Marilyn Strathern, Sarah Franklin, Susan Merrill Squire, Charis Cussons Thompson and others.

Gentile's volume does offer some sensitive and thoughtful discussions of clinical encounters and experiences which involve ARTs, and it would have done well to limit itself to this area, for it is precisely the reasons *why* it thinks it is the 'first inter- and transdisciplinary exploration of ARTs [...] integrating psychoanalytical and cultural theories' that form the core problems throughout the volume.

Karín Lesnik-Oberstein is Professor of Critical Theory and Director of the Graduate Centre for International Research in Childhood: Literature, Culture, Media (CIRCL) and its M(Res) in Children's Literature at the University of Reading, and author of *Children's Literature: Criticism and the Fictional Child* (Clarendon Press, 1994) and *On Having an Own Child: Reproductive Technologies and the Cultural Construction of Childhood* (Karnac, 2008).

A Place for Practice

Sheena Culley

Debra Benita Shaw and Maggie Humm (eds), *Radical Space: Exploring Politics and Practice*, London and New York, Rowman and Littlefield International, 2016, 222pp; £24.95 paperback.

The 'spatial turn' in the humanities and social sciences has been influenced by a range of thinkers, from the work of its 'traditional' founders - Merleau Ponty's phenomenology, Michel Foucault's writing on institutional space, Michel de Certeau's focus on everyday lived space, and Henri Lefebvre's work on the production of social space - to the more recent ideas explored through New Materialisms, topology and digital space. In light of so many developments in ideas surrounding the spatial since these founding authors, it will perhaps surprise the reader of *Radical Space* to discover that the ideas of thinkers such as Foucault and de Certeau feature prominently in this volume, over more current theorists of the spatial such as, for example, Peter Sloterdijk, Donna Haraway and Rosi Braidotti. The radical component of this collection is therefore not to be attributed to its theoretical or philosophical approach to the spatial. *Radical Space* is, in fact, not an attempt to 'do' theory. Rather, as Shaw and Humm state in the first page of their introduction:

> *Radical Space* conceives of 'radical' to encompass new political uses of space outside of capitalist and neoliberal organisations, new radical interpretations of space and new and radical imaginaries.

Readers should therefore be mindful that this volume does not aim to define radical space, theorise space in a radical fashion, nor draw upon the latest spatial theories. Indeed, the focus on more 'traditional' spatial theorists can be accounted for in the aims of the Radical Cultural Studies series that this volume belongs to. With the recognition that the discipline of Cultural Studies has been extended to areas such as celebrity and game culture, the series 'encourages a return to the core project of Cultural Studies: to examine the culturopolitical, sociopolitical, aesthetic and ethical implications of international cultures'.[1] The outcome of a 2013 conference held at the University of East London, organised by the editors, this collection is instead focused on the spatial in relation to political activism, creative interventions, quotidian spaces and cityscapes, aiming to move beyond the 'core spatial disciplines' such as geography and architecture. The volume is split into three parts: Art, Public Space and the Body, Heterotopias, and Extraterritorialities. Thus, the question of place becomes equally as important as space for many

1. http://www.rowmaninternational.com/series/radical-cultural-studies

of the contributing authors, as they disaffirm normative ways of occupying and using spaces by rupturing these configurations with their practices and insights. Useful for all who have teaching and research interests in the spatial, and the relationship between theory and practice, this text will particularly appeal to those who appreciate the tradition of British Cultural Studies, as defined by the Birmingham School, whilst engaging in its multi-disciplinary contemporary debates.

The book opens with a gripping and thought-provoking chapter by artist Joanna Rajkowska, the conference's keynote speaker, and Maggie Humm, who introduce many of the themes explored in subsequent chapters, including migration, national boundaries, public art and public space. This immediately conveys one of the book's key strengths - that it allows artists and practitioners a space to talk about their work, combining theory, practice and experience in ways that do not necessarily privilege one over the other. This element also comes through strongly in Zlatan Krajina's wonderfully articulated chapter, 'An Alternative Urbanism of Psychogeography in the Mediated City', where the recordings from participants of the project are transcribed next to citations from theorists to form compelling collages. Indeed, urban space and psychogeographies are an important component of this volume, which also features Matt Fish's piece on squatting, again written from the dual perspective of activist and theorist, as well as Angie Voela's chapter on 'Camp for Climate Action', in which she discusses the 2009 occupation of the site in Blackheath, London, in relation to heterotopias and Lacanian psychoanalysis.

The thread of public space traverses this volume eloquently. Connell Vaughan's chapter on public art and public space enters neatly into dialogue with Rajkowska's work. Vaughan draws on the idea of curation, coming from the Latin *curare*, to care. When thinking about curation in terms of works of art, activities such as preservation, presentation and organisation also come to mind (p28). Curation of public spaces, as observed by Vaughan, can then become defined as sinister, as curation becomes part of a normalising process. Public art, often thought of as art in the public realm, should instead be conceived of as 'productive of public space' (p22). This idea sits well in conversation with Rajkowska, whose work was met with such animosity from the local community that the planned installation did not happen, as the meaning given to her work 'The Peterborough Child' by the local council and community detracted from the artist's intentions, leading to hostility and misunderstanding.

Carl Lavery et al.'s chapter 'Return to Battleship Island' further draws on the ideas of heterotopia, whereby the authors uncover the ruin of Hashima Island, excavating histories of forced Korean and Chinese labour masked by a UNESCO World Heritage site status and industrial success. Particularly interesting here was the transition between forced mining labour of the period between the 1880s and 1945, and employment post-1950, where the Mitsubishi company needed to encourage a new workforce to settle on Hashima, selling the aspirational island lifestyle via images of 'heroic work and laid-back consumerism' (p101). Given that this chapter is part of the 'Heterotopias' section, a reflection on the differences between the utopic and heterotopic stands out as a missed opportunity here alongside the mention of the creation of a 'worker's utopia' during this time period. However, the interspacing of film stills, notes from the fieldwork, dreams, and reflections on themes such as trauma and nostalgia make this chapter rich and imaginative.

The introduction tells us that the 'situation of bodies' is an urgent concern of the volume. In particular, two of the contributions make this theme explicit: Victoria Hunter's 'Radicalising Institutional Space', and Kat Deerfield's 'Gravity Gender and Spatial Theory.' Hunter's practice of Phenomenological Movement Inquiry provides an excellent introduction to both Phenomenology and dance philosophy, where participants in her study were encouraged to challenge normative ways of moving against the backdrop of institutional space. This is a timely study, drawing on the ideas of embodied and choreographic knowledge that are pertinent to other dance theorists and practitioners such as Wayne McGregor and William Forsythe. Deerfield's chapter provides an original perspective on the gendering of bodies, showing us that the tendency to take gravity for granted in our view of the body leads to the representation of bodies in two dimensions. Furthermore, Deerfield uncovers the impact of the masculine perspective of the female body as mysterious and unknown on twentieth-century space travel, which was used as grounds to exclude women from participating in this activity. These two chapters go the furthest theoretically in contesting the body as docile and questioning the space of the body itself. It is perhaps implicit in this volume that bodies which are part of projects involving 'activism' should be seen as 'active' or non-docile, which could have been problematized and discussed in more detail, in both the introductory or concluding remarks.

Whilst this volume does not theorise, or aim to define radical space, Dimitris Papadopoulos's 'Composting Space' serves as a manifesto of the spatial for 'Generation M', the dedicatee of the book. This chapter is perhaps the most engaged in current thinking around the spatial, hinting at the intersubjective, material, ecological and post-anthropocentric. Whilst these themes should not be thrown in simply because they are fashionable, some of these exciting theoretical ideas about the spatial could have featured more prominently, such as Sloterdijk's and Haraway's work on immunity, post-Deleuzian schools of thought such as New Materialisms, and thinking around non-human space and the topological. With Shaw's work on technocultures and her focus on the connection between science and culture, this volume could have opened up more conversations between these themes and the spatial and political. The intersection between culture, science and technology does not necessarily need to convey Cultural Studies' more recent focus on media-related areas such as celebrity or game culture, but can form part of rigorous projects faithful to understanding the everyday and practices of inhabiting spaces. Yet, with its conscious positioning away from certain theoretical elements, and focus on practice and activism, *Radical Space* makes an important contribution to work on the spatial and political, taking a refreshing slant.

Sheena Culley was awarded her PhD by the London Graduate School, Kingston University. She is author of 'Killing Pain? Aspirin, Emotion and Subjectivity' in *Pain and Emotion in Modern History* ed. by Rob Boddice (Palgrave, 2014).

EXPANSION/EXPULSION

Kevin M. Potter

Thomas Nail, *The Figure of the Migrant*, Stanford, Stanford University Press, 2015, 295pp

As the twenty-first-century political and social climate continues to confront migration, displacement, and movement - especially with the persisting refugee crises unfolding in Europe and Africa - the struggle to comprehend the nature of global human migration seems to underlie the disturbing and panicked rhetoric within the news media.[1] Moreover, rarely do either academic or intellectual discourses attempt to conceptualise migration outside of the bounds of law and politics - both institutional paradigms that tend to represent people and human rights according to a matrix of *stasis*, territory, and legitimacy. Thomas Nail's *The Figure of the Migrant*, therefore, arrives at a perfect moment to give a unique insight into the phenomenon of movement in the present time. Utilising an historical materialist approach to migration, Nail advances a lucid vision of migration through a much-needed 'kinopolitics', or 'politics of movement', highlighting the fact that we live in a world where there is no 'social stasis, only regimes of social circulation' (p4). That is to say, the contemporary economic system of technologically accelerated mobility, globalised industrial expansion, and capital accumulation determines and compels motion on a large, critical scale. Since 'modernity', according to Zygmunt Bauman (one of Nail's major inspirations in the text), 'is the impossibility of staying put', a movement-oriented philosophy is necessary to theorise one of the figures who defines the twenty-first century.[2]

Nail concisely and rigorously analyses the mechanics of movement from the Neolithic age up through modernity. Relying upon the philosophical insights of Lucretius, Karl Marx, Henri Bergson, Gilles Deleuze, and Bauman, as well as the corroboration of historical records Nail sufficiently equips his conceptual schema with a thoroughly researched and consistent foundation. He then takes a section of the text to apply his conceptual and historical model toward Mexico-U.S. migration, analysing it as a major space of contemporary kinopolitics. The material forces of movement have historically played a key role in shaping societies and political regimes. These conditions include the struggle for resources, climate change, political and social conflict, and the accumulation of territorial, economic, and political control. The social forces of motion are qualitatively distinct, yet symbiotic conditions of movement that have had unique points of emergence throughout history; and the conceptual mechanics of social motion (flow, circulation, and junction) are necessary

1. Thomas Nail, 'The Hordes Are Banging on the Gates of Europe?', *History News Network*, 25 October 2015.

2. Zygmunt Bauman, *Postmodernity and its Discontents*, Cambridge, Polity 1997, p77.

furnishings to develop a framework within which the figure of the migrant manifests.

The migrant, of course, is defined by movement; and, more often than not, this movement is a coerced outcome of 'kinopower', a term which Nail uses to refer to the manner by which societies 'expand their territorial, political, juridical, and economic power through diverse forms of expulsion' (p24). According to Part II of *The Figure of the Migrant*, these forces of kinopower include: 'centripetal force', in which the accumulation of territorial kinopower pulls from the periphery inward (through, for example, land accumulation and territorial expansion); 'centrifugal force', whereby political kinopower generates outward-directed motion, using 'the power of an accumulated centre in order to expel from, or to, its periphery' (p189) - taking the form of de-politicisation, arrest, and eviction. Kinopower also generates 'tensional force', or a 'juridical power', that creates legal boundaries and varying degrees of inclusion, thereby intensifying displacement, political conflict, and social resistance; and 'elastic force', which has historically stopped, managed, or redirected social flows to avert economic catastrophe or collapse. Nail's development of these forces, conceptualised within a physics-based lexical frame, extends previous materialist theories of economic and political accumulation, as well as analyses of migration and movement. Nail makes careful use, for example, of Marx's theory of 'primitive accumulation' where, as a requisite condition for a powerful elite to gain capital ownership and amass private property, there must first exist a process of displacing indigenous people and peasants from their land, depriving them of any property ownership in the first place. Yet, Nail's emphasis on 'expansion by expulsion' consequently 'radicalises' (p24) the theory of primitive accumulation by developing more extensively the notion that economic and political kinopower constantly expands and contracts, circulates and recirculates, distributes and redistributes flows of motion throughout history and into the present.

Of course, the material conditions of motion constitute and determine the primary subject of Nail's text: the figure of the migrant itself. Yet, the figurations and shapes that the migrant takes are not merely products of kinopolitical conditions; rather, according to Nail, the migrant holds claim to its own 'pedetic social force'. The migrant's autonomous and active pedetic force performs a counter-movement that is unpredictable and undetermined, often inspiring an inclusive and collective social motion. In other words, the capacity to redirect or apply pressure upon kinopower stems from a social force of 'solidarity or collective disruption' (p127). Social unrest, discontent, and general outrage inspire a joined action to collide with, or even block entirely, the flows of expansion by expulsion. Different migrant figures react to kinopower in their own singular manner, operating with different provisions for pedetic social force. The four figures that Nail outlines in detail are 'the nomad', 'the barbarian', 'the vagabond', and 'the proletariat'. These figures each come from specific regimes of circulation that have forced them out of their home territories; yet they each, concurrently, produce waves of pressure against the material forces of growing territorial control, privatisation, and juridical power.

The pressure that migrants place on political kinopower exists in the real threat they produce in deserting the land and committing raids (in the case of the nomad), seeking refuge and enacting revolt (in the case of the barbarian), wreaking heresy through rebellion (in the case of the vagabond), and acting in resistance against economic control and political power (in the case of the proletariat). In each case, these forms of pedetic social force frustrate and undermine the domination of kinopower. The figures of the migrant push forcefully against the systems of consolidated power that displace and expel them, while similarly forging singular flows of their own. The apolitical disenfranchisement of the migrant results from a long history of being considered 'a failed citizen' (p3) - disruptive, aterritorial, unstable, or criminal; and this discursive and ideological bias has ultimately come to shape the historically violent and ethnocentric boundaries of state and citizenship. In terms of movement, though, the migrant's pedetic action - in other words, its unceasing migratory motion - has continually applied pressure against the kinopower that wishes to expand its reach. As migrants push against the flows of expansion by expulsion, the regimes of consolidated kinopower react as they historically have toward all figures of the migrant - with fear, control, violence, capture, enslavement, and arrest - without compromising the boundaries of citizenship or political territory. Nail thoroughly insists, therefore, on the empowering and revolutionary capacity of the migrant to carry out a pedetic social force, leading then to new flows and waves of motion.

As Nail develops his argument with these ideas tying together, one cannot help but notice a slight conflict internal to his thesis. Particularly in the transition from Part II to Part III of the text, where Nail outlines the move between 'expansion by expulsion' on the one hand, and the figure of the migrant on the other, there appears a gap in connecting these two conceptual pillars. I offer this criticism in the spirit of Étienne Balibar, who diagnosed a similar weakness in Marx's *Das Kapital*. One can recall that, according to Balibar, Marx seems to describe 'labour' under two irreconcilable characteristics; that the labour 'working class' emerges as a substratum determined by the material conditions of capital exploitation, yet also as the proletariat agents that bring about revolution. The problem is that these characterising features have different temporal and ontological attributes; and in order for us to distinguish between them, we are 'obliged to search for the conditions in a conjuncture that can precipitate class struggle into mass movements'.[3] I see a similar issue with the way in which Nail conceptualises the migrant. On the one hand, migrants are a product of kinopower and the regimes that force them into motion; yet, at the same time, we are to perceive that same migrant (in its various permutations) as the subject who is able to enact a pedetic social force (in rebelling, revolting, or resisting)

3. Étienne Balibar, *Masses, Classes, Ideas: Studies on Politics and Philosophy Before and After Marx*, J. Swenson (trans), New York, Routledge 1994, p147.

against kinopower. So, the movement that defines (and produces) the migrant somehow has to be distinct from the counter-movement that the migrant carries out *against* those same regimes of circulation. Unless it is possible to locate an eventual transcendental shift in the migrant's pedetic motion - one that can be disembodied from the material conditions of kinopower - it is not clear how they can necessarily be the same figure. Nail does not offer any real solution for how this redirection or junction is meant to occur in the contemporary state of kinopolitics and movement; and it is hard to see what political function the migrant has that can be ontologically distinct from its historical and material determinations.

Despite this minor gap (which Nail may address in his next volume, *Theory of the Border*), *The Figure of the Migrant* enriches the present understanding of movement and migration, offering a refreshingly clear analysis of and groundwork for a movement-oriented philosophy. Future discussions of migration and mobility would be poised to consider Nail's text, especially as developing fields are more frequently incorporating materialist and affective perspectives. Analysing a complex system of motion and migration, Nail carefully outlines these ideas in a manner that is comprehensible, yet rigorous and erudite. Nail contributes a unique vocabulary for conceptualising how movement operates in the modern age, doing so in a manner that is ambitious and inspiring.

Kevin Potter is a recent graduate from the Research Master's program in Comparative Literary Studies at Utrecht University in the Netherlands. He is currently seeking a Ph.D position.

BORIS GROYS: THE INTRUDER

Julia Vassilieva

Boris Groys, *In the Flow*, London, Verso, 2016.

Boris Groys, *On the New*, London, Verso, 2014.

Boris Groys, *Under Suspicion: The Phenomenology of Media*, New York, Columbia University Press, 2012.

Only a handful of philosophers have managed to make a successful transition from Eastern Europe into the Western context and make their impact there over the last one hundred years or so - Alexandre Kojève, Julia Kristeva, Slavoj Žižek, Boris Groys. To come from another cultural context and philosophical tradition is to be haunted by the spectre of otherness and to act, inevitably, as an intruder in the host culture. Boris Groys has managed to turn these circumstances - his appearance on the Western philosophical scene after his immigration from Russia to Germany in 1981 - into one of the most distinctive aspects of his strategy of inquiry.

Holding professorial positions in Karlsruhe and New York universities, while also being part of the European Graduate School as well as acting as a curator of projects ranging from documenta to the Venice Biennale, Groys has attracted a growing following since his *Gesamtkunstwerk Stalin* (1988), published in English as *The Total Art of Stalinism* in 1992, urged a radical reconsideration of the relationship between Stalin's totalitarianism and the Russian avant-garde. Fredric Jameson described the book as 'a remarkable act of interpretation' and credited it with a much-needed reinvigoration of the field of utopian studies.[1] Groys's thesis in that book was that, instead of being a mortal enemy of the Russian avant-garde of Malevich and the Constructivists, Stalinism represented its logical outcome, fulfilling the most profound avant-garde inspiration: the total transformation of reality in accordance with an aesthetic plan. By claiming for itself the role of demiurge previously occupied by God, the avant-garde prepared the development that Stalin brought to a logical conclusion by merging art and politics and thus achieved a realisation of a utopian vision in practice. Groys's analysis in *The Total Art of Stalinism* reversed the established understanding of continuity and rupture, and set up paradox as the main methodology of his philosophical work, an impulse that becomes even stronger in his later writing.

Groys is fluent in English and French but writes mainly in Russian and German. The complicated history of translation means that Groys's works often reach their Anglophone readership belatedly. Prompted by Verso's recent publication of his new book *In the Flow*, this article reflects on its

1. Fredric Jameson, *Archaeologies of the Future*, Verso, London 2005, pxiv.

relationship with two earlier monographs by Groys: *On The New* (1992/2014) and *Under Suspicion: The Phenomenology of Media* (2000/2012). All three deal with one of Groys's primary fields of inquiry: the constant movement and change within the realm of what Yuri Lotman would call the semiosphere, which includes art objects as well as their interpretations, products of mass media, the circulation of theories, and linguistic expression in general. *On the New* investigates what constitutes innovation in art, theory and thought; *Under Suspicion* looks at what animates this dynamic of change, or which forces operate beneath the media surface; while *In the Flow* engages with the recent transformations in art and media brought about by the emergence of the Internet and digitisation more generally. Groys's overriding explanatory logic in these works is based on an economic paradigm, but one that differs in significant respects from both the market economy and the notion of 'creative economies' now favoured in cultural studies.

On the New takes as its point of departure postmodern critiques of truth and their insistence on the inaccessibility of 'the signified, reality, being, meaning, evidence, or of the presence of the present' (*On the New*, p7) - a critique that for Groys, rather than making the question of the new impossible, allows us to pose it adequately for the first time. For, as Groys understands it, innovation does not imply that something has been created or revealed that was previously absent or hidden, but rather that something which has always been seen, known and open is *revalued*. To explain how the process of revaluation unfolds, Groys mobilises an economic logic: 'As a revaluation of values, innovation is an economic operation' (*On the New*, p10); but the notion of economy at issue is not the dualistic Marxian one of a determining economic base and a cultural superstructure. Rather, Groys sees culture itself as an economic realm constituted by relations of equivalence and exchange, comparison and trade, which ensure its inherent dynamism and constant fluctuations. Thus for Groys, 'the logic of the cultural development itself' represents 'an economic logic of revaluation of values' (*On the New*, p12). The valorising comparison is the sole source of the sense of the new. And this comparison takes place at the border between two broad domains: the domain of the profane and the domain of the archive or cultural memory. The domains are separated by the 'value boundary', an ever-shifting divide that is itself redrawn every time a value-judgement is made.

Groys conceives of the archive as a structure with a material existence, comprising museums, libraries and other institutions for the preservation of cultural information. The other domain, which consists of all the things not included in the archive, constitutes the profane, which therefore represents a depository of everything not categorised, judged as valuable, interesting, or significant. Things that constitute the profane are not worth preserving, and hence transitory and perishable. Yet it is the domain of the profane that provides a pool from which things are extracted to be categorised as valuable, significant and worth preserving. 'The source of the new', Groys writes, 'is the valorising comparison between cultural values and things in the profane realm' (*On the New*, p64).

One can discern here the legacy of the Russian formalists Viktor Shklovsky, Boris Eikhenbaum, Yuri Tinianov and Roman Jakobson and specifically their concept of '*defamiliarisation*', developed to account for the emergence of a sense of the new in art through challenging the artistic canon, often by drawing on marginalised, folk or primitive aesthetics. Groys also exhibits the formalists' total neglect of the social context, historical evidence, or technological changes underpinning artistic innovation. However, unlike the formalists who saw '*defamiliarisation*' primarily as an artistic device, Groys conceives of his process of revaluation as a universal mechanism of change capable of explaining innovations not only in art, but also in science, theory, and religion. The process of reassessment of profane objects as culturally valuable can explain, on the one hand, how Duchamp's ready-made strategy works, when utilitarian objects - from bicycles to urinals - are displayed in a museum space, and, on the other hand, how previously profane objects and figures acquire sacred meaning in religion - as when the cross and the 'singularly profane fate' of Jesus - 'the crucified criminal' - come to symbolise the exchange of the profane for the divine essence in Christianity (*On the New*, p145). In the realm of theory, Marx's and Freud's innovations can also be understood as a repositioning of the profane - namely, the proletariat's labour, in the first case, and the psychopathology of 'everyday life' and basic 'animal' urges in the second - and as a valorising of previously profane processes as new explanatory principles.

Yet, Groys's model shares the fundamental weakness of the formalists by reducing the process of innovation to an abstract dialectic of 'the negation of the negation', to use Tony Bennett's phrase.[2] Furthermore, the topological character of Groys's explanatory scheme brings with it a palpable sense of homeostasis typical of the models that privilege the synchronic dimension, as, for example, Vladimir Propp's model of narrative analysis did. As Paul Ricoeur has demonstrated, while the temporal dimension was not totally absent in such formalist models, it was a specific achronic temporality, divorced from the real contingency and incalculability of time.[3] The same criticism can be levelled against Groys's theory, which, while attempting to account for developmental progression, remains surprisingly static.

Arguably, it is in an attempt to address these tensions that in the very last chapter of *On the New* Groys reverts to the heuristic category of the author in response to the question 'Who innovates/ Who initiates innovative exchange?' Groys makes this move in the hope of animating his abstract structural scheme, which lacks an internal motor, engine, or driving force. He tries to solve this problem with the magisterial gesture of situating the author at the very centre of his system and proclaiming, 'The author is an agent of both tradition and innovation: he is sufficiently well defined by this role, the one he plays in cultural-economic strategy. […]. Beyond that role and outside it,

2. Tony Bennett, *Formalism and Marxism*, New York, Routledge 2003, p49.

3. Paul Ricoeur, *Time and Narrative*, (trans) K. McLaughlin & D. Pellauer, Chicago, University of Chicago Press 1984-1988.

the question "What is man?" is irrelevant to an understanding of cultural authorship' (*On the New*, p190). Granted, Groys's theorisation of authorship is sufficiently different from that of the romantic or humanist tradition; his author is a calculating agent whose task is to grasp the existing cultural norms and assess the probability of successfully repositioning 'things' from the realm of the profane into the realm of the culturally valuable (although no author can grasp in full where the value boundary lies at a given moment, since this positioning is 'inevitably evenmental' [*ereignishaft*] (*On the New*, p191)). Yet, the appearance of the figure of the author in a theory that strives to move beyond poststructuralist critique strikes one as incongruous. However, in the context of Groys's own analytical paradigm the figure is entirely logical - it was through placing Stalin as an author at the centre of his earlier analysis of Soviet utopia that Groys managed to resolve the tension between art and power, ideology and creativity within one seamless scheme.

Under Suspicion continues from where *On the New* left off. In *Under Suspicion* Groys argues that in order to understand how the archive emerges and functions we need to understand what guarantees its endurance - which is always under suspicion as it is threatened by the onslaught of time. The crucial question for Groys thus becomes: 'what medium sustains the archive and for how long?' (*Under Suspicion*, p7). The answer turns out to be not so much about media - which for Groys include the whole gamut of semiotic systems and symbolic expressions - but about what lies beneath the phenomenological surfaces, which he terms 'the submedial space'. Because this submedial space is by definition not open to the observer, 'the relation of the viewer to the submedial space of the carrier is thus a relation of suspicion - a necessarily paranoid relationship' (*Under Suspicion*, p11). This suspicion forces the observer to develop a thirst for uncovering 'what is "really" concealed behind the media surface of signs' (*Under Suspicion*, p11).

Groys's logic here mirrors Ricoeur's 'hermeneutics of suspicion', albeit without referring to it explicitly, and builds on critical insights of Marx, Freud and Nietzsche, who in various ways contributed to a distinctively modern style of interpretation that circumvents the obvious or self-evident meanings in order to draw out the hidden truth. Groys carries this logic to its limit: it is not the truth of signification that is at stake for him, as signs do not conceal the absence of the signified object; what they conceal is their very own media carriers buried in the submedial space that we are bound to perceive as suspicious and dark, inevitably suspecting manipulation, conspiracy and so on. Groys's model is essentially a surface-and-depth model in which what might be discovered beneath the surface of appearance is not essence, being, or God but an obscure submedial other, the suspected source of manipulation and intrigue.

Peculiarly, Groys doesn't discuss the relationship between his model and ideology, yet his depiction of the submedial space as a mysterious force that controls the vast range of social phenomena through manipulation of the media, broadly understood, resonates closely with the post-Althusserian critique of ideology. And just as for Althusser ideology is crucially implicated in the production of subjectivity, for Groys the mechanics of suspicion is constitutive of the sense of self. Subjectivity for Groys is the submedial space par excellence as 'it can never show itself on the medial surface' (*Under Suspicion*, p20), and it is called into being by the same suspicion and anxiety in the seeing subject as any other submedial space generates. The Other for Groys is 'a name for the submedial space of suspicion'.

The move to invoke the Other in relation to subjectivity, of course, predates Althusser. However, if for Bakhtin and Levinas, for example, the Other is crucial in the formation of subjectivity for his or her affirmative power - whether it is the source of truth about me or the source of ethical obligation - for Groys the Other enters the production of subjectivity through a distinctly negative intervention. It is this ontological fear 'of the hidden subject in the submedial space who is watching the movements of the individual from behind the medial surface' (*Under Suspicion*, p 29) that is constitutive of our sense of selves, our subjectivity.

Invoking the economic paradigm again, Groys argues that the seeing subject, as well as the world observed, all become functions in the economy of suspicion, which encompasses a constant involvement of its participants with one another and may cause occasional ruptures, in the form of 'truth effects'. These are dependent on the fact that the submedial subject can only reveal itself in an aporetic way: confirming media-ontological suspicion and at the same time overcoming it by creating an effect of sincerity, testimony, or access to its interior depth. However, for Groys, this is always only a transitory moment: 'this state of trust only lasts until the old suspicion reawakens, and the sign of sincere revelation is exposed as nothing but a sign among many other signs on the medial surface' (*Under Suspicion*, p50).

Truth is of the moment: as in *On the New*, Groys has to revert here to the category of the 'event' to animate the dead mechanics of his scheme. It follows from this that 'all works of art, like many other valuable objects in the archives of our culture, are nothing but souvenirs that remind us of such exceptional moments of insight' (*Under Suspicion*, p39). Interestingly, the objects most likely to generate truth-effects are characterised by the very same qualities that, in *On the New*, serve to facilitate their entry into the archive - they disrupt the work of tradition and are perceived as alien, primitive or vulgar, which in this context serves to guarantee their sincerity.

Having outlined the basic dynamics of the economy of suspicion and truth, Groys sets out to differentiate his economy from the market-dictated logic of circulation and exchange. He dedicates the second half of *Under Suspicion* to a search for models that can disrupt economic reciprocity: Mauss's concept of the gift, Lévi-Strauss's mana, Bataille's potlatch, Derrida's economy of the future and Lyotard's sublime.

Under Suspicion, like *On the New*, is at its strongest when providing specific readings of contemporary media phenomena. Groys's tendency to overgeneralise erodes rather than reinforces the explanatory power of his paradigm. When he includes under the category of signs 'mountains, planets, or living elephants - signs that are too big to be presented in the museum' - his media phenomenology starts to look more and more like the Borgesian *Celestial Emporium of Benevolent Knowledge* which lists in its classification of animals 'the innumerable ones' as well as 'those drawn with a very fine camel hair brush'.

Groys's emphasis on suspicion as the main driving force of subjectivity, as well as his emphasis on the operation of media through the 'economy of affect' rather than communication of knowledge, may be timely. However, in those quarters where discontent and weariness with postmodernism keeps rising and questions of truth, beauty and God generate renewed interest, Groys's system, in which truth or meaning as well as aesthetic or ethical judgment simply have no place, might be perceived as a dead-end of philosophical nihilism.

In the Flow continues to explore the themes of cultural value, archive, innovation, subjectivity and otherness. Here, in contrast with his earlier works, time comes to occupy centre-stage: *In the Flow* sets out to investigate 'art entering the flow of time', offering discussion of 'art as flowing'. Groys's interest in fluidity is not unique, of course: scholars ranging from Marshall Berman (author of *All that Is Solid Melts Into Air*) and Zygmunt Bauman (coiner of the metaphors of 'liquid modernity', 'liquid fear', 'liquid surveillance' and 'liquid time') to Catherine Malabou (in her more recent work on plasticity), all address an increasing 'liquidification' of the material conditions of contemporary life and subjectivity. Groys's inquiry is distinctive for its focus on one specific aspect of this increasing malleability, namely, how our relationship with art and media are being reshaped by the development of the Internet. In addressing this issue Groys does not valorise the border between the old and new media but rather seeks to uncover, in a way also adopted by such theorists of new media as Lev Manovich and Siegfried Zielinski, how the analogical past has led to the digital present. In a set of sharply argued essays collected in *In the Flow* Groys examines issues ranging from the difference between mechanical and digital reproduction to the emergence of Google and WikiLeaks.

His first essay, 'Entering the Flow', provides a conceptual framing for the collection as a whole. In it Groys argues that if premodern art and cultural and religious inquiry, more broadly, were concerned with the subject's contemplation of God or eternal ideas, contemporary art is concerned with the subject's dissolution in the material flow of life, brought to the fore by the capitalist mode of production. He further contends that the results of these historical endeavours are comparable in their futility: just as it was impossible to capture the moment of religious ecstasy or rational insight, so it is impossible to pin down the process of the dissolution of subjectivity. Artworks thus are mere testimony, material traces of such attempts, while their phenomenological side remains elusive. In contrast to earlier eras, however, contemporary art - assisted by the changing role of the museum as a place where things are not exhibited but where events occur, and by the ease of recording provided by the Internet and digital technologies - shifts its focus explicitly to the documentation of this experience, the experience of subjective dissolution. Further, the notion of documentation becomes crucial for Groys. By taking the place of art on the internet, documentation also changes its ontological status: if traditional art produced objects, contemporary art practices produce descriptions of art events.

Another essay, 'Modernity and Contemporaneity: Mechanical versus Digital Reproduction', revisits Walter Benjamin's notion of the auratic original, which, as Groys emphasizes, referred to the presence of the presence, and as such is indissolubly linked with time. The aura that, for Benjamin, the original possesses and the copy lacks was essentially tied in with the artwork's potential for being exhibited either in one designated place and time, or being topographically dispersed through copying. Explaining that digital reproduction relies not on a mechanical copying but rather on the execution of a 'command' or a script contained in an invisible digital file, Groys argues that digitization turns all visual art into performance art. The staging of a digital copy becomes an event that takes place in the here and now, and therefore restores the aura of originality. Groys sees this as a decisive break that separates contemporaneity from modernity - the age of purely mechanical reproduction. While some of these points have been made by other media theorists before now, Groys goes a bit further in thinking about their implications.

For example, he argues that the Internet reshapes authorship and subjectivity. Echoing the main theme of *Under Suspicion*, Groys argues that the contemporary subject is defined by a secret: a set of passwords that delineate his or her area of access. 'This area of access,' Groys writes, 'replaces today the unity of individual message, the personal authorial intention, the subjective act of thinking and feeling' (*In the Flow*, p177). In this digital landscape hacking becomes the new hermeneutic: by breaking the secret codes and passwords it is possible to gain control of the subject. Thus, proclaims Groys, 'the cyberwars are wars of subjectivation and desubjectivation' (*In the Flow*, p177). Privacy has already been significantly diminished by the Internet as any Internet-using creative worker automatically subjects himself or herself to the same or a greater degree of surveillance as installed by the Foucauldian panopticon. Furthermore, the internet opens up the possibility of a production of subjectivity divorced from identity, 'a neutral, anonymous subjectivity producing no original, individual meaning or opinions at all' (*In the Flow*, p159). Consequently, WikiLeaks represents the ultimate expression of the 'common telos of contemporary media by realising the goal of universal class, of the new universalisation of the world through the means of universal service' (*In the Flow*, p165).

Predictably, then, Groys's liquidification brings in its wake liquidation of subjectivity and meaning, taking his invocation of the category of negation to a new level. The digital flow intensifies the strategy of destruction ushered in by avant-garde art and finalises the 'destruction of the metaphysics of presence'. Yet, at the same time, it opens up new vistas for the utopian imagination.

In the Flow is engaging and provocative, formulating a range of precise, insightful and sometimes disturbing points. Arguably, the essayistic format of *In the Flow* works better for Groys than his previous attempts to create metatheoretical frameworks in *On the New* and *Under Suspicion*. It also addresses more specifically a particular historical moment, rather than claiming to explain the history of human culture in its entirety, a claim made in both the other works, without much substantiation. In terms of methods and strategy, however, all three of these texts bear the characteristic Groysian marks: his writing stages as much as it analyses the paradoxes he addresses, aiming not so much to provide answers but to unsettle, question, disrupt. As when watching the militant modernist films of Jean-Luc Godard, one is doomed to feel frustrated as much as rewarded by engagement with a text whose form constantly undermines its content.

Groys's writing is profoundly performative, but it performs all-too-well the negation that he sets out to describe, achieving at times an effect of self-annihilation. The very fundamental paradox that his writing embodies is the paradox of thought struggling to take shape and make meaning when the preconditions for this - the schemes, the knowledge, the certainties - have progressively been demolished, to a degree that they can no longer sustain philosophical inquiry as we used to understand it. Whether it is the agony of philosophy or clearing of the space for the new is for the reader to decide.

Julia Vassilieva is Australian Research Council Research Fellow at Monash University. She has double background in film studies and psychology and she works at the intersection of these two disciplines. Her publications have appeared in *Camera Obscura, Film-Philosophy, Continuum: Journal of Media & Cultural Studies, Screening the Past, Critical Arts, Kinovedcheskie Zapiski, Rouge, Lola, Senses of Cinema, History of Psychology* and a number of edited collections. Her most recent monograph *Narrative psychology*, Palgrave Macmillan, 2016 explores narrative and subjectivity.

Inventing New Lines

Conor Heaney

Gerald Raunig, *Dividuum: Machinic Capitalism and Molecular Revolution Vol. 1*, Aileen Derieg (trans.), South Pasadena, Semiotext(e), 2016, 208pp; £14.95 paperback

Gerald Raunig's *Dividuum* confronts any reviewer with numerous challenges, not least of which is how to begin. Raunig (and his co-authors, for 'the authorship of any book is divided' (p11)) offers us at least four different beginnings through which to slip into our navigation of this complex and ambitious text. Further, the book's inclusion of nine *ritornellos* scattered throughout - bursts of poetic philosophy which function simultaneously as experimental explorations of *dividuum* which obey their own narrative distinct from the other chapters in the text (and which are a homage to Deleuze and Guattari's concept of *la ritournelle* in *A Thousand Plateaus*) - divides the book even further. As such, *Dividuum* never really 'begins', but rather, its beginnings are split, distributed, or *divided*.

Despite this, any reviewer must still select certain components to create an impression of the text. We will discuss two here: Raunig's genealogy of the concept of *dividuum;* and his associated attempts to spur the 'invention and multiplication of revolutionary practices and narratives' (p184).

Any conceptual genealogy must pass through a genealogy of use, extracting how certain concepts become embedded in economic, political, and social practices. Here, Raunig extracts the usage of the Latin *dividuum* from Roman Comedy, used in reference to the division of property: division as that which governs exchange. Raunig positions *dividuum* as bound up with sociopolitical division and economic distribution, specifically, with money, goods (p26), slavery, and patriarchy (p33). *Dividuum*, in other words, is associated with the partition, division, and exchange of money, goods, slaves, and women. However, Raunig also emphasises the struggle for freedom of those subject to such partition (p35): their strategies of 'incompliant subversion' (p36), invention of new lines of flight, and the carving out of new existential territories beyond extant hegemonic modes of division and exchange.

Raunig situates the emergence of *dividuum* in philosophy (with Cicero's translation of Plato's *Timaeus* (p45)) in opposition to *individuum* in the context of a discussion of divisible and indivisible matter (p47). The relationship between *dividuum* and *individuum* will become crucial; and although Raunig situates *individuum*, etymologically, as a negation of *dividuum* (p39), the former has nonetheless tended to assume priority in philosophy (in debates on the indivisibility of the 'atom', 'soul', or 'being'; the Christian God's primary *in-*

divisibility in conjunction with, or in spite of, its divisibility in the Trinity (as in Boethius (pp52-54)); or on the nature of the individual person). Raunig traces a treatment of *dividuum* in the history of philosophy (undoubtedly indebted to Deleuze's *Difference and Repetition*) which subordinates it as a derivative or corruption of *individuum*. A 'subordination of the divisible under the indivisible' (p48), whereby *in-dividuum* is placed 'equiprimordially alongside *dividuum* as a quasi absolute word, resulting in the suppression of its positive' (p39).

The most substantive conceptual development of *dividuum* Raunig tracks is in his Talmudic reading of the work of Gilbert de la Porrée (1070/1080 - 1154), bishop of Poitiers (p55). Not only does Raunig find in Gilbert a thinker of dividuality, but also a thinker of immanence who does not subordinate *dividuum* to *individuum*, and is concerned instead with the 'singularity, concretion and immanence of all that "subsists"' (p55) in the secular realm, itself totally independent from the divine realm. Gilbert's work opens up a rich conceptual space - Raunig's reading of Gilbert constitutes one of the key successes of *Dividuum* - through which his notion of immanent ontological dividuality flows into discussions of singularity, connectedness, non-universalism, non-essentialism, connection, and conjunction: 'Whereas the concept of individuality tends towards constructing closure, dividual singularity emphasizes similarity in diverse single things, and thus also the potentiality of connecting, appending, concatenating' (p67). In this exploration of ontological dividuality, Raunig passes inevitably through the question of the individual subject, drawing on Nietzsche's critique of Western-Christian moral subjection and pastoral power as a process of 'self-division' through which subjects become divided internally within themselves (p87; pp92-94). It is through this question of the subject, and the splitedness or dividuality of both the subject (p100) and collectives (pp82-84), that Raunig brings us to the second component we will discuss: our dividuality today.

As Raunig pivots his attention to contemporary capitalism, it is not surprising that attention is paid to Deleuze's late essay 'Postscript on the Societies of Control', which famously argued that control societies are marked by the governance of *dividuals* (pp109-110).[1] Relatedly, in his discussion of our relationship to *machines* today, Raunig develops a concept of *machinic subservience* - a concept close to Maurizio Lazzarato's recent work on *machinic enslavement*[2] - proper to control societies. This brings Raunig through a wide-ranging discussion of social media (pp115-120), Big Data (pp123-127), algorithmic control and contemporary management structures (pp131-134); those 'machinic industries of recommendation' (p126) which both *pre-empt* and *produce* desire and consumption through techniques of dividual governance which govern us as 'objects of partition' (p33). Drawing additionally on the work of Stefano Harney and Fred Morton, Raunig notes:

> Where people once divested themselves of effort, now they are divesting

1. Gilles Deleuze, 'Postscript on the Societies of Control', October, 59, 1992, p5

2. Maurizio Lazzarato, *Signs and Machines: Capitalism and the Production of Subjectivity*, Joshua David Jordan (trans), Los Angeles, Semiotext(e) 2014

themselves of control [...] That dys- and pan-topic fantasy of logistics aims to limit human beings as 'controlling agents' as far as possible, to liberate the flow of commodities and weapons from human time and human error [...] The drone brings death or it brings mail from Amazon, based on algorithmically produced risk or potentiality profiles. (p114)

Raunig consistently emphasises the divided actualisations of our dividual governance. Or, to put this another way, that the modalities and intensities of contemporary control are differentially distributed. Raunig's reading - which leans on Brigitte Young[3] - of the subprime crisis is instructive in this regard insofar as it tracks the integration of gendered and racialised humans into the financial system as a process through which that very integration paved the way for further subjection, division, and exploitation in the context of the financial crisis (debt traps, foreclosure, etc.) (pp140-141).

3. Brigitte Young, 'Die Subprime-Krise und die geschechtsspezifische Schuldenfalle', in *Antworten aus der feministischen Ökonomie auf die globale Wirtschafts-und Finanzkrise*, Berlin, Ebert Stiftung 2009, pp15-26

To his credit, Raunig consistently attempts to carve new lines of flight as vectors of molecular revolution. In an attempt to rethink debt, Raunig begins to develop a notion of *queer debt* as a means to co-compose 'new forms of sociality' (p149). In an attempt to rethink Eurocentric law (centred on the individual person and property), Raunig envisages dividual law and processes of immanent law-making (pp174-175). In an attempt to rethink the putative individuality and sovereignty of the state, Raunig offers us a nuanced, if under-developed, notion of *radical inclusion* (p189). These are some examples of the revolutionary paths Raunig seeks to open, and it is of note that his conceptualisation of revolution is decidedly dividual and multiple: revolution 'becomes an unending chain of instituent practices [...] the institutionalization of the revolution becomes the invention of ever new monster institutions' (pp184-185). Such practices (the invention of multiple lines of flight) are positioned by Raunig as decidedly non-teleological: the process of *inventing the line* is more about the creation of new singularising curves and conjunctions - what he will at the end of the book call 'con/division' (p92) - not about arrival or completion (pp79-80).

There are, at least, three points which would be particularly worthy of exploration in future volumes of this projected series. For one, Raunig leans heavily (especially when he develops the notion of con/division) upon a notion of similarity which is subject to a number of separate, if brief, reflections (pp67-68; p150; p191). This type of similarity enables conjunction and connection, but cannot be reduced to sameness. Its repetition throughout the text highlights its importance in Raunig's conceptual scheme, and would have thus benefited greatly from a more thorough and extended discussion. Secondly, a future volume might pass through the question of the division of labour - the mechanisms through which global production and distribution are differentially distributed and divided - especially insofar as the vastly asymmetrical global labour conditions present a pertinent challenge to how any processes of con/division and molecular revolution might be ignited. While this is briefly gestured towards (pp185-186), it nonetheless would benefit from further exploration. The third issue relates to the notion of radical inclusion. In a global context where a new politics of *exclusion* is growing simultaneously with increased levels of displacement and refugee numbers, how might we invent new weapons, or co-invent lines of flight, in order to combat such exclusion? This pressing question is opened by Raunig but is not, unfortunately, deeply explored.

Dividuum is a challenging and, at times, exhilarating text, which manages to demand both slow reading *and* active practice in the world. True to his approach, Raunig does not ask readers to absorb compliantly and reproduce his method (he terms works that do as displaying 'method-fetishisms' (p191)), and as such, one of the key functions of *Dividuum* as a text-machine is as an invitation towards the invention of multiple new lines, the enunciations of new singularities, and new modes of existence: an invitation to make the multiple.

Conor Heaney is a PhD Candidate in Social & Political Thought at the University of Kent, Canterbury. His website is www.conor-heaney.com.

Psychoanalytic Stimulus Packages

Dougal McNeill

David Bennett, *The Currency of Desire: Libidinal Economy, Psychoanalysis and Sexual Revolution*, London, Lawrence and Wishart, 2016, 314pp+vii; £20 paperback

'What happens when we start to decode sex-talk as metaphoric money-talk?' (p2) This is the organising question running through David Bennett's finely-argued, wide-ranging and lively study *The Currency of Desire*, a history of 'libidinal economy', its thinkers and discontents, from the Enlightenment to the present day. Bennett's reading is capacious, taking in everything from Lawrence to Lyotard, Viennese Actionism to Christina Aguilera, and his pursuit of his subject energetic and expansive, travelling from the 'complex marriages' of the Oneida Community in nineteenth-century North America to the new money - crime - psychoanalysis circuit of Yeltsin's Russia from our own recent past. If the vastness and stretch of Bennett's interests give his text a sometimes baggy formlessness, each chapter comes studded with insights and asides enough to reward any reader's patience. Erudite, engaging, and sometimes drily funny, *The Currency of Desire* combines political seriousness with an admirably scrupulous regard for what sometimes seems, to us now, the absurdities and delusions of the past. Bennett's aim 'is to denaturalise [...] the language of libidinal economy and reopen it to critique by historicising, rather than parodying, it' (p38).

Contemporary consumer society, from the relationships column in the *Guardian* to dating apps Tinder and Grindr, is awash with money metaphors floating in the discourses of sexuality and sex talk swimming through the language of money. We 'invest' in relationships, see our erotic or cultural 'capital' rise and fall as we work over our personal 'brand' and online identity, our private lives all the while being commodified, measured and monetised by Facebook as our financial lives are subject to strictures for stimulus or austerity. Economic concepts, in Bennett's account, 'have permeated the vocabularies of both popular and scientific discourses on sexual anatomy, psychology, morality and politics for several centuries' (p7) and *The Currency of Desire* sets itself the task of carrying out 'the resurrection of dead metaphors, or the resuscitation of unconscious ones' (p36) in order that we might estrange and see afresh the libidinal economic terms informing our consumerist lives.

Sex and money have, after all, been talked about together for a very long time. They even share clichés, from money making the world go round to the various insinuations about the 'oldest profession'. All sorts of pimps and pamphleteers have seen the financial appeal of desire, while a century's worth of Freudian analysis has searched the money-world for evidence of libidinal drives and dynamics. As the cynical author of *The Wandering Whore Continued* (1660) put it, 'Mony and cunny are good commodities'.[1] Eschewing the twin temptations of 'biologising' money (the orthodox Freudian approach) or 'eroticising' capital (the project of both psychoanalytic dissidents such as Wilhelm Reich as well as neoliberal advertising and marketing gurus), Bennett insists instead that 'neither discourse can ultimately claim to "demystify" the other, or explain the other historically' (p80). At a certain historical moment 'the discourses of money and sex became inseparable', and it is this interconnectedness, and its consequences, which *The Currency of Desire* traces. Bennett 'traces the history of the exchange or intercourse between the languages of money and sex, economic and libidinal economy' (pp3-4), not in order for one to 'establish itself as the literal, rather than the metaphoric, voice of history' (p80), but rather so readers can trace how these two mutually-reinforcing discourses have shaped our accounts of selfhood and society together. Bennett's work is thus both psychoanalytic history and a history of psychoanalysis, a work of a discourse analysis and an analysis of discourse mutating and shifting through history. 'Just as the entities traded in the money economy have become progressively rarefied, abstracted and psychologised,' he observes, 'so there has been a progressive dematerialising, rarefying and psychologising of the presumed currency of the animal economy since the seventeenth century' (p11).

The Currency of Desire pursues this history by way of two linked approaches. The first, and most successful, is an exercise in intellectual history, tracing the birth of 'economic man' as a 'fully 'psychologised' and 'sexualised' subject' (p3) and following his construction through the paired histories of economics and sexology. Sexology and neoclassical economics were both, Bennett suggests, 'complementary "scientific" moments in a broader redefinition of the citizen-individual during the eighteenth century as primarily a subject of desire rather than of labour' (p74) and, as desire - the impulse to spend - replaces thrift or the desire to produce as the central feature of the citizen subject, modern economics and sexuality can be formed. Human energies, whether sexual 'spending' or labour power, were, from Aristotle to Galen, seen as finite and hard to replenish, forces carefully to be tended and conserved. Our contemporary views - of personal libido as much as, or, Bennett might suggest, in partnership with, social and economic 'stimulus packages' - were born in the break from this thought-world. Bennett follows the 'quantitative character of libido' (p22) and its role as a medium of universal exchange through nineteenth-century economics and sexology. There are plenty of stimulating asides along the way (my favourite being the connections between Orson Squire Fowler's 'sexual science' of 'animal electricity' and Whitman's poetics), as well as some drily amusing encounters with Lawrence at his kookiest, but Bennett's journey takes us through concepts of subjectivity still ordering political and personal life today. His insistence on a kind of

1. Anonymous, *The Wandering Whore Continued*, London, John Garfield, 1660, quoted in Matthew Beaumont, *Night Walking: a Nocturnal History of London*, London, Verso 2016, p56.

'surface reading', produced via some scholarly skirmishes, mainly confined to the footnotes, with Thomas Laqueur, makes for some startlingly intellectual *Verfremdungseffekte*. *The Currency of Desire* does not tell the 'hidden' story of sexuality and money but, rather, reveals what has been hiding in plain sight. Psychoanalytic hydraulic accounts of sexuality and the mind's drives would, for instance, be unthinkable without the Industrial Revolution and the development of the steam engine: links 'between energetics and economics are more literal than analogical' (p33).

Bennett then follows this history across the Atlantic, into the post-war world of pop Freudianism, advertising, and counter-cultural sexual dissidence. Freud's 'politically conservative libidinal economy [...] produced a petit-bourgeois psyche, managing its economy of energy as a self-employed businessman must,' Bennett claims, 'spending frugally, wherever possible reinvesting in increased productivity, eschewing conspicuous consumption and credit'. In contrast, the contribution of psychoanalysis's anti-bourgeois exponents, such as the one-time Communist Reich, served, in an irony *The Currency of Desire* serves up with melancholic relish, not to overthrow the petit-bourgeois patriarch of Freudianism or the repressive capitalist world but, rather, in their celebration of 'free' sexual spending, 'to develop libidinal economy in the direction of a fully-fledged consumerist culture that celebrated spending for spending's sake' (p139). Bennett has fascinating insights on the 'Freudianism-consumerism nexus' (p90) of the post-war years, as advertising, Keynesian economics, consumer society and sexual revolution all draw on shared sexual-economic metaphors of spending. The cunning of reason, in this exciting account, sees sexual revolution not so much undoing capitalist society as updating its order and stimulating it to further growth.

Sexual revolution's practice, and its tawdry aftermaths, is Bennett's second focus. Here the results are more uneven. Using case studies from nineteenth-century American Christianity, post-war European avant-garde communes and Yeltsin-era 'feral' (p252) analysis through post-Communism, Bennett follows in the tracks of heterodox libidinal economy. The histories internal to these communities reveal that 'the biopolitics of 'free love' movements are invariably no less regulated than the putatively free market, which is sustained by innumerable tariffs, imposts, quotas, taxes and barriers' (p222) while their history as it interacted with the wider world shows how 'utopian experiments in sexual and economic revolution ultimately functioned, despite themselves, as dress-rehearsals for the full-blown consumerist culture of administered enjoyment and disinhibited spending' (p229). The Oneida Community's 'complex marriages' may be gone, but their capital remains in the tableware manufacturer Oneida Ltd; one of the largest Mac consultancy and dealerships in the United States had its origins in the administration of a Californian free-love commune. These case studies are fascinating on their own, and provide plenty for the Utopian reader to ponder, but seem, as part of a unified book-length study, oddly under-rehearsed. Why these accounts and not others? Bennett's erudition is obvious, and rewarding, but the analytic thread he sews through these sections is not always clear. Questionable also is the book's periodising scheme. If the birth of 'economic man' can be traced to the 'European Enlightenment' (p3), why not push further back? What are the links between Enlightenment and bourgeois revolution? Shakespeare's fourth sonnet seems to me now, after Bennett, to be worrying at precisely the distinction between sexual 'spending' in a vagina and unproductive storing of money in a bank or fluids in a male body:

> Unthrifty loveliness, why dost thou spend
> Upon thyself thy beauty's legacy?
> Nature's bequest gives nothing but doth lend,
> And being frank she lends to those are free.
> Then beauteous niggard, why dost thou abuse
> The bounteous largess given thee to give?
> Profitless usurer, why dost thou use
> So great a sum of sums yet canst not live?

Having 'traffic with thyself alone', the poet tells the young man, will leave no 'acceptable audit'. The masturbator 'spending upon himself' wastes his investment; the father puts it usefully into circulation. This predates Bennett's case by some decades, but anticipates his argument. The gendering of my example is deliberate, and Bennett's history traces an exclusively masculine, and heterosexual, lineage. A wider consideration of queer and feminist accounting for spending, sexual and otherwise, alongside feminist critiques of sexual revolution more generally, would have added theoretical and political currency to this story. It is the sign of a fine piece of scholarship, however, that one is left with productive quarrels and questions, and these are quibbling objections to a finely-written study of cultural history.

Dougal McNeill teaches in the English Programme, Victoria University of Wellington, and is, with Charles Ferrall, author of *Writing the 1926 General Strike* (Cambridge University Press, 2015).

TRUST SYLVIA WYNTER

S. Trimble

Katherine McKittrick, ed., *Sylvia Wynter: On Being Human as Praxis*, Durham and London, Duke University Press, 2015, 290pp.; $25.95 paperback

In the acknowledgements to *Sylvia Wynter: On Being Human as Praxis*, editor Katherine McKittrick writes that '[a]ny engagement with Sylvia Wynter demands openness' (px). Thinking with Wynter demands openness because her insights, if we take them to heart, undo the disciplines that condition what we can know and say about the world. What Wynter wants is nothing less than a collective 'rewriting of knowledge as we know it' (p18), a challenge that asks us - thinkers, creators, knowledge-makers, storytellers - to accept disorientation in exchange for the possibility of exercising 'dazzling creativity' (p17) as we recalibrate our sense of who 'we' are. Wynter's project of completely transforming Western ways of knowing derives from her argument, following Frantz Fanon, that humanness is hybrid. We are, in Wynter's terms, both *bios* and *mythoi*; flesh-and-blood organisms that also (re)invent ourselves by telling stories of where we came from and what we are. What we need, then, are forms of knowledge that are adequate to the fact that '*humanness* is no longer a *noun. Being human is a praxis*' (p23, emphases in original).

So thinking with Wynter demands openness. And it takes time. In a brief introduction to the collection, McKittrick describes Wynter's anticolonial insights as 'knots of histories and ideas and relational narratives', the entangled results of Wynter's working across the natural and social sciences, the humanities, and the arts (p3). This knottiness makes itself felt even at the level of the sentence. The sixty-page call-and-response that anchors the book - an archive of interviews, discussions, and written exchanges between McKittrick and Wynter that began in 2007 - showcases the denseness of Wynter's mode of expression. Her sentences are thick with asides; long dashes that facilitate transdisciplinary leaps - from critical race theory to neuroscience and back again - allow her to loop more connections, more implications, into her claims. *Sylvia Wynter* thus invites the kind of slow, patient engagement that Sylvia Wynter's thinking demands. The collection begins with conversations and then unfolds into more conversations, each contributor thinking with a particular set of Wynter's knots. The result is that rather than offering a stabilizing 'overview' of Wynter's main ideas - a project that would run counter to the ethos of her work, which emphasizes intellectual creativity and epistemological mutation - McKittrick's collection puts them into play: unraveling, retying, riffing on Wynter. It's a project inspired by the closing line of Wynter's correspondence. "Yours in the intellectual struggle", McKittrick explains, 'bears witness to the practice of sharing words and letters while also drawing attention to the possibilities that storytelling and wording bring' (p7).

As a collaborative project, *Sylvia Wynter* opens up, again and again, the question of what ethical, epistemological, political, and imaginative possibilities emerge from thinking-feeling-living, as Rinaldo Walcott puts it, 'the human as an alterable species-subject' (p186). The alterability of the human derives from what Wynter describes as a biomutational 'Third Event', the origins of which she traces to the archaeological findings in Blombos Cave, South Africa. As she elaborates in conversation with McKittrick, if the First and Second Events entailed, respectively, 'the origin of the universe and the explosion of all forms of biological life' (p25), then the excavation at Blombos of a 100,000 year-old workshop containing tools used in the creation of paints indexes a Third Event: the inauguration of practices that facilitate 'the *symbolic transformation of biological identity*' (p67, emphasis in original). In other words, humanness emerges from a dynamic of rebirth. We're born into the world as biological beings and then reborn into an origin story that tells us who 'we' are and what 'we' do. What's more, the story of humanness into which we're reborn gets into our brains: it 'co-functions' with our 'neurochemical behavior regulatory system' (p11), rewarding us when we live, act, and feel according to the script of humanness into which we've been initiated and blocking neurochemical rewards when we fail to approximate or otherwise depart from this script. Wynter thus follows Aimé Césaire in proposing that the study of our biologies should *follow* from the study of our stories: a science of the Word.

While these origin stories that we live by are, in Wynter's terms, 'genre-specific' (p32), one of her key insights is that we're currently constrained by a single, now globally hegemonic story. The West's secular, liberal genre of humanness - Man - currently 'over-represents' itself as the only viable model of the human (cf. Wynter 2003). And since Man's story scripts humanness in purely biocentric terms, it crafts us as *homo oeconomicus*, a biological organism driven by the laws of natural scarcity and for whom 'salvation' lies in 'the unceasing mastery of natural scarcity by means of ever-increasing economic growth!' (p26). In place of *homo oeconomicus* Wynter offers *homo narrans*, the hybrid human-as-storyteller whose task - especially given the planetary costs of Man's dispossessing, extracting, accumulating activities - is to narrate humanness from a species, rather than genre-specific, perspective.

These are some of the knots that shape Wynter's anticolonial project; her search for a new science and story of the human, the seeds of which are located in the 'demonic' perspectives that emerge from the 'ex-slave archipelago' (p2). The contributors to *Sylvia Wynter* consider the vantage points that run slantwise across Man's worldview, from the Caribbean basin as a site of invention, experimentation, and 'new indigenisms' (Walcott p185;

Boyce Davies, Sharma) to the intersections of habitability and humanness in post-Katrina New Orleans (Ansfield). From such perspectives, the colonial underpinnings of the classical order are unveiled (Ferreira da Silva), 'epistemic disobedience' becomes possible (Mignolo, p106), and the '*Thing* of *Being Black*' - the lack that defines blackness within Man's worldview - can be contested and undone (Eudell, p229). From here, from the 'crisscrossing of science and poetics' enabled by the wrenching open of a closed epistemological system, 'bold as love' creative acts might usher in a completely unexpected story of what it means to be human (McKittrick, p160).

The contributors to *Sylvia Wynter* aim at the horizon of that unexpected story - one that might interrupt the still-unfolding histories of violence that shape Man's world by offering us, in Walcott's terms, 'something more possible' (p188). McKittrick's collection is rich with insights that, in the spirit of Wynter's work, can help to reshape urgent conversations by compelling us to ask different questions from different starting points. What does Wynter's rehistoricisation of the human - and her centring of coloniality - do to our thinking about the Anthropocene? What happens to conversations around climate change if we look at environmental catastrophe within a 'post-1492' timeframe? How might Wynter's reconceptualization of indigeneity - a rethinking spurred by the fact that transatlantic slavery 'enforced the necessity of blacks to plant themselves as indigenous to the New World' (McKittrick, p6) - contribute to discussions of decolonization, reconciliation, and reparations both within the academy and beyond? (For those who want to explore this and related questions further, a March 2016 special issue of *Small Axe* explores Wynter's unpublished 900-page manuscript, *Black Metamorphosis: New Natives in a New World*. McKittrick is also a contributor to that issue.) And, finally, what might Wynter's arguments about storytelling, culture, science, and knowledge offer to those who are struggling to reimagine teaching and learning in the context of a higher education system increasingly constrained by neoliberal ideologies?

In her own contribution to the collection, 'Axis, Bold as Love,' McKittrick remarks that 'if we *trust* [Wynter's] argument' (p152, emphasis in original), then it means nothing less than a complete reconceptualization of, among other things, political struggle, intellectual labour, and something called 'freedom'. *Sylvia Wynter* proposes that we trust Sylvia Wynter - that we be bold enough to breathe life into, and live by, new stories of humanness.

S. Trimble is an assistant professor at the Women and Gender Studies Institute at the University of Toronto. Her research has appeared in numerous cultural studies journals including, most recently, her co-edited special issue of *TOPIA* entitled 'The Work of Return' (Spring 2016).